Women and British Aestheticism

Women and British Aestheticism

Edited by TALIA SCHAFFER *and*
KATHY ALEXIS PSOMIADES

University Press
of Virginia

Charlottesville
& London

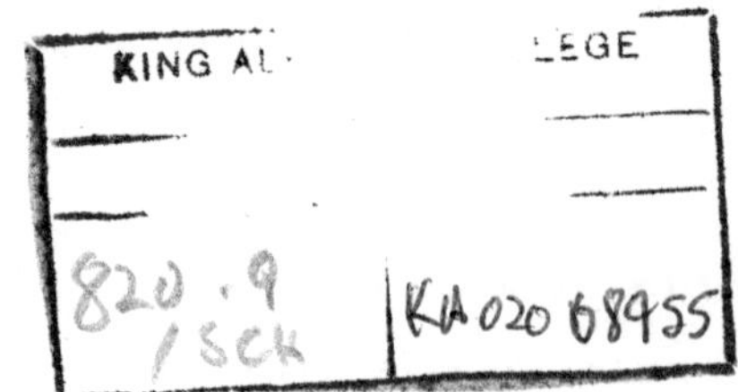

The University Press of Virginia

Printed in the United States of America

First published 1999

∞ The paper used in this publication meets the minimum requirements of the American National Standard for Information Sciences — Permanence of Paper for Printed Library Materials, ANSI Z39.481984.

Library of Congress Cataloging-in-Publication Data
Women and British aestheticism / edited by Talia Schaffer and Kathy Alexis Psomiades.
p. cm.
Includes bibliographical references and index.
ISBN 0-8139-1891-X (alk. paper) — ISBN 0-8139-1892-8 (pbk. : alk. paper)
1. English literature—19th century—History and criticism. 2. Aestheticism (Literature) 3. Women and literature—Great Britain—History—19th century. 4. Women and literature—Great Britain—History—20th century. 5. English literature—Women authors—History and criticism. 6. English literature—20th century—History and criticism. I. Schaffer, Talia, 1968– . II. Psomiades, Kathy Alexis, 1963– .
PR468.A33W66 1999
820.9'11—dc21 99-29825
CIP

For Ann and Benjamin Schaffer
and Christine Eames

Contents

III. Aesthetic Prose

IV. Aestheticism into the Modern

Acknowledgments

THAT THIS project has remained a pleasure from start to finish is due to the good humor, helpfulness, and support of our contributors, and we would like to thank all of them here. Particular thanks go to Margaret Stetz and Mark Samuels Lasner for their suggestions about cover art, to Regenia Gagnier for her support of the project, and to Linda Hughes for her practical advice about the publication process. The editors would also like to thank Joseph Bristow, Richard Dellamora, Jonathan Freedman, John Maynard, and Sally Mitchell for their encouragement and support of our work. We appreciate the friendship and collegiality of Kate Baldwin, Bonnie Blackwell, Bill Christmas, Eleanor Courtemanche, Theresa Krier, Diana Maltz, Anna Neill, Ellen Peel, Beth Sutton-Ramspeck, Cathy Shuman, Sheila Teahan, Pam Thurschwell, and Ewa Ziarek as well as the friendship and generous advice of Hilary Radner.

We are grateful to the anonymous readers for the University Press of Virginia for their helpful comments. Cathie Brettschneider has been a wonderful editor. Ellen Satrom moved the project along speedily, and Ingrid Sterner's meticulous copyediting is much appreciated. We would like to thank Cheryl Reed at the University of Notre Dame for her work preparing the manuscript. We would also like to thank the Institute for Scholarship in the Liberal Arts at the University of Notre Dame for a materials grant for the project. Special thanks go to George Musser Jr., Ann and Ben Schaffer, Jonathan Schaffer, George Musser, Judith Musser, and Bret and Eileen Musser.

Women and British Aestheticism

Introduction

THIS COLLECTION of essays aims to demonstrate that women's participation in aestheticism was widespread, significant, and controversial and that recognizing this participation will reshape our views of both aestheticism and the history of women's writing. Most of the scholarship on aestheticism has seen the movement as reflecting the masculine concerns of its male producers. By presenting scholarly work on a number of heretofore neglected women writers and on the cultural contexts in which they wrote, we seek to redress this imbalance.

Aestheticism both empowered and erased women writers. On the one hand, the aesthetes celebrated fields traditionally assigned to the women's sphere — including fashion, interior design, and decorative art — which meant that women's mastery of domestic minutiae gave them a kind of intellectual cachet within the movement. And aestheticism's emphasis on beautiful descriptions chimed in well with Victorian critics' requirement that women confine themselves to attractive writing styles. On the other hand, the aesthetes' valorization of professional artistic training often made women writers' domestic experiences seem glaringly amateurish. Furthermore, the aesthetes' growing interest in naturalist and decadent subjects — crime, opium addiction, disease, prostitution — posed a major problem for women writers who were not supposed to be aware of such issues.

It is not surprising, therefore, that women produced aestheticism according to a slightly different set of rules from their male counterparts'. The essays in this volume explore how women writers constructed a very inclusive form of aestheticism that endorsed nature as well as art (Barbara T. Gates, Ann Ardis), bourgeois culture along with cosmopolitan bohemianism (Annette R. Federico, Ardis), and alternative sexualities in the context of reputable historical or scientific study (Dennis Denisoff, Diana Maltz). That these women writers advocated apparently incompatible positions indicates just how useful aestheticism could be for women with mixed emotions about contemporary cultural and political movements and for women who found the strong political stance of the New Women novels foreign to their feelings. Aestheticism's inclusivity helps explain why aesthetic style was so popular, across virtually every genre, among late-Victorian women writers.

Using aestheticist discourse and empowered by aestheticist ideologies, the women discussed in these essays wrote novels, poems, domestic manuals, and philosophical tracts. The rediscovery of female aesthetes forces us to rethink the conditions of both aestheticism and women's writing during the latter half of the Victorian era. These essays give some idea of what female aesthetes can tell us about contemporary gender debates, the development of protomodernist literary techniques, the significance of nonnormative sexualities and ethnicities, the divide between mass readers and their elite counterparts, and the ramifications of an increasingly commodified culture. In the rest of this introduction we situate these essays and the women they discuss in the context of scholarship on British aestheticism and on women's writing. We explain how female aesthetes largely escaped the attention of scholars in both fields and indicate how their work might challenge existing scholarly paradigms. Finally, we provide an overview of the central concerns of the volume.

Defining Aestheticism

In this volume *British aestheticism* refers to a cultural movement occurring from the second half of the nineteenth century into the early part of the twentieth.[1] This movement, loosely connected to the phrase "art for art's sake," manifested itself not only in poetry, painting, and literary essays but also in dress, furniture design, and popular genres like the advice book, humorous magazine article, and best-seller.

Aestheticism began to emerge around midcentury in John Ruskin's claims for the importance of art and prescriptions for improving the beauty of everyday life and in the poetry, paintings, designs, and prose of Pre-Raphaelites like Dante Gabriel Rossetti, Christina Rossetti, Algernon Charles Swinburne, and William Morris. It was even more fully articulated in the 1870s and 1880s by Walter Pater and Oscar Wilde. Beginning in the 1870s the word *aestheticism* came to be used to indicate not only a certain style of painting, or way of writing, or set of ideas but also the popular manifestations of a belief in art's ability to make life more beautiful and to allow the beholder to achieve transcendence. The Grosvenor Gallery displayed aesthetic paintings; William Morris and other Arts and Crafts artists produced furniture, textiles, and glass; Charles Locke Eastlake published *Hints on Household Taste;* and peacocks' feathers, willowware, and aesthetic dress became fashionable, along with advice manuals on decorating and fashion. In *Punch* George Du Maurier's cartoons satirized aesthetic style, while William S. Gilbert and Arthur Sullivan's operetta *Patience* poked fun at the new movement.[2] In 1882 Walter Hamilton set out to explain aestheticism to those who might only have encountered these satiric images of effeminate men and gaunt drooping beauties in weird costumes. In *The Aesthetic Movement in England* Hamilton connected the popular manifestations of the movement in changes in dress and decor to the work of artists and poets like Dante Gabriel Rossetti, Swinburne, Morris, and Edward Burne-Jones.[3] In so doing, he articulated a central feature of aestheticism — its status as both a high-art and a mass-cultural movement.

During the rest of the century aestheticist ideas, images, designs, and fashions permeated the culture. Wilde became the visible embodiment of the movement and *The Picture of Dorian Gray* its central text, while the green carnation replaced the sunflower as the floral emblem of aestheticism. Decadence, with its fascination with the unnatural, death, decay, the body, and the exotic other, continued aestheticism's interest in artifice, intense experience, the mixing of beauty and strangeness, and the desire to experience life itself as art. Writers and artists of the 1890s like Wilde, Ernest Dowson, Max Beerbohm, Aubrey Beardsley, and Arthur Symons produced work clearly influenced by Pater, Rossetti, Swinburne, and Burne-Jones, as well as by French writers associated with *l'art pour l'art.*

At every stage of this process women writers and artists contributed to aestheticism. Christina Rossetti and Elizabeth Siddall wrote early aestheticist verse, sensation novelists like Mary Elizabeth Braddon popularized Pre-Raphaelite beauty in the 1860s, and best-selling novelists like Ouida disseminated aesthetic taste in countless novels. Artists like Marie Spartali Stillman and Evelyn De Morgan painted huge aestheticist canvases, which they exhibited at the Grosvenor Gallery.[4] Many women were involved in design work, book illustration, and the manufacture of textiles, pottery, and other aesthetic objects for the home.[5] Throughout the 1870s, 1880s, and 1890s Mary Eliza Haweis, Graham R. Tomson (Rosamund Marriott Watson), Rhoda and Agnes Garrett, Elizabeth Robins Pennell,

Gertrude Jekyll, and Lucy Crane wrote about aesthetic dress, decorating, cuisine, gardening, and art appreciation. Vernon Lee (Violet Paget) wrote art criticism, an anti-aestheticist novel, *Miss Brown,* and decadent short stories about ghosts, murder, passion, and depravity. By the 1890s women participated in all genres: Graham R. Tomson, Michael Field (Katherine Bradley and Edith Cooper), Sarojini Naidu, Laurence Hope (Adela Nicolson), Olive Custace, and others wrote aesthetic poetry; Ouida, Marie Corelli, John Oliver Hobbes (Pearl Mary Teresa Richards Craigie), and Lucas Malet (Mary St. Leger Kingsley Harrison) wrote novels on aesthetic themes; George Egerton (Mary Chavelita Dunne Bright), Una Ashworth Taylor, and Mabel E. Wotton wrote aesthetic short stories; Vernon Lee propounded new theories of psychological aesthetics; Netta Syrett, Ella D'Arcy, and Ella Hepworth Dixon wrote for the *Yellow Book;* and numerous women published under John Lane's aesthetic imprint.[6]

Though critics predicted that Wilde's spectacularly scandalous fall and the end of the nineteenth century itself would finish off aestheticism, its influence continued. Whereas male modernist writers often disavowed that influence, women writers continued to find in aestheticism a rich resource for the production of art and an alternative tradition with which to combat high-modernist misogyny. Syrett wrote on aestheticist themes into the 1930s; Virginia Woolf was influenced by Alice Meynell, Pater, and Lee; H. D., as Cassandra Laity has argued, drew on poets like Swinburne and Dante Gabriel Rossetti.[7]

Our definition of aestheticism accommodates this wide range of genres, figures, audiences, and eras. We read aestheticism as a movement ranging broadly from the 1850s through the 1930s, manifesting itself both in high art and in popular culture. We have tried to avoid the tendency to locate aestheticism's origins in high forms and to see popular forms as secondary, debased manifestations of high-art ideas, a critical practice that has sometimes devalued even a central figure like Wilde into a mere popularizer of Pater and Ruskin. Finally, we have set the movement's parameters unusually broadly because the addition of women's writing to the corpus of aestheticist work seems to require some redefinitions and reperiodizations.

Another definition of aestheticism implicit in many of the essays in this volume comes out of a marxist cultural critique: aestheticism is not just a series of texts but also a particular historical condition of art in bourgeois culture. In his *Theory of the Avant-Garde* Peter Bürger described how in bourgeois culture art is separated and freed from the constraints of church, court, and state and, distributed through the capitalist marketplace, becomes autonomous. In the early stages of its autonomy bourgeois art still has political content, but in the second half of the nineteenth century, in aestheticism, "the contents also lose their political character, and art wants to be nothing other than art." Thus "the apartness from the praxis of life that had always constituted the institutional status of art in bourgeois society now becomes the content of works."[8] Aestheticist art thus makes reflection on its own separate status its subject matter. For Bürger aestheticism is the historical stage that makes the "self-criticism" of art under the avant-garde possible.

Scholars writing about aestheticism have criticized as well as drawn on Bürger's work. Jonathan Freedman and Regenia Gagnier have shown how aesthetes like Wilde were engaged in the kind of attempt to merge art and the praxis of everyday life that Bürger ascribed to the avant-garde rather than the aesthetes.[9] Theodor Adorno linked aestheticism's focus on the autonomous, decontextualized art object to consumerist sensibilities, claiming that, "to that extent, the codeword of *l'art pour l'art* is the opposite of what it claims to be."[10] What is important about this definition is that it sees aestheticism not merely as a collection of texts and images but as an example of the problem of what it means to claim autonomy for a category of existence called the aesthetic in a culture increasingly under the market's sway. Whether aestheticism is seen as a claim for the absolute autonomy of art, a critique of that claim, or the moment at which art abandons itself wholeheartedly to the world of commodities while pretending not to, more is at issue than a particular language or set of images.

The women who produced and consumed aestheticism were deeply concerned with art and daily practice, whether they were involved in the aestheticization of the everyday through dressing, decorating, and gardening or intent on portraying the comic or tragic collision of the aesthetic and the "real" in parody or anti-aestheticist fiction. Their work makes important contributions to the discussion of art's relation to commodity culture. Yet for years this work was unknown, forgotten, or ignored. How did women get left out of our account of aestheticism, and why bring them back in now? To answer these questions, we need to look at how aestheticism has been constructed as a literary-historical category based in a highly gendered critical language and how more recent events in the study of aestheticism have compelled us to examine the work of women writers and artists.

Aestheticism and Its Critics

As Freedman has pointed out, much of our thinking about aestheticism has to do with its relation to modernism. Much of the early work on aestheticism was done from the perspective of modernism, so it is not surprising that the two central critical narratives that still structure our discussions should have so much to do with modernist anxieties. In the first critical narrative aestheticism signals the moment at which art begins to contemplate its separation from everyday life. In the second critical narrative, which details the relation between art object and commodity, aestheticism signals art's increasing involvement with commodity culture and consumerism. The notion that aestheticism implies a retreat into an unreal fantasy world at the expense of involvement with real life and that for this reason art must be rescued from the sterile, enfeebling enclosure of aestheticism by modernist rigor is one version of the narrative of withdrawal. The association of the movement with decoration, the repeated assertion that aestheticist artists merely pandered to nouveau-riche patrons, the denigration of aestheticism's poetry and paintings for being merely pretty are all gestures that refer to the narrative of commodification. Both narratives look back from modernism and locate in aestheticism one or the other side of a modernist great divide between art and mass culture. In the first narrative the aesthetes are the doomed but necessary precursors of the avant-garde; in the second they are the ultimately all too successful precursors of mass culture and the culture industry. Whether it is perceived as too separate from bourgeois culture to do it any good or too connected to its central sites, aestheticism bears the weight of modernist anxieties about mass culture.

Aestheticism thus often is portrayed as feminine or effeminate in contrast to modernism's masculine rigor. This sense of aestheticism's inadequacy carries over into the work of the New Critics, who tended to denigrate aestheticist poetry for its lack of complexity and content. For a while aestheticism seemed more interesting as good gossip, colorful and scandalous stories about flamboyant people, than as an aesthetic practice. Wilde enjoyed a revival among the flappers and dandies of the 1920s, who admired his flawless effrontery.[11] As new biographical material about Wilde began to appear (mostly either generated or contested by Lord Alfred Douglas), his reputation as a charming, doomed, stylistic hedonist spoke to Jazz Age sensibilities and influenced young writers like Ronald

Firbank and the Sitwells. Popular when defined as an insouciant fashion, aestheticism appeared weak and ineffectual as an intellectual movement.

In the years after World War II, when Romantic and Victorian poetry enjoyed a critical renaissance, the fortunes of aestheticism began to rise. Yet aestheticism was still caught up in a narrative implicitly about masculinity: no longer seen solely in the context of modernism, aestheticism became Romanticism's last hurrah. Graham Hough's *The Last Romantics* (1949) remains a central text in the study of aestheticism, and its linking of aestheticism to Romanticism was explicitly tied to a Freudian narrative of masculine development by Harold Bloom in the 1960s and 1970s.[12] In these narratives aestheticism is the late and somewhat enfeebled version of a Romanticism that has its vigorous beginnings in William Wordsworth and John Keats and may be traced, growing ever more exhausted, through Alfred, Lord Tennyson into Rossetti and Swinburne, then into the decadent poets, before its transformation in William Butler Yeats, T. S. Eliot, and Ezra Pound into modernism. Again, this is primarily a masculine trajectory and speaks mainly to poetry and a few high prose texts.

The 1960s saw a revival of interest in aestheticism: many of the anthologies of Pre-Raphaelite and aestheticist poetry and editions of the letters, poetry, and other writing of aestheticist poets and prose writers still in use today date from this period. Cecil Lang's *The Pre-Raphaelites and Their Circle* (1968), Jerome Buckley's *The Pre-Raphaelites* (1968), Karl Beckson's *Aesthetes and Decadents of the 1890s* (1966), and R. V. Johnson's *Aestheticism* (1969) date from this era.[13] The focus on aestheticism is primarily on its poetry in this decade as well, and it is interesting to note that both Lang and Buckley include Christina Rossetti in their anthologies, even as they downplay her involvement in aestheticism. Beckson includes a few 1890s women poets as well. In the 1970s work on individual figures in aestheticism — Rossetti, Swinburne, Pater, and Wilde — flourished. Ian Small's *The Aesthetes: A Sourcebook* appeared in 1979 with excerpts from poetry, prose, and popular aestheticist and anti-aestheticist texts, including Lee's *Miss Brown.*[14] What is remarkable about many of these anthologies, from Beckson's to Small's, is the extent to which they still bear the marks of aestheticism's denigration. Often the introductions are apologetic, careful to point out the moral problems aestheticism poses and to make clear that many of the texts presented are not what the editor feels are good art.[15] Often too, aestheticism's good points are either its most romanticist or its most modernist moments. Aestheticism as fashion, and especially as associated with perverse sexuality, often meets with the same anti-aestheticist arguments that many of the women writers we discuss here put forward a hundred years ago.

Yet the availability of texts for teaching aestheticism marked a real renaissance of scholarship on aestheticist writing and art. John Dixon Hunt's *The Pre-Raphaelite Imagination, 1848–1900* (1968) was followed by countless volumes of criticism on aspects of the movement and on the work of individual writers.[16] Pre-Raphaelite poets, Pater, Wilde, Beerbohm, and others received careful critical attention. By the 1970s and early 1980s feminist criticism began to address aestheticism's use of feminine images — among the central texts were Griselda Pollock's groundbreaking essays on Dante Gabriel Rossetti and much of the criticism on Christina Rossetti's poetry.[17] During this period critics began expanding our notion of aestheticism's cultural context. Margaret Stetz and Mark Samuels Lasner revealed the intricate dynamics of 1890s publishers, while Linda Dowling set aestheticist texts in the framework of larger linguistic, philosophical, and educational paradigms.[18] These exceptions aside, however, aestheticism itself received less attention than did individual authors, and, generally, the critical paradigms through which critics thought about aestheticism remained relatively stable: aestheticism as art for art's sake, aestheticism as late romanticism, aestheticism as the abandonment of moral and political responsibility, aestheticism as a step toward the autonomy aesthetic. And then, beginning in the mid-1980s, the paradigms began to shift.

Two central innovations reshaped the study of aestheticism and, along with the innovations of feminist criticism and theory, made possible the essays in this volume. The first was a shift toward considering the relations between aestheticism and commodity culture, the second a shift toward considering the relations between aestheticism and sexuality. The first approach looked to marxist and postmarxist theory to see aestheticism "not simply as a literary or artistic tendency or movement, but rather as an intricately articulated arena in which new definitions of the aesthetic and its relation to the social were negotiated and renegotiated."[19] Interestingly, this new version of aestheticism was articulated as such in two books that focus on single authors: Gagnier's *Idylls of the Marketplace: Oscar Wilde and the Victorian Public* (1986) and Freedman's *Professions of Taste: Henry James, British Aestheticism, and Commodity Culture* (1990). Gagnier demonstrated aestheticism's complex relation to the marketplace as she traced Wilde's strategic courting of different kinds of audiences and his manipulation of a growing culture of celebrity.[20] Freedman redefined aestheticism by claiming for it a mobility, a willingness to live with contradiction, and a critical engagement with commodity culture that he associated more with postmodernism than with a high-modernist drive toward totality. Both Gagnier and Freedman saw aestheticism as engaged with the marketplace yet critical of it, producing a poetry of consumption and a critique of the inequities capitalism metes out. This focus on the relations between the aesthetic and the social, on aestheticism as a broader cultural movement, puts into play a rationale for the reading of popular aestheticist writing by both men and women. It also opens up questions about bourgeois men's and women's different relations to commodity culture.

The year Freedman published his work also saw the appearance of Richard Dellamora's *Masculine Desire: The Sexual Politics of Victorian Aestheticism,* which helped redefine aestheticism as a privileged space in which desire between men was celebrated and valued.[21] If for Gagnier and Freedman aestheticism was to some extent the art of the culture of consumption, for Dellamora it was the art of the culture of sexuality. Aestheticism's connections to Oxford, to classical education, and to the formation of male homosexual identity have been further explored by Dowling, Thaïs Morgan, and others.[22] By taking aestheticism's obsession with sexuality seriously, this approach has shed new light on something about aestheticism that criticism had always noticed but usually turned away from: its tendency to celebrate nonnormative sexuality. Drawing on the historical and theoretical work of Michel Foucault and on Eve Kosofsky Sedgwick's literary criticism, Dellamora and others traced connections between male-male desire and ideas about art and artists from Romanticism's valorization of androgyny, through Tennyson, Swinburne, Gerard Manley Hopkins, Pater, and Wilde. In the process they demonstrated how the modernist recoil from aestheticism involved an attempt to erase an age-old connection between art and homoeroticism and how the reception of Pater and Wilde has been shaped by the attempt to erase or ignore the central erotic concerns of their work. Whereas this approach still produces an all-male canon of aestheticist writing, it also often involves attention to the implications new forms of masculinity might have for women — Dellamora, for example, read Swinburne and Pater as advocating departures from normative femininity alongside their concerns about masculine desire; Morgan focused on the conjunction of the celebration of male-male desire and misogyny.

Recent feminist work on aestheticism has concerned itself with issues of economics and issues of sexuality but hardly at all with the status of women as cultural producers of aestheticism. In *The Gender of Modernity* (1995) Rita Felski argued that aestheticism is characterized by a certain strategic identification with the feminine on the part of male artists. Yet this identification ultimately says more about the complex relationship between capitalism and bourgeois masculinity than it does about any solidarity between women and men: indeed for Felski aestheticism is constructed by men, for men, and involves an intense misogyny. The aesthetes who identify as somehow feminine or effeminate lay claim to a cultural mobility and power they would deny women.[23] By contrast, Cassandra Laity argued in *H. D. and the Victorian Fin de Siècle* (1996) that the decadent topoi of the femme fatale and male androgyne were enabling for modernist women poets like H. D., allowing them to counter "the major male modernists' anti-Romantic theories of impersonality."[24] In *Beauty's Body: Femininity and Representation in British Aestheticism* (1997) Kathy Alexis Psomiades claimed that aestheticism uses eroticized feminine images to separate the aesthetic from the economic and mediate between them. By representing itself through figures of beautiful women and feminized men, aestheticism as produced by both men and women is able to hold the contradictions of art and commodity culture in suspension.[25] All three feminist discussions of the ideological work femininity performs in aestheticism have fascinating implications for the work of women aesthetes, who explicitly address aestheticism's gender politics and its use of feminine images. More important for our purposes, the work of women aesthetes allows us to examine how women were also responsible for producing aestheticism's tropes and strategies in ways hitherto unrecognized. In the rest of this section, then, we will briefly sketch out some of the ways in which the work discussed in this volume challenges existing critical paradigms.

Aestheticist women's writing challenges the literary histories of aestheticism based exclusively in masculine traditions. Several alternative literary histories of aestheticism emerge. First, we can construct a different genealogy for aestheticist poetry, with its origins in a Romanticism that includes the work of both men and women. When Tennyson began to produce the feminine figures for art and artistry (like "The Lady of Shalott") that so fascinated the Pre-Raphaelites and their heirs, he drew not only on a masculine Romantic tradition that includes figures like Shelley's "highborn maiden" in "To a Skylark" but also on the popular women's poetry of the 1820s and 1830s written by Felicia Hemans and Letitia Landon that made women's emotional experiences the ideal subject matter of poetry.[26] Of all aestheticist poets, Christina Rossetti is in some respects the most Tennysonian, but her focus was primarily on preserving her heroines' interiority and radical separation from the world, even if such preservation comes only in death. In turn, her influence on Swinburne helps explain his focus on feminine dreaming and liminal states, a focus that continued in the work of later aesthetic poets like Michael Field, Marriott Watson, Dowson, and Symons. Such a history must recognize that both men and women read and drew inspiration from the work of both men and women: Swinburne may have been influenced by Rossetti and gone on to influence not only men like Symons or Eliot but also women like H. D. The essays in this collection dealing with poetry — those by Psomiades, Linda K. Hughes, and Edward Marx — make contributions to a new genealogy for aestheticist poetry.

Second, we can give the prose genres of aestheticism some long-overdue attention. When we see aestheticism as the blending of high and popular texts by both men and women, we can add to the poetic trajectory traced above figures like Haweis and Eastlake; we can read Pater and Wilde alongside Lee; we can place popular novels by Ouida, Corelli, Malet, and Syrett alongside novels by Thomas Hardy and Henry James. This history would recognize that many women wrote in a variety of genres and solicited a range of audiences, that women were particularly and intensely engaged with the literary marketplace and traversed the boundaries between high and low (Stetz, Gates, Alison Victoria Matthews, Margaret Debelius). This history would further revise our account of the relation between aestheticism and modernism by showing how women aesthetes developed new prose strategies that prefigured modernist achievements (Talia Schaffer, Denisoff). In novels, domestic manuals, and essays, aestheticist writers were able to satisfy both elite and popular readers while conveying innovative ideas with nonrealist techniques. The next generation of modernist writers derived many of their strategies from these forgotten aestheticist predecessors.

Third, we can read aestheticism as the celebration of "perverse" sexuality in ways that take into account desire between women as well as between men. In this account, Michael Field, Malet, and Lee would appear alongside men like Swinburne, Pater, and Wilde. It is important here to remember that people do not consume images or texts in predictable ways: the very paintings of beautiful women or descriptions of lesbians that critics argue are designed to reinforce dominant ideologies of gender and sexuality — by constructing women as the objects of masculine desire, or vilifying women who desire other women — may have exactly the reverse effect. Women might very well look at the women in aestheticist art and literature from the perspective of desire rather than of identification; they might, as Martha Vicinus has shown, look at beautiful young men as figures not of male-male but of female-female desire.[27] Women might also be as interested as men in developing ways of writing that use homoerotic codes: Lee, for example, like Pater and Wilde, wrote both for a general audience and for a particular, intimate, same-sex audience.

Finally, the connections between aestheticism and imperialism beginning to come to the fore today have implications for women as well as men. For the aesthetes the East was not only the origin of the elegant, disciplined Japanese art they so admired but also the pleasurable or terrifying site of sexual anarchy in which dancing girls and boys whirl by with promises for either sex or both sexes. The source of sensually satisfying material objects — kimonos, Indian cottons — was also the fearful locus of the barbarism that some decadents sought to fight. Much current work on aestheticism and imperialism has looked at the ways in which aestheticism contributed to the male-male bonds that made the empire run and has seen aestheticism's use of the exotic as bound up in its attempt to provide alternative erotic scenarios. Yet as Marx's essay shows us, we might want to look at aestheticism as it appears from the outside. As Marx demonstrates, aestheticism could offer women from the colonies, whether British settlers or Indian women, a means of gaining cultural capital and entry into a powerful literary community. A new history of aestheticism would ideally see the work of women as well as men in a global context.

Feminist Criticism and Aestheticist Women Writers

If scholarship on aestheticism can be reformulated to include women, so too might feminist criticism be reworked to include aestheticism. It is easy to understand how criticism that focused on a high-art movement in poetry might have overlooked aestheticism's popular, prose-oriented, commodity-culture attributes; but how could feminist criticism, which for decades has devoted itself to uncovering neglected women writers, have overlooked such a prominent, ambitious, and important group of women writers? In fact, feminist scholarship surprisingly parallels scholarship on aestheticism. In each case the field had already formed its central presuppositions by the end of the modernist period; in each case certain assumptions about the late Victorians created a selective reading effect.

Women's lifestyle aestheticism — chinamania, gardening manuals, dress patterns — seemed just as frivolous to feminist scholars as to other literary critics. If aestheticism's critics were looking for serious aesthetic philosophy, feminists sought texts connected to sustained political activity. The female aesthetes seemed to have written minor, embarrassingly feminine texts — a historical irony, considering that many women deliberately produced this effect in order to get their work past the Victorian reviewers. The reputations of many of the female aesthetes deteriorated during the modernist era, when bold, daring, radical styles and ideologies gained prominence. When feminist scholars began to pore through archives fifty years later, they were still looking for passionate feminist pronouncements in the style the modernists prized.

The neglect of women's writing began with the first histories of aestheticism, which were mostly written by men who had been active in the movement and who recorded primarily the activities of their own predominantly male circles. Yeats, Holbrook Jackson, Richard Le Gallienne, and Osburt Burdett, writing in the early years of the twentieth century, all recorded an aestheticism that centered mostly on tragically short-lived male poets.[28] The one moderately sympathetic account of women's writing, W. L. Courtney's *The Feminine Note in Fiction* (1904), also advanced theories about the particular weaknesses, foibles, and limitations of female-authored fiction.[29] Nor did Courtney consider his subjects participants in aestheticism or, indeed, in any larger intellectual movement. Female aesthetes penned their own accounts of the movement from the 1910s through the 1930s, but since they were incorporated in personal memoirs (in the cases of Pennell and Dixon) and semiautobiographical novels (in Syrett's case), these narratives seemed too idiosyncratic to qualify as literary history.[30] Meanwhile, the main female literary historian of the 1930s, Amy Cruse, was not particularly interested in women's work and wrote a fairly traditional version of the period in *After the Victorians* (1938).[31] And when Woolf issued her famous plea for a women's literary history in *A Room of One's Own* (1929), she ignored the female aesthetes' generation altogether; her feminist historiography leaps from Charlotte Brontë straight to her own contemporaries. In the 1930s and 1940s the last generation of female aesthetes died, and subsequently both feminist scholarship and the scholarship on aestheticism developed without any reference to these women.

From the 1940s through the 1970s most scholars followed *A Room of One's Own* in seeing the period between George Eliot and Woolf as a break in what had otherwise been a fairly consistent history of successful women writers. Feminist scholars sought to explain this failure. Perhaps the most influential of these explanations was Elaine Showalter's *A Literature of Their Own* (1977). Showalter argued that the 1880s marked the end of the "feminine" period, with its cautious conservative texts, and the 1890s marked the beginning of the "feminist" period.[32] The groundbreaking nature of *A Literature of Their Own* can hardly be overemphasized, for the book delineated a strong tradition of women writers so persuasively that it still shapes much scholarship and pedagogy. Thus Showalter's early belief that during the 1880s and 1890s traditional women writers disappeared, to be replaced by passionate feminist voices, continues to influence feminist historiography even though Showalter herself has subsequently expanded her view of the range of women's work at the fin de siècle.[33]

We can see the reverberations of this idea in the ways recent feminist criticism has diverged — either celebrating the feminist energy of 1890s novels or lamenting the virtual disappearance of ambitiously literary late-Victorian women writers. Felski, David Weir, and Peter Keating have revealed the extent to which fin-de-siècle gender judgments impeded women.[34] Naturalists, decadents, and early modernists all believed they were fighting for art against a specifically female mass readership who insisted on conventional romances or crude New Women potboilers, and they consequently expressed hostility toward women as both writers and readers. Whereas Weir and Keating have seen misogyny accounting for the apparent decline of women writers, most other histories of late-Victorian literature have simply assumed that no women writers existed in the period. And critics who disbelieve in the possibility of strong women writers tend not to search for them.

However, an alternative feminist criticism has emerged in the last twenty years. In the 1970s and 1980s New Women criticism, as practiced by Gail Cunningham, Penny Boumelha, David Rubinstein, and others, revolutionized the study of late-Victorian women's fiction, for it not only recovered previously unknown writers but also provided a new critical context within which to understand them. Boumelha, in particular, explored the ways in which New Women novels challenged narrative conventions. But critics of the 1970s and 1980s often presented New Women writers as minor precursors to the major late-Victorian men.[35] This set a defensive tone in New Women criticism, in which many scholars have refused to address the question of their subjects' literary value, or have urged the reader to admire political rather than literary qualities, or have praised one writer at the expense of others. In spite of this hesitancy to proclaim New Women worth reading, however, Cunningham and the critics who followed her succeeded in alerting readers to the fact that a noteworthy corpus of fin-de-siècle women's writing existed.

Contemporary New Women criticism has spectacularly compensated for such earlier self-doubts. In the 1990s Ann Ardis's *New Women, New Novels: Feminism and Early Modernism* and Lyn Pykett's *The "Improper" Feminine: The Women's Sensation Novel and the New Woman Writing* offered ambitious new modes of reading the work of these forgotten women writers.[36] Ardis presented an encyclopedic account of the varieties of New Women fiction, demonstrating that a commitment to political projects existed throughout this fiction. Pykett emphasized that journalistic transparency of language and political univocality of plot could be legitimate literary goals. Both Ardis and Pykett challenged readers' reliance on largely unexamined canonical standards, and their delineation of new evaluative modes has enabled Jane Eldridge Miller's *Rebel Women: Feminism, Modernism, and the Victorian Novel* and other substantive critical work that accords late-Victorian women writers attention and respect.[37]

New Women criticism, however, has not managed to find a niche for the female aesthetes. Although individual women writers whom we might consider aestheticist, like Egerton, have received some consideration, it is usually on the grounds of their feminism rather than their aestheticism — and most of the women discussed in this volume, including Syrett, Jekyll, Malet, Ada Leverson, and Lee, are neglected in discussions of New Women. The problem is that, whereas New Women criticism often seems to include all of the women writers of the period, it tends to discuss only those with strong feminist or political credentials. This selection effect drastically skews our sense of the period, for it tacitly ignores the majority of late-Victorian women writers whose writing does not fit twentieth-century activist criteria.

Female aesthetes will continue to fall through the cracks of a New Women criticism that requires evidence of political enthusiasm — and that is precisely how it should be. New Women and female aesthetes often embraced widely differing opinions about literature and gender, and they ought to be read according to different criteria (Lisa K. Hamilton). These criteria are beginning to emerge, and their further development is one of the central projects of this collection. In her brief introduction to the anthology *Daughters of Decadence,* Showalter described the work of some of the major neglected women writers of the period. Some feminist critics have produced important scholarship on individual female aesthetes — Hughes's recent articles on Tomson and Stetz's work on Egerton are good examples.[38]

Aesthetic women used a variety of experimental literary styles, including fragmented writing, stream of consciousness, dislocated point of view, an unreliable narrator, oblique description, and nonrealist passages. They did so precisely because they were not New Women: in other words, because they could not face public outrage over plain speaking, because their politics were too embattled and intermingled to permit them to write from a clear platform, because they followed high-literary rather than journalistic models, because they were attracted to Pre-Raphaelite notions of beauty. For a brief moment at the end of the nineteenth century a new field of writing opened up to women, and the women who flocked to aestheticism did so because it gave them a language complex enough to express their characteristically ambivalent, sophisticated, and intellectual views.

What does it mean for the history of women's writing to recover the female aesthetes? First, the belief in the absence of ambitious women writers between Eliot and Woolf will have to be abandoned. Eliot had many heirs. In fact, Malet and Mary Ward were often compared to Brontë and Eliot, respectively. Malet, Ward, Lee, Meynell, Margaret L. Woods, Ethel Lillian Voynich, Ouida, Mary and Jane Findlater, Syrett, Tomson, Egerton, and Olive Schreiner constitute an impressive group of ambitious women writers who enjoyed strong sales and critical acclaim. Their work satisfies older canonical criteria of complex structure and symbolic and figurative language and speaks to newer interests in marginalized subjects and formal innovations. By any measure, then, the generation after Eliot's death in 1880 forms a strong link in the chain of women writers.

Second, we need to abandon the idea that Woolf's modernist generation arose ex nihilo, spontaneously generated from a mess of decrepit traditional forms. The modernists famously liked to present themselves as living after "the great divide," in Andreas Huyssen's phrase, writing in a wartime era when, as Woolf put it, "human character changed."[39] Thus modernists often tended to denigrate books from their parents' generation in order to maintain a sense of their own modernity. The idea that the modernists' work evolved slowly and naturally from earlier texts threatens this foundational chasm metaphor. We are implying not that there was some sort of reprehensible conspiracy on the part of modernist writers and critics to suppress their predecessors but rather that, as the modernists' self-image developed, potentially contradictory evidence tended to get forgotten or explained away and that the aesthetes happened to be the primary victims of this modernist self-fashioning.

Third, we need to reconsider the parameters of New Women criticism or to make its standards more explicit. Heretofore, New Women criticism has been the only mode of reading fin-de-siècle women writers. It would enhance the specificity and historical accuracy of New Women discourse to treat it as a mode of analysis particularly suited to the work of overtly political writers, while other critical approaches might be mobilized for some of the other varieties of women's writing during the period. Moreover, by considering the late-Victorian era as a time when a wide variety of women writers were operating, we will enrich both our view of the era and our understanding of its complex gender politics.

What, then, might such an alternative mode of criticism look like? We may answer that question best by turning to an overview of the essays in this volume.

Women and British Aestheticism

The essays in this collection treat a range of writers over a range of genres. Our aim has been to convey the pervasiveness of women's participation in aestheticism as well as the variety of forms that participation took, from the enthusiastic embrace of aestheticism to an equally fervid rejection.

We begin with fin-de-siècle fiction because so many women wrote about aestheticism in the 1890s in both short stories and novels. Indeed, Talia Schaffer has claimed that the aesthetic novel is one of the central contributions women writers made to aestheticism and was a recognizable genre with a feminine tradition stretching back to the early novels of Ouida.[40] The essays in this section show how women writers took up a range of positions in relation to the aestheticism of the 1890s: Margaret Stetz discusses the critique of aestheticism's sexual politics from within, Talia Schaffer the ways in which the aesthetic novel offered women writers an important (if problematic) alternative to New Womanism and naturalism. Lisa K. Hamilton shows how new ideas about evolution and degeneration gave New Women writers something in common with the male aesthetes they criticized. Annette R. Federico demonstrates how the popular novel could make use of aestheticism as well, as a marketing device, playing off the anti-elitist sentiments of its readers while recognizing the allure of aestheticist language, plots, and concerns. That so many different kinds of women writers engaged with aestheticism suggests that its representational techniques and focus on sexuality and gender were extremely productive for them, whether they saw themselves as supporters or opponents, and that engaging with aestheticism enabled women to place themselves advantageously in the literary marketplace.

We turn next to poetry by women that consciously situates itself in the high traditions of Pre-Raphaelitism and decadence. Kathy Psomiades shows how Christina Rossetti constructed the aestheticist woman poet as drawing authority from her privileged relation to aestheticism's feminine images. Linda Hughes describes how Marriott Watson adapted the conventions of decadent poetry — its treatment of the city, of the femme fatale — to her own use, contesting decadent misogyny. Edward Marx analyzes the ways in which Naidu and Nicolson took advantage of the decadent interest in "exotic" Indian femininity to make a place for themselves as cultural producers. Thus, although the sexual politics of aestheticist poetry seems to relegate women to the status of mute erotic objects, Rossetti, Marriott Watson, Naidu, and Nicolson all took advantage of the conventions of this poetry to write about feminine desires and passions. By mingling the aesthetic and the erotic, aestheticism could provide women, as well as men, with a language in which to celebrate and value desire.

Nonfiction prose forms are central to women's participation in aestheticism, whether in the advice-book genre, travel narratives, parody, or aesthetic theory. Aestheticism was a lived practice as well as a high-art theory, and these two realms intersected in unexpected ways. The essays in this next section are centrally concerned with the relation between art and the daily lives of women and men. Barbara T. Gates shows how Jekyll's garden writing aestheticized nature and in the process contributed to the ongoing discussion of the art-nature binarism in aestheticism. Alison Victoria Matthews examines aestheticist ideologies of color taste, as expressed both in painting and in advice literature like that of Haweis, and locates the material bases of these ideologies in the technological innovations that made possible cheap synthetic dyes. Margaret Debelius treats Leverson's parodies of Wilde, which juxtapose high language with everyday situations to make a double gesture of admiration and aggression. Finally, Diana Maltz analyzes the collaboration between Lee and Clementina Anstruther-Thomson on a theory of psychological aesthetics that combined a Ruskinian concern for the poor with a Paterian foregrounding of pleasure and the creation of solidarity in a same-sex elite. In this section the real range of women's participation in aestheticism is visible, as are the connections between widely different genres.

The final group of essays look forward into the twentieth century to texts written within the time period assigned to modernism that review, revise, or renovate aestheticist concerns, themes, and images. Ann Ardis demonstrates how Syrett rewrote fin-de-siècle aestheticism as respectable by allying it with, rather than against, middlebrow bourgeois culture. Dennis Denisoff shows how aestheticism continued to provide a rich resource for women modernists like Woolf and demonstrates the continuing influence of Lee, one of aestheticism's most respected and prolific cultural critics. These essays reveal that modernism was not entirely a rebellion against aestheticism, but in fact incorporated the aestheticist legacy, and that aestheticism provided a powerful discourse for women's self-definition in the early twentieth century.

Finally, Regenia Gagnier addresses the ways in which the turn in scholarship toward issues of consumption and sexuality tends to shift the focus of cultural criticism from the laboring to the desiring body and the ways in which the work of women writers might help us to reexamine aestheticism's implication in commodity culture. Gagnier's essay, like all the essays in this volume, reveals how the very notion of a female aestheticism enables us to rethink historical constructs of nineteenth-century culture and to revise our own contemporary critical paradigms. We hope that readers will find these essays a suggestive starting point for the recovery of a lost generation of women writers.

Notes

1. The difficulties of defining aestheticism are discussed in Ruth Temple, "Truth in Labelling: Pre-Raphaelitism, Aestheticism, Decadence," *ELT* 17 (1974): 201–22. For an excellent, exhaustive definition of aestheticism, see Jonathan Freedman, *Professions of Taste: Henry James, British Aestheticism, and Commodity Culture* (Stanford, Calif.: Stanford University Press, 1990), 1–78.

2. For extended discussions of popular aestheticism, see Ian Fletcher, "Some Aspects of Aestheticism," in *Twilight of the Dawn: Studies in English Literature in Transition,* ed. O. M. Brack Jr. (Tucson: University of Arizona Press, 1987), 1–33; Elizabeth Aslin, *The Aesthetic Movement: Prelude to Art Nouveau* (New York: Praeger, 1969).

3. Walter Hamilton, *The Aesthetic Movement in England* (London: Reeves and Turner, 1882; reprint, New York: AMS Press, 1971).

4. For women artists, see Jan Marsh and Pamela Gerrish Nunn, *Women Artists and the Pre-Raphaelite Movement* (London: Virago, 1988).

5. For more on aestheticist craftswomen, see Anthea Callen, *Women Artists of the Arts and Crafts Movement, 1870–1914* (New York: Pantheon, 1979). Also see Lionel Lambourne, *The Aesthetic Movement* (London: Phaidon, 1996).

6. Talia Schaffer, "The Women's World of British Aestheticism, 1870–1910" (Ph.D. diss., Cornell University, 1996).

7. Cassandra Laity, *H. D. and the Victorian Fin de Siècle* (New York: Cambridge University Press, 1996).

8. Peter Bürger, *Theory of the Avant-Garde,* trans. Michael Shaw (Minneapolis: University of Minnesota Press, 1984), 26–27.

9. Freedman; Regenia Gagnier, *Idylls of the Marketplace: Oscar Wilde and the Victorian Public* (Stanford, Calif.: Stanford University Press, 1986).

10. Theodor Adorno, *Aesthetic Theory,* trans. C. Lenhardt (London: Routledge and Kegan Paul, 1984), 339.

11. Martin Green, *The Children of the Sun: A Narrative of Decadence in England after 1918* (New York: Basic, 1976).

12. Graham Hough, *The Last Romantics* (London: Duckworth, 1949); Harold Bloom, *The Visionary Company: A Reading of English Romantic Poetry* (Ithaca, N.Y.: Cornell University Press, 1961); ibid., *Yeats* (Oxford: Oxford University Press, 1970).

13. Cecil Lang, ed., *The Pre-Raphaelites and Their Circle* (Chicago: University of Chicago Press, 1968; 2d ed., 1975); Jerome H. Buckley, ed., *The Pre-Raphaelites* (New York: Modern Library, 1968; reprint, Chicago: Academy Chicago, 1986); Karl Beckson, ed., *Aesthetes and Decadents of the 1890s* (New York: Vintage, 1966); R. V. Johnson, *Aestheticism* (London: Methuen, 1969).

14. Ian Small, *The Aesthetes: A Sourcebook* (London: Routledge and Kegan Paul, 1979).

15. This apologetic, even hostile, attitude toward aestheticism is not peculiar to the editors of anthologies. For example, Christopher Nasser, in *Into the Demon Universe: A Literary Exploration of Oscar Wilde* (New Haven, Conn.: Yale University Press, 1974), while praising Wilde's writing, quite literally demonized his homosexuality.

16. John Dixon Hunt, *The Pre-Raphaelite Imagination, 1848–1900* (Lincoln: University of Nebraska Press, 1968).

17. Griselda Pollock, *Vision and Difference: Femininity, Feminism, and Histories of Art* (New York: Routledge, 1988).

18. Margaret Stetz and Mark Samuels Lasner, eds., *England in the 1880s: Old Guard and Avant-Garde* (Charlottesville: University Press of Virginia, 1989); ibid., *England in the 1890s: Literary Publishing at the Bodley Head* (Washington, D.C.: Georgetown University Press, 1990); ibid., *The Yellow Book: A Centenary Exhibition* (Cambridge, Mass.: Houghton Library, Harvard University, 1994); Linda

Dowling, *Language and Decadence in the Victorian Fin de Siècle* (Princeton, N.J.: Princeton University Press, 1986); ibid., "Ruskin's Pied Beauty and the Constitution of a 'Homosexual' Code," *Victorian Newsletter* 75 (spring 1989): 1–8.

19. Freedman, xvi.

20. Gagnier. Gagnier's more recent work on aestheticism, in addition to the essay in this volume, includes "A Critique of Practical Aesthetics," in *Aesthetics and Ideology*, ed. George Levine (New Brunswick, N.J.: Rutgers University Press, 1994), 264–82, and "On the Insatiability of Human Wants: Aesthetic and Economic Man," *Victorian Studies* 36 (1993): 125–53.

21. Richard Dellamora, *Masculine Desire: The Sexual Politics of Victorian Aestheticism* (Chapel Hill: University of North Carolina Press, 1990).

22. A small sampling of this work would include: Linda Dowling, *Hellenism and Homosexuality in Victorian Oxford* (Ithaca, N.Y.: Cornell University Press, 1994); Thaïs Morgan, "Lesbian Bodies: The Construction of Alternative Masculinities in Courbet, Baudelaire, and Swinburne," *Genders* 15 (1992): 37–57. Dellamora's own *Apocalyptic Overtures: Sexual Politics and the Sense of an Ending* (New Brunswick, N.J.: Rutgers University Press, 1994) is also important.

23. Rita Felski, *The Gender of Modernity* (Cambridge, Mass.: Harvard University Press, 1995).

24. Laity, xii.

25. Kathy Alexis Psomiades, *Beauty's Body: Femininity and Representation in British Aestheticism* (Stanford, Calif.: Stanford University Press, 1997).

26. See Angela Leighton, *Victorian Women Poets: Writing against the Heart* (Charlottesville: University Press of Virginia, 1992), for sustained discussions of Hemans and Landon.

27. Martha Vicinus, "The Adolescent Boy: Fin-de-Siècle Femme Fatale?" *Journal of the History of Sexuality* 5 (1994): 90–114.

28. W. B. Yeats, *The Autobiography of William Butler Yeats* (New York: Macmillan, 1938); Holbrook Jackson, *The Eighteen Nineties* (London: Grant Richards, 1913); Richard Le Gallienne, *The Romantic Nineties* (London: Putnam, 1951); Osburt Burdett, *The Beardsley Period* (London: John Lane, 1925).

29. W. L. Courtney, *The Feminine Note in Fiction* (London: Chapman and Hall, 1904).

30. Elizabeth Robins Pennell, *Nights: Rome and Venice in the Aesthetic Eighties, London and Paris in the Fighting Nineties* (Philadelphia: Lippincott, 1916); Ella Hepworth Dixon, *As I Knew Them: Sketches of People I Have Met on the Way* (London: Hutchinson, [1930]); Netta Syrett, *Strange Marriage* (London: Bles, 1930).

31. Amy Cruse, *After the Victorians* (London: Allen and Unwin, 1938).

32. Elaine Showalter, *A Literature of Their Own: British Women Novelists from Brontë to Lessing* (Princeton, N.J.: Princeton University Press, 1977).

33. See Elaine Showalter, *Sexual Anarchy: Gender and Culture at the Fin de Siè-*

cle (New York: Viking Penguin, 1990); and ibid., ed., *Daughters of Decadence: Women Writers of the Fin de Siècle* (London: Virago, 1993).

34. Felski; David Weir, *Decadence and the Making of Modernism* (Amherst: University of Massachusetts Press, 1995); Peter Keating, *The Haunted Study: A Social History of the English Novel, 1895–1914* (London: Secker and Warburg, 1989).

35. Gail Cunningham, *The New Woman and the Victorian Novel* (New York: Harper and Row, 1978); Penny Boumelha, *Thomas Hardy and Women: Sexual Ideology and Narrative Form* (Sussex, U.K.: Harvester, 1982); David Rubinstein, *Before the Suffragettes: Women's Emancipation in the 1890s* (New York: St. Martin's, 1986).

36. Ann Ardis, *New Women, New Novels: Feminism and Early Modernism* (New Brunswick, N.J.: Rutgers University Press, 1990); Lyn Pykett, *The "Improper" Feminine: The Women's Sensation Novel and the New Woman Writing* (London and New York: Routledge, 1992).

37. Jane Eldridge Miller, *Rebel Women: Feminism, Modernism, and the Victorian Novel* (London: Virago, 1994).

38. Linda K. Hughes, "A Female Aesthete at the Helm: *Sylvia's Journal* and 'Graham R. Tomson,' 1893–1894," *Victorian Periodicals Review* 29 (summer 1996): 173–92; ibid., *Strange Bedfellows: W. E. Henley and Feminist Fashion History,* Occasional Series, no. 3 (London: Eighteen Nineties Society, 1997); ibid., "A Fin-de-Siècle Beauty and the Beast: Configuring the Body in Works by 'Graham R. Tomson' (Rosamund Marriott Watson)," *Tulsa Studies in Women's Literature* 14 (spring 1995): 95–119; Margaret Stetz, "Keynotes: A New Woman, Her Publisher, and Her Material," *Studies in the Literary Imagination* 30 (spring 1997): 89–106.

39. Andreas Huyssen, *After the Great Divide: Modernism, Mass Culture, Postmodernism* (Bloomington: Indiana University Press, 1986); Virginia Woolf, "Mr. Bennett and Mrs. Brown," *Collected Essays* (1925; reprint, New York: Harcourt, Brace and World, 1966), 1:320.

40. Schaffer, "The Women's World."

PART I

Fin-de-Siècle Fiction

MARGARET D. STETZ

Debating Aestheticism from a Feminist Perspective

IN *A Fair Deceiver* (1898) by George Paston (Emily Morse Symonds), the upper-middle-class hero grows testy and irritable as he suffers through tea with an aesthete. So violent is his reaction to Mr. Leckerby, a contributor to the *Magenta Magazine* (that is, the *Yellow Book,* the influential magazine of art and literature issued by the Bodley Head, 1894–97), that "[h]is feet tingled to kick that corpulent body, his hands itched to . . . shake him till all his affectations fell away." The aesthetic young man is there to pay respects to the hero's fiancée, Lesbia, and to her sister Magda — a visit that Lesbia frames with the following wry commentary: "He professes to be a great admirer of mine. . . . But he scarcely ever addresses a word to me personally. He only discusses me with Magda as if I were a work of art, or not there at all. You can't think how funny it is." Her lover replies, "I should probably call it highly impertinent. . . . But I suppose women really like that sort of thing."[1]

In fact, the anti-aesthetic man has misjudged what "sort of thing" Leckerby provides that "women really like." Lesbia is not swayed by compliments to her beauty, nor is she blind to the aesthete's intellectual shortcomings and ready to be his disciple. She exhibits a shrewd apprehension of the narrowness of Leckerby's intellectual preoccupations, while hinting at the breadth of her own, saying, "The first time he came here he discoursed eloquently upon the works of Pater, Paul Verlaine, Tolstoi and Ibsen. I was rather impressed. . . . [T]he next time . . . he held forth again about Tolstoi, Verlaine, Pater and Ibsen, but he hadn't anything fresh to say about them, and he appears to have read very little else."[2]

Nevertheless, she is pleased to entertain Leckerby, even in the face of philistine disapproval. The exchange with her fiancé that follows explains why: "I never did profess to understand women's ways, but how you can encourage that animal to come and sprawl in your chairs, and pour out his drivel by the bucketful, while you listen patiently and even look as if you liked it, is one of the mysteries that I can never hope to fathom," he declares. Lesbia responds, "If you lived all the year round at Berrymead you would be ready to welcome any novelty with enthusiasm — even a dancing bear. . . . Besides, men and women are not amused or irritated by the same things and persons."[3]

Here, Emily Morse Symonds, a New Woman, or feminist of the 1890s, touches on contemporary dynamics between male authors of the aesthetic school and society women of their circle, who usually were not writers themselves. Such women were, she suggests, well aware of being used as inspiration and decoration and even contemptuous of the role of *tableaux vivants,* or living works of art, to which they were assigned by these "admirers." But they remained more conscious still of the limitations imposed by the norms of their social sphere — norms dictated by both gender and class — and grateful to the aesthetes, who brought variety to their restricted lives and paid lip service, at least, to women's importance, when other men did not. To have someone break the monotony of the drawing room, deliver gossip fresh from the world of avant-garde culture, and address the hostess seriously on Tolstoi, Verlaine, Pater, and Ibsen was no small diversion.

Symonds's 1894 *A Modern Amazon* had already delineated the alternative to the aesthetes' entertaining company, for women of a certain socioeconomic level. In that novel Regina Haughton gives up her literary ambitions upon marrying Dr. Humphrey Kenyon, who considers it "unnatural and unseemly" that "a lady by birth and education . . . should have to earn her living by writing for newspapers and should be forced to wander about alone and unguarded among all sorts and conditions of men."[4] After their wedding he subjects his bride to the physical and intellectual stasis of cloistered, upper-middle-class domesticity. Frustrated, she abandons her husband, only to return penitently later. Her actions, though, receive this sympathetic gloss from Sir Gregory Linkwater, an author himself: "If Humphrey chose to take to wife a modern woman like you, with a mind and character of your own, he ought to have known that you could not be made happy with a comfortable home and plenty of pin-money. He should have allowed you to share his work and his interests, or else encouraged you to find work and interests of your own. But . . . he wanted to . . . keep you in a bandbox."[5] Elevation on a pedestal by attentive aesthetes — even if it came with a price — could seem preferable to enclosure in a box by men who left to pursue "work and . . . interests" from which women were barred.

This was the message reiterated by Lucy Clifford, a prolific author of fiction and plays as Mrs. W. K. Clifford. Her *Mere Stories* (1896) contained the tragicomic "Mr. Webster," the narrative of a woman of means who abandons her marriage and is unrepentant for doing so. She is driven to desperate measures by a bourgeois martinet of a husband, who forbids her to pursue aesthetic accomplishments and banishes the literary company she entertained before her marriage. "I wish you would not talk quite so much at dinner, Emily, when any one is here," her bridegroom informs her peevishly. "I dislike women who express definite opinions —." "I only do it about books, and pictures, and things in my own line," she pleads.[6] But so far as the philistine is concerned, she can have no such "line": "'[D]omestic duties . . . ought to provide enough interest for any ordinary woman. Duty,' he added, with solemnity, 'is the pivot on which the world turns.'"[7] Her flight with an old lover — an aesthete — is the only way out of a life bound not merely by oppressive rules but by tasteless and ugly surroundings. Of the summer "cottage" to which her husband confines her, she notes, "The furniture was highly respectable, durable . . . in the drawing-room the chairs were covered with maroon velvet, in the dining-room with green leather. . . . On each bedroom mantelpiece there were two china vases. Emily looked at the staircase when she went up, and again when she came down, and wondered foolishly whether her coffin would be carried down it or down the one in the Adelaide Road. 'But I don't care which it is, for I shall be a rejoicing corpse inside,' she thought."[8] Lucy Clifford herself, widow of an eminent mathematician, preferred the rarefied, art-loving milieu of Henry James, and the attachment was mutual between the aesthete and the well-connected woman whom Leon Edel has called "one of his [James's] oldest and most cherished London friends."[9]

Throughout the 1880s and 1890s, many real-life counterparts to Clifford's Emily and Symonds's Lesbia were cooped up and restlessly eager to be amused by aesthetes. Among the aristocratic classes, women associated with the group known as the Souls were particularly keen to divert themselves, in their country houses, with avant-garde male artists. There was, for instance, Frances Graham, who, as the wife of the politician John Fortescue Horner, played "lady of the manor" at Mells Park. Having grown up in a household frequented by painters and critics — her father was a National Gallery trustee[10] — she was distressed when she "came to

Mells as a bride [and learned] . . . that she had married into a . . . narrowly puritanical family in which even cycling seemed a dissipation."[11] But she "found her release in art" or, more precisely, in close relations with artists of the aesthetic school, especially Edward Burne-Jones, for whom "[h]er splendid gold hair . . . [and] graceful figure in flowing gowns of sage green and russet made her an ideal model."[12] Similarly, Ettie (Ethel) Fane put Taplow, the hereditary estate of her husband, William Grenfell (later Lord Desborough), at the disposal of aesthetic characters, who kept her supplied with "confidences and compliments" while her husband occupied himself in Parliament; as a friend observed cattily, "What a comfort it is to be cleverer than one's husband."[13] Among those to enjoy her hospitality was Oscar Wilde, who paid her back in flattery, as this 1891 note suggests: "I am publishing shortly a new volume of fairy tales. . . . One of the stories ["The Birthday of the Infanta"], which is about the little pale Infanta whom Velasquez painted, I have dedicated to you, as a slight return for that entrancing day at Taplow. . . . I want you to see it and to like it."[14]

The dynamics of the relationships between male aesthetes and women of the genteel or aristocratic classes were complex and finely nuanced. What Phyllis Rose has observed of Victorian marriage was also true of intersexual friendships: "Traditional marriage shores up the power of men. . . . So that women who are sensitive to power negotiations in their relationships — and women seem to be particularly sensitive to power — may prefer men with some handicap."[15] Often, the female halves of these pairs enjoyed greater social or economic advantage, even when no direct patronage was involved. Many aesthetic male friends were poorer and of humbler origins (for example, Richard Le Gallienne, William Sharp) or branded as interlopers in English society from Ireland (George Moore, Oscar Wilde, William Butler Yeats) or from America (James Abbott McNeill Whistler, Henry Harland, Henry James). Most were looked on scornfully by male contemporaries as effeminate. As Alan Sinfield explains, however, "[T]he aesthete was regarded as effeminate — but not . . . as distinctively homosexual. That was lurking in potential; for some people it was more; but excessive concern with women was still the mainspring."[16] Aesthetes were "handicapped" in the eyes of other men by their very connection with women — feminized and thus despised by association — which, in turn, helped to equalize the balance of power in intersexual friendships.

Nevertheless, male aesthetes also exercised considerable superiority. Although seemingly disadvantaged, they were still men and had the distinct edge provided by better educations, even university degrees; most benefited from unrestricted foreign travel, unlike their chaperoned female counterparts; and all could obtain access to important arts clubs and societies closed to women. Ladies may have ruled drawing rooms and at homes, but they depended on aesthetic male visitors to mediate between them and the influential sites where opinions and works were actually produced and from which they were shut out as effectively as from the spheres of business and commerce. As the male aesthetes moved, during the 1880s and 1890s, into positions as editors of magazines, manuscript readers at publishing firms, critics and reviewers for newspapers, and members of "hanging" committees for art exhibitions, they consolidated their power and controlled portals of admission for women with ambitions in the arts. As arbiters, moreover, of what constituted the Beautiful, they could bestow or withdraw that designation, bringing coteries to one woman's drawing room or putting another's off limits with the label of "second-rate."

The story of the dynamics between male aesthetes and women of the upper-middle and gentry classes is, therefore, tangled, and the subject of women and aestheticism already complex. The complexity increases, however, in the relations between aesthetes and professional women authors, many of whom, like their male peers, were from the middle classes or from abroad and were rising economically and socially through literary pursuits. As women, they may have been the objects of aesthetic valuation and worship, but as artists, they also occupied a different category. Laboring to survive, they did not need visits from men of the avant-garde to relieve the boredom of leisure; they could afford to cast a colder eye on the aesthetes' behavior and the assumptions — especially the sexual ideologies — informing it. Unlike Symonds's Lesbia, these women did not confine themselves to being silently "amused" by condescension. They were as philosophically invested in the principles of aestheticism as were their male contemporaries and stood ready, therefore, not merely to object to specific practices of the men of that movement but to interrogate and correct those practices in their own writings.

Often, women authors issued critiques in the same publishing venues that promoted the men they were targeting. Their corrections of aestheticism appeared side by side with texts illustrating the causes of these objections. Women were, indeed, enabled and even encouraged to speak out by male editors and publishers' readers who were aesthetes themselves — sometimes, the very figures under censure. As Oscar Wilde's Lord Henry

Wotton says, in another context, "[T]here is only one thing in the world worse than being talked about, and that is not being talked about."[17] The male aesthetes' insatiable desire for publicity combined well with their shrewd grasp of consumerist principles, especially of how to sell controversy as a public spectacle. (This apprehension reached an apex in 1895–1896 with volumes 7, 9, and 10 of the *Yellow Book,* featuring epistles that sniped at aesthetic contributors to the magazine — epistles penned pseudonymously by the *Yellow Book*'s own editor, the American aesthete Henry Harland!) Making aestheticism receptive to revisionist voices and broadcasting such voices only strengthened the movement's position in the literary marketplace. Disagreements among aesthetic colleagues could sell books; disagreements between men and women could sell even more books.

Thus a gendered dialogue about aestheticism ran throughout print culture at the fin de siècle, especially in magazines and publishers' lists controlled by the avant-garde. Like other examples of work by late-Victorian women, much of the female side of this exchange has been lost. But once acknowledged, the existence of this conversation ought to cause literary historians to rethink British aestheticism itself — to see it as a movement that was far from monolithic and that allowed for self-criticism and internal dissent. Reviving and re-viewing feminist pronouncements on aestheticism, which were often embedded in fiction rather than in the more obvious vehicle of essays, should also further an understanding of how broad and numerous were the intersections between the literature of the New Woman and the literature of the aesthetic movement.

That aestheticism was contested ground throughout the 1880s and 1890s is a commonplace in studies of Victorian cultural history. Everyone today knows of contemporary attacks on the aesthetes from without: assaults by the bourgeois caricaturists of *Punch,* the muscular imperialists of W. E. Henley's *National Observer,* and the mainstream satirists of the D'Oyly Carte. Less familiar, however, are attacks from within, especially by women writers affiliated directly or peripherally with the aesthetic movement, such as Ella Hepworth Dixon, Ethel Colburn Mayne, and Ella D'Arcy. Many of these women shared, in the 1890s, a connection with John Lane (the publisher of Oscar Wilde, Richard Le Gallienne, Henry Harland, Max Beerbohm, and other aesthetes), either as authors of Bodley Head titles or as *Yellow Book* contributors, which suggests again the deliberate "courting" of feminist criticism by the men who marketed aestheticism.

Unlike those positioning themselves as aestheticism's enemies, female participant-critics were out not to overturn the principle of art for art's sake but to revise the practices, in both literature and life, of its male advocates. Chief among their concerns was the objectification of women in the act of "appreciation," a form of masculine connoisseurship dependent on silent and passive female spectacles. Their goal was to rescue the worship of beauty, so prominent in aesthetic doctrine, from its association with the exploitation of women as nothing more than beautiful "occasions" for masculine discovery, theorizing, and reverie. They wished, moreover, to rescue women themselves from the consequences of an exoticized and demonized vision of female sexuality that had established itself as a cliché in aesthetic literature.

These revisionist female authors were impelled in their efforts by their own dual allegiances. Often, they were not only aesthetes but also New Women, conscious of the political implications of unequal relations between men and women and working actively, through their writing, to restructure social institutions. As Deborah Cherry notes about female painters in the later nineteenth century, "a fragmentary, decentered subjectivity" was the norm, rather than the exception, and "a woman could inhabit quite diverse positions, not only sequentially but at the same time" in her art and politics.[18] Certainly, female proponents of aestheticism and of feminism demonstrated such a multiplicity of loyalties and purposes. In denouncing the misuse of women by male aesthetes and in suggesting possibilities for a more feminist practice of aestheticism, they simultaneously opened up larger questions about gender hierarchies, especially in middle- and upper-middle-class British life, and struggled toward change.

I would like to examine a few of these feminist-revisionist critiques of aesthetic practice. What they share with better-known attacks by male "outsiders," such as William S. Gilbert, is frequent recourse to humor. But as Emily Morse Symonds reminds us helpfully in *A Fair Deceiver*, "men and women are not amused or irritated by the same things." In works by female writers affiliated with aestheticism, the satire is directed much more specifically against male aesthetes' conduct toward women, particularly the treatment of them as mere texts to be interpreted, circulated, consumed, and discarded.

One such "inside" critique is Ella Hepworth Dixon's *My Flirtations* (1892), an episodic comic novel issued under the pseudonym Margaret Wynman shortly after Dixon contributed to Oscar Wilde's magazine,

Woman's World. Dixon frequented the circle of Max Beerbohm, the highly aesthetic wit, and counted among her intimates William Heinemann — the publisher and friend not only to her but to many aesthetes. For the *Yellow Book,* she would write "The Sweet o' the Year," a story set in that most aesthetic of locations, a painter's atelier in Paris, and reflective of her own Parisian schooling in the visual arts. It was, therefore, as a once and future member of the aesthetic milieu that she devoted two chapters of *My Flirtations* to scourging first Valentine Redmond, an Oscar Wilde doppelgänger, and then Claud Carson, a composite poet owing much to Richard Le Gallienne — the aesthete who did, in fact, pen "an extempore poem" about Dixon at a country-house party.[19] These figures have in common a callous exploitation of the very women they profess to hold up as incarnations of the Ideal and as inspirations for their literary productions.

The more harmless Val Redmond — who presents himself as the narrator's worshiper but clearly has no wish to be a suitor — makes use of women as decoration and as the currency of social exchange in the homoerotically linked band of aesthetes that he leads: "He brought all his boys to see me . . . and insisted that they should admire me as much as he did; which was as tiresome for them, poor things, as for me. My photograph . . . was, for exactly five weeks, a conspicuous object on his drawing-room table; after which, for a fortnight, it stood on a cupboard in a dark corner, and finally, I hear, disappeared altogether — to the limbo where the rest of his departed 'enthusiasms' languish."[20]

Potentially more dangerous, however, is Claud Carson, who dedicates to the narrator his volume *Roses of Passion* in these pseudo-Paterian words: "Perfect soul, framed in your strange, subtly-sweet beauty, I worship you from without, with never a thought of earthly guerdon."[21] Despite that disclaimer, his intentions toward the narrator remain murky; at times, he appears to be a heterosexual predator-in-sheep's-velvet-breeches. That reading is reinforced through the narrator's accidental observation of the allegedly unattached Mr. Carson emerging from a very inartistic, suburban house in Hammersmith, with an aitch-dropping wife or mistress and a child in tow. Although his passport to fame is an aesthetic self-presentation that deliberately blurs gender lines, Carson's actions bespeak a most conventional adherence to dichotomies in which working-class women are used for sex and upper-middle-class women are used for "soul," but no honest dealings with either are required of men. The literary consequence of such assumptions is an unconsciously self-revealing hypocrisy of sentiment that disfigures *Roses of Passion,* from which Dixon shows Carson reading to public acclaim at a soiree. His swooning recital becomes a calculated attempt at mass seduction of the female audience's emotions, and thus a betrayal of the principle of art for art's sake. And, as the narrator remarks dryly, "I was the only woman in the room who laughed."[22]

Dixon would turn again to the theme of the politically unreliable male aesthete who conceals behind the rhetoric of art and liberty a wholly retrograde sexism. "The Disenchantment of Diana," from *One Doubtful Hour* (1904), provided a further satirical send-up of the type. This time it was embodied by Astel Verlase, another feminized male poet with "a beautiful head . . . and the full lips of a voluptuary" — lips that signal his appetite for devouring the women around him.[23] A man of fifty, Verlase has a wife whom no one in society has met, "a dipsomaniac, put away in a Home."[24] As the narrative unfolds, the audience sees why she might have had recourse to drink. Following her sudden death, the poet chooses a "bride-elect" thirty years his junior and subjects her to the iron whims that regulate his gloomy, stifling household, with its "dingy" rooms furnished by William Morris and its routines dictated by the poet's hypersensitive digestion.

The narrative analyzes mercilessly the unwholesome dynamics that entrap Diana Bethune as "bride-elect" — dynamics directly related to the position of the Beautiful Woman vis-à-vis male aesthetes. "Diana's strange type of beauty," as the narrator explains, "had made her, at twenty, the fashion in a little set . . . in which famous poets dine, and great painters, who disdain the cheap successes of the Royal Academy, find inspiration for their work." As acknowledged leader of this hierarchical group, the poet appropriates Diana for himself: "Verlase's next volume contained a sonnet-sequence about a certain 'Lily-maid.' . . . [Y]ounger poets came and sat at her feet, noting what the master admired, and piping minor lays about Verlase's Lily Maid. . . . That the poet should have lived more than half a century, and that his love should still be in her teens, mattered nothing to his disciples."[25] Neither does that matter to her guardian, who is eager to fraternize with artists and not above using his niece as an aesthetic commodity to be exchanged between himself and the men whose company he seeks.

What rescues Diana is her own aestheticism — a growing confidence in the right to assert her variant notions of beauty, in opposition to the poet's. She begins in the position to which she has been consigned by male aesthetic practice, silent and passive. But her first sight, as future wife, of the house that she will inhabit awakens her critical visual sensibility and, with it, her rebelliousness. She clashes with Verlase initially over the Woolfian room of one's own, "the little sitting-room which was to be hers": "She glanced round the room at the paper, with its meaningless apples meandering over a sage-green ground, at the faded peacock-blue curtains, and at the autotypes of simpering virgins. . . . 'I think I should like Empire!' said Diana with a sudden impulse. 'It is gay, don't you think in a dull world? Why not,' she went on, gazing at the dolorous draperies, 'have little mirrors with fluted gilt frames, and a sofa or two with pretty striped brocades?'"[26]

Soon, there is no stopping Diana's spiraling hostility to playing "Lily Maid" languishing among the autotypes. A shopping trip for household goods ends in flight. "Never . . . had she desired anything so ardently as to escape from this place, from the man she was with, and to be alone in her own house with leisure to look her future in the face."[27]

Dixon and other feminist revisionists used fictions such as this not only to argue against patriarchal practices by their aesthetic contemporaries but also to argue for the recognition of women as aesthetes themselves. Doing so countered the exclusionary tendencies of masculine artistic circles, as well as the theories of end-of-the-century sexual "scientists," who classified gender roles and published biological evidence of female incapacity in artistic matters. Havelock Ellis, for instance, had made a stir with *Man and Woman: A Study of Human Secondary Sexual Characters* (1894), in Walter Scott's Contemporary Science Series, by confidently affirming, in a chapter titled "The Artistic Impulse," that "there can be no doubt whatever that if we leave out of consideration the interpretive arts [i.e., performing arts], the artistic impulse is vastly more spontaneous, more pronounced, and more widely spread among men than among women. There is thus a certain justification for Schopenhauer's description of women as the unaesthetic sex."[28]

The reasons for this disparity were clear to scientific observers. Ellis cited Guglielo Ferrero, coauthor of *La donna delinquente: La prostituta e la donna normale* (1893), to inform readers that "Ferrero has sought the explanation of the small part played by women in art, and their defective sense for purely aesthetic beauty, in their less keen sexual emotions. This is doubtless an important factor. The sexual sphere in women . . . is less energetic in its manifestations. In men the sexual instinct is a restless source of energy which overflows into all sorts of channels."[29] Yet, as Dixon's protagonists demonstrate, women possessed the very "sense for purely aesthetic beauty" that science declared it impossible for them to manifest and used this, moreover, for emotional, creative, and even political expression and liberation.

A female writer who inhabited the split subject positions of aesthete and New Woman and was in search of male allies would find no welcome among scientists, with their insistence on biology as destiny. But male aesthetes had already opposed the limitations of nature and lauded the individual's power to fashion new, limitless selves. Could they be taught to apply this same perspective to their female contemporaries and colleagues? Could they be laughed out of their exploitation of women as mere occasions for the production of their own art and made to endorse less oppressive aesthetic practices, while accepting female practitioners as artists and equals? The frequency with which fin-de-siècle women authors satirized male aesthetes, for the purpose of correction, and then placed their comedies in publishing venues read by the targets of their laughter suggests a strong interest in such reeducation. Feminist writers may have wished for the luxury of creating art for its own sake, which their male contemporaries enjoyed. They recognized, nonetheless, that their own pursuit of the ideal had to be accompanied by a pragmatic struggle for change in the literary and social worlds, before their aesthetic accomplishments could be received and acknowledged in the first place. New opportunities were emerging, and this "'widening sphere' may have encouraged a false sense" in some male observers "that all doors were open to women" as producers and interpreters of art, but women themselves knew better.[30]

Thus, they took their efforts to the venues where these could have the broadest influence, such as the *Yellow Book,* which embraced the deliberate contradiction of being a mass-circulation magazine of avant-garde high culture. Numerous satires, both gentle and bold, of the men who led the aesthetic revolution appeared there, produced by female participants in the same movement and circulated in a format designed to draw other insiders. Perhaps no women occupied more privileged inside positions than Ethel Colburn Mayne and Ella D'Arcy, each of whom worked as an assistant editor at the quarterly during some stage of its three-year existence and used her vantage point to deliver a corrective message to her male associates.

Around 1927 Ethel Colburn Mayne (whose early pseudonym was Frances E. Huntley) would compose an adulatory reminiscence of Henry Harland, the long-dead literary editor of the long-dead *Yellow Book,* emphasizing his dedication to artistic perfection.[31] From a distance of thirty years, Harland embodied for her the ideal of the end-of-the-century male aesthete as a literary knight engaged in a holy quest. But in 1896, while under the management of the Bodley Head men, Mayne published a comic skewering in "Lucille," for volume 8 of the *Yellow Book.* In Mr. Transfield, the narrator who defines his identity through his connection with the journal "*The Appreciator,* most modern of modernities, most *connaisant* of connoisseurs," Mayne offered her male contemporaries an acid portrait of themselves as fatuous, self-absorbed, and unable to understand or support the female artists whose talents they claimed to "appreciate."[32]

Readers watch in horror as Transfield treats the lonely and despairing poet Lucille Silverdale, whose family considers both her and her gifts an "inconvenience," as merely a fascinating visual spectacle. So charmed is he with his own sensitivity to the sight of her that he never responds to her evident misery or tacit appeals for help. When she flees her family through the only means left, becoming engaged to a very ordinary suitor and ending her literary career, all that Transfield can muster is baffled anger. As Susan Waterman says of Mayne's narrator, "His determination to play the aesthete is pivotal to why he makes no move to court Lucille, despite his protestations of adoration; clearly, he prefers her as 'the riddle . . . of my life,' his Paterian Mona Lisa, rather than as an earthly human being."[33] Clearly, too, he prefers appropriating and narrating her story himself to making it possible for her to further her own art. The female poet and her poetry are annihilated by the man from the *Appreciator,* who has absorbed both into "the little comedy-tragedy that I had (I might say) written, or, at any rate, conceived, entirely by and for myself."[34]

As Jan Marsh observes, "[T]he story of women and art in the nineteenth century is not a simple one of linear, if gradual, progress towards equality," for even new movements and institutions "became more misogynistic as . . . [they] went on."[35] It usually fell to women themselves to arrest and reverse this process. Joining Mayne in this endeavor was the other assistant editor under Henry Harland, Ella D'Arcy. Like Mayne, who came from Ireland, D'Arcy, the child of Irish parents, was an outsider by birth; later, she chose the Channel Islands and Paris over London. But in English aesthetic circles, D'Arcy was as inside as a woman could be — doubly so, as employee of and regular contributor to the *Yellow Book* and also as an author on John Lane's Bodley Head list.

D'Arcy's "The Pleasure-Pilgrim" (1895) appeared in the *Yellow Book* before its reprinting in *Monochromes,* a collection dedicated to "THE CHIEF"

— D'Arcy's name for Harland, the expatriate American aesthete who affected French mannerisms and sat at the feet of Henry James. The story is filled with allusions to the literary milieu in which both she and her editor were immersed. In this narrative, D'Arcy revisits the territory of James, a prized *Yellow Book* contributor, and uses the gendered transatlantic terrain of *Daisy Miller* (1878) as a backdrop for her assault on the aesthetic practices of a male fiction writer, which prove fatal to a beautiful woman.

The story attacks on several fronts, hitting first at habits of appreciation — especially, of women as decorative objects — on which Campbell, the unmarried English aesthete, prides himself. When, at a German castle turned into a resort, Campbell meets his fellow "pleasure-pilgrim," the red-haired young American Lulie Thayer, she represents an occasion for spectacular Paterian connoisseurship: "Her strange little face . . . began to please him. . . . He felt an immense accession of interest in her. It seemed to him that he was the discoverer of her possibilities. . . . Her charm was something subtle, out-of-the-common. . . . Campbell saw superiority in himself for recognising it, for formulating it; and he was not displeased to be aware that it would always remain caviare to the multitude."[36]

The narrator's language exposes the easy slippage from the seemingly apolitical world of art collecting and accessions to imperial conquest and domination, as Campbell fancies himself the "discoverer" of, quite literally, virgin territory. Either way, Lulie functions as visual property, seized through the power of Campbell's superior eye. In D'Arcy's satirical hands, masculine aesthetic spectatorship of women reveals itself as narcissism, meant to reflect well on the artist figure's own refinement. It is no more appealing than the middle-class complacency and self-regard against which the aesthetes railed.

Further assaults on aesthetic practice begin with the arrival of Mayne, Campbell's married male friend. At first, the opportunity for shared spectatorship that Lulie supplies merely strengthens the men's homosocial bond. D'Arcy presents their conversations about Lulie's beauty as a form of competitive sport, a game played at women's expense; Mayne tops Campbell's assertion that "I discovered that she is positively quite pretty" by assuming the posture of the more cultivated critic with a better vocabulary at his command: "'Pretty, pretty!' he echoed in derision. 'Why, *lieber Gott in Himmel,* where are your eyes? Pretty! The girl is beautiful, gorgeously beautiful; every trait, every tint, is in complete, in absolute harmony with the whole. . . . You speak of Miss Thayer's hair as red. . . .

[But] what a red . . . as though it had been steeped in red wine.' 'Ah, what a good description,' said Campbell, appreciatively. 'That's just it — steeped in red wine.'"[37] Mayne, artist manqué, wins this round from Campbell, a published novelist, in the contest of rhetorically appreciating the female body.

But tragic complications ensue when Mayne also claims Lulie as a site for displaying his virtuosity in interpretation and narrative. He imposes on Campbell his vision of Lulie not as a virgin discovery but as a fallen woman. She becomes, in Mayne's overheated tale of the female sexual predator, the vampire who haunts the aesthetes' more sinister imaginings, the woman who seduces "for devilry, for a laugh."[38]

Campbell has been primed to accept this reading by his own rather clichéd Paterian fantasies of strangeness in Lulie's beauty, particularly in her eyes, which he finds "slit-like," exotic, and almost inhuman, with their "narrow, red-brown glances."[39] Not content to call Lulie a siren, Mayne labels her "the newest development of the New Woman,"[40] employing the term as Jude Burkhauser has described its use, "as insult to any female seen to be pressing too far the existing gender boundaries."[41] Unable to shake the "disgust" that Mayne's accusations have aroused and fearful of being "fooled" by a woman, Campbell avoids Lulie. When she breaks out of her assigned role as the passive occasion for male observation and actively expresses romantic interest in Campbell, he recoils from her as from a serpent.

As Lulie's declarations of love increase — as she not only speaks her own desire but thwarts his attempts to silence her, saying "Don't!"[42] — Campbell's rejections grow nastier. Finally, during an afternoon amusement of target practice, Campbell answers her romantic appeal to him by shouting, "[I]f you had any conception of what the passion of love is, how beautiful, how fine, how sacred . . . you would feel yourself so unworthy, so polluted . . . that . . . by God! you would take up that pistol there, and blow your brains out!" The narrator remarks that "Lulie seemed to find the idea quite entertaining," and with a "tragic air which seemed so like a smile disguised," she fires the weapon into her chest.[43] Afterward, Mayne — whose interpretation is opposed by that of Lulie's female confidante but neither countered nor endorsed by an external narrator — continues to insist that Lulie never loved Campbell. Her suicide, he declares, merely showcased her "histrionic sense," for "[s]he was the most consummate little actress I ever saw."[44]

Mayne's denigration of her, even beyond the grave, makes plain the threat she has embodied for these male aesthetes. For Lulie Thayer proves not merely an erotic rival, fracturing the homosocial pairing, but an artistic competitor. Ella D'Arcy creates a female character who is an aesthete in her own right, usurping the male prerogative of appreciating. Susan Casteras has described how late-Victorian middle-class women were reined in and thwarted when trying to exercise their right to visual spectatorship:

> [W]omen were consumers as well as makers of art, although their roles were typically trivialized and underplayed. . . . As spectators of art they were also vulnerable to attack. . . . They were instructed to rely on male criticism . . . and discouraged from competing with men for prizes and commissions. Women were urged to keep their gaze averted in social contact and, symbolically, in art as well, especially from seeing the nude. Although they were frequent visitors to the Royal Academy exhibitions and galleries, even this activity was gendered. The act of looking at art seemed exclusively male to many; thus, the motives imputed for feminine vision or consumption of art were ridiculed.[45]

D'Arcy's American "pleasure-pilgrim," traveling in Germany, understands neither these gendered rules of vision by which the two English male aesthetes live nor the dire consequences of flouting them. From her opening speech, Lulie lays claims to spectatorship, declaring the castle "wonderfully picturesque," and announces her search for fresh impressions and sensations to fuel her imaginative verbal scene painting. She shows an easy familiarity with the aesthetic credo, preferring artifice to nature and the ancient to the modern in architecture and decoration. Clothed in "extravagant" velvet costumes, she proffers judgments confidently, even to a male audience, and disagrees with Campbell in their first conversation. Worst of all, she takes up the privilege of treating men as aesthetic occasions, as they treat her; picking a periwinkle for Campbell's lapel, she says admiringly, "It's just as blue as your eyes. . . . You have such blue and boyish eyes, you know."[46] For these crimes against the gendered code of the aesthetes, Lulie Thayer must die.

But death fails to erase her, either from the narrative itself, which ends with multiple speculations on her suicide, or from the consciousness of readers of the *Yellow Book,* who would have included many male aesthetes. Ella D'Arcy employs her female protagonist, just as she uses satirical representations of masculine aesthetic practices, to rebuke, disturb, and correct her male contemporaries. For the version of the story in *Monochromes* (1895), D'Arcy would produce an important new passage of dialogue, signaling her intentions yet more openly. There, Campbell confronts Lulie with a question that reveals that Mayne has been speaking ill of her. Lulie reacts forcefully: "She flashed him a comprehending glance from half-shut eyes. 'I think men gossip a great deal more than women,' she observed, 'and they don't understand things either. They try to make all life suit their own pre-conceived theories.'"[47]

Was it unrealistic of D'Arcy and other women writers, at the center or fringes of aestheticism, to expect to make their male contemporaries "understand things"? Perhaps not. They had before them the inspiring example of at least one site where artists who advocated aestheticism gathered and where the atmosphere was female-friendly: the Slade School of Art. From its opening in 1871, its "expressed intent" had been to offer "the same opportunities to both men and women for a professional art training." As Alison Thomas notes, it proved "the answer to many young women's secret prayers," including those of the painters Gwen John and Edna Clarke Hall, because of its "supportive and encouraging environment." In the 1890s, it even broke with the gendered rules of looking that had permitted working-class women to model for life class but had kept middle-class women art students from drawing nudes alongside their male colleagues: "By the time that Frederick Brown became the Slade's third professor in 1893 . . . Brown and his two assistants, Henry Tonks and Philip Wilson Steer, happily mixed with the women in the Life Room. Indeed, they were particularly supportive of the women's struggles to be accorded the same educational opportunities as the men . . . [and] maintained their interest in and support of many of the women beyond their student years."[48] Steer was not merely a teacher; he was also a painter, whose work appeared in five of the first six issues of the *Yellow Book,* and he was part of the *Yellow Book* circle. For female writers in that milieu, encountering men such as Steer, who had moved beyond seeing women only as models for their own art and toward accepting them as fellow artists, must have been a powerful incentive to convert their literary brethren to such an enlightened position.

Although some New Women authors primarily addressed female audiences, others directed their work simultaneously to male readers.[49] Certainly this was true of writers who were both New Women and participants in aestheticism, a movement dominated by men. To read their novels and short stories is not merely to hear the double voice of these texts but to become aware of the multiple voices — including feminist voices — within aestheticism itself. With this new knowledge, we may at last redefine British aestheticism at the end of the nineteenth century as more than a precious or static side note to cultural history and instead view it as a complex and engaging movement made up of controversies and countercurrents, as diverse as the modern age it heralded.

Notes

1. George Paston [Emily Morse Symonds], *A Fair Deceiver* (London: Harper and Brothers, 1898), 178–79.
2. Ibid., 177–78.
3. Ibid., 186–87.
4. George Paston, *A Modern Amazon: A Novel* (London: Osgood, McIlvaine, 1894), 1:81–82.
5. Ibid., 2:280–81.
6. Mrs. W. K. Clifford, "Mr. Webster," in *Mere Stories* (London: A. C. Black, 1896), 33–34.
7. Ibid., 52.
8. Ibid., 45.
9. Leon Edel, *Henry James. The Master: 1901–1916* (Philadelphia: J. B. Lippincott, 1972), 5:26.
10. Penelope Fitzgerald, *Edward Burne-Jones: A Biography* (London: Michael Joseph, 1975), 145.
11. Jeanne MacKenzie, *The Children of the Souls: A Tragedy of the First World War* (London: Chatto and Windus, 1986), 19.
12. Ibid., 18.
13. Ibid., 25–26.
14. Wilde to Mrs. W. H. Grenfell, 12 November 1891, *More Letters of Oscar Wilde,* ed. Rupert Hart-Davis (London: John Murray, 1985), 100.
15. Phyllis Rose, *Parallel Lives: Five Victorian Marriages* (New York: Knopf, 1983), 268–69.
16. Alan Sinfield, *The Wilde Century: Effeminacy, Oscar Wilde, and the Queer Moment* (New York: Columbia University Press, 1994), 90.
17. Oscar Wilde, *The Picture of Dorian Gray,* ed. Donald L. Lawler (New York: Norton, 1988), 8.
18. Deborah Cherry, "Women Artists and the Politics of Feminism, 1850–1900," *Women in the Victorian Art World,* ed. Clarissa Campbell Orr (Manchester: Manchester University Press, 1995), 51.

19. Ella Hepworth Dixon, *"As I Knew Them": Sketches of People I Have Met on the Way* (London: Hutchinson, 1930), 136.

20. Margaret Wynman [Ella Hepworth Dixon], *My Flirtations* (London: Chatto and Windus, 1892), 57.

21. Ibid., 83.

22. Ibid., 79.

23. Ella Hepworth Dixon, "The Disenchantment of Diana," in *One Doubtful Hour and Other Side-Lights on the Feminine Temperament* (London: Grant Richards, 1904), 34.

24. Ibid., 33.

25. Ibid., 32–34.

26. Ibid., 49–50.

27. Ibid., 53.

28. Havelock Ellis, *Man and Woman: A Study of Human Secondary Sexual Characters* (London: Walter Scott, 1894), 326.

29. Ibid., 326–27.

30. Claire Richter Sherman, "Widening Horizons (1890–1930)," *Women as Interpreters of the Visual Arts, 1820–1979,* ed. Claire Richter Sherman with Adele M. Holcomb (Westport, Conn.: Greenwood, 1981), 56.

31. Margaret D. Stetz and Mark Samuels Lasner, *The Yellow Book: A Centenary Exhibition* (Cambridge, Mass.: Houghton Library, 1994), 18–19.

32. Frances E. Huntley [Ethel Colburn Mayne], "Lucille," in "Two Stories," *Yellow Book,* January 1896, 57.

33. Susan Winslow Waterman, "Ethel Colburn Mayne: Unheralded Pioneer of Modernism" (master's thesis, Georgetown University, 1995), 72.

34. Huntley, 52.

35. Jan Marsh and Pamela Gerrish Nunn, *Women Artists and the Pre-Raphaelite Movement* (London: Virago, 1989), 119.

36. Ella D'Arcy, "The Pleasure-Pilgrim," *Yellow Book,* April 1895, 39–40.

37. Ibid., 41.

38. Ibid., 46.

39. Ibid., 48.

40. Ibid., 46.

41. Jude Burkhauser, "The 'New Woman' in Glasgow," in *"Glasgow Girls": Women in Art and Design, 1880–1920,* ed. Jude Burkhauser (Edinburgh: Canongate, 1990), 45.

42. D'Arcy, 51.

43. Ibid., 65.

44. Ibid., 67.

45. Susan P. Casteras, "From 'Safe Havens' to 'A Wide Sea of Notoriety,'" in *A Struggle for Fame: Victorian Women Artists and Authors,* by Susan P. Casteras and Linda H. Peterson (New Haven, Conn.: Yale Center for British Art, 1994), 14–15.

46. D'Arcy, 57.

47. Ella D'Arcy, "The Pleasure-Pilgrim," in *Monochromes* (London: John Lane, 1895), 150.

48. Alison Thomas, *Portraits of Women: Gwen John and Her Forgotten Contemporaries* (Cambridge, U.K.: Polity, 1994), 3.

49. Margaret D. Stetz, "Keynotes: A New Woman, Her Publisher, and Her Material," *Studies in the Literary Imagination* 30 (spring 1997): 100–102.

Chapter 2

TALIA SCHAFFER

Connoisseurship and Concealment in *Sir Richard Calmady*

Lucas Malet's Strategic Aestheticism

In describing the enormous importance of *The History of Sir Richard Calmady* by Lucas Malet (Mary St. Leger Kingsley Harrison), it is tempting to place the novel in the context of how fin-de-siècle women writers critiqued, undermined, and rewrote aestheticism. But it is also possible to read *Sir Richard Calmady* as the epitome of a female corpus of aesthetic thought, which was, in some ways, the dominant tradition against which male aesthetes were battling. Other articles in this volume show how crucial women's writing was in the genres of aesthetic poetry and prose, but there was also a strong tradition of best-selling female-authored aesthetic novels, developed by Ouida (Marie Louise de la Ramée) and climaxing in the work of Lucas Malet. Malet's 1901 masterpiece, *The History of Sir Richard Calmady,* stages some of the central ways that women could find aestheticism liberating but also critiques and ultimately repudiates this movement. *Sir Richard Calmady* offers some idea of why women found aesthetic discourse so enabling, how a women's aestheticism functions differently from the men's version, and why the recovery of this lost history is so crucial for both literary and feminist historiography.

When she wrote *Sir Richard Calmady,* Malet was already one of the best-respected authors in England. The daughter of Charles Kingsley, niece of Henry Kingsley, and cousin of the African explorer Mary Kingsley, she belonged to a considerable literary dynasty. Her early novels, *Mrs. Lorimer* (1882), *Colonel Enderby's Wife* (1885), and *A Counsel of Perfection* (1888), were widely admired by critics, but it was *The Wages of Sin* (1890) that placed her with a new rank of writers. Malet became known as "the lady who had the audacity to write *The Wages of Sin* — the first of the modern school of lady novelists to throw a literary bomb into the centre of squeamish people loaded with what she called 'the great and cruel riddle of sex.'"[1] The story of a tortured, masochistic artist torn between a delicate cosmopolitan lady and a strong, kindly peasant woman, *The Wages of Sin* broke new ground in the English novel and deeply influenced Thomas Hardy when he began writing *Jude the Obscure* two years later.[2] *The Wages of Sin* was, according to one critic, "a work which, in my humble judgment, surpasses in psychological insight any English novel published since the death of George Eliot."[3]

When *Sir Richard Calmady* was published in 1901, it cemented Malet's status as the leading psychological novelist of the period. The critic Justin McCarthy stated: "None of our later writers of fiction takes higher rank than that which has been won by Lucas Malet."[4] Reviewers also singled out *Sir Richard Calmady* as the last hurrah of an unrepentant, shocking aestheticism. In 1932 Janet E. Courtney recalled that *Sir Richard Calmady* was one of many aesthetic scandals: "Close on the publication of *The Wages of Sin* came the decadent Beardsley 'Yellow-Book' period, followed by the violent revulsion of 1895 after the Oscar Wilde scandal. That had to be let die down, but even five years later *Richard Calmady* raised a storm of its own."[5] As we shall see, given the subject matter of the novel, it is not surprising that *Sir Richard Calmady* "raised a storm" — if anything, it is surprising that such a novel was published, circulated, and praised.

The novel's first few chapters describe the fairy-tale life of the elder Sir Richard Calmady and his wife, Katherine, who live in an Elizabethan mansion called Brockhurst. When Katherine is several months pregnant, Richard gets trampled by a horse, his leg is amputated, and he dies in pain. Katherine's baby turns out to be a lovely child who carries Richard's name and face — but also inherits his father's dismemberment. He is born with his legs missing below the thighs, leaving him with feet growing where his knees should be. His life is a series of struggles to cope with this condition. At one point he arranges an engagement with Lady Constance Quayle, but she breaks it off because his body disgusts her. Constance's confession of revulsion unhinges Richard and sends him reeling off to all sorts of erotic, anarchistic, atheistic adventures. The dirty, painted, unhealthy, gaudy city of Naples provides an appropriate setting for his growing faintness from typhoid fever and his growing sexual need for his married cousin Helen de Vallorbes. After the delirious climax of "Book IV: The Rake's Progress," Richard slowly realizes that he must learn to accept his body without shame. His difficult climb to emotional equilibrium wins the admiration, and finally the love, of the pure woman Honoria St. Quentin.

The text works through three central paradigms: formalist, political, and economic. In formalist terms *Sir Richard Calmady* combines several genres, creating a kind of culmination of the radical literary innovations of the late nineteenth century. It is indebted to the tradition of gothic fiction; it is heavily influenced by French naturalism; and it is a prime example of the Jamesian psychological novel; at the same time, its language is steeped in semi-archaic, luxuriously descriptive aesthetic discourse. This creative combination of genres was, in itself, a remarkable achievement.

But Malet suffered under the disadvantage of being a woman who was expected to write only about pretty subjects. Unlike other authors of 1890s horror fiction, such as Oscar Wilde, H. G. Wells, Richard Marsh, and Robert Louis Stevenson, she was not supposed to be acquainted with the inmost feelings of male monsters. This problem reveals why Malet needed to become an aesthete and demonstrates at least one way in which the aestheticism of women writers functioned differently from that of their male counterparts. In *The Picture of Dorian Gray* Wilde used aesthetic images to enhance the gothic atmosphere, but in *Sir Richard Calmady* Malet deployed aesthetic visions for the opposite reason: to conceal horrors. She was able to placate her critics by situating her shocking tale in a charming, time-mellowed aristocratic mansion, emphasizing the magnificent antiques and priceless garments of her characters, and framing the whole story in lush, archaic "almost Elizabethan prose."[6] (For instance, the opening chapter, which describes Brockhurst mansion, is titled "Acquainting the Reader with a fair Domain and the Maker thereof."[7]) One of the most perceptive critics of *Sir Richard Calmady* explained that it is "a tragedy so horrible that it must somehow be relieved and ennobled, and that is what Lucas Malet has bent herself to do."[8] So Malet manages to weave pleasing aesthetic images into the painful description of the elder Richard Calmady's operation:

> The logs burning in the grate had fallen together with a crash, sending a rush of ruddy flame and an innumerable army of hurrying sparks up the wide chimney. All the mouldings of the ceiling — all the crossing bars and sinuous lines of the richly-worked pattern, all the depending bosses and roses of it, all the foliations of the deep cornice — sprang into bold relief, outlined, splashed, and stained with living scarlet. And this universal redness of carpet, curtains, furniture, and now of ceiling, even of white-draped bed, suggested to

> Katherine's distracted fancy another thing — unseen, yet known during her other hour of waiting — namely blood (1:73).

The lovely red of the flames both distracts from and denotes the other, unspeakable red of blood. In another example, even as the elder Richard lies dying, Malet draws our attention to the intersecting circles of light from the silver candelabra along with the ghastly pallor of the drawn face that they illuminate. One can fully understand Janet E. Hogarth's judgment: "There are pages which, if read at all, can only be read through the eyelashes. They hurt like the sudden view of a street accident, they are as intolerable as the sight of a surgical operation. But side by side with them are pages, and those the majority, quite as beautiful, perhaps more beautiful, than anything to be found in [her] earlier novels."[9]

Malet's political achievement was her development of aesthetic diction as a strategy to permit a wider range of topics than ever before, especially for women writers. This technique had a history, of course; Ouida was particularly adept at offering extended catalogs of beautiful boudoirs to cover her critiques of the cold-blooded way Victorian society traded on women's sexuality. And other female aesthetes, including Graham R. Tomson (Rosamund Marriott Watson), John Oliver Hobbes (Pearl Mary Teresa Richards Craigie), and Alice Meynell, made good use of this descriptive strategy. But in *Sir Richard Calmady* Malet pushes the very limits of acceptability. This novel addresses deformity, atheism, physical abuse, incest, adultery, premarital sexuality, oral sex, and lesbianism, not to mention the permissible but still dubious topics of socialism, the New Woman, feverish hallucinations, and family conflict. In a period when New Women novelists were getting in trouble simply for acknowledging that they knew about syphilis, it is instructive to notice what a rich and varied range of unpopular interests authors could explore simply by using the techniques of aesthetic fiction. Not only did Malet manage to treat more daring subjects than the much-excoriated New Women novelists, but she also got the critical respect they never received. *Sir Richard Calmady* is a textbook case of why female aestheticism was so useful. Indeed, Malet's techniques may have worked too well. Today, when feminist scholars are searching for revolutionary work by women writers, *Sir Richard Calmady* still successfully dodges behind its rich cloak of aesthetic language, still manages to camouflage itself as a charming period piece.

If read as a parable of economic change, *Sir Richard Calmady* rehearses one of the major shifts in thought at the end of the nineteenth century. In

"Productive Bodies, Pleasured Bodies: On Victorian Aesthetics," Regenia Gagnier discusses the fin de siècle as the moment when a shift away from production and toward consumption begins to dominate both economic and aesthetic theories. Gagnier's idea has obvious gender correlations, since throughout most of the nineteenth century masculinity was associated with economic productivity, while femininity was associated with the pleasurable exercise of taste. But during the fin de siècle male aesthetes expressed a decided preference for connoisseurship, consumerism, and, often, nonreproductive or "perverse" sexuality, which conflicted with the Victorian valorization of productive work and reproductive success.[10] Gagnier cites Hardy's Jude Fawley as a prime example of the clash between these two aesthetics — Jude lives as a hardworking laborer but yearns for a life of free, varied sensations at Oxford — but Richard Calmady seems an equally tortured example, and, indeed, Jude's counterpart. Whereas Jude cannot achieve a purely pleasurable, consumerist existence, Richard cannot find anything else. From birth Richard's deformity has placed him outside economic and patriarchal viability. Through most of his life he imagines himself only in consumerist terms, as either a collector or a collectible. Thus Richard manages to live the life of pleasurable aesthetics, complete with "perverse" sexuality, unrestrained spending, and extraordinary possessions, but only to despise it and himself. Ultimately, he renounces this life, aiming instead for a largely symbolic entry into the normative world of Victorian masculinity. Unable to be a laborer, he can only devote himself to helping those men, like Jude, who participate in an authentic life of work. At the end of the novel he must be folded back into the productive economy, which also requires a proper gender identification and socially appropriate sexual behavior. Indeed, at the end of this novel all three of Malet's major projects intertwine, as Richard's struggle to reach a normative male identity has to fight the narrative itself. The very aesthetic diction that enabled Malet to write the novel, and that gave Richard a sense of self, has to disappear.

We can see how narrative and economic questions converge by looking at Malet's descriptions of the Long Gallery, which is both library and museum, surely an appropriate locale for so aesthetic a novel. Most evidently, it is the site of collections, which demonstrate the family's taste, cosmopolitanism, and ancestry. It is significant that young Richard grows up in what is essentially a museum, for it teaches him to view himself as another objet d'art. Richard's condition requires that his mother and the servants lift him, carry him, and place him. After a brief period of struggling for autonomy, when he insists on learning to ride horses and on struggling up into window seats on his own, Richard resigns himself to the status of an item on display — a useless, static object, alienated from himself and others.

The room contains a Murillo painting of a dwarf, which Richard regards as a strange, skewed mirror of himself. In this uncanny version of Lacan's mirror stage, young Richard learns to identify himself not as a self-contained, attractive ideal but as a repulsive, ominous body. Furthermore, Richard is indeed a creature of art, not of nature. His body has been portrayed by Murillo and predicted by the ancient vellum book that contains the family curse; he comes of art and literature, not of mother and father.[11] Denied normative social interactions, young Richard finds his peers, his family, and his sense of self in the museum.

The room is "cool, faint-tinted, full of a diffused and silvery light," with delicate stone mullions in its lofty windows and misty sunshine coming through the antique leaded panes; along with the painting of the dwarf, it contains ancient books, a marble Buddha, souvenirs from Polynesia and Canada, a bronze Antinoüs, oriental jars (1:41). "It was . . . a harbour of refuge for derelict gods, derelict weapons, derelict volumes, derelict instruments which had once discoursed sweet enough music but the fashion of which had now passed away. The somewhat obsolete sentiment of the place harmonised with the thin, silvery light and the thin sweetness of spices and dead roses which pervaded it" (1:42). The museum description participates in a recognizably 1890s rhetoric that praises half-tones, delicacy, historical obsolescence, and gracious decay. It is in passages like this that *Sir Richard Calmady* justifies its claim to be an aesthetic novel. And if there are hints of brutality beneath the refined, faded description — if the Antinoüs is roughened with rust, if the Polynesian souvenir is a sharp spear, if the Murillo dwarf looks out from embittered, tragic eyes — what are these but the very points that give the frisson to the picture? The objet d'art's coexistence with half-concealed violence makes the scene all the more poignant, just as the embroidered purple cloth shrouding Dorian Gray's infamous picture gives its image a special savor. At least at the beginning of the novel, the steely points of sadism underlying the aesthetic loveliness of faded treasure do not undermine its aestheticism, but intensify it.

The coexistence of aesthetic loveliness with bitter ugliness characterizes Richard Calmady's body, as well as the prose style of the novel. With his body divided between a classic head and grotesque legs, Richard's behavior is half courteous, half satanic. "The indissoluble union in one body of elements so noble and so monstrous" governs his character too (2:49). From the waist up "he might indeed, not unfitly, have been compared to one of those nobly graceful lads, who, upon the frieze of some Greek temple, set forth forever the perfect pattern of temperance and high courage, of youth and health" (1:227). From the waist down Richard is merely "a living creature . . . slow of pace, strange of shape," shuffling like "some strayed animal" (2:303). Usually a good-tempered, thoughtful man, his Rake's Progress is a rebellious adolescent period during which he systematically engages in every kind of sexual vice he can imagine.

He is able to do this because he is so profoundly alienated from his own body. As a man, Richard is frustrated by his inability to participate in the economic activities going on around him, either agricultural labor at Brockhurst or industrial work in urban areas. He tries to compensate for his enforced economic passivity by engaging in maniacally energetic, repetitive sexual activities. But his sexuality, ironically, only ends up replicating his sense of sterility. Since women will not sleep with him voluntarily, Richard hires prostitutes — and thus finds himself in the situation, yet again, of a collector who objectifies and consumes bodies. Even when he gets engaged to Lady Constance, he eventually concedes that she had been bought by the Calmady wealth and name. Richard, in his sexually active adulthood, perpetuates the dehumanizing pattern of connoisseurship, this time placing himself in the collector's position of power instead of the objet d'art's position of passivity.

Malet's symbolism is more than clear in creating a character whose genital area is hideously deformed, especially since she nicknames him Dickie too. Indeed, Richard's sexual needs are the unspoken obsession of almost everyone in the novel. The construction of this character owes something to the mermaid or siren tradition of a lovely woman who is monstrous below the waist, as in William Makepeace Thackeray's famous description of Becky Sharp. But *Sir Richard Calmady* would have been only a titillating decadent novel had it been solely about the sexual acrobatics of a dwarf. Dickie Calmady functions as a kind of everyman, made typical, paradoxically, by what seems to set him apart. In fact, his deformity makes him a sort of priapic figure, a caricature of the male sexual body. Through her depiction of this grotesque body, Malet both constructs male heterosexual activity as repulsive and hints darkly at the dangerous appeal of other "perversities."[12] Richard can only accept his physical deformity when he accepts the social rules for the use of his sexuality; he must reject adolescent transgressive extramarital sex for the more properly controlled fate of marriage to the chaste girl next door. Once he gets integrated into the Victorian structure for male heterosexual relations, his body finally becomes acceptable. ("I am grateful, being as I am; grateful for everything, it being as it is" [3:310].) At once a monster and the average man, Richard Calmady implies that the average man is, in fact, a monster — until marriage, which makes him a patriarch, a properly reproductive and productive subject.

Part of Richard's monstrosity is his incestuous closeness with his mother. Katherine Calmady sees Richard in a double way, for while his deformity makes him a perpetually dependent child, his appearance, name, and character make him an eerily perfect substitute for his missing father. When Richard falls ill, "she saw now, not Richard Calmady her son . . . but Richard Calmady her husband, the desire of her eyes, the glory of her youth" (3: 135). When Katherine and her son reconcile during his fever, she leaps onto his bed to embrace him, crying: "My beloved is mine — is mine! . . . and I am his" (3:138). Meanwhile, Richard's deformity makes him gloat over Katherine's perfectly proportioned limbs. Each night she visits her son's bedside, her hair loose, wearing a delicate robe. On these visits Richard "gazed at her, kissed her hair, and gently touched her arms, where the open sleeves of her white dressing-gown left them bare, in reverential ecstasy" (1:252–53).

Mother and son circle each other in this incestuous dependence, which is based on their simultaneous, tacit erasure of Richard's deformity. Richard can only break out of this cycle by brutally condemning his ugliness, insisting that his deformity makes him nonsubstitutable for his father: "You as good as own it an outrage to your taste, and your affections, that so frightful a thing, as I am, should venture to range itself alongside your memories of your husband" (2:246). In order to direct his desires outside the family romance, he has to emphasize his monstrous difference from Katherine's real object of desire.

Richard's affair with his cousin Helen is a kind of warped mirror of his relationship with his mother. He is attracted to Helen as an accessible version of Katherine: "it struck Richard that she bore a certain resemblance to his mother, though smaller and slighter in build. Her mouth was less full, her hair fairer — soft, glistening hair of all the many shades of heather honey-comb, broken wax, and sweet, heady liquor, alike" (2:279–80). And Richard reconstructs Helen to resemble his mother morally as well as physically. As he tells his mother, "I care enough for her to hold her honour as sacred as I do your own — for ever inaccessible" (2:260).

But Helen's investment in Richard is very different from Katherine's. Helen has an aesthetic interest in him: she sees Richard as a rare collectible. "Your loving is unlike any other. It is unique, as you yourself are unique. I — I want more of it," she pleads (3:104). Helen is a kind of epicure of sex, a courtesan who seduces everyone, from decadent poets to Russian princes, a connoisseur of bodies and desires. Her curatorial attitude is dangerously compelling for Richard, who grew up seeing himself as an objet d'art. Richard's involvement with Helen represents the acme of his alienated, masochistic vision of himself as a consumer item designed to be lifted, carried, and displayed, for he passively lets Helen "collect" him.[13]

Helen's narcissism makes her a fit match for Richard, whose deformity not only makes him wholly self-centered but also makes him admire Helen's perfect body nearly as much as she does herself. Helen constantly examines herself in the mirror. Her beauty guarantees her continued power to seduce: "She leaned forward, gazing intently into her own eyes — meeting in them, as Narcissus in the surface of the fatal pool, the radiant image of herself. And this filled her with a certain intoxication, a voluptuous self-love, a profound persuasion of the power and completeness of her own beauty. She caressed her own neck, her own lips, with lingering finger-tips. She bent her bright head and kissed the swell of her cup-like breasts" (2:275). Helen's narcissistic self-fixation is both a traditional symptom of the Victorian wanton and an appropriate aesthetic response to her own beauty. She is such a ravenous collector that she even objectifies her own body.

Helen is one of the "mondaines," to use Ouida's term, who dominate women's novels of the 1890s.[14] Extraordinarily beautiful, she is also brilliant enough to manipulate the Oxford-educated scholar Dickie Calmady. Helen comes of an English family, but she lives in Paris, and her English is faintly inflected with French rhythms. Her modern rootlessness and epigrammatic wit would be enough to establish her as a female aesthete even if she did not possess a wardrobe and a countenance that rival Dorian Gray's. (She wears a crocus-yellow silk-brocade gown embroidered with peacock feathers and pomegranates, hung about with strings of seed pearls, modeled on a seventeenth-century Venetian design; her wardrobe also includes pink topazes that burn with yellow flame and Nile-green gowns.) Like Dorian, she has absolutely no moral sense, and she engages in sexual adventures whose excess belies her innocent demeanor. In her blithe consciencelessness Helen enjoys inventing stories about herself, which she considers "delightful improvisations, her talented *vivâ voce* improvements on dryasdust fact" (3:31). In other words, she is also an aesthetic writer who constantly rewrites the ever-fascinating tale of her own life. She is, in short, a symbol of one pole of the aesthetic movement as Malet perceived it.

By writing Dickie's relationship to Helen, Malet was able to work through her own attitude toward aestheticism; the sexual relationship between Helen and Richard stands in for the literary interaction between author and genre. Like Richard, Malet goes through all the stages of profound attraction, an important period of engagement that enabled unprecedented, rule-defying liberties, followed by a repudiation of what she saw as dehumanizing falseness. When Richard ultimately rejects Helen, it is at the same time and for the same reasons that Malet disengages herself from aestheticism. Dickie and Helen's relationship represents and works through the novel's own engagement with the genre in which it participated.

The height of Helen's power emerges in the consummation of her affair with Richard in Naples. In a tour de force of writing, Malet weaves the symbolism of the city in with the characters' growing sexual obsessions and Richard's worsening fever.[15] Just as Helen is at the acme of her career in this chapter, so too the novel's aesthetic language is most triumphant here; extraordinary descriptions of exotic objects come to dominate all aspects of the text, including Richard's view of himself. Richard's night with Helen unhinges him and loosens him into a terrifyingly unrestrained, hallucinatory world where there is no reality, only art.

The episode is described in terms of gowns, colors, weather, and scents. Helen, in her sea-green robe, exposing "all the secret loveliness of her body and her limbs," pads barefoot toward Richard's bed. "Not till the grey of a rain-washed, windy morning had come, and Naples had put off its merry sinning, changing from a city of labour, and, too often, of callously inflicted pain, did Helen de Vallorbes leave the cedar-scented library" (3:64). The shift from Helen's loveliness to a gray morning signifies Richard's shift from desire to disgust and his full entry into a surreal world where apparently "real" events and people become objects representing his feelings. Richard now experiences the most abject and repulsive aspects of Naples — its poisonous harbor, filthy with oily pollution, coal dust, poverty, curses, and screeching — as his mind wanders helplessly in fever. He now views his ideal, Helen, as a filthy woman, and when he reviews his adultery he feels "an immense private shame and immense self-condemnation, a conviction of outlawry and a desolation passing speech" (3:68).

We are somewhere outside realism here. In Richard's hallucinatory stream of consciousness, "formless thoughts pursued one another, as with the hurry of rumoured calamity, through his mind" (3:60). He confuses the heat of fever with the flames of desire; he sees events and objects as defective. He dimly perceives "beings maimed as he was himself, but after a more subtle and intimate fashion — a fashion intellectual or moral rather than merely physical" (3:61). Richard begins to see everyone, not just himself, as flawed objets d'art. In a sense, his fever gives him the capacity to read his "reality" as a series of symbols. In other words, he examines the people around him as if they were characters in a novel — as if he is in an aesthetic world where there is nothing but art. This leap to the reader's perspective is a frighteningly alienating one, because it profoundly undermines the novel's reality effect. And as Dickie enters an entirely aesthetic worldview, he achieves a kind of radical epistemological dislocation, for both himself and the reader, that is unprecedented in the history of the aesthetic novel, which usually constructs a "safe" aesthetic space within a house but assumes that ordinary life goes on outside it.[16] In his feverish hallucinations, for instance, Richard sees two sides of Helen: "He beheld a being, exquisitely formed, perfect in every part, step forth from between the lips of the woman fashioned in ivory and gold. It knelt upon one knee. . . . It was naked and unashamed. It was black — black as the reeking, liquid lanes between the hulls of the many ships, over which the screaming gulls circled seeking foul provender, down in Naples harbour. — And he knew the fair woman it came forth from for Helen de Vallorbes, herself, in her crocus-yellow gown sewn with seed-pearls" (3:94–95). When Richard sees Helen as a fair body encasing an oily body, this literalization of the governing metaphor for Helen is just as disturbing as *Vanity Fair* would be if Joseph Sedley suddenly glimpsed Becky Sharp's mermaid tail under the Sedleys' mahogany table.

Richard's cloudy reasoning impels him to go to the opera house, where he has a revelatory hallucination that gives *Sir Richard Calmady* the dimension of an ideology critique. In this moment he understands his personal tragedy as an inevitable result of his class position. The opera-house revelation is the moment when Richard and the novel itself repudiate the aesthetic world generally, which is seen here to consist of the exploitative practice of unrestrained, parasitic consumption in which people can only imagine themselves as objets d'art that someone else might want to consume or, at best, as collectors buying other bodies. Like *Dorian Gray,* then, *Sir Richard Calmady* is an aesthetic novel that critiques the dangerous excesses of aestheticism.

Dickie sees the opera boxes as the tiers of a gigantic honeycomb, where the worker bees are about to swarm against their rulers:

> For they were all peopled, these cells of the honeycomb, and — so it seemed to him — with larvæ, bright-hued, unworking, indolent, full-fed. Down there upon the *parterre,* in the close-packed ranks of students, of men and women of the middle-class, soberly attired in walking-costume, he recognised the working bees of this giant hive. By their unremitting labour the dainty waxen cells were actually built up, and those larvæ were so amply, so luxuriously fed. And the working bees — there were so many, so very many of them! What if they became mutinous, rebelled against labour, plundered and destroyed the indolent, succulent larvæ of which he — yes, he, Richard Calmady — was unquestionably and conspicuously one? (3:86–87)

Richard hopes desperately for this revolution to cleanse society and offers himself as the sacrificial victim; as a useless, decadent aristocrat, he has to be destroyed by the buzzing, swarming masses. His vision critiques the lovely objects with which the novel has otherwise softened the impact of its story. The daintiness of Helen's yellow brocade, of the heirlooms in the Long Gallery, of Richard's cedar-scented library, becomes a sign of "sinfulness and uselessness" (3:90). The "beehive" vision is the point where the novel turns on itself and externalizes, embodies, and repudiates its own aestheticism.

Richard's beehive vision reveals that labor makes the rarefied aesthetic world possible — that the gray slums of Naples produce the city's beauty, that Helen's prostitution buys her splendid dresses. At this moment Richard realizes that he must return to the productive aspect of the economic world instead of being entirely a consumer; as Gagnier reminds us, "surely people are *both* producers and consumers, workers and wanters, sociable and self-interested, vulnerable to pain but desirous of pleasure, longing for security but also taking pleasure in competition." When Richard recognizes this fact, he begins to see how he can insert himself into the productive economy, too. He flees toward a life of productivity — to reproductivity, in the form of Honoria, and to supporting economic production, even if he cannot initiate it, by founding a home for victims of disfiguring industrial accidents. Richard insists on recognizing his kinship with these laborers: "After all, I am . . . a bit of human wreckage myself, with which, but for the accident of wealth, things would have gone pretty badly" (3:277). His recognition of equality with those who are, supposedly, his social inferiors is precisely the kind of radical equation Malet liked to place at the heart of her novels.[17]

Thus the part of *Sir Richard Calmady* after the beehive vision works to repair things in several ways: it remasculinizes Richard in order to regularize his sexuality, to place him in a properly productive regime, and to develop an appropriately honest discourse. The novel also rejects the feminized realm of aestheticism, associated with unbridled license, dangerous exoticism, dehumanizing connoisseurship, and deceptive language. In order to reform both its subject and its narrative, *Sir Richard Calmady* replaces Helen with a more acceptable object of desire: Honoria St. Quentin (clearly a substitute for Helen de Vallorbes, as another cousin of Dickie's, a friend of Helen's, and a woman with a similar name). Honoria represents a different set of discourses: New Woman fiction and naturalism. Through the characteristics associated with Honoria — honesty, political engagement, straightforwardness, naturalness, and healthiness — Malet tries to find a different direction for the novel. But the transition is not easy; in order to present Honoria, Malet still has to use the strategic tricks of aesthetic language.

On the surface Honoria St. Quentin seems the embodiment of nature itself. She loves trudging over fields and feeding animals; her eyes are the green color of the forest gloom, and her serviceable tweeds are always stained with mud and scented with fresh air. She is figured as a kind of Artemis, goddess of virginity. Richard admires her "superb chastity — he could call it by no other word" (3:220). Honoria is also his mother's closest friend. In these respects she is the wholesome English girl, healthy and pure.

Yet in reality Honoria's character pretty thoroughly violates the usual definitions of the good Victorian girl — and transgresses these definitions so deftly that no contemporary reviewer noticed how problematic she might be. She retains her heterosexual chastity not because of her sexual purity but because of her homoerotic desires. Honoria falls in love with Katherine Calmady.[18] In marrying Honoria, Richard perpetuates the family romance, for Honoria and Richard view each other as substitutes for their real but unattainable object of desire, Katherine Calmady.

Honoria and Richard are an ideal match, for each provides the properly gendered behavior the other so problematically lacks. Honoria's masculine activity allows her to pursue goals that Richard's deformity makes impossible. As she herself says, she can shoot, fish, break horses to harness, sail, handle an ax, play tennis and billiards, but she cannot sew (3:121). Honoria has an angular, boyish body and often refers to herself as a man. ("I'm not what you call a marrying man," she tells a suitor [2:315].) At the same time Richard represents the "feminine" part of Honoria. He is domestically oriented, weak, passive, and cared for by his mother and servants. By marrying Honoria, Richard can symbolically acquire her masculine self-reliance, while the marriage helps Honoria appropriate the passive, trapped femininity of Richard's life.

That the two are counterparts of the same psychological whole is shown by their parallel acts. After his Rake's Progress, Richard decides to imprison himself in his bedroom, unwilling to show his deformity in public. At the same time that Richard commences his seclusion, Honoria makes an odd declaration: "The woman in me must continue to be kept in the back attic. She shall be denied all further development" (3:142–43). Indeed, just when Richard emerges from his rooms to begin courting Honoria, she feels the madwoman in the attic start tearing off the yellow wallpaper, as it were: "It so happened that the woman in her whom — to use her own phrase — she had condemned to solitary confinement in the back attic, beat very violently against her prison door just then in [*sic*] attempt to escape" (3:221). Honoria finally merges with this "woman" inside when she enters a linen closet that is literally a back attic. In this tiny, safe, womblike space she confronts her love for Richard. Although the metaphor demands that the woman be released, the narrative implies that Honoria has turned into the imprisoned woman incarcerated in the closet. And Honoria's entrance into normative heterosexuality is connected with highly ambiguous images. The visible signs of her desire for Richard are her swollen, reddened eyelids and her face oddly thickened with a rush of blood, as if she were in pain. Victorian narrative demands this kind of retraining of rebellious subjects; but Malet allows us to see how pathologically it functions, and how emotionally painful it feels, for its unwilling participants.

Richard's new idea of working for disabled laborers chimes in with Honoria's radical politics. She is a socialist who sees factory work as human sacrifice and a feminist who struggles to unionize women workers (3:242–43; 2:64). Honoria is, in other words, a New Woman, and the discourse she brings into *Sir Richard Calmady* is that of the New Woman novel. Independent, politically active, fearlessly transgressing gender and sexual lines, Honoria St. Quentin is exactly the kind of woman that Eliza Lynn Linton labeled a "shrieking sister" and that was commonly perceived as sterile, unnatural, and fatal to the race.[19] This fact makes it all the more remarkable that Honoria's character was universally praised in reviews of *Sir Richard Calmady.*[20] By constantly focusing the reader's attention on Honoria's appearance, Malet successfully distracts her readers from Honoria's profoundly transgressive character. For instance, she describes Honoria's dark-red gown knotted with black silk in such loving detail that we hardly notice the problematic fact that its wearer is running straight from the fields into the dining room yelling that she is hungry (3:201).

Sir Richard Calmady's canny deployment of images like Honoria's red gown makes it an aestheticist novel that both uses and critiques aestheticism. Helen de Vallorbes, fair on the outside, a mass of seething sexuality within, is indeed a good figure for the female aesthetic novel. *Sir Richard Calmady* uses its semi-Elizabethan language and longing descriptions of museum-quality objects as a shield for its interest in transgressive sexualities. In the literary climate of 1901, no writer, particularly no woman writer, could have published this novel without its saving aesthetic face. Malet's crucial political achievement was to violate all the critical canons governing women's writing with complete impunity.

Richard's painful journey toward self-exposure was also the journey that *The History of Sir Richard Calmady* had to take. When Richard realizes that he must treat his deformity openly and unashamedly, we can read this as not only his psychological growth but also a self-reflexive description of the novel's growing acceptance of its own naturalism. But given the contemporary critical bias against women's naturalism, the novel had to resist its own imperative toward revelation. In the last few chapters, after Richard decides to stop hiding himself, the narrative goes to great lengths to keep our attention away from his body. Our point of view shifts to Honoria's, who, to the very end of the novel, resists looking at Richard's legs. In other words, at the end of the novel we are more or less in the world of the New Woman novel, but we cannot fully inhabit its outspoken language.[21] When Richard learns to stand on his own two feet, the novel must either follow him or end — and in 1901 it had to end.

Sir Richard Calmady, who tries to hide his diseased, sexualized body under an embroidered coverlet, is no bad figure for the female aesthetic writer herself, who used archaisms, adjectives, humor, and fantasy to express yet conceal what she was not supposed to know (1:288). For women writing at the end of the nineteenth century, then, aestheticism became a privileged locus for self-expression because it was the most critically acceptable way to explore alternative topics and the most self-consistent way to investigate a new culture of consumption. Women writers found in aestheticism a complex style, subject, and system within which they were able to produce remarkable novels in a way no other turn-of-the-century genre permitted. In *Sir Richard Calmady* Malet utilized aestheticism to produce a radical text that anticipates modernist ideas. It is perhaps relevant to look back to *Dorian Gray, Dracula,* and *Dr. Jekyll and Mr. Hyde,* which coped with the threat of moral chaos by producing reassuring endings in which the monstrous invader is ejected from an essentially purified society. But the female aesthetic version of the monster narrative indicates that we are all monsters; that in a new world of warped sensibilities and surreal representations, the morally and physically deformed figure must be our role model, not our threat. *Sir Richard Calmady* insists that the unproductive, suffering body is "no longer abhorrent but of mysterious virtue and efficacy, endued with power to open the gates of a way, closed to most men, into the heart of humanity" (3:195).

Notes

1. Harry Furniss, *Some Victorian Women: Good, Bad, and Indifferent* (London: John Lane, 1923), 19–20.

2. Talia Schaffer, "Malet the Obscure: Thomas Hardy, 'Lucas Malet,' and the Literary Politics of Early Modernism," *Women's Writing* 3, no. 3 (1996): 261–86.

3. Canon Malcolm MacColl, "Morality in Fiction," *Contemporary Review* 60 (August 1891): 252.

4. Justin McCarthy, *Reminiscences* (New York: Harper and Brothers, 1899), 2:236.

5. Janet E. Courtney, "A Novelist of the 'Nineties," *Fortnightly Review* 137 (1932): 237.

6. William Barry, *Bookman* 14 (November 1901): 255.

7. Lucas Malet, *The History of Sir Richard Calmady,* 3 vols. (Leipzig: Bernhard Tauchnitz, 1901), 1:7. All further citations will be noted parenthetically in the text and are taken from this edition.

8. Stephen Gwynn, "Sir Richard Calmady," *New Liberal Review* 2 (1901–2): 483.

9. Janet E. Hogarth, "Lucas Malet's Novels," *Fortnightly Review* 77 (1902): 540.

10. In this article I am treating these as chronologically distinct movements, but of course the reality was somewhat more complex. Both movements were present

within aestheticism, in two conflicting strands of thought: Paterian and Ruskinian aesthetics. Walter Pater praised art for inviting viewers to live a life of pure sensation, while John Ruskin emphasized that art derived from, and incited viewers to, socially responsible work.

11. The family curse is that the owners of Brockhurst will die violently until a strange child is born, half angel and half monster, who can redeem the family.

12. The two most obvious forms of "perverse" desires represented in the novel are fetishism and incest, for Helen de Vallorbes is clearly aroused by Dickie's deformed feet, while Richard's mother has a problematically close bond with him. Dickie also admires the sinewy bodies of male relatives, and in the aftermath of the Wilde trial any aesthetic novel depicting a man's voracious and shameful sexual appetite (especially in an exotic locale) carried overtones of "the love that dare not speak its name."

13. In this respect it is fitting that when Helen seduces Richard he is lying passively on the sofa.

14. In Ouida's novels, the "mondaine" is a witty, rootless socialite whose overwhelming beauty, aristocratic hauteur, and razor-sharp tongue give her complete dominance over her social scene. The ladies who exchange tea-table repartee in Wilde's *Dorian Gray* and his plays are watered-down versions of this figure, while the femme-fatale characters who appear in so many late-Victorian texts bear some relation to her.

15. Malet's depiction of a dangerous fever combining with an erotic obsession predates Thomas Mann's use of the same theme in "Death in Venice" by eleven years.

16. In *The Picture of Dorian Gray,* Dorian's, Lord Henry's, and Basil's houses are beautiful spaces, but there is an unromantic real world that includes opium dens, tawdry theaters, and poor lodgings. In J.-K. Huysmans's *À rebours,* Des Esseintes makes his house into a self-contained aesthetic fantasy world but increasingly has to hide himself inside it, as the external world becomes too hostile in its ugliness. Even his servants have to wear artistically medieval gowns when they pass his windows to keep up the illusion.

17. Similarly, in *The Wages of Sin* Malet works toward an equation between the "angel" and the "whore." See Schaffer, "Malet the Obscure."

18. "'Does it displease you? Does it seem to you unnatural?' Honoria asked quickly. 'A little,' Lady Calmady answered, smiling, yet very tenderly" (2:324).

19. Eliza Lynn Linton, "The Partisans of the Wild Women," *Nineteenth Century* 31 (1892): 455–64.

20. For instance, Justin McCarthy called Honoria "a beautiful and gifted young woman" (Justin McCarthy, *Independent* 53 [1901]: 2624). The author of a stridently anti–New Woman article, W. F. Barry, felt that *Sir Richard Calmady* "justified the very highest praise" (255).

21. This ambivalence is typical of the female aesthetes. Torn between the liberated, witty, urbane, strong New Woman and the gracious, lovely Angel in the House/Pre-Raphaelite lady, the female aesthetes tried to forge a compromise identity. Women authors of aesthetic fiction frequently stage a competition between representatives of these two realms, a way of working through their own indecisiveness about women's proper role.

Chapter 3

LISA K. HAMILTON

New Women and "Old" Men

Gendering Degeneration

Critics have often conceived of the distinction between decadence and degeneration as the difference between a literary and philosophical movement and a pseudoscientific rhetoric of decay or as the difference between the cultivation of decline and the unintended slide into it. David Weir opened his study of decadence with a provocative aphorism: "Decadence and degeneration have little in common: one refines corruption and the other corrupts refinement."[1] Oscar Wilde, however, explored the representational possibilities of describing decadence through allusion to degenerationist rhetoric in his novel *The Picture of Dorian Gray* (1891), in which the growing ugliness and decay of the painted Dorian express the corruption of his soul. The flaws and deformities in the painting represent Dorian's sins according to the pervasive nineteenth-century model of reading the body, which linked moral and physical traits in order to discover physical manifestations of morality and immorality. While theories about the correlation of the inner self and the body have existed since antiquity, the formal codification of this myth of recognizability that arose in the late eighteenth century with the systematization of Lavaterian physiognomy as a scientific way of reading character on the body was refined by the post-Darwinian culture of scientific materialism. In his late-nineteenth-century fable about the visibility of vice, Wilde retained the essential degenerationist connection between vice and physical decay but suggested an entirely different evaluation of sin itself, as Dorian becomes aesthetically enthralled by the painting's intensifying ugliness.

The flood of degenerationist writings, both literary and scientific, that began at midcentury and peaked before World War I reflects a pervasive fascination with physical deviations as simultaneously the source and the marker of mental and moral inferiority.[2] When difference is pathologized — that is, when features of a population's physiognomic variation are thought to encode normalcy and deviancy — a mind-set is established in which novelists and clinicians looking to mark and separate out certain groups (ill people, foreigners, criminals) have recourse to elaborate descriptions and discussions of physical features that appear to represent the feared characteristics. Degenerationism's tenure as reigning cause and symptom — a brief fin-de-siècle moment preceding the ascendancy of Freud — arose out of and perpetuated a culture that regarded bodily pathology as the cause and result of immorality. Rita Felski has noted that even though the decadent movement in general disdained "the rationalist claims of science, aestheticism was nonetheless deeply suffused by its organicism and pathological metaphors and by Darwinian notions of evolutionary development."[3] Moreover, the literary degeneration that critics like Felski have seen as part of a late-century style in which "'organic' narrative" decomposes into "detail" draws the reader's attention away from plot and focuses it on description.[4]

Into this singular descriptive universe arrive the New Women writers, early feminists whose work addressed the political, social, and moral conditions of the fin-de-siècle female. One of the most prominent New Women writers, Sarah Grand, in her popular 1893 novel, *The Heavenly Twins,* paid particular attention to the health of middle-class women threatened by syphilis contracted through marriage and by the more generalized degeneracy of their husbands. The stereotypical physical markers with which Grand branded her syphilitic and degenerate male characters were drawn from scientific and medical tracts and from the literary works of her contemporaries, the decadent writers, all of whom partook in "the late-nineteenth century obsession with visible vice."[5] Grand, however, as a protofeminist who was influenced by the midcentury purity campaigns that focused obsessive attention on the issue of male sexuality, countered the decadents' transvaluative approach to degenerationism and issues of morality and recognizability by reaffirming the connection between vice and appearance assumed by the racial and sexual sciences of the age. In response to the culturally enforced innocence of many women and their resulting failure to recognize and read properly signs of their husbands' potential disease, Grand emphasized sexual awareness and a high level of diagnostic sophistication in the service of both personal protection and purity.

Critics have commented on the relationship between New Women and decadents ever since the fin de siècle itself. Linda Dowling has noted that Victorian observers "persistently identified the New Woman with the decadent, perceiving in the ambitions of both a profound threat to established culture." But, in her attempt to map out a coherent genealogy of the avant-garde, Dowling has emphasized their shared "revolutionary" tendencies at the expense of their fundamental differences in aesthetic strategy and cultural ideals.[6] That the New Women even *had* an aesthetic strategy has been doubted.[7] However, recent critics have rethought this idea. For example, John Kucich and Teresa Mangum have explored what has often been perceived as shoddy craftsmanship in New Women novels and have argued that their mix of politics and fiction resulted from a rejection of the art for art's sake attitude of the decadents and produced what Mangum has called "the ethical aesthetics of the New Woman."[8] The literary projects of the aesthete and the New Woman involved a heightened awareness of sexuality and of gender, both of which were expressed in highly visible, physical terms — in the content of their literature and in their choice of clothing and mannerisms. But I want to examine the *differences* between the two by comparing the ways in which decadents and New Women writers (specifically, Wilde and Grand) manipulated descriptive tropes drawn from sciences like physiognomy and degenerationism: while the decadents felt free to play with stereotypes and to embrace what society considered dangerous and pathological, New Women writers generally accepted the authority of pseudoscience, used it to underpin their warnings about dangerous sexual liaisons, and thereby disseminated its conclusions.

The disparity and the unevenness of the "revolutionary" commitment — falsely perceived by Dowling to constitute "real coherence" — of *both* New Women and aesthetes become clear when their positions are viewed through the prism of degenerationism and its anxious focus on anarchic sexuality and gender roles. A New Woman writer like Grand tended to reinforce a conservative reading of the genders as stable and stereotypical opposites, while the decadents, as Felski has argued, took on idealized feminine traits but rejected any association of sophistication or artistic and cultural value with women. Moreover, the variant uses of scientific discourse in the writings of both groups reveal their relative positions within the dominant culture. The decadents, writing from a position of greater sophistication, education, and privilege within British society, relied on parodic inversion and the transvaluation of both literary and scientific terminology and social and discursive paradigms, while the New Women authors sought to shore up their culturally marginal position and attain legitimacy through the straightforward use of scientific discourse.

Although the decadents aspired to cultural marginality through their assumption of feminine characteristics and their antibourgeois sentiments, their secure position at the center of culture allowed them to flourish despite attacks from critics.[9] Cultural marginality worked against the effectiveness of New Women critiques because their work seemed to lack the subtlety and complexity of the decadent writers'; the anxious didacticism of their writing often appeared simpleminded in comparison with the sophistication and wit of cultural insiders. But of course their anti-aesthetic aesthetic was also an attempt to define themselves against the decadents and to distinguish themselves *morally* as well as artistically. For example, while contemporary critics tarred all sexually explicit work with the same brush, Grand was careful to distinguish her brand of sexually frank writing from that of both the decadents and the French school of naturalists, especially in her 1897 novel, *The Beth Book,* in which both her New Woman, Beth, and Beth's literary mentor, Sir George Galbraith, read but reject the sexual explicitness of Zola: Galbraith disapprovingly notes that France's "lascivious authors and artists . . . are sapping the manhood of the country and degrading the womanhood by idealising the self-indulgence and mean intrigue."[10]

Dorian Gray's double life became a model on which both decadent and New Women writers drew for the expression of degeneracy and for the possibility of its concealment. But Dorian's degenerate offspring inhabit New Women novels in the service of a project entirely different from and even incompatible with that of decadent writers like Wilde.[11] New Women novels are cautionary tales warning women about how the degeneracy of potential spouses can adversely affect their health and educating them about how to read the male body in order to recognize even the faintest symptoms of vice. By shifting the focus from aesthetic fable to diseased reality, New Women writers critiqued the romanticization of illness and degeneracy through graphic depictions of the real-life consequences. With this critique of cultural and literary mores, New Women writers juxtaposed the decadents' aestheticism and their own practical politics and exposed the extent to which aestheticism had repressed or attempted to contain a troubling social situation, the reality of illness as a result of vice.

Deciphering the New Women writers' stance on gender issues is difficult because, although they were reformers who argued for an active and informed female population, they retained traditional expectations about gender behavior in their writing, though somewhat inconsistently. Because they violated the Victorian ideology of separate spheres — which considered the realm of public life and political action a masculine fiefdom — politically active reformers, suffragists, and New Women were stigmatized as manly and therefore "decadent."[12] This stigmatization influenced early feminist writers' attempts to reinforce the decadence and effeminacy of the male in their writings in order to shift the charge of degeneracy away from themselves. Their writings reflect anxiety about the upending of traditional social roles, as some New Women writers lamented that the late-Victorian period was "effeminate."[13] For example, in the *North American Review* Grand admonished men who "snarl" about "the end of all true womanliness" and who complain about women who have not remained in their proper "[s]phere . . . with shades over our eyes so we may not see [man] in his degradation." Grand dismissed their predictions that such women would be "afflicted with short hair, coarse skins, unsymmetrical figures, loud voices, tastelessness in dress, and an unattractive appearance and character generally." While she rejected the physiognomic threat that women were thought to face because of *their* transgression of the separate spheres, she concluded in the terms of the stereotypical gender dichotomy: "the trouble is not because women are mannish, but because men grow ever more effeminate."[14] Grand urged men to reclaim masculinity, thereby reinforcing the definition of effeminacy as a negative quality.

The cultural cognates of effeminacy in late-nineteenth- century culture, and the feminized ideals that the decadents both aspired to and despised, have been described by recent critics as evidence of the decadents' participation in the feminized world of commodity culture (Felski and Regenia Gagnier), as a rhetoric of illness and the occupation of the female body (Barbara Spackman), as a kind of dandiacal theatricality (James Eli Adams), as a moment of masculine crisis (Richard Dellamora), and as a carefully crafted counterdiscourse of spiritual, hellenized love in response to a classical republican theory of degeneration and weakness (Dowling).[15] However, decadent effeminacy was not always the revolutionary act that some critics might wish it was, for as Joseph Bristow has noted, dandies were not necessarily "sexual radicals" and in fact tended "to define their preoccupation with a dissident masculine style against an often aggressive and despicable contempt for women,"[16] while Felski has argued against those who attempt to align the decadents' "parodic subversion of gender norms" with an enlightened attitude toward women.[17] That New Women writers wanted to distance themselves from decadence and its stated positions about women (who were described by Wilde, for example, as "charmingly artificial" but with "no sense of art") comes as no surprise, and that they wanted to repudiate the appropriation of effeminacy as a femaleness divorced from the "vulgar" female body and the "unsophisticated" female mind is perhaps even more understandable.

But the alignment of women with nature and the body was a cultural commonplace, so in assuming some of the traits of the feminine, decadents also attracted attention to their bodies as sites of "sexual anarchy," to use Elaine Showalter's term. As Ellen Moers has shown, through excessive attention to clothing, the body, and forms of cosmetic artifice — all of which were thought to be the province of women — dandies called attention to the male body and to what it meant to be masculine or not. This was, in fact, the decadents' fatal mistake, emblematized by the aftermath of Wilde's spectacular sodomy trial in 1895. Dowling has argued that before the trial the term *effeminacy* was merely part of an ongoing debate about the vitality of the state, rooted in the classical republican theory of the *effeminatus* as a symbol of "civic enfeeblement" that had little to do with gender in the modern sense.[18] But at the moment when this disembodied theorizing of effeminacy and homosexuality collapses, at Wilde's trial, Dowling's analysis fails adequately to account for the negative public response to Wilde. The public was outraged because the idea of effeminacy, no longer limited to intellectual revisions of classical republican discourse, had spread to the larger culture, through popular scientific texts and novels, which portrayed it as dangerous and perhaps even homosexual, as Max Nordau did when he invoked "Sodom and Lesbos" in his scathing assessment of Wilde and his contemporaries.[19] The representation of sexual degeneracy as effeminacy, symbolized by the confusingly gendered body of the decadent male, signaled a fear about the decline and extinction of the race through syphilis, hereditary illnesses, and sterility. For example, in *The Heavenly Twins* the effeminacy of a potential husband is indicated through his use of makeup, which marks him as sexually dangerous and syphilitic. In drawing attention to their transgressively gendered physical presence, decadents in the 1880s and 1890s demonstrated that effeminacy was physical as well as theoretical. The spectacle of the feminized male was reinterpreted by conservative critics and their anxious public not as a liberatory philosophical position but as a real pathological threat to the health and robustness of the body politic — or, as the prosecutor in Wilde's trial described the defendant's sexual practices, "a sore which cannot fail in time to corrupt and taint it all."[20]

In examining degeneracy and effeminacy as parts of a descriptive discourse on legible and symptomatic bodies, it is possible to distinguish the goals and strategies of two groups falsely seen as complementary. Both New Women and decadent writers found that degenerationism and its physiognomic mode of analysis were useful for categorizing physical characteristics and compressing descriptive language. Grand's unironic physiognomic descriptions reaffirm the *reliability* of this mode of reading the body.[21] In the fin de siècle's hysteria over illness the potent combination of physiognomy and degenerationism promised recognizability and diagnostic certainty: in a "sick" society the dangerous elements can be identified and avoided. In *The Heavenly Twins* Grand used the scientific language of evolution and degeneration to describe the physical decline of men in the English colony of Malta: "There were elephants once in Malta, I am told, . . . but they dwindled down from the size which makes them so useful by way of comparison, till they were no bigger than Shetland ponies, before they finally became extinct. And there is a set in society on the island now . . . formed of representatives of old English houses that once brought men of notable size and virile [*sic*] into the world, but are now only equal to the production of curious survivals, tending surely to extinction, and by an analogous process" (184–85). When New Women writers wished to describe the degenerate male body in particular, they appropriated the tropes of the decadents as well as the pervasive codes of degenerationism. Decadent writers had already performed a complicated cultural transvaluation in appropriating the language of decline from the very writing that condemned them; their descriptions of the degenerate are informed by antidecadent degenerationist critiques but reworked to invert cultural norms and celebrate their own deviancy *as deviancy* in the language of the "normal" culture. Because of their need to educate readers about the dangers of syphilitic husbands, New Women novelists relied on not only the language but the *conclusions* of the pseudoscientific model of description drawn from physiognomy and degenerationist theory that by the late nineteenth century were cultural clichés. Grand reinforced the myth of recognizability by reconnecting vice and the appearance of vice on the countenance, which, in *The Picture of Dorian Gray,* is displaced from the person to the painting. New Women writers also sought to clarify the system of fin-de-siècle aesthetics that produced the shifting boundaries of the beautiful and the ugly in decadent art and blurred the distinction between good and evil. That is, they attempted to remove decadence from the realm of aestheticism and give it a face.

Decadents perversely assumed the mantle of effeminacy, and the qualities stereotypically attributed to the feminine — illness, alterity, and marginality — as the signifier of their degeneracy. This strategy, which Barbara Spackman has described as "the occupation of the woman's body," follows on the decadents' own demasculinization and eviration.[22] Degenerate feminization became a symbol of otherness, representing a spectrum of possibilities for oppositional identities that involved differences in gender behavior, sexual practice, and literary strategies. Decadents also valued their cultural exquisiteness, their art for art's sake philosophy, which placed their cultural production outside the emphatically work-oriented bourgeois Victorian sphere.[23] Along with their appropriation of femininity as a paradox of weakness and divinity, decadents (despite their largely middle-class origins) espoused an aristocratic, antibourgeois attitude, which arose out of their general abhorrence of "uniformity, mediocrity, and vulgarity,"[24] words often used to label middle-class women writers as overidentified with the commodity culture of the masses that the aesthetes despised, as sentimental, and as vulgar.[25] In celebrating their counterintuitive cultural presence, decadents perversely utilized the tropes of illness and effeminacy in their descriptions of degenerate aristocrats, for example in *The Picture of Dorian Gray* and Joris-Karl Huysmans's *À rebours.* Huysmans's famous decadent, Des Esseintes, the "prefiguring type" for Dorian,[26] is the weakened product of a long line of aristocrats in which "the degeneration of this ancient house had clearly followed a regular course, with the men becoming progressively less manly . . . using up what little vigour they had left."[27] Des Esseintes, with his "thin, papery hands," resembles a portrait of one of his ancestors that displays the courtier's "pale, drawn features; the cheekbones punctuated with cosmetic commas of rouge, the hair . . . plastered down and bound with a string of pearls."[28] The charge of effeminacy (highlighted by the suggestion of makeup) and the degenerate and aristocratic ancestral stock are common tropes of degenerationism, as is Des Esseintes's subsequent behavior — he cultivates the most extreme connoisseurship, sexual deviance, love of the unnatural, and fascination with his own ill body. Wilde's Dorian begins life less exhausted but no less effeminate: as a painter's muse, he is described in terms befitting a medieval maiden, looking "as if he was made out of ivory and rose-leaves" (25), with a demure blush and "finely-curved scarlet lips" (39). The decay that comes with sin and age is averted by the sorcery that stains the portrait but not him, as he continues "unspotted" in "the bloom of boyhood" and retains the "purity of his face" as a rebuke to his companions in vice (227, 159). The "monstrous" and "misshapen" figure in the portrait displays "the signs of sin" (usually read as marks of syphilis), which are horrible to Dorian (159), even as he finds "real pleasure" in watching the picture change (136). Dorian's fascination with the representation of his own decaying body as an emblem of sin provides the clearest example of the transvaluation of morality and illness found in decadent writing. This description of Dorian's portrait echoes through other representations of the degenerate: the figure has something loathsome in its expression, as well as "thinning hair" and "sodden eyes" (189). Contemporary reviews were critical of the "unmanliness" and the "effeminate frivolity" of the book, as Dorian was interpreted as an unnatural creation and rejected as antithetical to public morals and the ideal of Victorian robustness.[29]

Grand is representative of the strain of New Women writers who reconceived the decadent male as the moral and philosophical heir of the eighteenth-century libertine, a marked and dangerous man to be avoided at all costs. She crafted *The Heavenly Twins* as a rebuke to the heroicization of the libertine in the eighteenth-century novel, but she described him in the loaded symptomatological terms of the late nineteenth century.

When Grand's heroine, Evadne, learns of her husband's "wild" past, she refuses to live with him and reproaches him for not remaining celibate until marriage. Here Grand suggests that, had Evadne been properly educated, she would have recognized that her husband is a degenerate; Evadne's ability to read physical features as signs of character is limited at first by her inadequate education. Although Evadne is widely read in science, knowledge of sexual matters has been withheld from her. Before her marriage her primary impression of her husband's physique is vague and incomplete: she is aware that he is "a big blond man, with a heavy moustache, and a delicate skin that flushed easily" (53). The engagement is short, and Grand makes it clear that Evadne "did not actually *see* much of Major Colquhoun in the days that followed . . . but such timid glances as she stole satisfied her" (54). These oblique and girlish glances do not allow Evadne accurately to judge her future mate. Immediately after the wedding Evadne receives a letter which informs her that her husband has a disreputable past. After reading the letter, her sight becomes sharper, and "she noticed that his hair was thin on his forehead, and there was nothing of youth in his eyes" (64). It is only *after* she has been made aware of the possibility of her husband's degeneracy that she sees its signs on his body. Only in retrospect does she understand what certain traits signify, noticing that "although his face is handsome, the expression of it is not noble at all" (79). The narrator attributes his enervated attitude to "a want of proper healthy feeling, for he was a vice-worn man, with small capacity left for any great emotion" (66).

Evadne's refusal to live with her husband shocks her family, who admit to her they knew about her husband's past, which they euphemistically describe as "wild." Evadne's indignation at their indifference to her health reflects the text's indictment of a larger systemic evil: she exclaims, "I would stop the imposition, approved of custom, connived at by parents, made possible by the state of ignorance in which we are carefully kept — the imposition on a girl's innocence and inexperience of a disreputable man for a husband" (78). In refusing to live with Colquhoun, Evadne takes precautions against becoming sick herself, branding him "a moral leper" and not only arguing the moral point that "marrying a man like that . . . is countenancing vice" but insisting on the contagious medical language by which to understand it (79). Vice is a term of opprobrium and a code word for syphilis (and its subsequent congenital dangers); hence Evadne's proposition that "there is no past in the matter of vice. The consequences become hereditary and continue from generation to generation" (80). That the dissolute aristocrat, hero of much eighteenth-century fiction, has become in Grand's text the vice-ridden villain of the late-nineteenth-century novel, is demonstrated by Evadne's remarking of her husband that "in point of fact his mode of life has very much resembled that of one of those old-fashioned heroes, Roderick Random or Tom Jones, specimens of humanity whom I hold in peculiar and especial detestation" (84). By stigmatizing these characters as old-fashioned and by proposing a model of an enlightened marital relationship of equality and bilateral purity, writers like Grand hoped to prevent unnecessary illness and to allow the Clarissas to be succeeded by the Evadnes.

Edith is Grand's other test case in *The Heavenly Twins,* the protagonist of her sadder and more cautionary tale. In her state of ignorance, Edith marries a degenerate aristocrat, Sir Moseley Menteith, an act that Evadne, now an experienced reader of vice-ridden men, strongly opposes. When Evadne and Edith meet Menteith at a dance, Grand presents Evadne's description of him: she notices "something repellent about the expression of [his] mouth" and opines that "his eyes were small, peery, and too close together, and his head shelved backwards like an ape's" (178). Later she also notices "a suspicion of powder on his face" (189), an attempt to conceal facial flaws that is a highly questionable practice for a soldier in nineteenth-century minds not only in its hint of vanity and effeminacy but in its suggestion that Menteith has something serious to hide — perhaps sores. Except for one other remark on the small size of his head, the highly critical description of Menteith is exclusively Evadne's, its specificity and disgust born of her firsthand experience with her husband. Menteith is introduced into the narrative with a far more bland and superficial description: "He was extremely spic-and-span in appearance, and wore light-coloured kid gloves" (178). In the same way that Evadne rereads the features of her husband as symbolizing exhaustion and degeneracy, she then reads the features of Menteith to mean the same, providing a cautionary corrective to the more general description of him that is first offered. Menteith's cleanliness, his "spic-and-span" appearance, is now suspect on two levels, moral and hygienic. He is also judged in explicitly physiognomic terms in the reference to the shape of his face and forehead, and the judgment marks him as a reversionary type, an ape. Evadne urges Edith not to marry Menteith because he is "a dreadful man," but she can offer no proof of his dreadfulness beyond hints dropped by her husband and "a vague consciousness which informs [her] of things which [her] intellect cannot grasp" (232). Edith's child displays the stigmata of congenital syphilis, thereby lending weight to the common assertion that syphilis produced hereditary exhaustion: "Although of an unmistakable type, he was apparently healthy when he was born, but had rapidly degenerated, and Edith herself was a wreck" (277). Although the father appears symptomless now, the child suffers from a congenital taint that renders him small and prematurely old-looking, a "little old man baby" who is "exhausted with suffering" (288–89).

The detailed physiognomic judgment of Menteith that the *reader* hears Evadne make — his eyes too close together, his sloping forehead, his "repellent" expression — is one that she cannot communicate to Edith and her mother. Although Evadne recognizes the signs of degeneracy as a result of her experience, they are not yet communicable in recognizable, discursive terms; it is precisely this incommunicability that Grand's novel sets out to repair. Grand works to establish a noneuphemistic language for women, one that will identify men not as "wild" but as "degenerate." The difference between the descriptions of Colquhoun and Menteith is crucial, however, since Menteith seems to display not just the effects of vice and rough living that the "vice-worn" Colquhoun does but a clear physiognomic predisposition to sin in the strong suggestion of effeminacy.[30] In describing him, Grand demonstrates that a particular *kind* of body is dangerous; it is his inborn *potential* for vice, not just its effects, that are evident on his face. The taxonomic markers of degeneracy that Grand lists, therefore, indicate both latent and active degeneracy and are of three distinct but related kinds: physiognomic (the fixed features of the face), pathognomic (facial expression), and generally degenerationist (the aura of agedness, exhaustion, and physical decay).

Reading the features of the face, the positioning of the eyes or the shape of the forehead, is troubling to modern readers in that it accesses the racist and classist rhetoric of physiognomy inherent in degenerationist theory, a rhetoric that argued for the fixed and identifiable nature of entire categories of persons. Although Colquhoun and Menteith *appear* to be acceptable mates, Colquhoun is Irish, a race from which the British spent much time differentiating themselves morally and physically,[31] and Menteith is an aristocrat, a member of a group, along with the degenerate city-dwelling masses of the lower orders, was stigmatized by middle-class writers and scientists as visibly weak and degenerate. In outing Colquhoun and Menteith not only as vice-ridden but as members of problematic racial and class groups, respectively, Grand suggests that the proper mates for British middle-class women are British middle-class men. The solution to the problem of male degeneracy, according to Grand, is most often found within British bourgeois society. But even within Britain's middle class lurk apparently decent men poisoned by diseases contracted through impure behavior, behavior that shatters the illusion of their middle-class status after a careful reading of their bodies reveals them to be members of unacceptable races or classes.

The damage done to Evadne and Edith, Grand argues, is the result of the dangerous conduct of men. However, the frequent separation of the fin-de-siècle world into sexually adventurous aesthete and asexual, prim female reformer creates a false dichotomy: Grand represents women who have sexual desires they would like to have met, but met on *their* terms. She describes Evadne as "a nineteenth-century woman of the higher order with senses so refined that if her moral as well as her physical being were not satisfied in love, both would revolt" (345). The onset of Evadne's nervous condition after the quick collapse of her first marriage appears to be the result of an incomplete life that does not include healthy sexuality. The difference between the *kinds* of sexual transgression in which New Women and decadents were engaged becomes clear: the decadents were interested in a parodic mimicry of femininity as an oppositional political strategy, while New Women used discussions of sexuality in their novels for educational purposes — warnings, not wordplay.

A discussion of the differences in the projects of decadents and New Women, in response to a tendency to group them together as sexual and gender radicals, is complicated by anomalous moments in their texts in which they appear to take on characteristics of the other — when Wilde, for example, produces a morality play, or when Grand includes in her novel a fantasy interlude of cross-dressing and sexual desire. In the interlude in Grand's novel, Angelica, the female child of the twins referred to in the book's title (she is large and unruly, while her brother, Diavolo, is effeminate), cross-dresses as a boy to get nearer to a visiting musician, the Tenor. The relationship between Diavolo and the Tenor is filled with references to the boy's delicate "womanish" form and bearing, signaling the Tenor's illicit desire for Diavolo, which is necessarily redirected toward Angelica, but as idolatry, not friendship. Because of this, Angelica feels that the way to achieve a relationship of respect and equality with the Tenor is to dress up as her brother. The complicated circulation of sexual energy within this threesome, with its suggestion of repressed and redirected homosexual desire, is also paradoxically a fantasy of an escape from gender: after her unmasking, Angelica tells the Tenor, "The best pleasures in life are in art, not animalism; and all the benefit of your acquaintance, I repeat, has consisted in the fact that you were unaware of my sex" (459). The first part of Angelica's statement could have been made by a decadent writer who wished to focus on the ideal, not the vulgar, while the second half expresses the fantasy of some late-century feminists who wished that women could step outside gender and the body; here the twist is that Angelica wishes to do this in order to enter the world of art and ideas. In defense of her cross-dressing stunt, Angelica argues that "as a woman I could not expect to be treated by men with as much respect as they show to each other" (451), thereby revealing the underlying desire of this apparently transgressive gender moment to be much of a kind with the didacticism that drives the rest of the novel. Here indeed are some of the "revolutionary" attitudes and the ideological use of sexuality to which some critics have pointed as links between decadents and New Women, but one must take into account that in *The Heavenly Twins* Angelica's gender charade kills the object of her unconventional desire, since the Tenor dies from a cold he catches rescuing her from an overturned boat. Grand's strange interlude proposes and then repudiates, through its tragic outcome, the decadent route of gender masquerade as a solution to the problem of women's position in society.

Grand's flirtation with a decadent literary style and with decadent subject matter in the interlude reflects her awareness of and willingness to experiment with other literary strategies. But she consistently distanced herself from what she considered improper sexuality, since her male characters, like the dandy figure Alfred Cayley Pounce and Major Colquhoun, are censured for their association with French novels. Finally, Grand needed to stigmatize degenerate men (and by extension, societal decadence, decadents, and the decadent movement) and define her literary output against that of the aesthetes because of the socially marginal place of women and of early feminists especially. Like that of a number of New Women novelists, Grand's attempt to carve out a space in which the degeneracy of men exceeds that of women was a response to the pervasive stereotyping of women, especially prostitutes, as the chief carriers of disease and the loci of degenerate sexuality.

The recognition that men could be responsible for disease, however, did nothing to make *effeminacy* any less of an epithet implying degeneracy or to moderate the conception of women as representative of the body and its pathologies. Even though men were identified as the culprits in spreading disease, the label *effeminate* did not lose its metaphorical connotations as a catchall cognate for diseased and different. Why the troubling and insistent connection that linked the feminine with bodily weakness went unchallenged by New Women in their attempt to refigure men as the locus of degenerate sexuality is best understood by examining nineteenth-century gender stereotypes. Masculinity represented strength, vigor, self-control, and positive, desirable qualities, while femininity was characterized by small size, weakness (both moral and physical), illness, and harmful, negative qualities, making it the converse of masculinity. To be a man in decline was to become like a woman, and while women in decline could become manly, this was not an advantage but a grave category error, despite the uniformly positive assessment of what it meant to be masculine. The problematic characterization of weak men as feminine, which degraded the symbolic meaning of the female, was of secondary interest to early feminists, since they were continually defending themselves against charges of masculinism.[32] Counter to the critics who have found similarities in the cultural and sexual politics of the New Women and the decadents as proof of an alliance, the attempt in early New Women novels to stigmatize men as degenerate and implicitly effeminate arose to offset the characterization of New Women as unwomanly and even as dangerously masculine.

In claiming the place of healthy, innocent victims and by deflecting critical attention about the upending of traditional gender roles onto men, New Women anxiously hoped to reposition themselves as the unthreatening norm. They were aided in this attempt by the fact that decadents advertised certain bodies, especially those of artists, aristocrats, and slum dwellers, as always already decadent; it was not difficult for New Women to capitalize on the weakness and moral laxity implied in decadent portrayals and manipulate the stereotypes for their own ends. The hint of makeup visible on Menteith signifies effeminacy first and vice second; the persistent identification of one with the other reaffirms that degeneracy and effeminacy are one and the same. But in New Women writing any charge of effeminacy against potential husbands remains subsumed under the language of weakness and disease, for the degenerate man must be clearly gendered and clearly heterosexual in order to be a physical threat to women. In emphasizing the hallmarks of heterosexuality by making these men suitors and roués, New Women avoided any extensive or explicit discussion of feminized "illness" and "womanish" moral weakness, as it might connect the men *too* closely with certain aspects of decadence. The alchemy through which New Women authors transformed the figure of the feminized and degenerate decadent into a husband rested on this erasure of any hint of "deviant" sexuality, namely homosexuality. The term *degenerate* had already acquired explicitly homosexual overtones, as critics like Nordau charged that sensuality only finds admission into decadent works "when disguised as something unnatural and degenerate" and that "[v]ice looks to Sodom and Lesbos" for its embodiments.[33] Grand presented the degenerate as a heterosexual male because of her focus on the plight of women who marry syphilitics but also because she did not wish to address the homosexual implications of the "celibate" stereotype with which New Women were often labeled. In the cultural imagination New Women and decadent men were forcibly paired because they both were perceived as being of indeterminate gender — effeminate men and masculine feminists — which appeared to make them perversely complementary. In insisting on the heterosexuality of both the New Woman and the degenerate, and in rejecting the phantom pairing of themselves with decadents, the New Women symbolically rescued the degenerate from the charge of perversion while they saved themselves from the fate of odd women (that is, permanent spinsterhood).

But the attempt by New Women writers to reinscribe the rhetoric of degeneration onto the bodies of men merely replicated the impulse that previously stigmatized women, for as Sander Gilman has pointed out, "in male medical writers, the trope of decay is most often associated with the female."[34] Although New Women writers appropriated these ideas for the benefit of women, they participated in further disseminating and popularizing a suspect system of identifying degeneracy, reformulating a set of diagnoses that had once stigmatized their own sex. Moreover, fin-de-siècle writers who identified with decadence were largely but not exclusively male, and, as in the writings of their scientific, medical, and cultural counterparts, their graphic portrayals of total degeneracy (a degeneracy that retains no positive connotations) were often located in the female — in the actress or the prostitute — even their portrayals of decadent men appropriated the rhetoric of degenerate effeminacy as a celebration of countercultural otherness. A woman writer caught inside such a discursive structure could not ignore that both scientific and cultural constructions of the female and effeminacy were being used to define and enforce essentialism and to establish the differences between the sexes as again beneficial to men, especially the differences in their modes of transgression. In evolutionary theory women were considered less evolved, above apes and "savages" but below men. In physiognomy and degenerationist theory male facial and physical traits marked positive qualities, while supposedly female characteristics, when found on either men or women, were negatively evaluated. In decadent literature women are left out of the celebration of perversity for their lack of imagination and artistry even as they are cannibalized for their coveted traits of "artificiality" and social marginality. Women, however, could not win even if they acquired desirable masculine traits, for transgressiveness of traits, such as women with masculine features or men with feminine ones, was insistently defined as abnormal and undesirable: New Women and the novels that described them were "socio-literary portrait[s] of anarchy."[35]

Grand's attempt to counter the charges of unnatural and degenerate masculinity made against early feminists and reformers had the dismaying effect of locking New Women back into a system of stifling binarism and of positioning them firmly within a vocabulary of evaluation that would always revert to defining the norm as male, middle-class, and British.[36] On a representational level the attempt to fix degeneracy as a set of recognizable symptoms proved futile, since any system that purports to be able to identify and translate moral character into a visual signifier is doomed by the circular logic of physiognomically influenced thought, and is an example of the representational ambiguity that many narratives of the late nineteenth century failed to avoid. Despite their laudable attempts to protect the health of women, the inability of New Women writers like Grand to imagine a new paradigm that would overcome gendered stereotypes positioned them against the next wave of more radical feminists and New Women of the later "bachelor girl" school, who began to look beyond traditional gender roles and conventional marriage to celibacy and other unorthodox practices as political strategies and who, in mirroring the decadents' appropriation of effeminacy as a positive trait, were no longer afraid of claiming the transgressive cultural power associated with the term *masculine.*

Notes

1. David Weir, *Decadence and the Making of Modernism* (Amherst: University of Massachusetts Press, 1995), ix.

2. See Daniel Pick, *Faces of Degeneration: A European Disorder, c. 1848–c. 1918* (Cambridge, U.K.: Cambridge University Press, 1989).

3. Rita Felski, "The Counterdiscourse of the Feminine in Three Texts by Wilde, Huysmans, and Sacher-Masoch," *PMLA* 106, no. 5 (1991): 1098.

4. Ibid.

5. Elaine Showalter, *Sexual Anarchy: Gender and Culture at the Fin de Siècle* (New York: Penguin, 1990), 177.

6. Linda Dowling, "The Decadent and the New Woman in the 1890's," *Nineteenth Century Fiction* 33, no. 4 (1979): 435.

7. See Elaine Showalter's early dismissal of New Women writers in *A Literature of Their Own* (Princeton, N.J.: Princeton University Press, 1977).

8. See John Kucich, "Curious Dualities: *The Heavenly Twins* (1893) and Sarah Grand's Belated Modernist Aesthetics," in *The New Nineteenth Century: Feminist Readings of Underread Victorian Fiction,* ed. Leah Harman and Susan Meyer (New York: Garland, 1996); and Teresa Mangum, "Style Wars of the 1890s: The New Woman and the Decadent," in *Transforming Genres: New Approaches to British Fiction of the 1890s,* ed. Nikki Lee Manos and Meri-Jane Rochelson (New York: St. Martin's, 1994), 49.

9. Linda Dowling's *Hellenism and Homosexuality in Victorian Oxford* (Ithaca, N.Y.: Cornell University Press, 1994) illustrates how writers like Wilde and John Addington Symonds used their access to cultural institutions to occupy a secure position at the center of culture.

10. Sarah Grand, *The Beth Book* (New York: Appleton, 1897), 367.

11. For the sake of this argument I am claiming Grand as a representative New Woman, but I would reiterate Richard Dellamora's observation that, in regard to New Women, "neither the type nor the fiction are uniform."

12. Sandra Siegel, "Literature and Degeneration: The Representation of 'Deca-

dence,'" in *Degeneration: The Dark Side of Progress,* ed. J. Edward Chamberlin and Sander Gilman (New York: Columbia University Press, 1985), 209.

13. See Lyn Pykett, *Engendering Fictions: The English Novel in the Early Twentieth Century* (New York: St. Martin's, 1995), especially chap. 2, "Gender, Degeneration, Renovation: Some Contexts of the Modern," for a good discussion of the troubled relationship of ideas of masculinity and femininity to degeneration.

14. Sarah Grand, "The New Aspect of the Woman Question," *North American Review* 158 (1894): 274–75.

15. See Rita Felski, *The Gender of Modernity* (Cambridge, Mass.: Harvard University Press, 1995); Regenia Gagnier, *Idylls of the Marketplace: Oscar Wilde and the Victorian Public* (Stanford, Calif.: Stanford University Press, 1996); Barbara Spackman, *Decadent Genealogies: The Rhetoric of Sickness from Baudelaire to D'Annunzio* (Ithaca, N.Y.: Cornell University Press, 1989); James Eli Adams, *Dandies and Desert Saints: Styles of Victorian Masculinities* (Ithaca, N.Y.: Cornell University Press, 1995); Richard Dellamora, *Masculine Desire: The Sexual Politics of Victorian Aestheticism* (Chapel Hill: University of North Carolina Press, 1990); and Dowling, *Hellenism.*

16. Joseph Bristow, *Effeminate England: Homoerotic Writing after 1885* (New York: Columbia University Press, 1995), 9.

17. Felski, "Counterdiscourse of the Feminine," 1094.

18. Dowling, *Hellenism,* 5–6.

19. Max Nordau, *Degeneration* (New York: Appleton, 1895).

20. Dowling, *Hellenism,* 1.

21. Sarah Grand, *The Heavenly Twins* (New York: Cassell, 1893). For example, one doctor notes about her heroine, Evadne, that "the balance of brow and frontal development are perfect" (97). All further citations will be noted parenthetically in the text and are taken from this edition.

22. Spackman, 11.

23. See Adams for a study of the dandy and the identification of social and economic utility with masculinity.

24. Ellen Moers, *The Dandy: Brummel to Beerbohm* (Lincoln: University of Nebraska Press, 1984), 264.

25. Felski, "Counterdiscourse of the Feminine," 1094.

26. Oscar Wilde, *The Picture of Dorian Gray* (London: Penguin, 1985), 158. All further citations will be noted parenthetically in the text and are taken from this edition.

27. Joris-Karl Huysmans, *Against Nature,* trans. Robert Baldick (London: Penguin, 1959), 17.

28. Ibid.

29. Felski, "Counterdiscourse of the Feminine," 1098; Gagnier, 59.

30. Brooke's characters are even more openly effeminate: the aristocratic Lord Heriot giggles and repulses others with "his moist palm, his vile eyes, and his

heavily scented apparel" and is described as having "a tall head with retreating forehead bald at the temples, the hair limp, fair and thin, the nose small, narrow and mean, the eyes old, and the lips wandering and feeble" (Emma Frances Brooke, *A Superfluous Woman* [New York: Cassell, 1894], 120, 243).

31. See John Beddoe, *The Races of Britain: A Contribution to the Anthropology of Western Europe* (Bristol, U.K.: Arrowsmith, 1895), for a discussion of the "degeneracy" of the Celts.

32. Cesare Lombroso's influential studies of the "moral physiognomies" of female criminals made much of their "virility": as Spackman points out, he finds "criminality in the abolition of difference" between the genders but, unlike Nordau, only when it is women who "'exhibit a strong tendency to be confused with the male type'" (25).

33. Nordau, 13.

34. Sander Gilman, *Health and Illness* (London: Reaktion, 1995), 61.

35. Ann Ardis, *New Women, New Novels: Feminism and Early Modernism* (New Brunswick, N.J.: Rutgers University Press, 1990), 13.

36. Pykett has made a similar observation about the effects of certain female strategies on New Women: "social purity feminists . . . redefined femininity by appropriating traditional gender stereotypes and deploying them . . . against the patriarchal order. . . . Their version of the New Woman has some striking resemblances to the womanly woman of the anti-feminists" (38).

Chapter 4

ANNETTE R. FEDERICO

Marie Corelli

Aestheticism in Suburbia

POPULAR, SATIRICAL treatments of the aesthetic movement in the 1880s and 1890s — George Du Maurier's drawings of the aesthete Maudle in *Punch,* William S. Gilbert and Arthur Sullivan's operettas, and the countless advertisements, ballads, songs, and novels aimed at Oscar Wilde and his followers — confirm that for all of its silliness aestheticism was a regenerative force in Victorian society. Indeed, Lionel Lambourne has claimed that the most "remarkable thing about the satirical comment upon the Aesthetic Movement is that it is remembered more vividly than the subject satirized."[1] Such industrious appropriations of aestheticism by philistines suggest a certain Victorian self-consciousness and resiliency. They also demonstrate the adeptness of an advanced consumer society in transforming an oppositional art movement into a commodity. Yet aestheticism undoubtedly raised popular awareness about the growing distance between utilitarian and commercial concerns and the world of beauty, intellect, and emotion. The complex relationships between literature and commerce, between design and production, between art and life caused by industrial and technological progress were rendered visible and accessible to many people because of the flamboyance of aesthetes, dandies, and decadents.

Despite this apparently democratic function, aestheticism also helped to mythologize and circulate in popular forms a mystique of the artist as a poor bohemian who was a martyr to beauty or a cultivated aristocrat with taste. The word *genius* is often used to evoke the extraordinary talent and vision of the *artiste,* who is inevitably misunderstood by commoners and only appreciated by an informed elite.

In this essay I am interested in the tension between the democratic impulse of aestheticism and its often explicit scorn for bourgeois education, tastes, and modes of living. Marie Corelli (1855–1924) is an interesting mediator in these ideological contradictions. As the best-selling novelist of late-Victorian and early-twentieth-century England, she would seem the antithesis of aesthetic style: the astonishing sales of her romances surely disqualify her from being either avant-garde or decadent, bohemian or aesthete.[2] In fact, Corelli's immense popularity was consistently identified with the zeal and directness with which she spoke to the democratic feeling of the British middle class. She certainly believed she had a genuine affinity and commitment to what she called "the people." Yet for all her moral confidence, Corelli's passionate interest in sin and sexuality, literature and commercialism, spirituality and death struck some critics as more than melodramatic excess. Her popularity was seen by some as evidence of the triumph of the "degeneration of the last twenty years," and she was even accused of plagiarizing the works of one "French decadent" and another "degenerate writer of Paris."[3] These are interesting accusations because Corelli repeatedly expressed her disgust with literary decadence and the French school of art, and throughout her career she was openly laughed at by the majority of English critics, who thought her tawdry, unsophisticated, and even ungrammatical.

Corelli had a conspicuous role in the changing functions of literature in social formation at the turn of the century. Debates about whether popular literature, especially fiction, systematically lowered cultural standards or, conversely, stimulated intellectual appetites were widespread. The tone in many articles about and reviews of her books reveals acute anxiety about the menacing encroachments of popular taste. H. G. Wells, to take one example, explicitly connected democratic reforms and literary mediocrity in 1896:

> The passing of the Education Act in 1870 and the coming to reading age in 1886–1888 of multitudes of boys and girls have changed the conditions of journalism and literature in much the same way as the French Revolution changed the conditions of political thought and action. . . . And while the male of this species has chiefly exerted his influence in the degradation of journalism, the debasing influence of the female, reinforced by the free libraries, has been chiefly felt in the character of fiction. 'Arry reads *Ally Sloper* and *Tit-Bits,* 'Arriet reads *Trilby* and *The Sorrows of Satan.*[4]

Interestingly, both *Trilby* and *The Sorrows of Satan* were popular novels that exploited the public fascination with art and artists stimulated by aestheticism. *Trilby* (1894), the highly successful novel by George Du Maurier about English artists in bohemian Paris, is set in the 1850s, but it is as much a novel of 1890s aestheticism as Wilde's *Picture of Dorian Gray* (1891) — in fact, the American painter James Abbott McNeill Whistler quite justly threatened Du Maurier with a libel suit.[5] *The Sorrows of Satan* (1895) was Corelli's eighth best-selling novel and had an initial sale greater than any previous English novel, even though its author, fed up with the critics, refused to send out copies for review. The book is about a struggling male novelist who falls under the spell of an aristocratic Satan and is exposed to the destructiveness, greed, and immorality of the late-Victorian publishing world. He is finally redeemed by the honesty and sweetness of his rival, the popular novelist Mavis Clare, whose books radiate goodness and truth instead of atheism and despair.

I will look at *The Sorrows of Satan* alongside other Corelli novels later in this essay. But first H. G. Wells's claim that Corelli's principal reader is "'Arriet of the Board-school" needs further scrutiny, for Corelli gained the admiration of quite a few celebrities: the Prince of Wales asked her to dine, Gladstone came to call, Queen Victoria had all of Corelli's books sent to Balmoral, there were fan letters from Queen Margherita of Italy and from the empress of Austria; besides these figureheads, Oscar Wilde invited her to write for *Woman's World,* she was introduced to Robert Browning and Algernon Charles Swinburne, Dame Ellen Terry adored her, and Lillie Langtry asked to perform in dramatizations of her novels.

This extraordinary attention baffled journalists and literary men who confidently classified Corelli's fiction as low art — or, as one reviewer put it, "pure bosh."[6] Critics and writers who thought they understood their society's tastes and reading habits were bewildered by the Corelli phenomenon. In 1909 the *Bookman* published a long and appreciative profile defending Corelli's popularity from her snobbish detractors:

> The superiority of your very superior literary person depends upon his being able to maintain that literature is not for all the world, but is a sort of exotic that can only be cultivated and appreciated in select holes and corners. In the interest of this gospel — for popularity is an offence to those who cannot obtain it — no living author has been more persistently maligned and sneered at and scouted by certain sections of the Press — by the presumptuous and struttingly academic section of it particularly — than has Miss Marie Corelli, and none has won (by sheer force of her own merits, for the press has never helped her), a wider, more persistently increasing fame and affection among all classes of that intelligent public which reads and judges books, but does not write about them. "Yes," say her detractors, "she is the idol of Suburbia — the favourite of the common multitude. . . . She is suburban and the delight of

> Suburbia"; so that when you find, on making inquiries, that everything she has written has been translated many times into so many varied languages and dialects, that there are some five or six hundred translations of her books selling all over the world, you can only ask yourself, if this is suburban, which one of our novelists may be regarded as approximately cosmopolitan?[7]

Sorting out the differences between suburban and cosmopolitan literature, the "mass culture/modernism dichotomy," has been an important project for cultural studies.[8] Clearly, it was important to Victorian critics and writers, too, and their confusion invites more questions: What were some late-Victorian constructions of suburban taste and sensibility, and how do these assumptions contribute to fears about the decline of literature? Are reading habits accurate indicators of social class? How do judgments about literary value reflect expectations based on gender as well as class?

Corelli offers an exceptionally interesting case for studying the way these questions were approached by writers, literary men, and consumers in the 1890s. She is a curious example of cultural crossover, not just in her appeal across classes but in her literary works, where the virtue of simplicity is extravagantly dramatized through the vices of the upper crust and the interests of artists and writers are played against the narrowness of the "aesthetic" critics and reviewers she knew from personal experience. In *Literary Capital and the Late-Victorian Novel* Norman Feltes discusses Corelli's success in the context of late-Victorian publishing, pointing out that she was frequently attacked for her mistakes, her "vulgarities," her ignorance of languages, history, and grammar and that these attacks imply a "patriarchal/class judgment."[9] Indeed, that male literary critics felt compelled to locate Corelli's audience suggests that a writer's legitimacy was partly based on the Victorian consumer, on class, and on gender. For example, a hostile critic wrote that Corelli's readers were from the "unthinking classes," "undoubtedly . . . members of her own sex, in middle-class society, and from the working classes — shop girls and young men of the large towns."[10] But a sympathetic journalist claimed, "[M]any of her most enthusiastic admirers are men of the professional classes — doctors, barristers, lawyers, writers, men of education and intelligence."[11] While one corner asserted that a Corelli novel appealed only to readers in Camberwell and Brixton, Corelli countered by insisting, "Camberwell and Brixton must be included in the London radius; and I believe the Prince of Wales, who has always been most kindly in his appreciation of my books, has property there!"[12] Once we discuss shopkeepers in the same breath as royalty, suburbia begins to look rather indeterminate or, as the historian H. J. Dyos has written, "a curious blend of romantic idealism and hard-headed realism."[13] The suburban dweller wanted not only the Englishman's castle and the pleasures of the countryside but also affordable lodging and a location convenient to his work. Thus the suburban sensibility is divided between a desire for privacy and a love of ostentation, for "individual domesticity and group-monitored respectability."[14] As a contributor to *Architect* wrote in 1876, "A modern suburb is a place which is neither one thing nor the other."[15]

Coincident with the rise of the aesthetic movement (the Grosvenor Gallery had its first exhibition in 1877), the suburbs became "objects of ridicule and even contempt" and were "associated less with a geographical expression than an attitude of mind and a species of social as well as economic behaviour."[16] The suburban mind was considered petty, unimaginative, and without social, cultural, and intellectual interests, in direct contrast to the cosmopolitan emphasis on art, variety, and urban sophistication. This reduction relies less on actual economic status than on cultural emphasis: bohemians without a shilling can become alienated artists in the hands of French decadents, but they become something else in the hands of the bourgeoisie — they become Little Billie and the Laird in *Trilby.* The suburban/cosmopolitan construct gives cultural privilege to aestheticism, associated with young men, explorations of life, and "the wizardry of cities," rather than to suburbia, associated with feminine domesticity, homogeneity, and the delights of nature (or, at least, of a small garden).[17] This opposition was commonplace by the 1890s. Thus a critic of new fiction writing in the *Westminster Gazette* in 1895 asserted that the once scandalous "yellow-back" novels have been left behind "in a kind of stranded respectability, for the consolation of those households which the emancipated youth calls 'suburban.'"[18]

Though it was upheld by those "presumptuous and struttingly academic" male reviewers and by certain "emancipated youth," the dichotomy I have described was anything but clear-cut, and in fact aestheticism was "essentially a middle-class movement."[19] The pose of the dandy may have been "antithetical to the democratizing ethos of the middle-classes," but the sheer fame of the dandy-aesthete seems to have compelled the bourgeoise to adopt a pose of her own out of cultural resistance.[20] And this is what is most interesting about the success of Corelli as the "idol of Suburbia," for in her books and in her public image she reconstructed the identity of the artist for an audience who, as typical suburbanites, desired both celebrity and conservatism. For twenty years Corelli negotiated images of the artist that both reflect and refute the social and literary assumptions of aestheticism.[21] If literary value was associated with suggestiveness, nuance, the half tints of Whistler's nocturnes or Arthur Symons's desire to "spiritualise literature," such fine distinctions were useless for a writer with a moral and democratic mission.[22] "Have you noticed how fond some people are of the word '*subtle*'?" Corelli wrote to her publisher, George Bentley. "Tell them a book is *subtle* and they will rave over it instantly!"[23] This "subtle" taste belonged to university men, not to the masses. Even reviewers recognized this dichotomy (if Corelli herself did not): "Democracy has not a discriminating taste . . . Marie Corelli is clever enough to be a perfect literary purveyor to public taste. As an artist she paints with a brush as big as a bill-sticker's."[24]

Socially, too, the "greenery-yallery Grosvenor Gallery foot-in-the-grave young man," famously satirized in Gilbert and Sullivan's *Patience* (1881), was Corelli's nemesis, for, in the light of the aesthetic movement, this parasitic Oxonian had come to represent artists in the view of ordinary people. Corelli created a persona in opposition to the prevalent starving male artist manqué, for to her middle-class work ethic this pose was simply irresponsible. In an essay in the *Idler,* published in 1893, she wrote:

> It is an unromantic thing for an author to have had no literary vicissitudes. One cannot expect to be considered interesting unless one has come up to London with the proverbial solitary "shilling," and gone about hungry and footsore, begging from one hard-hearted publisher's house to another with one's perpetually-rejected manuscript under one's arm. One ought to have consumed the "midnight oil"; to have "coined one's heart's blood" (to borrow the tragic expression of a contemporary gentleman-novelist); to have sacrificed one's self-respect by metaphorical crawling on all-fours to the critical faculty; and to have become aesthetically cadaverous and blear-eyed through the action of inspired dyspepsia.[25]

Corelli was proud to have done none of these things; she simply worked patiently and wrote from the heart, and the public response was warm and rewarding. Corelli was the feminine alternative to the foot-in-the-grave young man: the healthy, earnest, hardworking writer, clear-eyed and unashamedly populist.

Her publisher's concern about the tone and subject matter of some of her novels, therefore, is rather interesting. Bentley frequently worried that

Corelli would either offend readers with her fervid exposures of adultery and vice or invite malice from critics who found her view of reality distorted, to say the least. Corelli was fiercely defensive about both the morality and the honesty of her books and took herself very seriously as a writer. If Bentley feared her books would be condemned by the critics, she retaliated by calling his attention to her "artistic" competitors (among them, the "sickening" Rider Haggard), for example in a letter of 1890, when she published her melodramatic attack on absinthe-drinking Parisians, *Wormwood*: "The press that deifies a 'Rudyard Kipling' and hovers between fits of ecstasy and opprobrium over Zola and Tolstoi and Ibsen, is such an utterly worthless thing now-a-days to sway an author's fame one way or the other. The 'public' is a different matter. That has forgiven me my sins always, and I hope and believe it will understand my motive in having struck the key-note of French morbidness — the partial secret of national decay."[26]

Can there be any doubt that Corelli viewed this novel as a moral reprimand to the decadent? Yet in her directions to Bentley, she sounds like a contributor to the *Yellow Book:* "The covers of the book should be pale green: the colour of Absinthe, with the title running zig-zag across it in black letters — an adder or serpent twisted through the big *W.*"[27] The antidecadent novel is packaged as the very flower of decadence — even down to the color green, which Wilde popularized as the "sign of a subtle artistic temperament."[28] She even sent a copy of *Wormwood* to Arthur Symons in February 1891, apparently because she thought it would impress him.[29]

Wormwood: A Drama of Paris is a fascinating example of middle-class curiosity about and appropriations of decadence, and it particularly dwells on the widespread use of absinthe among artists and bohemians in Paris, the morbid imaginations of French poets and painters, and the erotic dimensions of crime. The narrator, Gaston Beauvais, becomes an "absintheur" when his beloved Pauline confesses that she is in love with her cousin, Silvion Guidèl, an exceptionally beautiful young man who is studying to be a priest. Beauvais's first experience with "the Green Fairy" is on the night Pauline breaks his heart, when he meets the poor painter André Gessonex on the Champs-Elysées and ends up drinking absinthe with him at a café. The rest of the novel describes the moral deterioration of the narrator under the influence of absinthe: he commits a foul murder, coolly witnesses two suicides, takes part in lurid scenes at the morgue and the immoral cancan rage, and experiences horrible "brain phantasms," including one that involves a leopard with green eyes following him through the streets of Paris.

Corelli's stated intention in her "Special Preface" to the authorized American edition of *Wormwood* was to bring this "fatal brain-degradation" before French authorities and so put an end to its destructive progress.[30] But even her publisher worried that the novel would be read less as a moral tonic than as an engrossing account of the Parisian underworld of artists and absintheurs. Despite Corelli's status as a best-selling novelist and her ostensible missionary purpose, *Wormwood* is completely dependent on decadent tropes. Her artist André Gessonex, for instance, is the stereotypical debauchee, with long hair, "in strict adherence to true artistic tradition," and a battered hat, soiled collar, and red flannel tie (114). He is a "genius" but cannot sell his paintings because the ignorant masses only want representational art. "I am not to blame if these people who want to buy pictures have no taste! I cannot paint Dutch interiors, — the carrot waiting to be peeled on the table, — the fat old woman cutting onions for the *pot-au-feu* . . . I can only produce grand art!" (114–15). André's story has a predictable trajectory. He paints a magnificent, dark painting of a priest wrenching open the coffin of the woman he once loved, whose decomposed face is just visible. Written beneath it in blood-red paint are the words, *"O Dieu que j'abjure! Rends-moi cette femme!"* (226). André declares that he would rather "starve like a rat in a hole" than sell the painting to philistines. Later at a café, while drinking absinthe, he tells Beauvais he envies an artist who drew a political cartoon in the *Journal pour Rire.* "*You* envy the foul-minded wretch who polluted his pencil with such a thing as that?" asks Beauvais. "Assuredly," André replies. "He dines, and I do not — he sleeps, and I do not, — he has a full purse, — mine is empty! — and strangest anomaly of all, because he pays his way he is considered respectable, — while I, not being able to pay my way, am judged as quite the reverse! Foul-minded? Polluted? Tut, *mon cher!* there is no foul-mindedness nowadays except lack of cash — and the only pollution possible to the modern artist's pencil is to use it on work that does not *pay*!" (266–67). After this speech André calmly walks over to a kiosk, picks up the *Journal pour Rire,* laughs harshly at the cartoon, and shoots himself with a pistol. To guarantee his fame, he had bequeathed his masterpiece to France.

This episode is more complex than I am allowing, for throughout the novel Corelli offers competing interpretations of artists. Although André is unappreciated by the vulgar masses while he is alive, Corelli portrays his addiction to absinthe, his filthy lodgings, and his trips to the morgue as morally repulsive. For Corelli even aesthetic feeling cannot excuse such a life. And when Beauvais becomes obsessed with viewing Pauline's corpse at the morgue, after driving her to suicide, he ironically justifies his compulsion not as an absintheur but as an aesthete: "The girl, though dead, is beautiful! I am an artist! — I have the soul of a poet! . . . I love beauty — and I study it wherever I find it, dead or living" (321).

Like many Corelli novels, *Wormwood* is stocked with biting allusions to the school of Zola, that "literary scavenger of Paris" whose "pitchfork pen turns up under men's nostrils such literary garbage as loads the very air with stench and mind-malaria!" (280, 237). But *Wormwood* also cites appreciatively and at length the verse of French decadent writers. The most conspicuous example is that of the poet and inventor Charles Cros, a friend of Arthur Rimbaud's who reportedly drank twenty absinthes a day and died at the age of forty-six.[31] Beauvais recalls the first stanza of a poem by Cros:

> Avec l'absinthe, avec le feu
> On peut se divertir un peu
> Jouer son rôle en quelque drâme![32]

In a book condemning the effects of absinthe, it seems peculiar to insert verse evoking its seductive powers. Even more paradoxical is Corelli's footnote about Cros, a gloss on another poem she quotes in full. There is no question that she writes here not as Beauvais but as Marie Corelli:

> This exquisite poem, entitled "L'Archet," . . . was written by one CHARLES CROS, a French poet, whose distinctly great abilities were never encouraged or recognized in his lifetime. Young and still full of promise, he died quite recently in Paris [1888], surrounded by the very saddest circumstances of suffering, poverty, and neglect. The grass has scarcely had time to grow long or rank enough over his grave; when it has, the critics of his country will possibly take up his book . . . and call the attention of France to a perished genius. (55)

Even though Corelli must have known Cros was addicted to absinthe and a follower of Rimbaud and Paul Verlaine, she was susceptible to the myth of "perished genius." And she places the responsibility of honoring Cros's genius on the critics who will gather public recognition, even though later in *Wormwood* the narrator lashes out against the so-called experts:

> I ought to keep to the thread of my story, ought I not, dear critics of the press? — you who treat every narrative, true or imaginative, that goes into print, as a *gourmet* treats a quail, leaving nothing on the plate but a fragment of picked bone which you present to the public and call it a "review!" *Ah mes garçons!* — take care! . . . The Public itself is the Supreme Critic now, — its "review" does not appear in print, but nevertheless its unwritten verdict declares itself with . . . an amazing weight of influence. (295)

The contradictions and paradoxical treatments of Parisian decadence in *Wormwood* exemplify the problems of cultural classifications, for surely in this last outburst on the "Supreme Critic" Corelli has her own ax to grind.

If *Wormwood* is Corelli's somewhat naive manipulation of literary decadence (ostensibly as a warning against drug addiction and all things French), her long engagement with English marketplace aesthetics inevitably provokes more direct attacks. By 1896 Corelli was famous enough and experienced enough to devote two novels, *The Sorrows of Satan* and *The Murder of Delicia,* to her views on the literary life, critics, popularity, and, significantly, gender. In both novels she does not spare the reader her scorn for the immorality of modern art and literature. *The Sorrows of Satan* is especially successful at conjuring decadence while condemning decadent tendencies. The heiress Lady Sibyl, for example, leaves a sensational suicide note in which she explains how her training for the marriage market, combined with reading new fiction and too much Swinburne at an impressionable age, blackened her soul and chilled her heart: "Between their strained aestheticism and unbridled sensualism, my spirit has been stretched on the rack and broken on the wheel."[33] Although most of the novel is set in London, the dandy's cosmopolitanism is not adored for its stimulation and artificiality: the novelist Mavis Clare's Stratford cottage is the preferred retreat from "the restless modern Babylon" (209).

Indeed, *The Sorrows of Satan* goes after Victorian society with both barrels and not much subtlety: corrupt publishers, greedy advertisers, literary snobs, religious hypocrites and heartless atheists, aristocratic scoundrels, Darwinists, feminist extremists, and, not least, minor poets and writers of new fiction are all targets of Corelli's reformist zeal. The novel strains after bourgeois sanity and health against the "decadent, ephemeral age," in which "Art is made subservient to the love of money" (78). The sweetly feminine novelist Mavis Clare (very likely a self-portrait) is the personification of middle-class virtue. Much can be made here of Corelli's defensiveness and personal prejudices: powerful literary men such as Andrew Lang (McWhing) are represented as transparently corrupt; literary elitism is exposed as antidemocratic whining ("The public only cares for trash. . . . It is a pity you should appeal to them" [80]); the notion that "legitimate Literature" is written only by poor and struggling authors is revealed as a self-serving fiction (81). When the devil asserts that if a writer wants to be talked about, he needs to be "a judicious mixture of Zola, Huysmans, and Baudelaire" (63), Corelli targets not only the immorality of French decadents and their English imitators but also the depraved critics who scout them.

Yet many passages of "uncurtained" writing in *The Sorrows of Satan* underscore Corelli's participation in literary decadence. Just as she cites decadent French verse in *Wormwood,* she describes the irreparable harm of Swinburne's "Before a Crucifix" by producing four of the most offensive stanzas (394–95). But what is more interesting is how this novel harps on the commercialization of art. The link between money, class, and artistic success is one of its controlling themes, but Corelli's concern is not with the bohemian outcast. Her attempt to resolve the familiar conflict between the artistic value of autonomous literary texts and the monetary value of commodities relies on a valorization of the artist not as neglected genius, as in *Wormwood,* but as middle-class hero.

Geoffrey Tempest, the protagonist of *The Sorrows of Satan,* is a gentleman's son who emerges from Oxford with an idealistic desire for higher things, particularly the pursuit of literature. He soon discovers that society despises ardent young writers and that he cannot live by doing "'hack work' for the dailies" (8). Starving and poor, he finds that the music from a violin emanating from the room next door appeals to "the sensuous and aesthetic part" of his nature (13): Tempest is the familiar type of the sensitive, outcast artist, even down to his ulster, which is "an artistic mildewy green" (29). When he inherits his millions, however, he decides to gain revenge on the harsh industry that rejected his work and publishes his book himself (Satan helps him to "boom" it in prestigious journalistic circles). But his wealth and renown do not make Tempest happy. He has picturesque recollections of his former life: "I saw myself worn and hungry, shabbily clothed, bending over my writing in my dreary lodging, wretched, yet amid all my wretchedness receiving comfort from my own thoughts, which created beauty out of penury, and love out of loneliness" (72). Even more important, the book he writes when he is poor "propounded sentiments and inculcated theories" that he does not hold, chiefly a belief in God and in man's divine soul. The book seems to have been unconsciously influenced by a nobler instinct.

Starving in a garret is not the route to fame, but on the other hand wealth can corrupt, which also makes for bad art. Tempest's atheism and literary egotism surface when he becomes wealthy, showing the moral harm caused by both the commercialization of art and the seductions of wealth. Even though Tempest wishes to win fame legitimately, Satan tells him, "You can't! It's impossible. You are too rich. That in itself is not legitimate in Literature, — which great art generally elects to wear poverty in its buttonhole as a flower of grace" (81). The economic constraints of literary production, which are discussed obsessively in this book, contribute to social stratification, not the other way around. In other words, class does not *necessarily* define literature; neither who buys a book nor who writes it constitutes literary value. Rather, the literary industry is self-contained and self-perpetuating: the "six leading men who do the reviews" and their "comfortable little fraternal union" are the cultural authorities (100, 102).

Corelli had to tackle several contradictions here. Middle-class society may romanticize the artist who wears poverty in his buttonhole, but this genius will not be rewarded if his works are not well received by influential publishers. On the other hand, genius cannot be secured through buying up advertisers. "I am one of those who think the fame of Millais as an artist was marred when he degraded himself to the level of painting the little green boy blowing bubbles of Pears' soap. That was an advertisement," Tempest says pretentiously (99). Obviously, the dichotomy of high and low is connected with economics as much as with aesthetics. Corelli's faith lies in the tastes of the middle-class public, because then success is unmediated by critics and their assumptions of readers' social status. Mavis Clare represents the provincial writer who balances commercial success and artistic worth. She is inexplicably well loved. "She always 'takes' and no one can help it," says one bookseller. "You see people have got Compulsory Education now, and I'm afraid they begin to mistrust criticism, preferring to form their own independent opinions; if this is so, of course it will be a terrible thing, because the most carefully organized clique in the world will be powerless" (207–8). The seditious assumptions in this remark suggest that much is at stake — recall H. G. Wells's comparing the effects of mass education with those of the French Revolution. But with all of its decadent borrowings and allusions to the end of the world, its fierce attacks on wastefulness and privilege, its anguish at the gulf between rich and poor, and its criticism of every utterance opposed to the intelligence and good sense of the people, *The Sorrows of Satan* is far from revolutionary. Corelli romanticizes the artist by emphasizing familiarity, not alienation: the tolerant middle-class worker, represented in this novel by Mavis Clare and her faith in "the dignity of Literature as an art and a profession" (308), is the true redeemer of modern culture.

In the same democratic spirit Corelli wrote to Bentley, "After all, literature is the edifice, and authors only the working masons — if each one can add a fresh brick or stone to the building, that is something — and the builders should be too intent on the whole architecture to pause for an instant to criticize each other."[34] For Corelli rivalry, superficial evaluations of artistic merit, and arbitrary designations of "genius" are all forms of elitism generated by the aesthetic movement. But even if there is no place in aestheticism for her idiom of democratic cooperation in the name of art, the attitude of *service* to art, to something higher, is strikingly similar to that propounded by aestheticism. David Weir has discussed how the aesthete's pose may be construed as either an elitist rejection of democracy or "radical self-reliance and the expression of intense individualism" necessary for the cultivation of the aristocrat.[35] Corelli's popularity with the middle class and her intense faith in her personal mission, not to mention the persecutions she endured from masculine literary cliques, exemplify how the aesthetic pose could cut both ways — even for a writer who is not usually identified with aestheticism. Thus in *The Murder of Delicia* (1896) Delicia Vaughan's novels uplift her readers because she herself embodies virtue: her *moral* superiority (with which Corelli closely identifies) brings literary fame, compared with the vile band of male critics, reviewers, reporters, and paragraphists who lounge around The Bohemian, a London literary club. These pretenders dismiss Delicia as one of the "female *poseurs* in literature, whose works appeal chiefly to residents up Brixton and Clapham way."[36] In this novel Corelli's scorn is directed at self-promoting fakes who adopt the attitude of the fashionable aesthete in an effort to win approval from gullible publishers and readers. The phony Aubrey Grovelyn is one of these villains, "a long-haired 'poet' who wrote his own reviews" (98). "This son of the Muses" is "an untidy, dirty-looking man" who sets himself up to be (what else?) "a genius" (98). But, Corelli notes, the public sees he is a humbug and avoids his books "as cautiously as though they had been labeled 'Poison'" (99).

The Murder of Delicia is almost entirely without irony. Corelli writes with the bitterness of an outsider, and by 1896 she had had enough of insulting reviewers and sexist critics. If she was partly in collusion with aesthetic doctrines in her commitment to art and her own mythology of artists, her love of spirituality and the imagination, and her critiques of commercialism, Corelli was also in collusion with an advanced consumer society that had become very successful at condensing and marketing ideas. Despite the emergence of high and low art at the turn into modernism, these categories were still under revision, and borrowings from aestheticism are ubiquitous in mass fiction, just as aestheticism does some borrowing in return. The whole idea of decadence as an *aesthetic* category falls *socially* between romantic bohemia and avant-garde belle epoque: "Sometimes the decadent may pursue a bohemian life-style, but he always imagines himself a cultural aristocrat, while being, at base, thoroughly bourgeoisie."[37]

Victorian suburbia and Victorian mass commodity fiction shared the contempt of the cultural elite, and yet, as Holbrook Jackson writes in *The Eighteen Nineties,* eventually "even poets fell before the seductions of suburban life. . . . Bohemians cut their locks, shed their soft collars and fell back upon Suburbia."[38] How fitting that the first planned garden suburb, Bedford Park, was built in the 1870s as a kind of artists colony and satirized as the "aesthetic Elysium."[39] Even Arthur Symons admitted, in his classic treatise on decadence, *The Symbolist Movement in Literature,* that "the desire to 'bewilder the middle classes' is itself middle-class."[40]

Esmé Amarinth, the aesthetic hero of Robert Hichens's satire *The Green Carnation* (1894), utters the lament that is the epitaph to aestheticism's elitist pretensions: "I have been an aesthete. I have lain upon hearth-rugs and eaten passion-flowers. I have clothed myself in breeches of white samite, and offered my friends yellow jonquils instead of afternoon tea. But when aestheticism became popular in Bayswater — a part of London built for the delectation of the needy-rich — I felt that it was absurd no longer, and I turned to other things."[41]

However much it was regretted by the artists and intellectuals who were its initiators, aestheticism's success was marked by the many ways its tenets were absorbed into the Victorian middle class. Modernism possibly constitutes a reaction to the triumph of philistine taste and is being reassessed by postmodernist, feminist, and cultural critics for this very reason.[42] Corelli's popular appeal may have caused her eviction from the towers of high art in the 1890s and after, but by reading her novels again we can begin to reexamine the various shifts in emphasis, the teasing dialogues, the adaptations and contrivances that constitute an interesting continuum between the masculine world of "taste" and the feminine world of "trash" — between the consummately aesthetic and the utterly bourgeois.

Notes

1. Lionel Lambourne, *The Aesthetic Movement* (London: Phaidon, 1996), 114.

2. In his 1978 biography, *Now Barabbas Was a Rotter: The Extraordinary Life of Marie Corelli* (London: Hamish Hamilton, 1978), Brian Masters states, "At least half of her thirty books were world best-sellers. About 100,000 copies were sold every year" (6–7). Masters compares this figure to Hall Caine's 45,000, Mrs. Humphry Ward's 35,000, and H. G. Wells's 15,000. Norman Feltes gives a materialist explanation for Corelli's fame: the collapse of the three-volume novel and the introduction of the single six-shilling volume in the 1890s. See chap. 4, "The Process of Literary Capital in the 1890s: Caine, Corelli, and Bennett," in *Literary Capital and the Late-Victorian Novel* (Madison: University of Wisconsin Press, 1993).

3. J. M. Stuart-Young, "A Note upon Marie Corelli by Another Writer of Less Repute," *Westminster Review* 167 (1906): 687, 689.

4. H. G. Wells, *H. G. Wells's Literary Criticism,* ed. Patrick Parrinder and Robert M. Philmus (Sussex, U.K.: Harvester, 1980), 74.

5. Edward L. Purcell, "*Trilby* and Trilby-Mania: The Beginning of the Best-seller System," *Journal of Popular Culture* 11 (1977): 63.

6. Quoted in Masters, 59.

7. A. St. John Adcock, "Marie Corelli: A Record and an Appreciation," *Bookman* 36, no. 212 (1909): 59–60.

8. Andreas Huyssen, *After the Great Divide: Modernism, Mass Culture, Postmodernism* (Bloomington: Indiana University Press, 1986), 19.

9. Feltes, 125.

10. Stuart-Young, 683.

11. Adcock, 78.

12. Arthur H. Lawrence, "Miss Marie Corelli," *Strand* 15, no. 91 (1898): 24.

13. H. J. Dyos, *Victorian Suburb: A Study of the Growth of Camberwell* (London: Leicester University Press, 1966), 23.

14. F. M. L. Thompson, "The Rise of Suburbia," in *The Victorian City: A Reader in British Urban History, 1820–1914,* ed. R. J. Morris and Richard Rodger (London: Longman, 1993), 159.

15. Quoted in Thompson, 151. Given this identity crisis, it is fitting that the most famous account of late-Victorian suburban life is George and Weedon

Grossmith's *The Diary of a Nobody,* published serially in *Punch* in 1892. Along with describing the comical mishaps at the Pooters' Holloway villa (and the popularity of aesthetic decor among the suburban middle class — the Pooters have Japanese pictures, muslin curtains over the folding doors, and an arrangement of fans on the mantelpiece), *The Diary of a Nobody* testifies to the perceived gulf between middle-class philistinism and aesthetic sensibility. "*Revenons à nos moutons.* Our lives run in different grooves. I live for MY ART – THE STAGE. Your life is devoted to commercial pursuits," Mr. Burwin-Fosselton tells Pooter. "Cannot even you see the ocean between us?" And when a savvy American, Mr. Hardfur Huttle, makes a speech equating middle-class respectability with "miserable mediocrity," he asserts that such a man "will spend the rest of his days in a suburban villa with a stucco-column portico, resembling a four-post bedstead. . . . That sort of thing belongs to a soft man, with a soft beard, with a soft head, with a made tie that hooks on" (*The Diary of a Nobody* [London: Everyman, 1992], 107, 172).

16. Dyos, 26.

17. Holbrook Jackson, *The Eighteen Nineties* (New York: Capricorn, 1966), 107.

18. J. A. Spender, *The New Fiction and Other Papers,* in *Degeneration and Regeneration: Texts of the Premodern Era,* ed. Ian Fletcher and John Stokes (London: Garland, 1984), 82.

19. Lambourne, 13.

20. Jonathan Freedman, *Professions of Taste: Henry James, British Aestheticism, and Commodity Culture* (Stanford, Calif.: Stanford University Press, 1990), 49.

21. "Marie Corelli" was the creation of Mary Mackay, the daughter of Charles Mackay, a Scottish journalist, poet, and balladeer. After the publication and unexpected success of her first novel, *A Romance of Two Worlds* (1886), she satisfied the curiosity of her publisher, George Bentley, with an elaborate self-mythology: she said she was Venetian by birth (and took ten years off her age) and traced her heritage back to Arcangelo Corelli, the famous musician; she claimed that she had a godfather in Rome, that her mother had died in England, and that she was residing *en famille* with the Mackays. She also claimed that she was presented to Queen Margherita as a child. See Masters, especially chap. 1.

22. Arthur Symons, *The Symbolist Movement in Literature* (New York: Dutton, 1958), 5.

23. Corelli to Bentley, 11 May 1888, Marie Corelli–George Bentley Correspondence, Beinecke Rare Book and Manuscript Library, Yale University.

24. "Miss Marie Corelli: A Character Study by a Reader of Books," *Daily Mail,* 2 August 1906.

25. Marie Corelli, "My First Book," *Idler* 4 (1893): 239.

26. Corelli to Bentley, 8 September 1890, Marie Corelli–George Bentley Correspondence.

27. Ibid., 5 August 1890.

28. Oscar Wilde, "Pen, Pencil and Poison," in *The Artist as Critic: Critical Writings of Oscar Wilde,* ed. Richard Ellmann (Chicago: University of Chicago Press, 1969), 324.

29. Arthur Symons, *Selected Letters, 1880–1935,* ed. Karl Beckson and John H. Munro (Iowa City: University of Iowa Press, 1989), 76.

30. Marie Corelli, *Wormwood: A Drama of Paris* (New York: Burt, 1890), 4. All further citations will be noted parenthetically in the text and are taken from this edition.

31. Barnaby Conrad, *Absinthe: History in a Bottle* (San Francisco: Chronicle, 1988), 47.

32. Here is the complete poem in translation, quoted in Conrad, 48.

With Flowers, and with Women,
With Absinthe, and with this Fire,
We can divert ourselves awhile,
Act out our part in some drama.

Absinthe, on a winter evening,
Lights up in green the sooty soul;
And Flowers, on the beloved,
Grow fragrant before the clear Fire.

Later, kisses lose their charm
Having lasted several seasons;
And after mutual betrayals
We part one day without a tear.

We burn letters and bouquets,
And Fire takes our bower;
And if sad life is salvaged
Still there is Absinthe and its hiccups. . . .

The portraits are eaten by flames . . .
Shriveled fingers tremble . . .
We die from sleeping long
With Flowers, and with Women.

33. Corelli, *The Sorrows of Satan* (Philadelphia: Lippincott, 1895), 404. All further citations will be noted parenthetically in the text and are taken from this edition.

34. Corelli to Bentley, 6 April 1887, Marie Corelli–George Bentley Correspondence.

35. David Weir, *Decadence and the Making of Modernism* (Amherst: University of Massachusetts Press, 1995), 93.

36. Marie Corelli, *The Murder of Delicia* (Philadelphia: Lippincott, 1896), 76. All further citations will be noted parenthetically in the text and are taken from this edition.

37. Weir, xv.

38. Jackson, 116.

39. Lambourne, 86–87.

40. Symons, 4.

41. Robert Hichens, *The Green Carnation* (New York: Appleton, 1894), 196.

42. Most recently, Rita Felski's *The Gender of Modernity* (Cambridge, Mass.: Harvard University Press, 1995) includes a brilliant chapter on Corelli. R. B. Kershner has also written about Corelli and modernism; see his "Joyce and Popular Literature: The Case of Corelli," in *James Joyce and His Contemporaries,* ed. Diana A. Ben-Merre and Maureen Murphy (New York: Greenwood, 1989), 213–26, and "Modernism's Mirror: The Sorrows of Marie Corelli," in *Transforming Genres: New Approaches to British Fiction of the 1890s,* ed. Nikki Lee Manos and Meri-Jane Rochelson (New York: St. Martin's, 1994), 67–86.

PART II

Aesthetic Poetry

Chapter 5

KATHY ALEXIS PSOMIADES

Whose Body?

Christina Rossetti and Aestheticist Femininity

THERE IS perhaps no cannier representation of Christina Rossetti as aesthete than Max Beerbohm's cartoon in *Rossetti and His Circle* (1922). Its caption reads:

> Rossetti, having just had a fresh consignment of stunning fabrics from that new shop in Regent St., tries hard to prevail on his younger sister to accept at any rate one of these and have a dress made out of it from designs to be furnished by himself.[1]

Brother and sister stand in a paneled room with indecipherable pictures on the walls. The room is full of chairs draped with swags of material in brilliant colors. In the center the Rossettis face each other — Gabriel in a black smocklike garment over trousers, Christina in a black bonnet, shawl, and gloves and holding an umbrella. Gabriel frowns and gesticulates, saying, "What *is* the use, Christina, of having a heart like a singing bird and a water-shoot and all the rest of it, if you insist on getting yourself up like a pew-opener?" Christina replies, "Well, Gabriel, I don't know. I'm sure you yourself always dress very quietly."

At first glance this cartoon appears to represent yet another woman writer's refusal to accept aestheticism's tendency to turn women into beautiful erotic objects. But as we continue to examine it, a more complex picture emerges. Beerbohm seems to be portraying Christina Rossetti's complicated engagement with aestheticism. In this cartoon Rossetti can be said to have two bodies — the respectable, black-clad body she presents to the world, and the imaginary body of the aestheticist art object. This imaginary body is seen partly as the product of masculine imagination — Gabriel urges Christina to make this body a reality with his intervention — and partly as an implication of Rossetti's own poetry: her poem "A

Birthday" begins with the lines "My heart is like a singing bird / Whose nest is in a watered shoot," and the second stanza describes the use of gorgeous materials in creating a stage for self-display — "Raise me a dais of silk and down."[2] So the body urged on Christina by Gabriel in Beerbohm's cartoon is one she herself has helped to create, and her refusal to occupy it in real life is not the same as the refusal of such a body *tout court.*

Furthermore, Gabriel attempts to use bolts of cloth to materialize the aesthetic realm in the everyday world. Yet here the attempt to aestheticize daily life connotes participation in commodity culture — the heart like a singing bird comes from the realm of art, but the fabrics come from a new shop in Regent Street. They are described as "stunning," a word that is both part of the shopper's common parlance and reminiscent of Dante Gabriel Rossetti's use of the word "stunner" to describe women, words, and art objects. So, in an odd way, rather than refusing aestheticism, Christina Rossetti insists on an aestheticism more perfect than her brother's, one that does not traffic so much in the market, one whose lushly beautiful objects are not for sale.

Finally, the cartoon ties the two Rossettis together, both by having Christina compare Gabriel's appearance to her own and by making the poets into black shapes that face each other. Dressing quietly, the two poets mark themselves out as producers rather than consumers, as workers rather than pleasure seekers. By refusing brightly colored clothing, loose hair, a relaxed posture, Christina refuses a certain gender dimorphism; her phallic umbrella and Gabriel's feminine smock act to undercut the absolute difference between feminine art object and masculine artist that Gabriel's gesture seems to suggest. She thus takes up the dandy's attitude of extreme yet understated self-regulation.

What Beerbohm shows us here, in other words, is an aestheticism produced by both men and women and characterized by a particular way of using the feminine figure. He also provides a critical model of the double vision necessary for thinking about the work of the women who produced aestheticism. On the one hand, this model examines the different relations men and women might have to aestheticism's feminine images — no one suggests that Dante Gabriel try to look like the women in his paintings. On the other hand, this model observes the continuities between the work of men and women — both poets create aestheticism's feminine images, both have an investment in those images as the location of their art and artistry, both operate in the aestheticist tradition.

In this essay I want to follow Beerbohm's lead and demonstrate how

Christina Rossetti constructs the aestheticist woman poet as drawing authority from her privileged relationship to aestheticism's feminine images. Those images, I want to argue, are part of what makes it possible to imagine aestheticism as a tradition with both masculine and feminine practitioners. Many feminist scholars have seen aestheticism's tendency to construct and represent aesthetic value in feminine figures as oppressive to women. But to the extent that these figures value feminine interiority and reveal femininity's artificiality, they may also be enabling for women. Rather than assuming that aestheticism prescribes a version of femininity as the mute object of masculine desire, we might shift our focus to what it means to the men and women who produce culture that in aestheticism femininity signifies the power of the aesthetic.[3]

To address this issue is to move toward a new history of aestheticism, one that takes account of the contributions made by both men and women. By showing how Rossetti draws on and contributes to the aestheticist trope of Beauty's body — that is, the use of a feminine figure to embody and represent aesthetic experience — I will also show how aestheticism's feminine images invite women's participation in the movement. Ultimately, maintaining our double vision of women's participation in aestheticism means refusing to assume not only that we already know what aestheticism is about but also that we already know what women, or femininity, or women writers are about. In this way we might avoid inscribing in aestheticism the very gender binarisms it works to disrupt.

Queen of Pre-Raphaelitism: Christina Rossetti in the 1890s

What if we suspend for a moment what we know, and imagine a world in which Christina Rossetti is the inaugurator of British aestheticism? Such a world is not as far from reality as we might think, for if not hailed as the preeminent aestheticist poet of her day, Christina Rossetti was associated with Pre-Raphaelite aestheticism by reviewers as early as the 1860s.[4] Reviewers of *Goblin Market and Other Poems* (1862) and *The Prince's Progress and Other Poems* (1866) noted the illustrations by Dante Gabriel Rossetti and, particularly in America, used the word "Pre-Raphaelite" in relation to the poetry.[5] By the 1880s William Sharp was writing that Rossetti "has, as a poet, a much wider reputation and a much larger circle of readers than even her brother Gabriel, for in England and much more markedly in America, the name of Christina Rossetti is known intimately where perhaps that of the author of the *House of Life* is but a name and nothing more."[6] True, many reviewers do not mention the connection to Pre-Raphaelitism, placing Rossetti instead in the context of devotional poetry or poetry by women. But, as Antony Harrison has pointed out, to those associated with aestheticism in the 1880s and 1890s, Rossetti was an aestheticist poet. Richard Le Gallienne, Arthur Symons, Edmund Gosse, Alice Law, William Sharp, and Oscar Wilde all focused on her formal mastery, compared her work to that of men associated with aestheticism, and described her poetry in language associated with the aestheticist prose of Algernon Charles Swinburne and Walter Pater. Symons noted, "The thought of death has a constant fascination for her, almost such a fascination as it had for Leopardi or Baudelaire."[7] Gosse described "her habitual tone" as "one of melancholy reverie, the pathos of which is strangely intensified by her appreciation of beauty and pleasure."[8] Le Gallienne wrote, "The note of loss and the peculiar sad cadence of the music, even though the songs be of happy things, is the distinctive characteristic of Miss Rossetti's singing. . . . Her songs of love are nearly always of love's loss; of its joy she sings with a passionate throat, but it is joy seen through the mirror of a wild regret."[9] At her death in 1894, Rossetti was hailed not only as an important woman poet and writer of devotional verse but also as a major aestheticist poet.

Phrases like "Queen of the Pre-Raphaelites" or "High-Priestess of Pre-Raphaelitism" explicitly connect Rossetti's status as cultural producer to aestheticism's use of feminine figures. Both Rossetti's participation in the movement since the days of the *Germ* (the literary magazine of the Pre-Raphaelite Brotherhood) and the presence of imaginary women in Pre-Raphaelite poetry and painting come together in these phrases to make it possible to imagine a woman producing aestheticism. Similarly, aestheticism's association with passionate emotion and sensation, often seen as feminizing male poets and artists, also seems compatible with the participation of a woman poet. Symons wrote of Rossetti, "This motive, passion remembered and repressed, condemned to eternal memory and eternal sorrow, is the motive of much of her finest work."[10] Rossetti's repression of her passion does not erase that passion, any more than her plain clothing erases the idea of the beautiful aestheticist woman in Beerbohm's cartoon. Rather, repression acts further to interiorize and mystify that passion: in this way Rossetti's status as *woman* intensifies, rather than diminishes, her status as *aestheticist poet.* In short, we can see in many reviews of Rossetti's work a sense that she is peculiarly suited to write aestheticist verse *because* she is a woman, a sense that aestheticism's concern with femininity and its turn away from the productive masculine realm on some level invite feminine participation.[11]

Perhaps the most nuanced discussion of the relation between Rossetti's femininity and her aestheticism is Alice Law's eulogistic essay in the *Westminster Review* (1895). In the opening paragraphs of this essay Law asserts the aestheticism of Rossetti's verse — its polished finish, the inseparability of its form and content, its autonomy — by using language and imagery with feminine, as well as aestheticist, connotations: "The absence of all harsher and more rugged qualities, of all topical didacticism, of any rigid philosophical system on which we can lay hold, their seeming artless, yet aesthetic and finished perfection, all these combine to give the poems an air of elevated inaccessibility which renders critical approach difficult."[12] Later, Law employs a metaphor often used to connect femininity and artistry in aestheticist poetry: "Like some magic web, it seems woven of a substance so elusive, intangible, and of such an almost gossamer tenuity as defies handling, and constitutes at once the critic's ecstasy, wonder, and despair" (445). The absence of the harsh, rugged, and rigid and the presence of the elusive and intangible are, of course, characteristic of aestheticist poetry in general. But by showing how these feminine qualities make Rossetti's art resistant to critical consumption and co-optation, Law implies that Rossetti's femininity intensifies her aestheticism, making her poetry even more rigorously autonomous than aestheticist poetry generally is.

Law also uses vocabulary associated with male aestheticist writers like Swinburne, Pater, and Wilde to describe Rossetti's accomplishments:

> But the keynote of much of Miss Rossetti's word-music is its aesthetic mysticism and rich melancholy. It is associated here, as in the works of her brother and the other Pre-Raphaelites, with the deep medieval coloring, and quaint bejewelled setting of an old thirteenth- or fourteenth-century manuscript. . . . Neither dull English skies, nor any sort of Philistine environment, could damp the artistic ardor which burns in such exquisite similes as illuminate her pages. . . . But it is specially in the *Prince's Progress* that Miss Rossetti's subtle and mysterious art finds its most perfect expression. Here we seem to breathe the very atmosphere of old-world charm and mysticism: the stanzas as it were exhale that almost indescribable aesthetic aroma of mingled flowers and herbs — rosemary, thyme, rue, and languorous lilies. (447–48)

The words "aesthetic," "mysticism," "quaint," "exquisite," "subtle," "mysterious," and "languorous" underline Rossetti's status as a participant in a larger movement and insist on her work being considered along with the writing of her male contemporaries. Furthermore, by providing an occasion for Law to use this language, Rossetti enabled Law's participation in aestheticism as well, as an aestheticist critic.

Yet for Law, Rossetti's central achievement lies in her special relationship to aestheticist figures of femininity. At first Law seems to suggest a fairly straightforward connection between Rossetti's life and her art: Rossetti can convincingly give voice to the figure of the enclosed pining woman because she *is* that woman, because her art is the expression of her life. Yet in her references to aestheticist tradition, and in her use of formulations that simultaneously collapse and reinforce the distinctions between Rossetti and her feminine figures, Law also suggests that Rossetti's life is itself produced by aestheticism, that the links between life and art, real women and imagined women, are as much about femininity as artifice as they are about femininity as authenticity.

In the following passage, for example, Law claims not that Rossetti's poetry is autobiographical but that the aesthetic effects of this poetry depend on the conjunction of traditional tropes of femininity with the idea of a real woman:

> Not only is the atmosphere of her poems old-world, but in all Miss Rossetti's pages we seem to see the medieval heroine herself looking out at us, from an almost cloistered seclusion, with sad patient eyes. We hear the song of her overflowing heart, longing to spend and to be spent for love. There is nothing modern about this singing, unless it be its hopelessness, its troubled emotion and despair. The attitude is throughout that of the old-world heroine — pensive, clinging, *passive.* It is the tearful, uplifted accent of her who, in the silence of barred cell or rush-strewn chamber, weeps and prays for victory to crown the arms of others; of her whose only warfare is with the fears and fightings of her own bursting heart. It is the solitary singing of Shelley's
>
> High born maiden,
> In her palace tower,
> Soothing her love-laden
> Soul in secret hour
> With music sweet as love, that overflows her bower.
>
> The singing conveys all this, I think, and more; and yet, in hearing it, we are constrained to remember that the voice is none other than that of Miss Rossetti herself; that consciously or unconsciously she is her own medieval heroine. (449)

Law repeatedly conflates and separates the real and the aesthetic in this passage. The enclosed woman of art is distinguished from the real woman of the 1890s, yet the very language of the passage points to the similarities between the heroine and that other hopeless, troubled, despairing creature of suffering sexuality: the New Woman. By using the double entendre "to spend and to be spent," Law makes the desire of the medieval heroine as explicitly sexual (and thus as modern) as the desire of any New Woman. Furthermore, the passage depends on the uncanniness of the vivification of figures of poetic tradition. The heroine looking back at the reader from the page, or the sound of her singing reaching the reader's ears, produces an image not so much of authenticity as of art unexpectedly brought to life. So the poetry simultaneously constructs feminine figures that are recognizably part of a poetic tradition (the singing) and forces the reader to think of Rossetti (the voice) as bringing these figures to life in a new way. The phrase "consciously or unconsciously" introduces the same kind of doubling into the essay that Beerbohm introduced into his cartoon, allowing aesthetic agency to be conceived of as artifice and authenticity at the same moment. If Rossetti is unconsciously her own medieval heroine, the juxtaposition of real woman and feminine figure that occurs in her poetry is a function of her natural femininity. But if she is consciously her own heroine, then that juxtaposition is a function of art and a consciousness of femininity as artifice. By keeping both possibilities constantly in play, Law refuses to pin Rossetti to one model of femininity and poetic production.

Law sees as most typical of Rossetti's genius *The Prince's Progress,* a poem that both separates the feminine body of art from the feminine singer and contrasts masculine and feminine reactions to that body. The poem allows Law to situate Rossetti as aestheticist femininity and as singer and to situate herself as an aestheticist critic with a special relation to femininity. Law prefaces her review with a quotation from the last stanza of the poem, "You should have wept her yesterday," a line spoken by the attendants of a dead princess as a reproach to a prince who arrives too late. Law takes up the positions of both the prince to whom the line is addressed and the princess's attendant who utters it: she should have celebrated Rossetti while she lived, but now her essay can at least rebuke an insufficiently appreciative public. By doing this, Law places Rossetti in the positions of both the dead princess, who must be spoken for, and the attendants who speak for her: "In her lament for the Dead Bride of *The Prince's Progress,* she has, without knowing it, composed her own immortal epitaph" (449). Law places herself and Rossetti in the poem then in such a way as to connect them to and distance them from the aestheticist figure of the dead bride: as a modern woman of the 1890s, Law refuses to identify with the silent suffering object of the gaze, preferring to ally herself with the masculine gazer, but at the same time she and Rossetti are able to speak about femininity because they know it from the inside. If Rossetti is Pre-Raphaelite aestheticism, the full flowering of a tradition based on images of enclosed femininity, then she in turn authorizes Law as an aestheticist critic, who understands aestheticism all the better because of the double vision her femininity allows her.

My point here is simply that comparing Rossetti to a Pre-Raphaelite heroine and to the various feminine figures that people aestheticist verse does not just make her into an art object, on the one hand, or reduce her poetry to the authentic expression of natural emotions, on the other; instead it suggests a connection between aestheticism's uses of femininity and the ability to conceptualize the movement as one in which both men and women write. Aestheticism's tendency to think about the body of woman as mysterious surface always accompanied by some unknowable depth invites accounts of the experience of that body not only from the outside but also from the inside as the proper stuff of poetry. In so doing, it makes women aestheticist poets as imaginable as men. This is not to say that Beauty's body does not put demands on women that men do not experience. It is difficult to imagine Dante Gabriel Rossetti or Swinburne writing, as Christina Rossetti did, "If only my figure would shrink somewhat. For a fat poetess is incongruous, especially when seated by the grave of buried hope."[13] But even in this ironic comment, we can see a gesture of humorous identification and disidentification with the notion of being one's own heroine, one's own body of art.

Once She Was Fair: Aestheticism, 1866

The relation between Christina Rossetti's work and Pre-Raphaelite aestheticism has been characterized by scholars in two central ways. First, some of the best feminist criticism of Rossetti's work sees it as criticizing Pre-Raphaelitism's use of feminine images. In particular, Dolores Rosenblum has explored how participating in a movement that revolves around mute, mysterious feminine figures gives the female poet a consciousness divided between "the writer who sees and speaks, and the image/woman who is seen and is mute."[14] Second, some critics, notably Jerome McGann and Antony Harrison, see Rossetti as a recognized participant in Pre-Raphaelite aestheticism.[15] I would like to bring together these approaches in this reading of *The Prince's Progress* to suggest that what is aestheticist about Rossetti's poetry is not merely its turn away from the world in a movement of aesthetic and religious withdrawal but primarily its use of figures of femininity to think through the contradictory nature of art in bourgeois culture. As Law suggests, *The Prince's Progress* makes feminine artistry the logical outcome of aestheticist art. It may not be the "most perfect expression" of Rossetti's "subtle and mysterious art," but it is one of the most aestheticist of her poems.

The Prince's Progress and Other Poems was one of two major volumes of aestheticist poetry published in 1866; the other was Swinburne's *Poems and Ballads* (First Series). Each volume begins with a poem about the incompatibility of masculine heroism and erotic fulfillment: "The Prince's Progress" and "Laus Veneris" both explore the gendered and sexualized terrain of the aesthetic and make the sensational experience of a feminine body the central aesthetic moment. By tracing a dangerous but ultimately futile masculine journey to a private space constituted by an erotically charged and ultimately inaccessible feminine body, the poems meditate on the demands of self-enclosed eroticized aestheticist art and its incompatibility with the norms of bourgeois masculinity.

"Laus Veneris" is organized around the public space of a masculine quest, where knights ride and fight and pray, and the private space of femininity, art, and desire, where Venus slumbers in her Horsel.[16] Drawn out of the realm of masculine achievement by Venus's beauty, the poem's speaker unwittingly reveals that the masculine realm that he honors is a place of violence, hypocrisy, and tyranny, whereas the feminine realm of art and sex that he sees as his damnation is the location of the only real beauty and value. In Venus, Swinburne can claim that art is radically incompatible with the praxis of everyday life, based in the very instincts that always threaten to disorder civilization, and experienced, like sex, through the body.[17]

Venus's burning, scented, gorgeous flesh may seem at first to be miles away from the pining, dying body of a virgin princess. Yet Rossetti's poem also marks off two realms: a public masculine space of achievement, and a private feminine space of art and sex. As in "Laus Veneris," the valued space of art is grounded in a feminine body. From its initial association with flowers, gums, and juices, the princess's body brings together the erotic and the aesthetic:

> By her head lilies and rosebuds grow;
> The lilies droop, — will the rosebuds blow?

The silver slim lilies hang the head low;
  Their stream is scanty, their sunshine rare;
Let the sun blaze out, and let the stream flow,
  They will blossom and wax fair.

Red and white poppies grow at her feet,
The blood-red wait for sweet summer heat,
Wrapped in bud-coats hairy and neat;
  But the white buds swell; one day they will burst,
Will open their death-cups drowsy and sweet, —
  Which will open the first?[18]

Here the flowers that surround the princess are so weighted by poetic tradition that it is difficult to tell whether they are literally present or purely metaphorical representations of living and dead sex and virginity. They aestheticize the feminine body as they reduce its meaning to its erotic status.

By contrast, the prince is described surrounded by literal and mundane objects:

In his world-end palace the strong Prince sat,
Taking his ease on cushion and mat,
Close at hand lay his staff and his hat. (13–15)

The prince inhabits an oddly domestic world in which objects are used for his body's comfort but have neither aesthetic nor erotic significance. The very language of the passage is offhand and ironic, whereas the language used to describe the princess reverently invokes the elemental forces of nature and is the location of much of the poem's metaphoric energy.

The world of Rossetti's prince, like the world that Swinburne's knight gives up for Venus, is clearly not as valuable as the enclosed realm that contains Beauty's body. If for Swinburne the irony is that the masculine sphere of battle and religion is far more violent and just as sensual as the feminine sphere in which the knight now resides and about which he feels so much guilt, for Rossetti the irony is that the masculine sphere, whose activities are so important and on which the lovely bride waits, is silly and inconsequential. The prince of the poem's title is neither hero nor villain but a jolly incompetent, his quest a series of purposeless tasks that take him far too long. "Strong of limb, if of purpose weak" (47), he sets out only to find himself seduced not by a subtle temptress but by the first passing milkmaid. Finally breaking free, he journeys through a wasteland, arduous chiefly because there is no one to talk to: "Tedious land for a social prince" (152). Here he finds himself helping an alchemist make an elixir of life not because he has been enchanted, or because he really needs the elixir, or even because he has a greedy desire for knowledge, but because he is hungry and finds his solitude tedious. When the elixir is made and the magician dies, the prince rests another night before resuming his journey. Forthwith he is rescued from drowning by ladies and stays with them for a while because he cannot think of a polite way to refuse them. The events that in a traditional quest narrative prove the quester's moral fiber here are merely a series of procrastinations and delays. In short, the prince does not progress at all, and, indeed, his lack of progress trivializes masculine activity.

When the prince finally arrives at the princess's palace, he is, of course, too late:

> Day is over, the day that wore.
> What is this that comes through the door,
> The face covered, the feet before?
>   This that coming takes his breath;
> This Bride not seen, to be seen no more
>   Save of the Bridegroom Death? (469–74)

The question "What is this" echoes the "Who is this? and what is here?" that greets Alfred, Lord Tennyson's dead Lady of Shalott as she floats into Camelot. Here is the ideal opportunity for a Lancelot moment, the moment at which the obtuse male lover comes face-to-face with the dead body of the woman who has desired him. But the prince is never allowed the luxury of this moment, not the gazing on the dead face, the musing, or the final interpretive gesture. Instead, he finds himself addressed by the princess's attendants, upbraided for his part in the princess's story, the only story, the poem implies, that really matters:

> You should have wept her yesterday,
>   Wasting upon her bed:
> But wherefore should you weep to-day
>   That she is dead?
> Lo, we who love weep not to-day,
>   But crown her royal head.
> Let be these poppies that we strew,
>   Your roses are too red:

Let be these poppies, not for you
  Cut down and spread. (531–40)

As an aestheticist poem, then, *The Prince's Progress* makes a strong statement about the dangers of the autonomy aesthetic. The very isolation from the everyday world that keeps the princess pure and poetic threatens to destroy her entirely. The aesthetic and erotic experiences that the princess promises simply cannot compete with the stronger pleasures offered by objects and services of more immediate use — milk, magic, maidens — that can be had by anyone willing to pay for them. The philistine prince is above all else *bored;* like a model bourgeois consumer, he seeks to be amused and entertained.[19] By the time he finally decides he wants direct experience of the princess, there is no princess to be had. The greatest danger that everyday life poses to the aesthetic for Rossetti is not that it will, as in "Laus Veneris," attempt to stamp out the aesthetic realm but that, content with other amusements, it will simply not care enough about the aesthetic even to attempt to stamp it out. In an essay written in 1785 the German writer Karl Philipp Moritz makes a succinct statement about art's value that might serve as a proleptic gloss on Rossetti's poem:

> We do not need the beautiful object in order to be entertained as much as the beautiful object needs us to be recognized. We can easily exist without contemplating beautiful works of art, but they cannot exist as such without our contemplation. The more we can do without them, therefore, the more we contemplate them for their own sake so as to impart to them through our very contemplation, as it were, their true, complete existence.[20]

Beauty, like the princess, dies if left unvalued and unappreciated as easily as it dies if co-opted by the marketplace and seen in purely economic terms.

Despite its statement about autonomy's dangers, what makes *The Prince's Progress* aestheticist is its assertion that the aesthetic realm, attenuated and endangered though it may be, is still the location of all true value in the poem. It makes this assertion through the plot conventions of aestheticist narrative poetry, by producing a narrative that climaxes in the lyric contemplation of the dead or unconscious feminine body of art, a narrative that purports to explain but merely demonstrates the inexplicability of the lyric encounter. Aestheticist poems like Tennyson's "The Lady of Shalott," Dante Gabriel Rossetti's "Jenny," and Swinburne's "Laus Veneris," to name a few, share this structure. In these poems the inadequacy of the narrative as an explanation of feminine mystery marks out a further beyond that signifies art's inviolability even in the most compromising circumstances. *The Prince's Progress* further reorganizes the climactic moment of contemplation to place Beauty's body beyond the reach of heterosexual romance, intimating that a real understanding of Beauty's value is only available to those who have an understanding of femininity from the inside out.

The contemplation and celebration of the body of the dead bride occurs in the poem's final stanzas, which are spoken by the princess's attendants and set off from the rest of the poem by a longer stanza form. Written well before the rest of *The Prince's Progress* as a separate poem titled "The Fairy Prince Who Arrived Too Late," these lines form not only the poem's climax but its origin. (It was Dante Gabriel Rossetti who suggested that Rossetti "turn the dirge into a narrative poem of some length."[21]) These final stanzas depict a process of transformation in which the prince's neglect causes the princess's body to change. Withdrawn from aesthetic, erotic, and economic exchange, valueless in the real world, the body ceases to have the attributes of aestheticist femininity. Yet in their place, new attributes emerge that characterize an even more rigorous aestheticism.

Beauty, sexual exchangeability, and economic value typically come together in aestheticist figures of femininity, whose eroticism acts to manage the complicated relation between art and the market. Here, they appear as qualities gone:

> Is she fair now as she lies?
> Once she was fair;
> Meet queen for any kingly king,
> With gold-dust on her hair.
> Now these are poppies in her locks,
> White poppies she must wear;
> Must wear a veil to shroud her face
> And the want graven there:
> Or is the hunger fed at length,
> Cast off the care? (501–10)

Once beautiful, once admirably suited to sexual exchange, once covered in gold, the princess now wears a veil, or shroud, over her wasted face. Her sexual exchangeability, signified by the veil of virginity, is curtailed by death, as the veil becomes a shroud. The economic value sign of gold is replaced by the poppies that signify her radical unexchangeability. Her face, no longer lovely and thus no longer caught up in the desires of others, is hidden from view: it cannot function any longer as a figure of aesthetic value.

Yet the princess ultimately acts to signify the power of the aesthetic in bourgeois culture, even as she signifies its powerlessness in bourgeois systems of exchange. Because it is "[t]oo late for love, too late for joy," because she will never circulate as a value, the princess's body exists for its own sake. What it looks like is a sign not of the desires of others for it but of its own desires for fulfillment. As the attendants describe the dead princess as she was in life, they locate value in the her interiority, in her regulation of her own passions:

> We never saw her with a smile
> Or with a frown;
> Her bed seemed never soft to her,
> Though tossed of down;
> She little heeded what she wore,
> Kirtle, or wreath, or gown;
> We think her white brows often ached
> Beneath her crown,
> Till silvery hairs showed in her locks
> That used to be so brown.
>
> We never heard her speak in haste:
> Her tones were sweet,
> And modulated just so much
> As it was meet:
> Her heart sat silent through the noise
> And concourse of the street.
> There was no hurry in her hands,
> No hurry in her feet;
> There was no bliss drew night to her,
> That she might run to meet. (511–30)

Here the aging, wasting, self-regulating body comes to signify art's tragic isolation, but also its enduring value. Because this value comes from within, from feminine experience, it suggests that women, through their experiences with femininity, might have a special relationship to aestheticist art. No longer a value sign in the world of men, the princess ultimately becomes the sign of the singing maidens' superior artistry. Thus the final lines insist on the women's right to metaphorize the body with white poppies, flowers not usually invoked in poetry, rather than the conventional red roses. If red roses signify feminine beauty as the object of desire, white poppies seem to signify feminine desire unsatisfied, a yearning that ends only in death. The attendants' understanding of the princess makes their metaphors more original and exact than the trite and worn tribute offered by the prince. It is important to recognize that the two sets of flowers, the beautiful body and the pining body, are equally symbolic, equally textual. The pining body is ultimately no more and no less real than the blooming body, no more and no less a surface to be read. What is at issue is who writes and who reads the signs of femininity, who best understands them, and thus who best understands the truths about the aesthetic that they figure.

So in *The Prince's Progress* the princess not only serves as a figure for the aesthetic but also is the occasion for the poem's women singers to produce their own poetry. The singing women must make a double gesture toward the princess of identification and disidentification: they must be enough like her to be able to read the signs of her interior life on her body's surface but enough unlike her to survive. The double gesture of standing inside and outside the body of Beauty is echoed by Dante Gabriel Rossetti's illustrations for *The Prince's Progress and Other Poems,* which, far more than his illustrations for *Goblin Market and Other Poems,* locate Rossetti herself in the realm of art. In the illustration that appears on the title page along with Rossetti's name, the princess sits by a window, waiting, with long hair, full-sleeved robe, full lips, and eyes that gaze out on the landscape below. It seems to suggest that the volume will provide some access to the musing woman's thoughts. In the illustration for the poem's final scene, one woman is distinguished from the collectivity of attendants in the poem. She pushes the prince out the door of the crypt in which the princess lies shrouded in the background. The other maidens have the long, loose hair and full lips of Beauty's body, but the attendant who disposes of the prince turns away from the viewer, her hair hidden in a headdress. As she pushes the prince out the door, she seems to take his place; at the same time, in coming forward to meet him, she takes the place of the bride who would meet him were she alive. Significantly, it is with this figure that Rossetti partly identifies, remarking in a letter to her brother about an early version of this drawing, "Surely the severe female who arrests the Prince somewhat resembles my phiz."[22] By splitting the attendants into beautiful young women and a plainer, more mature figure,

Dante Gabriel projects the two bodies the poem locates in the princess onto the serving women, who in the poem remain an undifferentiated collectivity. In the process he makes the severe female into the musing princess's double and opposite. Together, princess and attendant both foster and thwart the reader's desires to see the woman poet as one who is or ought to be a version of the beautiful body of art.

Conclusion

What can Christina Rossetti tell us, then, about the relationship between aestheticism's use of feminine figures and the women who made aestheticist art? The answer depends on what we think aestheticism is and what we think women are. If we think that aestheticism is a masculine tradition that turns women into objects and that women authors only write to contradict the demand that women be silent, then what Rossetti tells us is that women aesthetes were participating in an inherently hostile tradition that they could only engage with in the mode of critique. The princess can only die of desire unsatisfied; her women can only weep. I would argue that, while this is by no means an entirely wrong view of aestheticism, it is a very partial one. If, to supplement this partial view, we think of aestheticism as a moment at which the idea of femininity became foundational to the conception of the aesthetic and if we think that women writers emerge in greater and greater numbers in the nineteenth century in part because middle-class femininity was increasingly the location of many different kinds of cultural authority, then we might see these images as connected not only to women's oppression but also to their increasing empowerment.

Aestheticism's concern with feminine images and later with traditionally feminine areas of expertise — dress, decor, gardening — meant that aestheticist and anti-aestheticist women writers alike could claim that their status as "real" women authorized them to speak about "imaginary" women and to give advice about traditionally feminine activities. The figure of the woman as silent art object may seem to have silenced women who would have been poets, but it also incited them to speech. The princess's attendants cannot be silent, cannot let matters rest; they must explain, exhort, interpret, claim the figure of Beauty as not the prince's but their own. If we read aestheticism's beautiful women not as incidental figures but as modes of grounding and representing art itself, then all discussions of aestheticist femininity are of necessity as much about art as about gender ideology. Because these discussions take place through the representation of a specific kind of femininity, they are discussions in which women, as well as men, speak. In short, the work of Rossetti and other women aesthetes allows us to see that arguments about representing and interpreting femininity are always also arguments about representation and interpretation, about art and artistry and their place in bourgeois culture as a whole. That femininity is the ground on which these arguments occur, their guarantee and their alibi, poses difficulties for women but also offers opportunities.

Notes

1. Max Beerbohm, *Rossetti and His Circle* (London: Heinemann, 1922; reprint, New Haven, Conn.: Yale University Press, 1987), 50.

2. Christina Rossetti, *The Complete Poems of Christina Rossetti,* ed. R. W. Crump (Baton Rouge: Louisiana State University Press, 1979–80), 1:36.

3. For more on the relation between femininity and aestheticism, see Kathy Psomiades, *Beauty's Body: Femininity and Representation in British Aestheticism* (Stanford, Calif.: Stanford University Press, 1997).

4. For accounts of Rossetti's reception in the nineteenth century, see Edna Kotin Charles, *Christina Rossetti: Critical Perspectives, 1862–1982* (London and Toronto: Associated University Presses, 1985), 23–67, and Rebecca Crump, *Christina Rossetti: A Reference Guide* (Boston: G. K. Hall, 1976), which lists reviews chronologically.

5. See J. R. Dennet, "Miss Rossetti's Poems," *Nation,* 19 July 1866, 47–48. In *Christina Rossetti in Context* (Chapel Hill: University of North Carolina Press, 1988), Antony Harrison points out that the review of *The Prince's Progress and Other Poems* in the *Athenaeum* (23 June 1866, 824–25) also judges it according to Pre-Raphaelite principles (27).

6. William Sharp, "The Rossetti's," *Fortnightly Review,* 1 March 1886, 427.

7. Arthur Symons, *Studies in Two Literatures* (London: Leonard Smithers, 1897), 142.

8. Edmund Gosse, "Christina Rossetti," *Century Magazine* 46 (June 1893): 215.

9. Richard Le Gallienne, "Review of *Poems,*" *Academy,* 7 February 1891, 132.

10. Symons, 138.

11. Tricia Lootens compellingly argues that fin-de-siècle criticism domesticates and naturalizes Rossetti's poetry. In many of the articles from which I quote, mention is made of Rossetti's narrowness, her technique, the connection between her poetry and her feminine experience. These gestures constitute a misogynistic minimalization of Rossetti's achievement. However, if we look at them in the context of nineteenth-century criticism of aestheticist poetry by men as well as women, we see that accusations of narrowness, of overworking or underworking

verse, even of sexual transgression, are made about aestheticist poetry generally. In other words, while these are responses to Rossetti as a woman poet, they are also responses to her as an aestheticist poet, a fact obscured by reading the criticism solely in the context of criticism on other women poets. See Tricia Lootens, *Lost Saints: Silence, Gender, and Victorian Literary Canonization* (Charlottesville: University Press of Virginia, 1996), 158–82.

12. Alice Law, "The Poetry of Christina Rossetti," *Westminster Review* 143 (1895): 444. All further references will be noted parenthetically in the text.

13. William Michael Rossetti, ed., *The Family Letters of Christina Georgina Rossetti* (London: Brown, Langham, 1908), 160.

14. Dolores Rosenblum, *Christina Rossetti: The Poetry of Endurance* (Carbondale: Southern Illinois University Press, 1988), 113. See also "Christina Rossetti: The Inward Pose," in *Shakespeare's Sisters: Feminist Essays on Women Poets,* ed. Sandra Gilbert and Susan Gubar (Bloomington: Indiana University Press, 1979), and "Christina Rossetti's Religious Poetry: Watching, Looking, Keeping Vigil," *Victorian Poetry* 20, no. 1 (spring 1982): 33–49.

15. See Jerome McGann, "Christina Rossetti's Poems: A New Edition and a Revaluation," *Victorian Studies* 23 (1980): 237–54, and "The Religious Poetry of Christina Rossetti," *Critical Inquiry* 10 (1983): 127–44, both reprinted in *The Beauty of Inflections: Literary Investigations in Historical Method and Theory* (Oxford: Clarendon, 1985). See also Harrison.

16. Algernon Charles Swinburne, "Laus Veneris," *The Poems of Algernon Charles Swinburne* (London: Chatto and Windus, 1904).

17. For an extended discussion of both "Laus Veneris" and the relations between Rossetti's and Swinburne's poetry, see Psomiades, *Beauty's Body,* 60–65, 79–93.

18. Christina Rossetti, *The Prince's Progress,* in Crump, 1: 95–110, ll.25–35. All further citations will be noted parenthetically by line number in the text and are taken from this edition.

19. Rossetti wrote to her brother about the stages of the poem: "1st a prelude and outset; 2nd, an alluring milkmaid; 3rd a trial of barren boredom; 4th the social element again; 5th barren boredom in a more uncompromising form; 6th a wind-up and conclusion" (William Michael Rossetti, ed., *Rossetti Papers* [London: Sands, 1903], 78).

20. "Versuch einer Vereiningung aller schönen Künste und Wissenschaften unter dem Begriff des in sich selbst Vollendeten" (*Schriften zur Ästhetik und Poetick,* ed. Hans Joachim Schrimpf [Tübingen: Max Niemeyer, 1962], 4). Quoted and translated in Martha Woodmansee, *The Author, Art and the Market: Rereading the History of Aesthetics* (New York: Columbia University Press, 1994), 32.

21. William Michael Rossetti, ed., *The Poetical Works of Christina Georgina Rossetti* (London: Macmillan, 1904), 461.

22. William Michael Rossetti, ed., *Rossetti Papers,* 84.

Chapter 6

LINDA K. HUGHES

Feminizing Decadence

Poems by Graham R. Tomson

We have known the female philanthropist who wrote . . . , the republican poetess, the poetess of the future, be she a Fourierist or a Saint-Simonist. But we have never been able to accustom our eyes . . . to all this solemn and repulsive behaviour . . . these sacrilegious imitations of the masculine spirit. — Charles Baudelaire

Decadents are always male and preferably noble.
— Richard Ellmann

It is equally important to acknowledge the female presence within those spheres often seen as the exclusive province of men, such as the realm of public politics or avant-garde art. — Rita Felski

British writers tended to adopt select conventions of French decadence rather than embrace the movement programmatically.[1] Arthur Symons, a case in point, established characteristic traits rather than philosophical underpinnings of decadence in "The Decadent Movement in Literature" (1893). Identifying two branches, "the truth of appearances to the senses, of the visible world to the eyes that see it; and the truth of spiritual things to the spiritual vision," he also associated decadence with a number of French authors and with "an intense self-consciousness, a restless curiosity in research, an oversubtilizing refinement upon refinement, a spiritual and moral perversity" — qualities found in the literature of Latin decadence — and "the diseased sharpness of over-excited nerves."[2]

Despite the fragmented practice of decadence in England,[3] it has often been considered monolithic in one respect, as a kind of exclusive male club.[4] Women poets of the fin de siècle thought otherwise, a point made clear in an 1892 causerie by Katharine Tynan in the *Speaker.* Surveying past and present women poets, Tynan concluded that younger women poets were ahead of the men: "The young school of women poets of our day is, to my mind, far in advance, both by nature and art, of the young school of men poets, where learns no possible great man, except one."[5] She identified Alice Meynell as the finest of these women for subtlety of thought and refined diction, praising as well Madame Darmesteter (A. Mary F. Robinson) and May Probyn for the musicality of their verse and E. Nesbit for her merging of social protest and lyric pathos. But she singled out Graham R. Tomson as a poet of decadence: "Mrs. Graham Tomson is very much the woman *fin de siècle* — nervously impressionable to the seen world and the unseen, finely touched to the magic of crowds, alert to the magnetism that is in the air of great cities, a maker of poetry whose very beauty tells us the writer is somewhat unstrung."[6] Tynan here recirculates decadent tropes first articulated by Baudelaire — the artist's capturing the evanescent and transcendent in evocative impressions, the artist as flaneur abroad on urban streets, and the artist's nervous sensitivity and disturbance — tropes restated by Symons in 1893.[7]

Following Tynan's lead and Felski's suggestion that we acknowledge the "female presence within those spheres often seen as the exclusive province of men," I examine in this essay how Graham R. Tomson initiated a dialogue with French decadence, appropriating the tropes of flaneur and vampire while interrogating the impetus toward autonomy lauded by many decadents and later exponents of high modernism. Her lyric "Of the Earth, Earthy" represents fleeting urban impressions but also a *flâneuse* whose connection to the urban crowd counters the aloof flaneur of Baudelaire. The female vampire of "Vespertilia," like decadent femmes fatales, haunts the male narrator of the poem and critiques inadequate male, rather than excessive female, desire. Such celebrations of communal, affective bonds, however, can also suggest the conventionally feminine duty to understand the self intersubjectively and place others' needs first. Tomson's decadent poems thus emerge as a complex web of female appropriation, resistance, critique, and complicity, a configuration that (as Felski might suggest) more nearly approximates women's relation to decadence than does a strict gender divide.[8]

In "The Decadent Movement in Literature" Symons distinguished Paul Verlaine, Maeterlinck, Joris-Karl Huysmans, and the Goncourt brothers as exemplars of decadence, while also mentioning Théophile Gautier, Gustave Flaubert, Baudelaire, and Stéphane Mallarmé, among others. Tomson knew the work of Baudelaire and Verlaine; she included poems by both (in French) in her 1892 anthology, *Concerning Cats,* which was illustrated by her second husband, Arthur Tomson, a member of the New English Art Club who specialized in impressionist landscapes.[9] Her knowledge of French literature appears to have been wide. Several of her ballades, triolets, and villanelles (as well as two Sicilian octaves) were included in an anthology of French verse forms edited by Gleeson White.[10] She was also tapped to review a volume bearing the impress of French decadence, the first *Book of the Rhymers' Club,* for the *Academy.*[11] Later, as Rosamund Marriott Watson, she corresponded with the Oxford professor Frederick York Powell (who entertained Verlaine at Oxford in 1893), the two discussing niceties of poetic translations from French in their letters.[12] She was, then, well positioned to adapt elements of decadence to her own work.

If "Of the Earth, Earthy," one of a number of city poems Tomson published, recalls Amy Levy's "A London Plane-Tree" or poems on omnibuses, it also adopts a stance analogous to that of Baudelaire, who identified modernity with the city and with an aesthetic based on the evanescent and dissonant, on intimate proximity fused with estrangement and anonymity. For Baudelaire the flaneur — a key figure in the discourses of decadence and modernity — is a "passionate spectator" for whom "it is an immense joy to set up house in the heart of the multitude, amid the ebb and flow of movement, in the midst of the fugitive and the infinite. . . . [always] at the centre of the world, and yet . . . hidden from the world."[13] Walking city streets posed problems for women writers because it could align them with prostitutes, but Tomson disregards danger in "Of the Earth, Earthy" and appropriates the role of *flâneuse* through recourse to the lyric moment rather than a narrative requiring explanation of motives for female street walking.[14] Tomson's speaker, like Amy Levy's in "Between the Showers," places herself squarely amid urban sights and a vision of beauty predicated on urban sensory experience, but like male decadents she celebrates the discordant and tawdry as well. Her sequence of images in the poem follows the path of an eagerly glancing eye that travels to the sky, the pavement, and those who surround her, her gaze falling equally on squalor and splendor:

> Never for us those dreams aforetime shown
> Of white-winged angels on a shining stair,
> Or seas of sapphire round a jasper throne:
> Give us the spangled dusk, the turbid street;

The dun, dim pavement trod by myriad feet,
Stained with the yellow lamplight here and there;
The chill blue skies beyond the spires of stone:

The world's invincible youth is all our own,
Here where we feel life's pulses burn and beat.

Here is the pride of Life, be it foul or fair,
This clash and swirl of streets in the twilight air;
Beauty and Grime, indifferent, side by side;
Surfeit and Thirst, Endeavour and Despair,
Content and Squalor, Lassitude and Care,
All in the golden lamplight glorified:
All quick, all real, hurrying near and wide.

Life and Life's worst and best be ours to share,
Charm of the motley! undefined and rare;
Melodious discord in the heart o' the tune,
Sweet with the hoarse note jarring everywhere!

Let us but live, and every field shall bear
Fruit for our joy; for Life is Life's best boon.[15]

The clear echo of Walter Pater's conclusion to *The Renaissance: Studies in Art and Poetry* in the second stanza ("Here where we feel life's pulses burn and beat") and of Baudelaire's insistence that beauty embrace the transitory as well as the eternal suggests Tomson's deliberate adoption of positions identified with decadence.

Even more decadent is the muted but unmistakable blasphemy in the poem.[16] Her title is drawn from 1 Corinthians 15, Paul's epistolary sermon on the Resurrection, in which Adam, the first man, is contrasted with the new order of life represented by Christ and the Resurrection: "The first man is of the earth, earthy: the second man is the Lord from heaven" (1 Cor. 15:47). This poem refuses the promise of an incorruptible heavenly body in favor of the delights of an earthly one and is structured as a secular text supplanting the sacred text alluded to in its title. Hence Paul's vision of the Resurrection is rejected as a dead, inert, past dream in the first three lines, which also repudiate John's apocalyptic vision of the New Jerusalem, with its foundations of jasper, sapphire, chalcedony, and emerald (Rev. 21:19). These formerly sacred images are appropriated for the poet's declaration of faith in fleeting life itself, the throng of "white-winged angels" transformed into the "myriad feet" of the crowd who tread on dun pavement rather than streets of gold, the noumenal jeweled throne displaced in favor of the phenomenal "spangled dusk" and "yellow" (not gold) lamplight that stains rather than purifies those walking in its glow. The secular heavens may be cold and remote, but they surpass a stone-cold religion that preaches denial of the present ("chill blue skies beyond the spires of stone"). Hence the strict binaries of the Last Judgment are replaced by yoked contraries glorified only by lamplight. Discord is the encompassing whole, the paradoxical harmony, this poet seeks ("Melodious discord"), an open and satisfying aesthetic system ("undefined and rare") whose cacophonies are welcome for their own sake ("Sweet . . . the hoarse note jarring"). Her secular sermon then ends with a lesson that is also a benediction: "Life is Life's best boon."

If this displacement of one text (the Bible) by another draws attention to textuality, the materiality of the poet's presence is also insisted on. Ghostliness is precisely what she does not yearn for here, preferring burning desire and beating pulses. No individuals stand out from the crowd, however — not even the poet. Masses of people become mere abstractions, representative types, in the third stanza ("Beauty and Grime," and so on), though they quickly dissolve back into diverse individualities ("All quick, all real, hurrying near and wide") — perhaps mirroring the crowd's modalities as a single mass and an amalgam of persons.

Another way in which Tomson differs from Baudelaire's flaneur, whose hauteur is that of a "prince," is in her suppression of an "I"; only a "we" exists.[17] This omission can be construed as a frightened retreat from visibility circumvented by the poet's losing herself in the crowd.[18] But given the freely adopted conventions of decadence elsewhere in the poem, this "we" may also function as a repudiation of the autonomy and elitism often sought in decadent literature.[19] In Huysmans's *À rebours* (*Against the Grain*), for example, an important influence on Oscar Wilde and Symons, Des Esseintes relentlessly pursues autonomy, or at least its illusion. He forces his servants to work noiselessly and, as much as possible, invisibly, requiring that the woman who must walk in front of his window to fetch firewood cloak her body and face.[20] Many English texts bearing the impress of decadence likewise privilege a persona of superior intellect and refinement who surveys the world as a lonely eye, or "I."

In this context "Of the Earth, Earthy" interrogates not merely the fiction of radical autonomy but also its desirability, insisting on connection and collectivity among human beings in keeping with the poem's secular vision, which admits of no angels protectively hovering over the saved: humanity must save itself. Socialist collectivity is perhaps implied as well, since Tomson was attending socialist meetings around the time of the poem's composition.[21] But her orientation might as readily derive from her socialization as a woman expected to fulfill obligations to others and sustain connections.[22] Hélène Cixous observes that women in patriarchal societies are necessarily "bisexual," perforce aware of female *and* male perspectives, whereas dominant masculinity usually excludes awareness of an other and thus can pursue the fiction of autonomy.[23] Paradoxically, however, by feminizing some decadent conventions in this poem, Tomson follows another dictum of Baudelaire's: "pure art . . . is the creation of an evocative magic, containing at once the object and the subject, the world external to the artist and the artist himself."[24] The crowd is a crucial part of the poem, as are sense impressions of the city and the poet's shaping powers; but it is impossible fully to distinguish her responses from those around her, who share, she argues, her essential condition in life. Tomson's achievement in this poem is to adopt the conventions of decadence while resisting its themes of alienation and elitism.

William Archer remarked that if the "town" was one theme of the poet he knew as Rosamund Marriott-Watson, another was the "supernatural." To represent her best work he selected "Vespertilia," the title poem of her 1895 volume, praising its handling of rhythm and diction as well as its eerie effects: "Alike in conception and in workmanship, the poem is masterly. It ranks among those which, once read, will haunt the memory for ever."[25] "Haunt" is an apt word since "Vespertilia" is a revenant poem, a favored decadent topos.

The publication history of this poem also suggests Tomson's participation in decadence, since her name changes at its various appearances inscribe her deviant sexuality. First publishing the poem as Graham R. Tomson — herself a former divorcée — in volume 4 of the *Yellow Book,* she then became Rosamund Marriott Watson (the name under which she published the poem in book form in 1895), after an extramarital affair with Australian-born novelist H. B. Marriott Watson, one of W. E. Henley's "young men." In the only extant account of the affair, given to Cyril Scott by Louisa Stevenson (the widow of Bob Stevenson, a cousin of Robert Louis Stevenson's), the affair is attributed to Graham Tomson's aggressive sexuality: "When she met Marriott she 'got mad about him' . . . and practically induced him to live with her."[26] Henley also privately characterized her in terms of devouring sexuality in a letter to Charles Whibley, remarking that Graham Tomson "hath evidently some filthy magic in her tail that makes men love to be less than themselves."[27]

Aggressive female sexuality was of course a staple of fin-de-siècle writing in the form of the fatal woman, one of whose incarnations was the female vampire who sucked a man's blood in an act erotic, destructive, and perverse.[28] Familiar to English readers from Pater's La Gioconda, the female vampire was also important to the work of Baudelaire and Gautier. In Baudelaire's "Le Vampire" the revenant is a trope for the (male) speaker's lover, who invaded him like the slash of a knife ("comme un coup de couteau"), who imprisoned him ("je suis lié / Comme le forçat à la chaîne"), and from whom escape is now impossible because of his own perverse desire. "Les Metamorphoses du vampire" emphasizes the putrefying body of the dead-undead, who is at once a seductive femme fatale and a disgusting mortal (and mortifying) body. Another Baudelaire poem ("Le Revenant") features a male revenant, but here, too, the supernatural is a sexually aggressive force that haunts and inspires fear. Tomson took up the figure of the revenant just when she was most susceptible to being troped as a vampirish woman by others, and Rosamund Marriott Watson made it central to her debut volume, *Vespertilia and Other Verses.* Tomson/Watson's comments about the poem, as well as its imagery, suggest a desire to align the poem with decadence, yet like "Of the Earth, Earthy," "Vespertilia" participates in yet deforms decadent conventions.[29]

Tomson/Watson overtly linked the poem to Gautier when she wrote to John Lane proposing its publication in the *Yellow Book:* "It is vampirical, of course, but not more so, I think, than Gautier's *La Morte amoureuse,* to which I would not dare liken it — I wish I could."[30] Gautier, in his 1868 essay on Baudelaire's *Les Fleurs du mal,* had identified key features of decadence that reverberate in Symons's essay of 1893:

> The poet of "Fleurs du Mal" loved what is improperly called the style of decadence, and which is nothing else but art arrived at that point of extreme maturity yielded by the slanting suns of aged civilizations: an ingenious complicated style, full of shades and of research, constantly pushing back the boundaries of speech, . . . struggling to render what is most inexpressible in thought, what is vague and most elusive in the outlines of form, listening to translate the subtle confidences of neurosis, the dying confessions of passion grown depraved, and the strange hallucinations of the obsession which is turning to madness.[31]

Not long before Tomson wrote "Vespertilia," Gautier's vampire tale had been brought before the English-speaking public through the 1889 translation of *La Morte amoureuse,* titled *The Dead Leman and Other Tales from the French,* by Andrew Lang and Paul Sylvester; given Tomson's close connection with Lang, this translation is another likely source for the Tomson/Watson poem.[32]

Gautier is best known for *Mademoiselle de Maupin* (1835) and its exploration of androgyny; *La Morte amoureuse* (1836) recuperates a more conventional sexuality. The tale is related by a parish priest who, at the moment of ordination, is awakened to sexual temptations by Clarimonde, a famous courtesan. Later called to her deathbed, he gazes on her naked body and succumbs to the overpowering desire to kiss her. She immediately awakens and tells him she may now visit him, becoming the vampire who haunts his dreams. By day the priest continues as a man of God, but at night, in sleep, he is a cavalier, sharing the voluptuous delights of Clarimonde's bed. After she avidly sucks the blood from a wound he suffers, he becomes suspicious and avoids drinking the wine she customarily gives him before they retire. His suspicions are confirmed when he sees her draw a pin, with which she intends to prick his arm in order to get blood to drink. Eventually the priest's abbé insists on exhuming Clarimonde's casket and uncovers her uncorrupted body; from her lips a drop of fresh blood oozes. When the abbé sprinkles holy water on her, she disintegrates, then reappears to the priest one last time, reproaches him for spurning her, and disappears forever. The story is ostensibly structured by the binaries of the sacred and the profane, priestly purity and demonic sexuality, but derives its power from locating these binaries in the body of the priest, who lives a double life and never forswears his love for Clarimonde. Nonetheless, Gautier's vampire functions as a woman of devouring sexuality who tempts and haunts her male lover.

"Vespertilia," like *La Morte amoureuse,* features a double setting; but whereas Gautier's story alternates between diurnal and nocturnal plots within a vaguely Early Modern historical era, Tomson/Watson's poem has one plot but merges contemporary and late-Roman time frames. Here the revenant is a Roman woman who left Italy to follow her lover to the colony of England and there died:

> And all her talk was of some outland rare,
> Where myrtles blossom by the blue sea's rim,
> And life is ever good and sunny and fair;

> "Long since," she sighed, "I sought this island grey —
> Here, where the winds moan and the sun is dim,
> When his beaked galleys cleft the ocean spray,
> For love I followed him."[33]

Her interlocutor, the poem's speaker, is a contemporary Englishman who strives to be true not (like Gautier's priest) to God but to the memory of his dead beloved. Though the Englishman occupies the privileged site of speaker, the poem's dual time frames suggest the perspective of the revenant, who embodies the distant past but resurfaces in the present. Laminating late-Roman and fin-de-siècle cultures also has specific resonance for decadence, since the later Roman empire and decadent Latin literature were invoked (by Huysmans's Des Esseintes, Gautier, and Symons) as precedents for modern literary decadence.[34] Tomson had used Greek myth for several narrative poems in 1889–90 but rarely turned to Roman classicism.[35] Her use of Roman materials thus underscores the poem's decadent overtones.

Even more important are the poem's eerie, disturbing boundary crossings between life and death, attraction and repulsion, which suggest (in Gautier's terms) an attempt "to render what is most inexpressible in thought, what is vague and most elusive," as in the poem's opening stanza:

> In the late autumn's dusky-golden prime,
> When sickles gleam and rusts the idle plough,
> The time of apples dropping from the bough,
> And yellow leaves on sycamore and lime;
> O'er grassy uplands far above the sea
> Often at twilight would my footsteps fare,
> And oft I met a stranger-woman there
>   Who stayed and spake with me:
> Hard by the ancient barrow smooth and green,
> Whose rounded burg swells dark upon the sky
> Lording it high o'er dusky dell and dene,
>   We wandered — she and I. (1)

At this Keatsian moment of fruition ("golden prime") and decay ("dusky-golden"), implements of harvest gleam in use while those of seedtime rot; nature sickens, turning yellow, while the ancient grave remains green and "swells" as if with sexual arousal or the double life of a pregnant belly. The entire scene is strange — estranging and uncanny — as is the woman who comes to meet the speaker. As Nina Auerbach remarks, "strange" was used by Algernon Charles Swinburne as a code word for homosexual, hence forbidden, love.[36] "Vespertilia" likewise turns on forbidden, transgressive erotic attraction. That a "stranger-woman" lingers to speak with an unknown man in open spaces evokes sexual danger and daring, as does their act of wandering — associated with errant morality as well as aimless sauntering. The supernatural Vespertilia, of course, is also a stranger because she is foreign, a revenant from another time and place.

Even more than the landscape, Vespertilia's body and garments are uncanny, charged equally with life and death. Her face is more alive, more natural, than the landscape yet suggests life perceived through a screen of death ("Her fair face glimmering like a white wood-flower / That gleams through withered leaves" [2]).[37] Her mouth, superseding nature ("Her mouth was redder than the pimpernel"), is itself unnatural (2); while her garments are at once winding sheets, their decay a metonymy for the rotting body, and a weirdly fashionable gilding for the beautiful body they enfold:[38]

> And all about her breast, around her head,
> Was wound a wide veil shadowing cheek and chin,
> Woven like the ancient grave-gear of the dead:
> A twisted clasp and pin
> Confined her long blue mantle's heavy fold
> Of splendid tissue dropping to decay,[39]
> Faded like some rich raiment worn of old,
> With rents and tatters gaping to the day.
> Her sandals wrought about with threads of gold,
> Scarce held together still, so worn were they,
> Yet sewn with winking gems of green and blue,
> And pale as pearls her naked feet shone through. (2–3)

In describing the garments the speaker also conveys his experience of the uncanny. He wills himself not to see what he sees, pretending that shrouds and putrescence are mere similes so that he can continue to gaze on "naked feet"; but the detail with which he registers her attire marks his tacit understanding of what she is. In the poem's final stanzas he refuses her allure and she disappears forever, but he cannot, like Gautier's priest, admit his desire and so continues the pretense of ordinary life:

> [A]ll my thoughts are of the stranger still,
> Yea, though I loved her not:

I loved her not — and yet — I fain would see . . .
Her dark veil fluttering in the autumn breeze. (5)

The falling trimeter lines punctuating the predominant iambic pentameter — suggesting variously pause, attenuation, decay — proliferate in this passage as if to represent the speaker's faltering assurance. In the end he seems to verge on madness, since Vespertilia, rather than residing in a confined body, now seems dispersed through all nature, from whence she haunts the man who spurned her:

Ever the thought of her abides with me
Unceasing as the murmur of the sea;
When the round moon is low and night-birds flit,
When sink the stubble-fires with smouldering flame,
Over and o'er the sea-wind sighs her name,
    And the leaves whisper it.

"Poor Vespertilia," sing the grasses sere,
"Poor Vespertilia," moans the surf-beat shore;
Almost I feel her very presence near —
    Yet she comes nevermore. (5–6)

Vespertilia becomes a fatal woman who preys on the speaker but is also represented as an innocent victim, a marked departure from decadent convention. The inscription of innocence within fatality is evident in another source of the poem, Tomson's 1889 two-part essay, "Beauty, from the Historical Point of View," in Wilde's *Woman's World.* Among the representations of beauty she surveys in this essay is the Lille Bust, sometimes attributed to da Vinci because of its enigmatic smile but perhaps, she suggests, merely a death mask:

> [S]ome say that this waxen bust is the death-mask of a beautiful young girl, whose corpse was accidentally exhumed centuries ago at Rome, and, strange to say, instead of crumbling away under the light of open day into a heap of grey ashes, remained calm and unchanged in its subtle loveliness, with the faint flush as of life yet lingering upon the lips and cheeks. So she lay in her stone sarcophagus, and all the city flocked to look on her and to marvel; and, alas! nearly all the city fell so desperately in love with her that the ecclesiastical authorities, seeing the demoralisation even of monks and priests, caused her body to be destroyed by fire, as being some work of the Evil One, and correspondingly "no canny."
>
> And, indeed, an intangible and indefinable, yet none the less real, *dead*

> look pervading the eyes, and the whole expression of the face, may furnish an excuse for this not too likely supposition. The smile, scarcely so pronounced as that of La Gioconda, is the smile of a dead woman; and it is from the dead that she comes to us.[40]

Like "Vespertilia," this description, in which Tomson draws on details common to Gautier's *La Morte amoureuse* and alludes to Pater's *The Renaissance: Studies in Art and Poetry,* occupies a borderline between life and death, the dead and the undead. Tomson, however, unlike Gautier or Pater, presents an innocent girl onto whose exposed body paranoiac suspicion is projected by patriarchal authority, which then destroys rare feminine beauty. Yet the girl is innocent *and* uncanny, coming to contemporary viewers "from the dead." Tomson neither returns the original of the Lille Bust to the world of ordinary reality nor accepts supernatural accounts that starkly oppose evil and good. Her stance is at once decadent and female-centered.

The same is true of "Vespertilia." The poem is laced with vampiric menace but tells even more about failed masculine love. When Vespertilia hears the nightingale one evening, she is moved by its passion to recall a lesson she once learned:

> "Now I remember! . . . Now I know!" said she,
> "Love will be life . . . ah, Love *is* Life!" she cried,
> "And thou — thou lovest me?"(3)

She offers love as a form of life, not living death, on the condition that the speaker embrace the "strange." He refuses, and his old love, more than the revenant, comes to represent the dead-undead:

> "Dear, but no love is mine to give," I said,
> "My heart is colder than the granite stone
> That guards my true-love in her grassy bed;
> My faith and troth are hers, and hers alone,
> Are hers . . . and she is dead." (4)

Vespertilia, humiliated by his refusal, rejoins, "Ah, hadst thou loved me but a little while, I might have lived again" (5). After she disappears, "gliding" away to the burial mound now described as "sullen," the narrator realizes that the memory of his beloved has begun to fade ("my true-love's memory / . . . Fades faint and far from me"), that of Vespertilia to intensify (5). But it is too late.

Here the tragedy is not a mortal's troth with a revenant but the missed opportunity to consummate love. The male narrator escapes the vampirical imprisonment Baudelaire represented in *Les Fleurs du mal,* but he goes mad and thwarts a loving woman's return to life. His failure also exposes the hypocrisy of his true-love relationship, for Vespertilia, herself emergent from the grave after having died for love, is a type or double of the other buried woman.

Bracketing vampiric sexuality and innocent love in "Vespertilia" may have been a form of oblique self-defense for Tomson/Watson, but it is more useful to view the poem's tangle of past and present loves and its Roman revenant in terms of the larger issues of serial love and divorce. In her feminist analyses of marriage and divorce from 1888 to 1894 (published in book form in 1897), Mona Caird remarked that laws allowing women to seek divorce in the Roman empire were far more liberal than those of subsequent regimes:

> The later Roman jurisprudence, inaugurated by Justinian, became singularly liberal in its treatment of women. In the time of Gaius, the system of perpetual tutelage fell entirely into discredit . . . the husband had no longer supreme power over his wife, since this was still held by the family, but the appointed guardians of the woman left her, to all intents and purposes, to do as she pleased. . . . Now, a form of civil union, which had previously not been considered entirely reputable, came into more general favour. . . . After the triumph of Christianity, there was a reaction against this liberty which the Roman women had attained, and against the easy laws of divorce.[41]

If the revenant's Latin heritage serves as a coded reference to Roman divorce laws, thereby enabling the poem to enfold New Woman discourse into decadent discourse, the poem's plot more directly impinges on divorce. The revenant and male narrator are, at the poem's outset, in thrall to dead loves, Vespertilia nostalgically remembering her melodramatic sacrifice of all for love of her centurion, the narrator invoking the sentimental Victorian tropes of his true love and her grassy bed. Vespertilia shakes off past ties and realizes that it is not fresh blood she needs to live but new love — or, rather, that new love functions as new blood: "Love *is* Life!" The narrator cannot surmount his ties to conventionality and loses all. Though the poem can stand on its own as a "vampirical" tale, its plot represents the essential condition of serial love and divorce. To embrace a new relationship after the failure of the old is to return "from the dead" to renewed loving and life, though ghosts of the old may haunt lovers, hence the curious doubling of the dead true love and the revenant. Remaining in a dead relationship, the poem suggests, embracing the corpse of love, is worse than embracing a stranger to one's past.

"Vespertilia" feminizes its treatment of the decadent revenant, then, by abjuring violence and a perversely evil fatal woman. Its revenant more closely resembles the friendly vampires Auerbach associates with the era 1820–70, since Vespertilia's major acts in the poem are to engage the narrator in long chats and ask for his love.[42] Like "Of the Earth, Earthy," "Vespertilia" critiques the desire for autonomy, making failed connection rather than intimate subjugation the crux of the poem and representing the stalwart male as well as the undead woman as a threat to life. Yet the poem is recognizably decadent in its hauntings and haunting articulations of the ineffable border between life and death and its complex psychological states, ranging from denial to neurosis. Insofar as it insists that ending old loves and embracing new ones is not profanation but a means to life, the poem is also a "perverse" representation of love and erotic relationships at odds with sacramental or sentimental conceptions of love and a defiant assertion of women's legitimate need to sustain sexual desire and fulfillment amid mutable relationships.[43] Yet again Tomson/Watson's feminizing of decadence — her insistence on connection to others — is also her means of extending its practices.

Tomson was indeed, as Tynan claimed, "impressionable to the seen world and the unseen, finely touched to the magic of crowds, alert to the magnetism that is in the air of great cities, a maker of poetry whose very beauty tells us the writer is [or at least appeared] somewhat unstrung." Though her work in the main is aligned with aestheticism,[44] she was familiar with decadent literary tropes and conventions and did not hesitate to deploy them when she wished to. Feminizing decadence enabled her to push the bounds of the sayable as woman and poet and advance her career by establishing her range and mobility. Her work also indicates that, if French and British decadence could be misogynistic, decadence did not exclude female participation altogether.[45] In this respect, Tomson's work provides an important link between aestheticism and modernism by suggesting the degree to which a fin-de-siècle woman writer could wrest the privileges granted the decadent and flaneur and remold these figures in female form — throwing them, so to speak, a curve.

Notes

I wish to thank the editors, for their suggestions regarding an earlier version of this essay, and Julie Smith and the TCU/RF Research Fund (grant 523812), for assistance with research. I am also grateful to the Pierpont Morgan Library, in New York, for permission to quote from the Gordon Ray Papers (MA 4500), and to the Harry Ransom Humanities Research Center, at the University of Texas at Austin, for permission to quote from the John Lane Papers.

1. See, for example, John M. Munro, *The Decadent Poetry of the Eighteen-Nineties* (Beirut: American University of Beirut, 1970), 58–59, and R. K. R. Thornton, *The Decadent Dilemma* (London: Edward Arnold, 1983), 34. Recently, British decadence has been usefully approached in terms of language theory (Linda Dowling, *Language and Decadence in the Victorian Fin de Siècle* [Princeton, N.J.: Princeton University Press, 1986]) and parodic discourse that destabilizes sexual identities and aesthetic surfaces (Richard Dellamora, *Masculine Desire: The Sexual Politics of Victorian Aestheticism* [Chapel Hill: University of North Carolina Press, 1990], Kathy Alexis Psomiades, *Beauty's Body: Femininity and Representation in British Aestheticism* [Stanford, Calif.: Stanford University Press, 1997]).

2. Arthur Symons, "The Decadent Movement in Literature," *Harper's New Monthly Magazine,* November 1893; reprinted in Karl Beckson, ed., *Aesthetes and Decadents of the 1890's,* rev. ed. (Chicago: Academy Chicago Publishers, 1981), 136, 135, 138. In stressing "nerves" Symons is participating in late-Victorian medical discourses that associated complex development of the nervous system with higher stages of evolutionary progress yet also considered advanced nervous structures more susceptible to disease and the stresses of modern urban life. See Janet Oppenheim, *"Shattered Nerves": Doctors, Patients, and Depression in Victorian England* (New York: Oxford University Press, 1991), 79–109, 265–92.

3. Symons, for example, cites W. E. Henley as a decadent poet, though in the *National Observer* Henley endorsed masculine aggression and ridiculed effeminacy, both counterdecadent strategies. See Linda K. Hughes, *Strange Bedfellows: W. E. Henley and Feminist Fashion History,* Occasional Series, no. 3 (London: Eighteen Nineties Society, 1997), 6, and Munro, 2.

4. See my first two epigraphs, the first of which is taken from Walter Benjamin, *Charles Baudelaire: A Lyric Poet in the Era of High Capitalism,* trans. Harry Zohn (New York: Verso, 1983), 93, the second of which is taken from Richard Ellmann, "The Uses of Decadence: Wilde, Yeats, Joyce," in *Studies in Anglo-French Cultural Relations: Imagining France,* ed. Ceri Crosby and Ian Small (Basingstoke, England: Macmillan, 1988), 17. Elaine Showalter, citing another misogynist remark by Baudelaire, attributes decadent misogyny to women's traditional association with nature rather than artifice in *Sexual Anarchy: Gender and Culture at the Fin*

de Siècle (New York: Viking, 1990), 170–74. Linda Dowling posits an alliance (if not identity) of British decadents and New Women writers as outsiders committed to transcending "nature" and repudiating the old order, in "The Decadent and the New Woman in the 1890's," *Nineteenth Century Fiction* 33, no. 4 (1979): 440–41. As Sally Ledger has noted, however, the historical practices of feminists, who usually distanced themselves from sexuality altogether, need to be distinguished from the yoking of decadents and New Women in the press; see "The New Woman and the Crisis of Victorianism," in *Cultural Politics at the Fin de Siècle,* ed. Sally Ledger and Scott McCracken (Cambridge: Cambridge University Press, 1995), 29. Like other female aesthetes, Graham R. Tomson was neither male decadent nor New Woman writer; Talia Schaffer pursues the implications of such a stance in "Malet the Obscure: Thomas Hardy, 'Lucas Malet,' and the Literary Politics of Early Modernism," *Women's Writing* 3, no. 3 (1996): 262.

5. K[atharine]. T[ynan]., "A Literary Causerie," *Speaker,* 29 October 1892, 535. Tynan presumably refers to William Butler Yeats, her friend and compatriot. Best known today for this association, she was a poet and journalist and close friend of Alice Meynell's.

6. Two books published during or shortly after the lifetime of Tomson, who was later known as Rosamund Marriott Watson, also align her with poets considered decadent. In 1911 W. G. Blaikie Murdoch asserted that, among poets published in the *Yellow Book,* "its finest worker was Ernest Dowson, while in this department must also be mentioned Father Gray and Mrs. Marriott Watson, and likewise Davidson and Mr. Symons"; see *The Renaissance of the Nineties* (1911; reprint, n.p.: Folcroft, 1970), 42. Seven years later Harold H. Williams similarly observed, "In poetry the most notable contributors to the *Yellow Book* were Mr. Arthur Symons, John Davidson, Ernest Dowson, Lionel Johnson, Laurence Binyon, Mr. W. B. Yeats and Mrs. Marriott Watson"; see *Modern English Writers: Being a Study of Imaginative Literature, 1890–1914* (London: Sidgwick and Jackson, 1918), xviii.

7. For Baudelaire beauty had both an eternal and an ephemeral element, the latter necessary to express the former, and the modern poet "distil[s] the eternal from the transitory" through expressive, flexible techniques that fix impressions in a verbal or visual medium. He also conceptualized the impressionist artist as a flaneur. See *The Painter of Modern Life and Other Essays by Charles Baudelaire,* trans. and ed. Jonathan Mayne (London: Phaidon, 1964), 3, 12, 4, 9.

8. Rita Felski, *The Gender of Modernity* (Cambridge, Mass.: Harvard University Press, 1995), 22. Margaret Stetz, Talia Schaffer, and Kathy Psomiades also view women aesthetes as working from within aestheticism but innovating and rewriting the modes usually adopted by male writers. See Stetz, "Debating Aestheticism from a Feminist Perspective" (paper presented at the annual meeting of the Modern Language Association, Chicago, December 1995), Schaffer, "The Woman's

World of British Aestheticism, 1870–1910" (Ph.D. diss., Cornell University, 1996), and Psomiades, 45–57.

9. *Concerning Cats: A Book of Poems by Many Authors,* ed. Graham R. Tomson, illus. Arthur Tomson, Cameo Series (London: T. Fisher Unwin, 1892). The volume includes Baudelaire's "Le Chat" and "Les Chats" and Verlaine's "Femme et chatte."

10. *Ballades and Rondeaus, Chants Royal, Sestinas, Villanelles, &c.,* ed. Gleeson White, Canterbury Poets (London: Walter Scott, [1887]).

11. Graham R. Tomson, review of *The Book of the Rhymers' Club, Academy,* 26 March 1892, 294–95. The review singled out the classic form, restraint, and deft impressionism of Lionel Johnson and the haunting cadences and Celtic imagination of William Butler Yeats. Symons came in for mention (and mild critique) in a single sentence; Ernest Dowson was merely acknowledged as a contributor.

12. See, for example, Oliver Elton, *Frederick York Powell: A Life and Selection from His Letters and Occasional Writings* (Oxford: Clarendon, 1906), 1:296–98.

13. Baudelaire, *The Painter of Modern Life,* 9.

14. Janet Wolff asserts, "There is no question of inventing the *flâneuse:* the essential point is that such a character was rendered impossible by the sexual divisions of the nineteenth century" ("The Invisible *Flâneuse:* Women and the Literature of Modernity," in *The Problems of Modernity: Adorno and Benjamin,* ed. Andrew Benjamin [New York: Routledge, 1989], 154). Elizabeth Wilson, Deborah Epstein Nord, and Rachel Bowlby admit the possibility of the *flâneuse* but emphasize that visibility on urban streets remained problematic for women writers. See Wilson, "The Invisible *Flâneur,*" *New Left Review* 1 (1991–92): 90–110, Nord, *Walking the Victorian Streets: Women, Representation, and the City* (Ithaca, N.Y.: Cornell University Press, 1995), 185–98, and Bowlby, "Walking, Women, and Writing: Virginia Woolf as *Flâneuse,*" in *New Feminist Discourses: Critical Essays on Theories and Texts,* ed. Isobel Armstrong (New York: Routledge, 1992), 26–47.

15. Graham R. Tomson, *A Summer Night and Other Poems* (London: Methuen, 1891), 8–9.

16. Compare Symons's linking of decadence to "spiritual . . . perversity" (135). It was unusual, however, for a woman poet openly to articulate irreligious sentiments (as seen in the suppression of Amy Levy's "A Ballad of Religion and Marriage" during her lifetime).

17. Baudelaire, *Painter of Modern Life,* 9.

18. See, for example, Nord, 197–98, 246.

19. As Regenia Gagnier argues, such self-enclosure was also implicitly critiqued by John Ruskin, William Morris, and Wilde, whose practical aesthetics emphasized art's fundamental connection to (and intervention in) everyday life and sensuous experience. See Gagnier, "A Critique of Practical Aesthetics," in *Aesthetics*

and Ideology, ed. George Levine (New Brunswick, N.J.: Rutgers University Press, 1994), 264–82.

20. Tellingly, those on whom he depends for food and daily services are also those who alert the doctor and care for him when Des Esseintes rapidly sinks from nervous and gastrointestinal distress. See Felski, 108–9.

21. John Lawrence Waltman, "The Early London Journals of Elizabeth Robins Pennell" (Ph.D. diss., University of Texas, 1976), 444–45.

22. Compare the "ethic of care" articulated in Carol Gilligan, *In a Different Voice: Psychological Theory and Women's Development* (Cambridge, Mass.: Harvard University Press, 1982).

23. Hélène Cixous, "Sorties," in Hélène Cixous and Catherine Clement, *The Newly Born Woman,* trans. Betsy Wing (Minneapolis: University of Minnesota Press, 1986), 63–132.

24. Baudelaire, *Painter of Modern Life,* 204.

25. William Archer, "Mrs. Marriott-Watson," *Poets of the Younger Generation* (1902; reprint, New York: AMS Press, 1970), 470, 477.

26. Cyril Scott, *My Years of Indiscretion* (London: Mills and Boon, 1924), 74. For further biographical details, see my "Rosamund Marriott Watson," in *Dictionary of Literary Biography: Late Victorian and Edwardian Women Poets,* ed. William Thesing (Detroit: Gale, forthcoming).

27. W. E. Henley to Charles Whibley, 14 May 1895, Pierpont Morgan Library, New York, MA 4500.

Elaine Showalter links misogynist comments, such as Henley's, and misogynist representations of female vampires: "The female vampire represented the nymphomaniac or oversexed wife who threatened her husband's life with her insatiable erotic demands. According to one gynecologist, 'just as the vampire sucks the blood of its victims in their sleep, so does the woman vampire suck the life and exhaust the vitality of her male partner'" (180). See also Oppenheim, 209.

28. See, for example, Bram Dijkstra, *Idols of Perversity: Fantasies of Feminine Evil in Fin-de-Siècle Culture* (Oxford: Oxford University Press, 1988).

29. Though it is clumsy, I designate the poet as "Tomson/Watson" while discussing "Vespertilia" to register the author's social and authorial acts in 1894–95.

30. G. R. Tomson to John Lane, undated letter, John Lane Papers, Harry Ransom Humanities Research Center, University of Texas.

31. Quoted by Havelock Ellis, introduction to *Against the Grain,* by J.-K. Huysmans (New York: Hartsdale House, 1931), 25–26.

32. Lang "discovered" Tomson and announced the arrival of a new poet in *Longman's Magazine.* H. B. Marriott Watson, introduction to *Poems of Rosamund Marriott Watson* (London: John Lane, The Bodley Head, 1912), viii.

33. Rosamund Marriott Watson, *Vespertilia and Other Verses* (London: John Lane, The Bodley Head, 1895), 3. All further citations will be noted parenthetically in the text and are taken from this edition.

34. Caesar invaded England before the birth of Christ. The poem fixes no precise date for imperial Rome, but its logic suggests an era sometime later, after colonization.

35. Linda K. Hughes, "'Fair Hymen holdeth hid a world of woes': Myth and Marriage in Poems by 'Graham R. Tomson' (Rosamund Marriott Watson)," in *Victorian Women Poets: A Critical Reader,* ed. Angela Leighton (Oxford: Basil Blackwell, 1996), 162–85.

36. Nina Auerbach, *Our Vampires, Ourselves* (Chicago: University of Chicago Press, 1995), 40.

37. These lines play on her name, since *vespertinal* connotes that which blossoms or is active at night, just as the wood flower to which she is compared glimmers in the muted light of evening or in moonlight. *Vespertinal* also connotes both organic life and night or death, as befits an undead woman who resembles a night blossom.

38. From 1889 to 1892 Tomson wrote a fashion column for Henley's *National Observer,* hence the vivid evocation of feminine garb. See Hughes, *Strange Bedfellows,* and Schaffer's chapter on fashion writing in "Woman's World."

39. This line is a witty inversion of Alfred, Lord Tennyson's "Slow-dropping veils of thinnest lawn" from the "Lotos-Eaters," another classical poem dealing with compulsion, forgetfulness, and the attractions of death. If nature (the waterfall) is transformed into linen in Tennyson's poem, linens here merge into nature and rot.

40. Graham R. Tomson, "Beauty, from the Historical Point of View," *Woman's World* 2 (July–August 1889): 537–38.

41. Mona Caird, *The Morality of Marriage and Other Essays on the Status and Destiny of Woman* (London: George Redway, 1897), 43–44. Caird and Tomson were friends in the late 1880s and early 1890s (see Waltman, 384, 391–92). The jurist Gaius was active from A.D. 130 to 180; Justinian lived from A.D. 483 to 565. Both periods were contemporaneous with Latin decadence. Petronius and Apuleius, two Latin authors beloved by Huysmans's Des Esseintes, for example, lived in the first and second century A.D., respectively. See also Symons, 148.

Vespertilia's historical era may carry a political valence, since it registers the fact that England, the imperial power of the 1890s, was itself once a colony.

42. Auerbach, 19, 60.

43. I discuss the censure of serial marriage, even among feminists, in "A *Fin-de-Siècle* Beauty and the Beast: Configuring the Body in Works by 'Graham R. Tomson' (Rosamund Marriott Watson)," *Tulsa Studies in Women's Literature* 14, no. 1 (spring 1995): 100. Jon Stratton has noted the challenge vampires pose to conventional marriage: "The agelessness of the vampire precludes the bourgeois idyll of growing old as a loving couple within marriage" (*The Virgin Text: Fiction, Sexuality, and Ideology* [Norman: University of Oklahoma Press, 1987], 173).

44. See Linda K. Hughes, "A Female Aesthete at the Helm: *Sylvia's Journal* and

'Graham R. Tomson,' 1893–1894," *Victorian Periodicals Review* 29, no. 2 (summer 1996): 173–92, and the chapters on interior decoration and fashion writing in Schaffer, "Woman's World."

45. Thornton, 18–19, 34. For the recurrent misogyny of French decadence, see Jean Pierrot, *The Decadent Imagination, 1880–1900,* trans. Derek Coltman (Chicago: University of Chicago Press, 1981), 38, 124.

EDWARD MARX

Decadent Exoticism and the Woman Poet

LITERARY HISTORIANS, until quite recently, have separated the writers of the 1890s into two opposing and overwhelmingly masculine camps: on one side, the aesthetes and decadents; on the other, the counterdecadents. Of these, the aesthetes and decadents, credited as the precursors of the modernist movement in their promotion of artistic autonomy and opposition to Victorian moralizing, have remained compelling to contemporary readers, while the counterdecadents, who "flaunted zesty attitudes in self-conscious repudiation of the aesthetic-decadent sensibility, which to them seemed effete," have come to be seen mainly as strident voices of patriotism, outworn Victorian morals, and imperialist expansion.[1] Contemporary readers generally find objectionable the imperialist propaganda of these writers, among whom are usually included Rudyard Kipling, W. E. Henley, Henry Newbolt, Alfred Austin, and William Watson. The decadent writers, with their aversion to realism and withdrawal into the realm of art, are typically thought to have insulated themselves from the now distasteful British obsession with imperial expansion.

This supposed disinterest is not, however, as simple as it appears on first glance. These writers were, in fact, deeply implicated in what I shall refer to in this essay as decadent exoticism, which in turn depended on a production of cross-cultural knowledge that was not only a by-product of empire but one of its most important operational strategies.

My interest in this essay is not to disparage the aesthetic movement by calling attention to its complicity in imperial expansion but to restore an aspect of its historical significance usually disregarded. Indeed, the idea of aestheticism's dependence on empire was first proposed by Holbrook Jackson as far back as 1913. "All so-called decadence," Jackson wrote, "is civilisation rejecting, through certain specialised persons, the accumulated experiences and sensations of the race":

> It is a demand for wider ranges, newer emotional and spiritual territories, fresh woods and pastures new for the soul. If you will, it is a form of imperialism of the spirit, ambitious, arrogant, aggressive, waving the flag of human power over an ever wider and wider territory. And it is interesting to recollect that decadent art periods have often coincided with such waves of imperial patriotism as passed over the British Empire and various European countries during the Eighteen Nineties.[2]

This is to say not that there were no differences between the decadent and counterdecadent camps, only that they were more closely intertwined than has usually been supposed. The professional and social associations of writers of the period, the Rhymers' Club, for example, cut broadly across the divide. It may be recalled that one of the most vocal of the counterdecadents, W. E. Henley, was quite close to both Oscar Wilde and William Butler Yeats. "I disagreed with him about everything, but I admired him beyond words," Yeats wrote in his *Autobiographies.*[3] Indeed, Yeats first met Wilde through Henley and was intrigued by the brief, close friendship between the two.[4]

Wilde and Yeats, though unified in their opposition to the British occupation of Ireland, were less vocal in their opposition to British expansion elsewhere. Both, however, drew inspiration from the non-Western cultures that Britain was then colonizing or attempting to colonize. Yeats's fascination in these early years was with India, via Madame Blavatsky and Mohini Chatterjee (and later Rabindranath Tagore). Later, the Noh drama of Japan became an object of interest. Wilde's non-Western enthusiasms were eclectic. His observations about Japan in *Intentions* — that "in fact, the whole of Japan is a pure invention" — are well known and, I shall argue later, perfectly characterize decadent exoticism's utter disregard for verisimilitude.[5] The Flaubertian Near Eastern orientalism of Wilde's *Salome* and the exotic opium-den atmosphere of *The Picture of Dorian Gray* have also been widely commented on. Curtis Marez has noted that "under Wilde's editorship, *Woman's World* published over thirty essays dealing with aspects of so-called exotic cultures and their ornaments. These articles, too numerous to name, include references to Eastern macramé and wallpaper designs; Persian, Egyptian and Indian appliqués; South African ostrich feathers for fans; South American perfume bottles; Egyptian and Indian shoes; Egyptian, Chinese and Japanese combs; Chinese screens; and Chinese, Egyptian, Turkish and Persian bridal costumes."[6] Zhou Xiaoyi points out that, for Wilde, "the exotic taste in house decoration is achieved by the consumption of Japanese commodities," creating a "juxtaposition of aestheticism and consumerism" that appears to militate against Wilde's efforts to detach art from commercial interests.[7] Wilde also wrote reviews of books on Chinese philosophy as well as of Pundita Ramabai Sarasvati's *The High Caste Hindu Woman* and Emily Ruete's *Memoirs of an Arabian Princess.*[8] For Wilde the unreality of non-Westerners did not diminish their fascination, and his autonomous exoticism was, at least for him, not incompatible with the belief that "criticism will annihilate race-prejudices, by insisting on the unity of the human mind in the variety of its forms. If we are tempted to make war upon another nation," he argued, "we shall remember that we are seeking to destroy an element of our own culture, and possibly its most important element."[9]

Thus, empire was not merely a preoccupation of the counterdecadent school but a critical field of influence for both the decadents and the counterdecadents. Decadent exoticism is therefore crucial to our understanding of the historical meaning and positioning of the aesthetic movement in England. At the same time it is significant that many of the important practitioners of the decadent exotic mode were women, following in the century-old tradition of exotic romance in which women writers had figured prominently.[10] This essay will focus on two late decadent women writers, Sarojini Naidu and Adela Nicolson (Laurence Hope), both of whom, I will argue, have strong claims to be included in the category of decadents.

Sarojini Naidu arrived in London as Sarojini Chattopâdhyây in 1895. A sixteen-year-old literary prodigy determined to be a poet, ostensibly studying at Girton and Cambridge on a scholarship funded by the nizam of Hyderabad, she quickly found her way into the literary circle of Edmund Gosse, where she developed an intimate friendship with the decadent poet-critic Arthur Symons. Brought up on the Victorian and Romantic classics, she soon discovered that her efforts in the styles of Alfred, Lord Tennyson and Percy Bysshe Shelley were of little interest to her literary mentors. "What we wished to receive," Gosse told her, was "some revelation of the heart of India, some sincere penetrating analysis of native passion, of the principles of antique religion and of such mysterious intimations as stirred the soul of the East long before the West had begun to dream that it had a soul."[11]

Sarojini strove to become the poet of the mysterious East that Gosse and Symons wanted her to be and was, at the same time, deeply influenced by the contemporary poetry scene in England. Her library, now in the collection of the Sarojini Naidu Trust in Hyderabad, offers a partial record of her literary interests from 1895 to 1898, when she left England. In her copy of Symons's *Days and Nights,* she wrote out the famous stanza from his poem "Art":

> All serve alike her purpose, she requires
> The very life-blood of humanity;
> All that the soul conceives, the heart desires,
> She marks, she garners in her memory.

But the counterdecadents are better represented among her books than the decadents are. Sarojini acquired four books by the pro-imperialist poets William Watson and W. E. Henley in 1895 and 1896, as well as books by Andrew Lang and Robert Louis Stevenson. Laurence Housman's *Green Arras* and another William Watson volume were acquired in 1897. The *Collected Poems* of the decadent Austin Dobson and George Meredith's *Selected Poems* were acquired in 1898, while the beginnings of her collection of contemporary women poets can be found in her copy of Alice Meynell's *Poems,* which she acquired in 1896, and two volumes — *Fair Shadow Land* and *In the Young World* — by the American poet Edith Thomas, whom she met in London in 1896. In a January 1896 letter to her future husband, Sarojini wrote of England's new poets:

> William Watson with his sublime, starry genius, Davidson with his wild, riotous, dazzling superabundant brilliance, Thompson with his gorgeous, spiritual ecstasy of poetry, Yeats with his exquisite dreams and music, Norman Gale, redolent of springtime in the meadows and autumn in the orchard, Arthur Symons, the marvellous boy, with his passionate nature and fiery eyes, all gathered together in the friendly house of that dearest and lovingest of friends and rarest and most gifted of [geniuses] Edmund Gosse.[12]

Nor is Naidu unfamiliar with "the older men, with their beautiful gifts — Swinburne, that grand old Socialist William Morris . . . that lovely singer Edwin Arnold and that graceful writer, the laureate of the English, Alfred Austin."[13] Undoubtedly, Gosse's more conservative tastes acted as a counterbalance to Symons's decadent interests, although even Symons evidently thought it necessary to shield the teenage poet from dangerous influences. In one letter quoted in Symons's memoir, Sarojini remarks on meeting Gabriele D'Annunzio in Florence: "I have never read anything of his, for the very good reason that you said you would not allow me to read his *Triumph of Death.*"[14]

The diversity of influences on Sarojini's poetic development helps to explain the divergences in her own poetic style. Her decadent tendencies are evident in poems such as "Eastern Dancers," published in the *Savoy* (which Symons edited) in 1896 (it appears as "Indian Dancers" in her collections):[15]

> The scents of red roses and sandalwood flutter and die
> in the maze of their gem-tangled hair,
> And smiles are entwining like magical serpents the
> poppies of lips that are opiate-sweet;
> Their glittering garments of purple are burning like
> tremulous dawns in the quivering air,
> And exquisite, subtle and slow are the tinkle and tread
> of their rhythmical, slumber-soft feet.[16]

Indeed, Sarojini so enthusiastically embraced the decadent style in this poem that it had to be toned down for publication: the dancers' "passionate bosoms aflaming with fire" being replaced with "passionate spirits."

The poems in her first volume, *The Golden Threshold* (1905), reflect the many styles that appealed to Naidu. Among those conspicuously of the decadent mode are "Nightfall in the City of Hyderabad": "See how the speckled sky burns like a pigeon's throat, / Jewelled with embers of opal and peridote" (71). An abundance of exquisite detail is found in these poems. In "Alabaster" the poet's heart is compared to an alabaster box "whose art / Is frail as a cassia-flower," "Carven with delicate dreams and wrought / With many a subtle and exquisite thought" (62). One may well suspect the poet of catering to Symons's fascination with gypsies in her poem "The Indian Gypsies,"[17] in which a gypsy girl "is twin-born with primal mysteries, / And drinks of life at Time's forgotten source" (70).

But these strongly decadent poems make up only about a third of *The Golden Threshold.* At the other extreme, poems like "To India" are written in an allegorical, didactic style perhaps borrowed from counterdecadents like Henley and Watson:

> Thy Future calls thee with a manifold sound
> To crescent honours, splendours, victories vast;
> Waken, O slumbering Mother, and be crowned,
> Who once wert empress of the sovereign past. (72)

Between these two extremes one finds poems in many styles: occasional poems, translations of folk songs and an Urdu ghazel, autobiographical lyrics, poetic fables, pastoral songs, and the scenes and sketches of Indian life that were Naidu's trademark. Coming to fin-de-siècle English poetry as an outsider, Naidu seems to have found it easier to blend styles that a British poet might have found incongruous.

The poet James Cousins noted of Naidu in 1918 that "in her life she is feminist up to a point, but in her poetry she remains incorrigibly feminine," a critique that has grown sharper among contemporary South Asian feminist critics.[18] But given the strong masculine biases of Naidu's decadent and counterdecadent models — the poets with whom she associated and in whose poetry she immersed herself during her English "apprenticeship" — it seems preferable to emphasize the extent to which her poetic representations of objects conventionally seen as exotic by the Western gaze, such as the female suttee, the *pardah nashin,* and the Indian dancing girl, incorporate the subjectivity of their personae and sometimes elude conventional patterns. Such a strategy can be found in the girl protagonist of her poem "Village Song," who disregards the call "[o]f bridal-songs and cradle-songs and sandal-scented leisure," objecting that "[t]he bridal-songs and cradle-songs have cadences of sorrow" and preferring instead to follow the "fairy-folk" and the "far sweeter sound" of "the forest-notes where forest-streams are falling" (60).

From Symons's perspective Sarojini was a precious object exuding "the magic of the East," as he titled his reflections about her in his memoir, *Mes souvenirs:* "She sat in our midst, an alien and judged us, and few, except myself, knew what was passing behind that face."[19] One can get a sense of Sarojini's importance to Symons from his late essay "A Neglected Genius: Sir Richard Burton."[20] Any account of the interrelations between the decadents and the counterdecadents would have to contend with the anomalous figure of Burton: the quintessential man of action and yet a man whose tastes — both personal and literary — secured him a special status among the aesthetes and decadents. With Algernon Charles Swinburne, his complete physical opposite, as it were, he had formed the Cannibal Club in the 1860s, an organization dedicated, it seems, to the delectation of the exotic and perverse. Nor did his contributions to the realm of erotic literature and his willingness to test the bounds of British censorship go unnoted by the decadents.

"A Neglected Genius" suggests that Sarojini was to Symons what Burton was to Swinburne: a personal link with the exotic. The aesthetic temperament, whether manifested in Swinburne's effete impishness or Symons's languid pallor, was, after all, almost by definition unsuited to excursions into the exotic real. Wilde philosophized about the unreality of the Japanese. Yeats, for all his fascination with India, never contemplated going there. Symons, however, not only idealized the journey to the East but even attempted it in 1902, spending September in Budapest and Constantinople before calling it quits.[21] The journey was brief but sufficient — or so he felt — to establish him as a card-carrying "exote," to use Victor Segalen's term.[22] In the Burton essay Symons refers to an incident at Scutari (a lake region between what were then Albania and Yugoslavia) during the trip:

> After seeing the howling Dervishes in Scutari in Asia, I can imagine Burton's excitement when in Cairo he suddenly left his stolid English friends, joined in the shouting, gesticulating circle, and behaved as if to the manner born: he held his diploma as a master Dervish. In Scutari I felt the contagion of these dancers, where the brain reels, and the body is almost swept into the orgy. I had all the difficulty in the world from keeping back the woman who sat beside me from leaping over the barrier and joining the Dervishes. In these I felt the ultimate, because the most animal, the most irrational, the most insane, form of Eastern ecstasy. It gave me an impression of witchcraft; one might have been in Central Africa, or in some Saturnalia of barbarians.[23]

Symons the writer idealizes the experience, and his pen revels in it; but Symons the traveler is, as always, the languid aesthete, observing from an intellectual distance a desirable (because intense) experience.[24] There is a suggestion that his female traveling companion might have potentially traversed this distance, being, presumably (according to prevailing beliefs about femininity), closer to the animal and irrational.

This recollection is the starting point for Symons's reflections about Burton's value as a writer of the exotic:

> There can be no doubt that Burton always gives a vivid and virile impression of his adventures; yet, as I have said before, something is lacking in his prose; not the vital heat, but the vision of what is equivalent to vital heat. I have before me a letter sent from Hyderabad by Sarojini Naidu, who says: "All is hot and fierce and passionate, ardent and unashamed in its exulting and importunate desire for life and love. And, do you know, the scarlet lilies are woven petal by petal from my heart's blood, those quivering little birds are my soul made incarnate music, these heavy perfumes are my emotions dissolved into aerial essence, this flaming blue and gold sky is the 'Very You,' that part of me that incessantly and insolently, yes, and a little deliberately, triumphs over that other part — a thing of nerves and tissues that suffers and cries out, and that must die tomorrow perhaps, or twenty years hence." In these sentences the

> whole passionate, exotic and perfumed East flashes before me — a vision of delight and of distresses — and, as it were, all that slumbers in their fiery blood.[25]

It is telling that in the paragraph that follows this one Symons quotes the famous "gem-like flame" passage from the suppressed conclusion to Walter Pater's *The Renaissance: Studies in Art and Poetry* — perhaps the quintessential English expression of the decadent aesthetic. Sarojini evidently cultivated this style at least partly because she knew how it delighted Symons, and, as the passage indicates, she succeeded in convincing him — if he needed convincing — that she and her vision of India were the living embodiments of an exotic intensity to which even a Western adventurer like Burton could only aspire.

When Sarojini's first volume of verse appeared in 1905 with an introduction by Symons, the 1890s long ago had ended and decadence fallen into some disfavor; Wilde and Aubrey Beardsley were dead, and Symons himself had criticized the movement in his 1899 *Symbolist Movement in Literature* as merely an "interlude . . . while something more serious" — namely the symbolist movement — "was in preparation."[26] But while it may be true, as R. K. R. Thornton, among others, has argued, that decadence as an English literary movement "was given a fatal blow" when Wilde was found guilty of acts of gross indecency in 1895, many of the movement's partisans continued to practice business as usual for many years, and decadent style lived on, in art nouveau, for example, for more than a decade.[27] Writers like Naidu, whose sensibilities had been formed during the 1890s, continued to write in the decadent and counterdecadent styles well into the Edwardian era.

Among the most popular of these late decadent poets was Adela Nicolson, a woman who had spent nearly all of the 1890s far from London among the remote military stations of central India, where her husband served in the higher ranks of the Indian army. Somehow — in part, perhaps, through her sister, Victoria Cross, who made her literary debut with a short story, "Theodora," in the *Yellow Book* in 1895 — news of the literary scene in London trickled in to the Indian army military cantonment at Mhow.[28] There Violet Nicolson (as she preferred to be called) was writing the poems that would compose her highly popular first volume, *The Garden of Kama,* published under the pseudonym Laurence Hope in 1901.

There is little that can be said with much certainty about Nicolson's formation as a writer.[34] Born Adela Florence Cory in England in 1865 while her father, Colonel Arthur Cory, was on leave from the Bengal army, she had been raised by relatives and schooled in Italy before joining her parents in Lahore at the age of sixteen. Perhaps she read Pater's *Renaissance* during those formative years; in any case, it would be difficult to find an English writer whose life and work demonstrate a greater determination to put into practice the Paterian credo: "to burn always with this hard, gem-like flame, to maintain this ecstasy, is success in life." Seizing on impressions, rejecting habit-bound behavior, Pater had suggested, "we may well grasp at any exquisite passion, or any contribution to knowledge that seems by a lifted horizon to set the spirit free for a moment, or any stirring of the senses, strange dyes, strange colours, and curious odours, or work of the artist's hands, or the face of one's friend."[30] In her life and in her poems Nicolson carried out Pater's search for exquisite passion well into the realm of decadent excess. "The tragic circumstances of her death," Thomas Hardy wrote, following her suicide in October 1904, "seem but the impassioned closing notes of her impassioned effusions."[31]

Nicolson's most famous poem, "Kashmiri Song," is among those most expressive of her decadent sensibility:

> Pale hands I loved beside the Shalimar,
> Where are you now? Who lies beneath your spell?
> Whom do you lead on Rapture's roadway, far,
> Before you agonise them in farewell?
>
> Oh, pale dispensers of my Joys and Pains,
> Holding the doors of Heaven and of Hell,
> How the hot blood rushed wildly through the veins
> Beneath your touch, until you waved farewell.
>
> Pale hands, pink tipped, like Lotus buds that float
> On those cool waters where we used to dwell,
> I would have rather felt you round my throat,
> Crushing out life, than waving me farewell![32]

These words, in Amy Woodforde-Finden's extremely popular musical setting, would for decades entice listeners with their distinctive suggestion of erotic strangulation amid exotic scenery.[33]

Eroticism and death are persistent themes in Nicolson's poetry. "Gathered from Ternina's Face" borrows its subject from Richard Wagner's *Tristan und Isolde* — "the redemptive eroticism" of which, Karl Beckson has noted, "especially beguiled Aesthetes and Decadents, as though justifying their personal visions" — as seen by Nicolson in a performance by the great Croatian soprano Milka Ternina.[34]

> Much may be done by those about to die,
> Much may be said by lips that say "Good-bye,"
> On which the Last Great Silence soon must lie,
> Tristan! (216–17)

Her vision of eroticism, death, and sacrifice is perhaps most characteristically and cogently expressed in her poem "Prayer":

> Give me your love for a day,
> A night, an hour:
> If the wages of sin are death
> I am willing to pay
> What is my life but a breath
> Of passion burning away?
> Away for an unplucked flower.
> Oh Aziza whom I adore,
> Aziza my one delight,
> Only one night, I will die before day,
> And trouble your life no more. (61)

Another poem, again on the subject of passionate death, is inspired by Maeterlinck's *Life of the Bee:*

> Oh for the death of a beautiful purple bee,
> Sailing away to the blue of a limpid sky;
> To have yielded up one's life in an ecstasy,
> And then, in the very climax of love, to die!
>
> To give oneself completely, once and for ever;
> Drink life at its utmost height as one laid it down;
> Spend one's soul in the rush of one last endeavour;
> And rule supremely in laying aside the crown. (307)

These poems stand out in their affinities with decadent works like Villiers's *Axel,* while some subjects treated by Nicolson speak to other decadent fascinations: opium smoking, erotic cruelty, the cult of youth, slaves and despotic rulers, dancing girls, and, above all, passion.[35] This was, in effect, the India of decadent exoticism, and its continuing appeal is suggested by a somewhat disparaging 1916 review in the *New Republic* of a new edition of Naidu's first book. Comparing Naidu to her British counterpart, the reviewer argued that "Laurence Hope, throbbing out her burning passionate soul, needed just India for a setting — needed the cruel heat of the Indian day and the hallucination of the Indian night," whereas "Sarojini Naidu's poems might have suggested themselves in Connaught or Cornwall or even in New Jersey."[36]

If Nicolson's exoticized female slaves and dancing girls, her typical poetic personae, seem unlikely candidates for feminist revival, one may at least point to the radicalism of her insistence on female sexuality in her characterizations. The bride in "Marriage Thoughts: by Morsellin Khan," for example, sings to her future husband,

> I may not raise my eyes, O my Lord, towards you,
> And I may not speak: what matter? my voice would fail.
> But through my downcast lashes, feeling your beauty,
> I shiver and burn with pleasure beneath my veil. (23)

Nicolson's women vehemently assert their capacity to experience emotional and physical intensities not often attributed to women even in decadent literature. Though strongly reinforcing patriarchal structures of male dominance in the most visceral manner (rendering them highly appealing to many male readers), the poems nevertheless represented a widening of the emotional range of women's poetry in the period. The female speaker of "Atavism," following "long dead instincts" — "the lure of my season's mate" and the "[s]cent of fur and colour of blood" — not only lays claim to a feminized version of Kipling's "law of the jungle" but scoffs at the conventionality of a colonial society that disparaged women "going *jungli*": "Pale days: and a league of laws / Made by the whims of men" (178).

"Laurence Hope is directly descended from the writers of the *Yellow Book* and *Savoy*," as an early literary historian of the period put it; "her background is different, but in psychological subtlety and frankness she was nearer to Mr. Arthur Symons than any other modern poet."[37] But Symons himself seems to have taken only a passing interest in this late arrival to the decadent camp. When news of her suicide in Madras came in 1904, he told Hardy he was "glad there are still people who can do such things" but ignored Hardy's suggestion that "the moment affords an opening for publishing a critical summary of her passionate verses by anybody who is acquainted with them, & may wish to do so."[38] It was left to Hardy — who had met Nicolson briefly at one of Blanche Crackanthorpe's literary salons in 1903 — to write her obituary for the *Athenaeum.*

The following year, however, Symons did contribute a fairly lengthy review of Nicolson's posthumously published third volume of verse, *Indian Love,* to the *Outlook,* calling her "one of the strongest personalities in recent English literature." Rather than reading her in the context of the poets of the 1890s, Symons chose to compare Nicolson with Emily Brontë. But even with Brontë, "their differences," he argued, "are greater than their resemblances," largely because "while Emily Brontë was of us, Laurence Hope was not." Though partly approving of Nicolson's otherness ("Our refusals, our conventions, our restraints, even our high notions of chivalry — at root so sound, but in their fruit so often weak and insincere — to her were foreign and intolerable"), he was ultimately compelled to draw the line. Citing her poem "Song of the Parao (Camping Ground)," in which the poet vehemently renounces West for East, he observed, "these, after all, are not the accents of the races that rule the world, and one might turn from them to the English woodnotes of far lesser poets with something of relief."[39]

Thus, what appealed to Symons about Naidu's poetry — "the wisdom of the East," as he called it in his introduction to *The Golden Threshold* — made him somewhat uneasy when encountered in the poems of the British Laurence Hope. One recalls the difficulty Symons allegedly had resisting the "contagion" of the dancing dervishes in Scutari and his greater difficulty in "keeping back the woman who sat beside me from leaping over the barrier"; here a British woman poet had clearly crossed the barrier — "gone native," as it were — and Symons could not fully approve. Though clearly fascinated with Nicolson's version of the decadent exotic — his comments on the "cold and studied cruelty" and "searing malice" of her notorious poem "Afridi Love," with its lingering depiction of the psychology of sexual assault, and the "raw, appalling . . . vividness" of "Sher Afzul," a revenge poem worthy of Edgar Allan Poe, are admiring rather than critical — he cannot help feeling that the poems, "into which she has breathed the very soul and colour of the East," ultimately "crave an antidote." The lines penned by Symons's friend Yeats — "Come near, come near, come near — Ah, leave me still / A little space for the rose-breath to fill!" — might well express Symons's perspective.

While Symons disapproved of Nicolson's going native, he also took issue with her philosophically. "In her philosophy," he observed, "passion came to seem the only reality . . . a reality to be sought and held, not in any spiritual or transcendental form, but in its elements." It seems at times, he argued, "almost an echo of Browning's belief in love as the climax of existence, the crucial test of soul, but simplified and de-spiritualised, and so inverted by the passive Eastern attitude that the crucial moment seems less life's test of the individual's worth than the individual's test of the worth of life." This lack of a spiritual vision of passion, he concluded, means that her poetry "never rises to the sublimity of the great love-poets." Symons had argued in *The Symbolist Movement in Literature* that passion, like religion and art, was a necessary escape from "sterile, annihilating reality" but that these forms of escape could only find their true expression in mysticism, "a theory of life which makes us familiar with mystery, and which seems to harmonise those instincts which make for religion, passion and art." "On this theory alone," he wrote, "does all life become worth living." In the poems of Laurence Hope, he argued in his review, there is "no sudden vision of eternity, such as crowns Catullus's most passionate love-poem."[40]

There is an element of truth in Symons's claim. One of Nicolson's juvenile verses asks skeptically:

> Is it that need of faith, innate in man,
> Which bends his stubborn knees and bids him pray,
> Which still surviving since his race began
> Forces him now to worship and obey?[41]

And there is little in her mature work to suggest a yearning for religion or an interest in spirituality for its own sake. Yet Nicolson's philosophy of passion was as complex as Symons's and certainly more intense; his passionate lyrics, the tales of excess in his *London Nights,* for example, seem tepid in comparison with her "passionate effusions." In rejecting the mysticism that held together Symons's tenuous approach to life, she was perhaps the more modern of the two, though it left her, as she wrote in one poem, "a broken boat / On a sea of passions, adrift, afloat" (16).

Symons's observation that Laurence Hope had captured "the very soul and colour of the East" was a common, though by no means universal, view. Indeed, the authenticity question dominated the reception history of her poems, and Hardy's 1904 observation that "we may at least go so far as to doubt if it will ever be precisely known how much in them was imitation and how much original work" remains true even today.[42] Pseudonyms, gender ambiguity, misleading labeling ("translated and arranged by Laurence Hope" reads the title page of her first volume), and blurred boundaries between what Symons recognized as her poems' "two broad types — ballads and songs and dramatic monologues, on the one hand; on the other, sad and passionate and ever unsatisfied, the cry of her own experience" — all contributed to the mystery of whether the poems were authentic translations or whether they were, as Hardy suggested, "dramatic" or "personative."[43] It is important to our understanding of decadent exoticism to recognize not only that no one could tell for certain whether the poems were authentic translations or not but also that it did not matter as much as one might expect, since a great deal of the period's cross-cultural literature operated in the epistemologically blurred space of Wilde's imaginary Japanese. Authenticity, for a surprising range of critics, was a subjective, rather than an objective, quality: if a work of literature, art, or music produced the appropriate "Oriental" feeling, then it *was* oriental. In the words of one critic, "it is not, of course, of the smallest importance whether her Oriental atmosphere and detail are in fact accurate and correct, any more than it matters whether the Celtic Revival school reproduce correctly the spirit of old Celtic literature."[44] The only serious attempt to disprove the poems' authenticity, in an essay evidently unnoticed outside India, was by an anonymous Indian writer in the *Calcutta Review.* "We cannot but resent," the critic wrote, "those who indulge a taste for the forbidden, and — indecent, by sheltering behind a misrepresentation of a country their knowledge of which may be summed up in the bare fact that it is the home of elemental passion."[45]

Naidu's reaction to Laurence Hope was ambivalent, as the notes contained in her copy of *The Garden of Kama* (now in the library of the Sarojini Naidu Trust in Hyderabad) indicate. Her attitude seems to be summed up in a comment scribbled at the end of "Malay Song": "I wish Laurence Hope would always sustain a style of hearty + [mythonic?] wealth of colour — unaffected + unmurdred [*sic*] by her usual vulgarity: such as we find in almost 3/4 of this book." We can glean some idea of what Naidu liked and disliked from her marginal notes to Nicolson's "The Temple Dancing Girl," a poem spoken by the dancing girl's lustful admirer, determined that he will possess her:

> You will be mine; those lightly dancing feet,
> Falling as softly on the careless street
> As the wind-loosened petals of a flower,
> Will bring you here, at the Appointed Hour.

Naidu marked this first stanza as "pretty." The second stanza, however, was less to her taste

And all the Temple's little links and laws
Will not for long protect your loveliness.
I have a stronger force to aid my cause,
Nature's great Law, to love and to possess!

The third and fourth lines, she noted, have "Beauty with a touch of vulgarity in them." The fourth stanza most met with Naidu's approval:

The clustered softness of your waving hair,
That curious paleness which enchants me so,
And all your delicate strength and youthful air,
Destiny will compel you to bestow!

This earned a "beautiful." The following lines, which mark the speaker's turn of thought toward what represents, for him, the erotics of resistance, "Refuse, withdraw, and hesitate awhile, / Your young reluctance does but fan the flame," were underlined without comment. But a few lines down, as the speaker's instructions become more explicit, Naidu's toleration came to an end:

Yet, make it not too long, nor too intense
My thirst; lest I should break beneath the strain,
And the worn nerves, and over-wearied sense,
Enjoy not what they spent themselves to gain.

"How vulgar!" she noted.

The 25 percent Naidu found pleasing is represented by the poem "Starlight," in which the eroticism is suggestive rather than explicit:

O beautiful Stars, when you see me go
Hither and thither, in search of love,
Do you think me faithless, who gleam and glow
Serene and fixed in the blue above?
O Stars, so golden, it is not so.

But there is a garden I dare not see,
There is a place where I fear to go,
Since the charm and glory of life to me
The brown earth covered there, long ago.
O Stars, you saw it, you know, you know.

Hither and thither I wandering go,
With aimless haste and wearying fret;

In a search for pleasure and love? Not so,
  Seeking desperately to forget.
    You see so many, O Stars, you know.

"This poem," Naidu commented, "would strike wondrous music on the chord of an artistically-moulded heart, that feels once for *one,* and in a state of unfulfilled desire, seeks desperate occupations."

That Naidu was content criticizing the vulgarity and admiring the beauty of Nicolson's verse, rather than attacking its cross-cultural pretensions (as the *Calcutta Review* had), seems significant and, I think, reinforces my point that Nicolson represented the fruition of the decadent exoticism espoused by Naidu's mentors. That Naidu implicitly recognized this fact, making room for the Anglo-Indian poet even while attacking her taste on purely aesthetic grounds, may be taken as a tacit admission that the success of her own poetry in the West depended on exoticism. Naidu's exoticism has led to some contemporary postcolonial critics dismissing her work for its imperialist complicity, and yet, this is, as I have argued here, to misunderstand the environment under which she developed as a poet and, as I have argued elsewhere, to ignore the difficulties of an Indian woman poet attaining a voice.[46] That Naidu was able to leverage her success as a poet to create for herself a role as one of India's most important female political leaders in the independence struggle calls into question the idea that her emulation of contemporary modes of exoticism was simply naive. "Mad dreams," she wrote in an early poem,

are mine to bind
The world to my desire, and hold the wind
A voiceless captive to my conquering song.[47]

It may be concluded that popular demand for exotic literature created opportunities for women writers like Naidu and Nicolson who possessed direct knowledge of exotic places. I have not touched on the extent to which women readers may have helped to promote exotic literature, but a gender-inflected reception history of exoticist writing — beginning at least as early as the late-eighteenth-century vogue for the oriental tale and comprehending such later forms as the Victorian "feminine picturesque," of which Sara Suleri has offered a useful account, the decadent exotic, and early-twentieth-century works such as E. M. Hull's *The Sheik* — would undoubtedly reveal the influence of a women's readership.[48] Yet one should not disregard persistent signs of a masculinist bias in examining the careers of writers like Nicolson and Naidu. The pragmatic wisdom of Nicolson's choice of a male pseudonym, though criticized by Hardy and others, was borne out by the persistently gendered critique of her work following the revelation of her identity as a woman. In Naidu's case the critical role played by her male patrons in establishing her career cannot be ignored. Thus, while exoticism presented opportunities for the woman poet, entering the field demanded a negotiation with its prominently masculine biases.

Notes

1. David Perkins, *A History of Modern Poetry* (Cambridge, Mass.: Harvard University Press, 1976–87), 1:12.

2. Holbrook Jackson, *The Eighteen Nineties: A Review of Art and Ideas at the Close of the Nineteenth Century* (New York: Kennerley, 1913), 64.

3. William Butler Yeats, *Autobiographies* (London: Macmillan, 1956), 124.

4. Ibid., 132.

5. Oscar Wilde, *Intentions* (New York: Dodd, Mead, 1894), 46.

6. Curtis Marez, "The Other Addict: Reflections on Colonialism and Oscar Wilde's Opium Smoke Screen," *ELH* 64, no. 1 (1997): 265.

7. Zhou Xiaoyi, "Oscar Wilde's Orientalism and Late Nineteenth-Century European Consumer Culture," *Ariel* 28, no. 4 (1997): 68.

8. Oscar Wilde, *The Works of Oscar Wilde* (New York: Lamb, 1909), 12:156–59, 280–90.

Wilde's authorship of a curious Burmese masque, *For Love of the King,* allegedly inspired by conversations with a noted Burmese lawyer, Chan Toon, and his British wife, Mabel Cosgrove, remains disputed. Mrs. Chan Toon herself is thought to have authored the work, and she did write a collection of short stories, *Told on the Pagoda: Tales of Burmah* (London: T. Fisher Unwin, 1895), and an autobiographical novel, *A Marriage in Burmah* (London: Greening, 1905), among other works.

9. Wilde, *Intentions,* 208–9.

10. See Martha Pike Conant, *The Oriental Tale in England in the Eighteenth Century* (New York: Columbia University Press, 1908).

11. Sarojini Naidu, *The Bird of Time: Songs of Life, Death & the Spring,* intro. Edmund Gosse (London: Heinemann, 1912), 5.

12. Quoted in *Sarojini Naidu: Selected Poetry and Prose,* ed. Makarand Paranjape (New Delhi: Harper Collins Indus, 1993), 8.

13. Ibid.

14. Symons, *Mes souvenirs* (Chapelle-Réanville: Hours, 1929), 39.

15. Sarojini Chattopâdhyây, "Eastern Dancers," *Savoy,* September 1896, 84.

16. *Sarojini Naidu: Selected Poetry and Prose,* 65–66. All further citations will be noted parenthetically in the text and are taken from this edition.

17. Symons contributed at least six articles to the *Journal of the Gypsy Lore Society* between 1908 and 1914. Much of his memoir of Naidu in *Mes souvenirs* is devoted to what she told him about gypsies. Symons regarded her stories as "one of the most valuable documents I possess in regard to a race I have always admired beyond all other races, and which I have often come in contact with almost all over Europe: they are the Eternal Wanderers, and they are our only link with the East, with Magic, and with Mystery" (*Mes souvenirs,* 38).

18. James Cousins, *The Renaissance in India* (Madras: Ganesh, 1918), 262.

19. Symons, 34.

20. Symons, it should be mentioned, also dedicated poems to Sarojini: "The Lover of the Queen of Sheba" (dated 28 May 1898), in *Images of Good and Evil* (London: Heinemann, 1899), 93–102, and "The Serpent," in *Knave of Hearts* (London: Heinemann, 1913), 27.

21. The dates are noted in Karl Beckson and John M. Munro, eds., *Arthur Symons: Selected Letters, 1880–1935* (Basingstoke: Macmillan, 1989), xix. Symons's "Notes on Constantinople and Sofia" appears in *Wanderings* (Letchworth, Hertfordshire: Temple, 1931), 141–49; an earlier account, "Constantinople: Three Aspects," was published in *Saturday Review* 95 (1903): 741–42.

22. Victor Segalen, *Essai sur l'exotisme: Une esthétique du divers (notes)* (Montpellier: Fata Morgana, 1978).

23. Arthur Symons, "A Neglected Genius: Sir Richard Burton," in *Dramatis Personae* (New York: Bobbs-Merrill, 1923), 254–55.

24. See also his poem "The Turning Dervish" (dated November 1902), in *The Fool of the World and Other Poems* (London: Heinemann, 1906), reprinted in *The Collected Works of Arthur Symons* (London: Secker, 1924), 2:227.

25. Symons, "A Neglected Genius," 255.

26. Arthur Symons, *The Symbolist Movement in Literature* (London: Heinemann, 1899), 8–9.

27. R. K. R. Thornton, "Decadence in Later Nineteenth-Century England," in *Decadence and the 1890s,* ed. Ian Fletcher (London: Edward Arnold, 1979), 15.

28. Oscar Wilde once remarked that "if one could only marry Thomas Hardy to Victoria Cross he might gain something of real passion with which to animate his little keepsake pictures of starched ladies" (Frank Harris, *Oscar Wilde, His Life and Confessions* [London: Constable, 1938], 331). On Victoria Cross, see Shoshana Milgram Knapp, "Victoria Cross," in *British Short Fiction Writers, 1880–1914: The Realist Tradition,* ed. William B. Thesing (Detroit: Gale Research, 1993), 75–84.

29. On Laurence Hope, see Leslie Blanch, "Laurence Hope — A Shadow in the Sunlight," in *Under a Lilac-Bleeding Star: Travels and Travelers* (London: John Murray, 1963), 184–208, and Edward Marx, "Reviving Laurence Hope," in *Gen-*

der and Genre: Women's Poetry, 1830–1900, ed. Isobel Armstrong and Virginia Blain (London: Macmillan, 1998), 230–42.

30. Walter Pater, *The Renaissance* (reprint, 1910 ed., London: Academy, 1977), 236, 237.

31. [Thomas Hardy], "Laurence Hope," *Athenaeum,* 29 October 1904, 591.

32. Laurence Hope, *Complete Love Lyrics* (New York: Dodd, Mead, 1929), 99. All further citations will be noted parenthetically in the text and are taken from this edition.

33. Amy Woodforde-Finden, *Four Indian Love Lyrics* (London: Boosey and Hawkes, 1902).

34. Karl Beckson, *London in the 1890s: A Cultural History* (New York: Norton, 1992), 273.

35. Auguste Villiers de L'Isle-Adam, *Axel* (Paris: Cres, 1890).

36. "Another Hindoo Poet," *New Republic,* 30 December 1916, 247.

37. Harold Herbert Williams, *Modern English Writers* (1918; Dallas, Tex.: Kennikat, 1970), 142.

38. For the first quote, see Thomas Hardy to Sir George Douglas, 26 October 1904, in *The Collected Letters of Thomas Hardy,* ed. Richard Little Purdy and Michael Millgate (New York: Clarendon, 1978–88), 3:143. For the second quote, see Thomas Hardy to Arthur Symons, 23 October 1904, in Hardy, *Collected Letters,* 3:142.

39. [Arthur Symons], "The Poetry of Laurence Hope," *The Outlook: A Weekly Review of Politics, Art, Literature, and Finance,* 26 August 1905, 261–62. Symons's authorship of this unsigned review is identified in Karl Beckson, Ian Fletcher, Lawrence W. Markert, and John Stokes, comps., *Arthur Symons: A Bibliography* (Greensboro, N.C.: ELT Press, 1990), 230.

40. Symons, *Symbolist Movement,* 172, 174, 175.

41. Laurence Hope, "To Myself," in *Laurence Hope's Poems* (New York: Reynolds, 1907), 19.

42. [Hardy], "Laurence Hope."

43. Thomas Hardy, "Preface [to the posthumous poems of Laurence Hope, written by request]," [1905], Dorset County Museum.

44. Brian Hooker, "Some Springtime Verse," *Bookman* (New York) 29 (1909): 371.

45. "Western Interpreters of Eastern Verse," *Calcutta Review,* April 1904, 478.

46. Edward Marx, "Sarojini Naidu: The Nightingale as Nationalist," *Journal of Commonwealth Literature* 31, no. 1 (1996): 59.

47. Sarojini Naidu, *The Sceptred Flute: Songs of India* (New York: Dodd, Mead, 1928), 36.

48. Sara Suleri, *The Rhetoric of English India* (Chicago: University of Chicago Press, 1992).

PART III

Aesthetic Prose

Chapter 8

BARBARA T. GATES

The Aesthetic in the Natural

Gertrude Jekyll's Garden Writing

WE HAVE always assumed that something discomforting happens at the end of a century — a sense of dis-ease, of loss, of disempowerment, emotions Elaine Scarry insightfully reviews in her essay "Counting at Dusk." Working with such assumptions, Scarry ponders the ways in which the final decade of a century tends to "disempower and reinvigorate the human will," particularly in men's poetry.[1] In *Victorian Suicide* I saw this time frame as symptomatic of what Thomas Hardy called "the coming universal wish not to live."[2] In my study men in particular are shown to look at the end of a century as lifeless. But a century's end also mixes and muddles categories; it confuses people. Thus Elaine Showalter envisions the nineteenth-century fin de siècle as a time of "sexual anarchy," when gender roles and sexual identities were questioned and reconstituted and when, in terms of literature, women were disengaged from their stronghold in the novel.[3]

I believe it is time to think about why none of this cultural confusion or doom and gloom pervades the work of women like Gertrude Jekyll and Vernon Lee, for whom the end of the century marked the beginning of two thriving careers. As the writing of these women confirms, there was a strong turn-of-the-century women's aesthetic based in perceptions of nature. It stemmed from British Romanticism but reentered Victorian culture not through the cities or through Oxford — as did the decadent fin-de-siècle aestheticism most often associated with Oscar Wilde — but through female literary and domestic spaces such as travel writing and horticulture.[4] In this sense it was akin to the travel and rustic writing of W. H. Hudson, Richard Jefferies, and Francis Kilvert, but it was not nostalgic for the British rural worlds that these men or Hardy celebrated.[5] Women like Jekyll and Lee were far more theoretically involved in describing and discussing beauty per se than in representing a disappearing British way of life.

Our failure to acknowledge that garden and travel writing like theirs encodes a natural aesthetic is one factor that has prevented us from more boldly inscribing women into late-century aesthetics. This failure has also encouraged frequent reappraisals of the longer-established, male, often homoerotic aestheticism, which is far more precious and world-weary. If we take Wilde, with his pronouncements that one "should either be a work of art or wear a work of art" and that "all art is quite useless," to represent this decadent aesthetic, it becomes clear that for the Wildean art has become allure, its object artificial or unnatural rather than natural.[6]

In contrast, the women I have mentioned were eager to aestheticize the natural and to promote their aestheticism socially and/or commercially. In this sense there was little that was precious about them. Jekyll both wrote about plants and began a flourishing business selling surplus plants from her home, Munstead Wood. In her later years she spent much of her time developing this nursery and answering correspondence about plants. Lee, like Jekyll, was a prodigious writer, every few years setting a new volume before the public. Thus if it was difficult for women at the end of the century to sustain their position in the lucrative area of what Gaye Tuchman calls the "high-culture novel," they were nevertheless successful — both critically and financially — in adding to the store of knowledge of natural aesthetics.[7] They revised the paradigm of woman as nature that had obsessed the Pre-Raphaelites and classical Victorian painters and was haunting the Viennese, proposing instead a paradigm of woman *in* nature — both domesticated and wild. These two women — one in all probability a lesbian, the other a spinster — were not obsessed with aestheticizing woman's nature in the form of either demon or Mother Nature. Instead they aestheticized nature as nature, domesticatable by art.

This use of nature as the stuff of art led both of them to a different sense not only of space but of time. As Scarry has shown, at century's end there is always a need to deal with the problem of calendar time. Time as human construct gets in the way of natural time, and the cycles of the moon and the seasons give way to a preoccupation with this human construction. Re-visioning space rather than time and addressing natural cycles of the vegetable year rather than apocalyptic endings, Jekyll's writing serves as a contrast to decadent fin-de-siècle writing, preoccupied as it often was with more linear time. For Lee, whose peak writing years overlapped Jekyll's, the nature that engulfed the place of travel offered a site parallel to the garden and a similar conception of time. Sunsets and sunrises over Italy and France recur in her writing; lizards come and lizards go. Even Lee's art history becomes more cyclical than linear as she circles back to ancient sites and relates time to life cycles — including her own — rather than to the linear calendar.[8] As Scarry says, "the evening voluntary and the garden voluntary, though never confined to the ends of centuries, continually recur there."[9] I would add that in the nineteenth century they recur most often in women's writing and that this is because at the end of Darwin's century women like Jekyll and Lee utilized, reconstituted, and embraced rather than feared nature. They naturalized both time and space.

In this essay I would like to focus on just one of these two authors, Gertrude Jekyll, in order to suggest that garden writing is as important to our understanding of aesthetics as are meditations on art or art history. Unlike Lee, who roamed Europe in search of the genius of various places, Jekyll was rarely far from the nature of which she wrote. Never separated from the practical implications of the gardens that she created for herself and for others, Jekyll returned to her own garden over and over again not through the scrim of memory and not just to plan or plant but to write on location. Twice a month she would pick a spot and sit there awhile, saturating herself in its sights and scents. Then she would begin an article for the *Guardian.* What emerged from these sittings were not just how-to essays but a unique kind of aestheticized nature writing that, like Jekyll's gardens, became her hallmark — an applied aesthetics based on her successive careers as painter and gardener.

During her lifetime Jekyll wrote fourteen books and more than two thousand notes and articles on gardening that offer insights into how this kind of writing transforms the natural into the aesthetic. When she translated the site of the garden into the symbolic structure of garden writing, she was performing a double translation. A garden is a representation of nature revised by culture, a site where an aestheticized nature is already in place. Garden writing sets out further to re-vision this nature as garden linguistically, a daunting task in many ways, especially for Jekyll. First, if the garden is a locus, the garden transformed into writing must become portable, representing a place but never literally tied to it. For a garden maker like Jekyll, this transformation could be particularly stressful. Unlike Andrew Marvell, for example, who in his "Garden" describes the garden work of someone else, Jekyll at Munstead was inscribing one of her own works of art. Artistic license was of little use to her; verbal accuracy was far more essential. Second, the garden is basically mute; it speaks primarily to the eye and the nose, not the ear. And because Jekyll saw the garden as something that yielded itself more readily to the sketch or photograph than to the word, garden writing presented challenges that in many ways exceeded those of laying out the garden itself. On the other hand, unlike Lee, who struggled to aestheticize places lost, Jekyll always had as her primary achievement the garden itself, her self-created and already beautified natural space. Her writing did not have to compensate for a personal loss of nature in quite the same way as did Lee's.

I would like to begin my analysis of Jekyll's garden writing with what Jekyll called her credo, something often reiterated in her essays and volumes: "I hold the firm belief that the purpose of a garden is to give happiness and repose of mind, firstly and above all other considerations, and to give it through the representation of the best kind of pictorial beauty of flower and foliage that can be combined or invented."[10] These two concepts underpinned all of Jekyll's work. What one reads first in this credo — the purpose of the garden — suggests her understanding of a commonplace in garden theory: the garden as artifice, harking back to Eden. The garden is made to deliver us for just a moment into a state of bliss that we can never really sustain. It is a place we can repair to to restore ourselves. But what one reads in the second part of the credo suggests the even greater allure of the garden for Jekyll. A painter before she was a professional gardener, Jekyll read color into the garden as no one before her or since. The garden for her was the place of artistic intentionality, a construction that above all else called for a painter's eye. A victim of failing eyesight that made it difficult to paint or to do other close work, Jekyll discovered in the garden a place where large-scale vision could find one of its finest expressions. In her gardens nature is not simply imitated but reinterpreted in terms of what she called "garden pictures."[11] "Planting ground," Jekyll expounded, "is painting a landscape with living things; and as I hold that good gardening takes rank within the bounds of the fine arts, so I hold that to plant well needs an artist of no mean capacity. . . . [H]is living picture must be right from all points, and in all lights."[12]

Because of her dedication to educating other people to see the garden properly, Jekyll freely used pictorial representations in her works, thinking of each book as a photography assignment that was also part of a teaching assignment. In *Wall and Water Gardens* she realized that photographs of gardens might be more instructive tools for learning about gardens than were the gardens themselves. Photographs could train the eye by setting a feature into bold relief or by providing a number of angles on one prospect or place. Through a photograph Jekyll could, for example, illustrate how improvements in landscape could be effected. Then she could revision the picture, sometimes with sketches and plans, sometimes with words, as in this passage, where a photograph reconstructs a scene that is then recaptured and refined verbally:

> Often one sees some piece of water that just misses being pictorial, and yet might easily be made so. Such a case is that of the sheet of water in the illustration. A great improvement could be effected by a moderate amount of navvy's work, if it were directed to running a sharp-pointed bay into the rising ground on the right, and tipping the earth taken out into the square corner on the near right hand; saving the bed of rushy growth and planting it back on the new edge and into the bay. The exact position of the excavation would be chosen by following any indication towards a hollow form in the ground above, and by considering how its lines would harmonize with the lines already existing. The two sides of the bay would also be eased down after the manner of those hollow places one sometimes sees by pond or lake in rising ground where cattle or wild creatures come down to drink.[13]

Jekyll was versatile with her use of photographs and at ease with a variety of audiences. In a later book, *Children and Gardens,* she photographed and whimsically described a love second only to the garden itself — the cats that inhabited her garden:

> One bank is covered with Cerastium; this [Tabby] thinks is just suitable for his bed. I often find him there, and though it is not quite the best thing for the Cerastium I cannot help admiring his beautiful rich tabby coat, with its large black clouds, so well set off by the velvety grey of the little downy plant.[14]

As here, artistic arrangement, color, and composition were ever Jekyll's primary concerns. Aesthetics were appropriate for children, as in this photographic and verbal revel, just as they were for landscape gardeners in the detailed description of how to make a body of water more pictorial. Tabby in the garden, his cloudlike patches of black set off by the gray cerastium, is an aesthetic portrait, a Whistlerian study in gray and black. Garden writing allowed Jekyll an alternative canvas.

Carefully evolved narrative strategies enhanced Jekyll's painting in words. In her most mature and beautifully written garden book, *Colour Schemes for the Flower Garden,* Jekyll continued to develop the art of word picturing along with the art of the imaginary walk. One technique gives us pause for taking in the static pictures that Jekyll wants us to linger with for the moment, the other kinesthetically moves her narrative forward. For example, she opens chapter 1 with a delivery of the "year's first complete picture of flower-effect in the woodland landscape":

> a place among silver-trunked Birches, with here and there the splendid richness of masses of dark Holly. The rest of the background above eye-level is of the warm bud-colour of the summer-leafing trees, and, below, the fading rust of the now nearly flattened fronds of last year's Bracken, and the still paler drifts of leaves from neighbouring Oaks and Chestnuts. The sunlight strikes brightly upon the silver stems of the Birches, and casts their shadows clear-cut across the grassy woodland ride. The grass is barely green as yet, but has the faint winter green of herbage not yet grown and still powdered with the short remnants of the fine-leaved, last-year-mown heath grasses. Brown leaves still hang on young Beech and Oak. The trunks of the Spanish Chestnuts are elephant-grey, a notable contrast to the sudden, vivid shafts of the Birches. Some groups of the pale early Pyrenean Daffodil gleam level on the ground a little way forward.[15]

With utter specificity, Jekyll's hyphenated adjectives direct our eyes into the scene, and her colors, though subdued, are intricately hued. The effect is again Whistler-like, an arrangement in browns, silvers, and silvery greens. But once we have this picture etched in our minds, we are moved on through a kind of garden gallery to a wider field of observation, and Jekyll begins our walk: through "dark masses of Rhododendron" on to a lawn, into a gray herb garden, on past some shrub clumps, and to a bulb garden. A plan of the bulb garden helps us on our way, as does a photograph of a magnolia. Successively, the colors brighten in the text:

> The colour scheme begins with the pink of *Megasea ligulata,* and with the lower-toned pinks of *Fumaria bulbosa* and the Dog-tooth violets. At the back of these are Lent Hellebores of dull red colouring, agreeing charmingly with the colour of the bulbs. A few white Lent Hellebores are at the end; they have turned to greenish white by the time the rather late *Scilla amoena* is in bloom. Then comes a brilliant patch of pure blue with white — *Scilla sibirica* and white Hyacinths . . . a long drift of white Crocus comes next.[16]

I have lingered here in the garden that opens *Colour Schemes* to indicate how very carefully one's eye is controlled in a mature Jekyll text. But this is all a trompe l'oeil. Jekyll realizes that her reader will never see the garden as she has painted it. Her text offers a Marianne Moore garden, "an imaginary garden with real toads in it," and Jekyll is a "literalist of the imagination."[17] What Jekyll establishes here then is a sense of immediacy that represents *her* having been in this place at this time. The innocence, the directness of all of this vanish when we begin to analyze exactly what is *not* going on here. Her readers are in all probability not in southern England in a bulb garden, nor were they there in her own time. Jekyll never lost sight of the illusions created by garden writing. This enabled her to describe not only the gardens she knew but the gardens she would never have nor ever make. In *Colour Schemes,* for example, she mentions that she does not have a rocky hillside in full sun and so cannot have something she can easily envision: "a rock garden on an immense scale, planted as Nature plants, with not many different things at a time."[18] The narrative of the spring garden in *Colour Schemes* was successfully mediated through rhetoric in much the same way as is Jekyll's nonexistent rock garden. In both cases we are in the presence of splashes of writing, not splashes of flowers, but Jekyll nevertheless works hard to bond her reader to her illusory garden spaces.

For all of her skill in writing the garden, Jekyll sometimes became frustrated with verbal representation. The imprecision of language in representing color caused her particular distress. In *Wood and Garden* she tells us that to practice the sorcery of word craft she placed herself before a juniper whose stems were clothed in lichen: "Standing before it (the juniper) and trying to put the colour into words, one repeats, again and again, pale-green silver — palest silvery green!"[19] Here she makes the reader work to capture this color in a mindscape. Then we authorize her because of her struggles; and so her verbal picture insists itself upon her readers. Her thoughts on the color gold illustrate another way in which this technique works. Again in *Wood and Garden* Jekyll emphasizes that no flower "matches or even approaches the true colour of gold" and derides the use of the word to describe what she calls "bright yellow." Pollen-covered anthers or dying beech leaves may approximate gold, but even they are not gold. But, she goes on, "in literature it is quite another matter; when the poet or imaginative writer says, 'a field of golden buttercups,' or 'a golden sunset,' he is quite right, because he appeals to our artistic perception, and in such case only uses the word as an image of something that is rich and sumptuous and glowing."[20] An image, not reality. All this time Jekyll is, of course, educating other eyes to work like hers in terms of both gardens and garden texts, for she believed that her work might train other human minds "to perception of beauty," so that they might "find more opportunity of exercising this precious gift."[21]

In her later books Jekyll was determined to educate her readers' eyes still further — to the tricks of perception. In *Colour Schemes* she shows how easily a gardener can manipulate color to fool the eye. After describing how an eye can become filled with gray and blue, she then shows what happens when it avidly seeks the brilliance of yellows, then "scarlets, blood-reds, clarets," and then yellows again. "Now the eye," she says, "has again become saturated, this time with the rich colouring, and has therefore, by the law of complementary colour, acquired a strong appetite for the greys and purples. These therefore assume an appearance of brilliancy that they would not have had without the preparation provided by their recently received complementary colour."[22] In such passages readers are not just witnesses to her gardening, as they are in the word pictures and walks; they are also potential painters of gardens. If Jekyll attempts to activate the artistic potential of the reader, she also reminds us how the same trompe l'oeil can be demonstrated scientifically, through colored words.[23] If we look for a long time at a word written in red and then shut our eyes, this same word changes to green in our mind's eye. When Jekyll paints with highly colored words, something of the same effect takes place: we are being impressed by the power of her expert gaze. Jekyll's words gain color through her knowledge of how the reader's mind works, and we in turn respond to passages like this one about the leaves of tree peonies:

> Their colour is peculiar, being bluish, but pervaded with a suspicion of pink or pinkish-bronze, sometimes of a metallic quality that faintly recalls some of the variously-coloured alloys of metal that the Japanese bronze-workers make and use with such consummate skill.[24]

In case we have come too completely to trust Jekyll's consummate skill in representing color through colorful words, in *Colour Schemes* she disillusions us when she muses:

> It is a curious thing that people will sometimes spoil some garden project for the sake of a word. For instance, a blue garden, for beauty's sake, may be hungering for a group of white Lilies, or for something of palest lemon-yellow, but it is not allowed to have it because it is called a blue garden, and there must be no flowers in it but blue flowers. . . . Surely the business of the blue garden is to be beautiful first, and then just as blue as may be consistent with its best possible beauty.[25]

The word is not the thing; naming is not being, nor does it bring anything other than words into being — and this includes colorful words. In the misunderstood blue garden word-deluded planners have mistaken the sign of the thing for the thing itself. Naming has distanced them from gardening. In this same chapter Jekyll returns to the word "gold," which had troubled her in her first book, *Wood and Garden.* Now an expert with words as well as with gardens, she relishes the metaphoric potential of the word and feels free to use it as poets might:

> The word "gold" in itself is, of course, an absurdity; no growing leaf or flower has the least resemblance to the colour of gold. But the word may be used because it has passed into the language with a commonly accepted meaning.[26]

Even we, the uninitiated in color and gardens, may use it. Words like "botany," as she tells children in *Children and Gardens,* are nothing to fear.[27] For Jekyll naming becomes a tool; she wants to keep it clean and sharp like a garden spade in order best to use it, not to be intimidated by it.

If Jekyll penetrates the power of language in order to present garden pictures — the second part of the credo with which I began my discussion — she also unmasks the power of the garden to instill the paradisial rest that she describes in the first part of that credo. If a feeling of paradise resides in the garden, it is a feeling brought about not just by the work of words, as I have been suggesting, but also by hard physical labor. Throughout her texts Jekyll discusses the physical aspects of gardening. With an air of Victorian classism, she assumes the role of overseer of workmen who need to be monitored at every turn by the educated eye and mind of a Gertrude Jekyll — or her intended, late-Victorian reader. Gardens do not just happen. They are planned, and then they are executed, and then maintained. Nor are they free from wild nature's encroachments. Sometimes wonderful effects appear that the gardener never could have imagined, as plants creep out of cracks or wander off into a different garden.

Just as words give only the illusion of gardens, gardens give only the illusion of paradise:

> The early summer air is of the perfect temperature, the soft coo of the wood-dove comes down from the near wood, the nightingale sings almost overhead, but — either human happiness may never be quite complete, or else one is not philosophic enough to contemn life's lesser evils, for — oh, the midges![28]

Here Jekyll resists her own constructions and deflates both of the premises in her credo. She eschews garden pictures, instead substituting images of sound and feeling, and sets out to undermine the illusion of paradise that she has created. Embedded in Jekyll's love of the arts was an understanding that it is the puppeteer who pulls the strings. As she reminds us in *Wood and Garden,* "it is not the paint that makes the picture, but the brain and heart and hand of the man who uses it."[29] This multitalented woman, who was never above filling in her gardens' bare spaces with potted plants and who counseled careful concealment of all garden props and stakes, was an aesthete in three media. All art must be illusion, said this discerning fin-de-siècle painter turned gardener turned writer. In her garden writing as in her gardening, Jekyll never lost sight of the fact that although the garden was art made from living things, it was unredemptive and reconstructible — nature understood and nature controlled. For her land did not resist aestheticizing. She had put the genius in the locus.

Notes

An earlier version of this essay appears as a portion of chapter 6 in my book *Kindred Nature: Victorian and Edwardian Women Embrace the Living World* (Chicago: University of Chicago Press, 1998).

1. Elaine Scarry, ed., *Fins de Siècle: English Poetry in 1590, 1690, 1790, 1890, 1990* (Baltimore, Md.: Johns Hopkins University Press, 1995), 10.

2. Barbara T. Gates, *Victorian Suicide: Mad Crimes and Sad Histories* (Princeton, N.J.: Princeton University Press, 1989), chap. 8.

3. Elaine Showalter, *Sexual Anarchy: Gender and Culture at the Fin de Siècle* (New York: Viking, 1990).

4. For Oxford aestheticism, see Linda Dowling, *Hellenism and Homosexuality in Victorian Oxford* (Ithaca, N.Y.: Cornell University Press, 1994).

5. See Glen Cavaliero, *The Rural Tradition in the English Novel, 1900–1939* (Totowa, N.J.: Rowman and Littlefield, 1977).

6. Oscar Wilde, *The First Collected Edition of the Works of Oscar Wilde,* ed. Robert Ross (1908–22; reprint, London: Routledge, 1993), 14:177, 12:xi.

7. Gaye Tuchman and Nina E. Fortin, *Edging Women Out: Victorian Novelists, Publishers, and Social Change* (New Haven, Conn.: Yale University Press, 1989), 5.

8. Vernon Lee [Violet Paget], *The Spirit of Rome: Leaves from a Diary* (London: John Lane, 1906).

9. Scarry, 23.

10. Gertrude Jekyll, *Wall and Water Gardens* (1901; reprint, Salem, N.H.: Ayer, 1983), 141.

11. Gertrude Jekyll, *Wood and Garden* (1899; reprint, Salem, N.H.: Ayer, 1983), 197.

12. Ibid., 156–57.

13. Jekyll, *Wall and Water Gardens,* 159.

14. Gertrude Jekyll, *Children and Gardens* (London: Country Life, 1908), 169.

15. Gertrude Jekyll, *Colour Schemes for the Flower Garden* (1908; reprint, Salem, N.H.: Ayer, 1983), 1–2.

16. Ibid., 6.

17. Marianne Moore, "Poetry," in *The Complete Poems of Marianne Moore* (New York: Viking, 1967), ll. 24, 20.

18. Jekyll, *Colour Schemes,* 40.

19. Jekyll, *Wood and Garden,* 31.

20. Ibid., 222.

21. Ibid., 10.

22. Jekyll, *Colour Schemes,* 40.

23. For a study of women in relation to science, particularly as popularizers of science, see Barbara T. Gates and Ann B. Shteir, *Natural Eloquence: Women Reinscribe Science* (Madison: University of Wisconsin Press, 1997).

24. Jekyll, *Wood and Garden,* 73.

25. Jekyll, *Colour Schemes,* 98–99.

26. Ibid., 108.

27. Jekyll, *Children and Gardens,* 86.

28. Jekyll, *Wood and Garden,* 220.

29. Ibid., 157.

Chapter 9

ALISON VICTORIA MATTHEWS

Aestheticism's True Colors

The Politics of Pigment in Victorian Art, Criticism, and Fashion

A symphony of blues and red —
The broad lagoon, and overhead
Sunset, a sanguine banner, spread.
Fretty of azure and pure gules
Are sea, sky, city, stagnant pools:
You, by my side, within the boat,
Imperially purple float,
Beneath a burning sail, straight on
Into the west's vermilion.
— John Addington Symonds,
"In the Key of Blue"

There is now a new class who dress after pictures, and ask, when they buy a new gown not — "Will it wash?" — or, "Will it wear?" — but "Will it paint?"
— Mrs. Oliphant, *Dress*

On a marble bench overlooking the sea, a young woman swathed in diaphanous robes lies caught in a web of sleep. Her eyes are closed, her body traces a serpentine line across the canvas. Oleander blossoms drape over the parapet and terrace adorned with Grecian scrollwork. Yet what first strikes the beholder contemplating Lord Leighton's *Flaming June* of 1895 is not the woman herself but the painting's brilliant palette.[1] The canvas is a symphony of flamelike oranges, golds, and ochers. Subtle hues play across the maiden's recumbent form; she dissolves into her surroundings until woman and world become one. As viewers, we are captivated by the gorgeous voluptuousness of this timeless idyll: no jarring contrasts of tint, no angular lines disturb the movement of our eye around the canvas. In

Leighton's painted universe all is harmonious, delicate, suffused with a gilded splendor.

Seductive beauty of palette and lack of narrative drive make *Flaming June* typical of late-Victorian art. The painter's insistence on the primacy of formal elements recalls the rhetoric of aesthetic criticism. In a discussion of Venetian Renaissance painting, Walter Pater wrote: "In its primary aspect, a great picture has no more definite message for us than an accidental play of sunlight and shadow for a moment, on the wall or floor: is itself, in truth, a space of such fallen light, caught as the colours are caught in an Eastern carpet, but refined upon, and dealt with more subtly and exquisitely than by nature itself."[2] Are we to read Leighton's canvas along Paterian lines, as a flickering dance of light and color, caught for a moment on the canvas? Or can we make more of both form and content? As happens in the paintings of society artists such as Alfred Moore, Leighton's images construct a specific type of allegorical femininity. They present the viewer with an endless stream of unnamed, interchangeable female figures, as bland and indistinguishable as the gaggle of toga-clad maidens descending Edward Burne-Jones's *The Golden Stairs.* The similarly abstracted *Flaming June* both elides the distinction between figure and ground and denies the individuality of its subject. The woman's body becomes a vehicle for the play of gemlike hues, her eyes are closed: she is unable to see or enjoy the radiant colors that envelop her. The slumbering woman is pure object: the passive recipient of the gaze and the polar opposite of the aesthete, whose supreme powers of vision this canvas celebrates.

Though Leighton, Burne-Jones, and Moore were influential figures in the late-Victorian art world, their canvases represent only one strain among many in nineteenth-century contests over gender and color. Their paintings of aestheticized women came at the end of a century of significant changes in color theory, technology, and consumerism. While scientific theories were beginning to locate color perception in the subjective experience of the beholder, technological innovations in the chemical industry led to the production of the first synthetic dyestuffs. These inexpensive aniline dyes made brightly tinted fabrics available to a broad cross section of the female population for the first time. Women soon became sophisticated consumers of these chemical hues, disseminating their knowledge through fashion publications and style manuals. In the face of this female appropriation of color, male aesthetes, artists, and poets used optical, physiological, and evolutionary theories to reclaim color as a domain of masculine expertise. The question of color and gender is further nuanced by its important role in the culture of homosexuality. Color provided a seemingly neutral, inherently sexless vocabulary with which aesthetes such as Vernon Lee and John Addington Symonds could paint their homoerotic desire. However, the same language that offered Lee and Symonds a safe narrative vantage was deeply inflected with the class rhetoric of "artistic" color. Through an analysis of color in late-nineteenth-century painting, literature, fashion, and aesthetics, I will try to tease out some of the complex and often contesting strands of meaning occasioned by shifts in the material bases of color, shifts that often perpetuated larger class and gender inequalities.

The writings of female aesthetes offer a strong counterpoint to the faceless seriality of Leighton's and Moore's paintings of aesthetic women. In the novel *Miss Brown* by Vernon Lee (a pseudonym for the lesbian author Violet Paget), Hamlin, an artist-aesthete figure, sketches a poor, half-Italian nursemaid, Anne Brown, and falls in love with her. He brings her to England, introduces her to the artistic set, and effects her transformation into an aesthete. In one passage Hamlin designs the heroine a dress that recalls the Flaming June's attire:

> Miss Brown was by this time tolerably accustomed to the eccentric garb of aesthetic circles, and she firmly believed that it was the only one which a self-respecting woman might wear; but when she saw the dress which Hamlin had designed for her, she could not help shrinking back in dismay. It was of that Cretan silk, not much thicker than muslin, which is woven in minute wrinkles of palest yellowy white; it was made, it seemed to her, more like a night-gown than anything else, shapeless and yet clinging with large folds, and creases like those of damp sculptor's drapery, or the garments of Mantegna's women.[3]

Hamlin is well pleased with the results of his collaboration with the Lyceum's stage dressmaker. He tells Anne how lovely she looks in his gown, a veritable Grecian sculpture in silk. However, when he leaves the room, Miss Brown questions the ravishing tableau that Hamlin has orchestrated. Not content to be a mere artist's model, she breaks her pose and vents her frustration: "Anne sat down. Why did that dress make such a difference to him? Why did he care so much more for her because she had it on? Did he care for her only as a sort of live picture? she thought bitterly."[4] Her angry musings question the aesthete's preference for surface beauty over emotional content. The novel as a whole narrates Hamlin's obsessive concern for Anne's Italianate beauty, her quaint aspect: as she puts it, her value as a "live picture." In one passage he sketches her in a verbal palette, describing her as she appears to him in an Italian church: "She was standing on the altar steps, whose orange-red baize cloth threw up faint yellowish tints on to her long dress of some kind of soft white wool, while the crimson brocade on wall and column formed a sort of dull red background. In the mixed light of the yellow tapers and the grey incense-laden sunbeams, her face acquired a diaphanous pallor, as if of a halo surrounding it."[5] Like the Flaming June, or Pater's "accidental play of sunlight and shadow" caught in an Eastern carpet, Anne melts into her surroundings as the whims of Hamlin's fantasy fashion her by turns into a Pre-Raphaelite angel and a picture of ancient beauty clad in creamy Cretan silk.

The aesthete's self-conscious orchestration of painterly coloristic symphonies contrasts with the realist painter's or poet's attempts to transcribe mimetically nature's local colors. This transition from realism to aestheticism parallels a larger shift in color theory and technology. In his influential book *Techniques of the Observer,* Jonathan Crary contends that the transition from Enlightenment to nineteenth-century concepts of color saw an epistemic rupture between color and its referents in the natural world. He writes: "Color, as the primary object of vision, is now atopic, cut off from any spatial referent."[6] In 1810 Johann Wolfgang von Goethe's publication of the *Theory of Colours* challenged Newtonian optical theories of local color. Unlike Newton, Goethe situated color not in the external world but in the subjective experience of the viewer: "Let the observer look steadfastly on a small coloured object and let it be taken away after a time while his eyes remain unmoved; the spectrum of another colour will then be visible on the white plane. . . . [I]t arises from an image which now belongs to the eye."[7] In optical theories at least, Crary argues, color had shifted from an absolute to a relative value, located in the eye of the beholder.

Though Crary traces the shift from objective to subjective models of color vision in the domain of optical theory, he passes over a dramatic change in the substance of color in the nineteenth century. The perceptual separation of color from content and its emergence as a formal, atopic phenomenon was contemporary with a complete revolution in color's material bases. The first synthetic dyes were produced at the beginning of the century, and as chemical industries began to search in earnest for new hues, traditional recipes for colors were replaced by scientific formulas.

The major catalyst for these technological innovations was the textile industry. Most natural pigments, such as the indigo and madder red used to dye military uniforms, were relatively expensive and time-consuming to produce, and many hues were derived from plants or minerals that had to be imported to England.

The discovery by William Henry Perkin (1838–1907) of aniline dyes in England in 1856 represents the final stage in nineteenth-century transformations in color technology.[8] Because the British dye industry was at the forefront of international production until the end of the century, its colors became a source of national pride in progress; previously foreign pigments could now be replicated through native ingenuity.[9] For example, dye works such as Levenstein and Sons at Blackley and Middleton exported its aniline colors through depots in Paris, Vienna, and Boston.

Artificial mauve, or Roseine, the first aniline dye to come on the market, was produced in 1856, soon followed by magenta, or Fuschine, and an entire spectrum of chemical colors. By the end of the 1860s most natural colors could be reproduced synthetically. Aniline dyes were especially vivid, even lurid, and became comparatively inexpensive to produce. They proved fairly colorfast in dyeing silk, wool, and cotton and were quickly adopted by the booming textile industry. With his commercial recipes for new hues, the industrial chemist had superseded the painter as the colorist of the nineteenth century.

The democratization of color also affected the fine arts. Transparent dyes or lakes produced for textiles could be mixed with a mineral base and made into artists' pigments.[10] Firms specializing in artists' colors, such as W. and T. Reeves and Winsor and Newton, prospered as the number of amateur painters increased. Their products were marketed and distributed through professional "colourmen," who stocked and sold the products of several firms.

The price difference between natural and synthetic pigments becomes evident when one examines two price lists from the early 1870s. According to the 1874 price list of Newman's artists' supplies, small cakes of madder red and pure scarlet watercolor cost five and four shillings, respectively, as opposed to a cake of mauve, which sold for only one. A cake of Newman's pure ultramarine cost the tidy sum of thirty-one shillings.[11] By contrast, Levenstein's aniline dyes were sold not by the cake but by the pound. Reds were among the least expensive colors in their spectrum, and in 1871 an entire pound of scarlet cost a scant seven shillings, while similar amounts of Violet de Paris (another name for mauve) and magenta could be obtained for twenty-five and ten shillings, respectively. Hence the cheapness of modern synthetic dyes was reflected in the aesthete's disdain for them as common, gaudy colors. The metaphoric associations of color were inextricably tied to its value on the market.

Class distinctions are clear in literary constructions of women's taste in color. In "Lizerunt," Arthur Morrison's working-class narrative first published in *Tales of Mean Streets* (1894), the heroine dreams of owning the fashion accessories of a "lady." This fantasy scenario involves the possession of a gaudy plush hat: "Now, it is not decent for a factory girl from Limehouse to go bank-holidaying under any but a hat of plush, very high in the crown, of a *wild* blue or a *wilder* green, and carrying withal an ostrich feather, pink or scarlet or what not" (italics mine).[12] Lizerunt (a contraction of the name Elizabeth Hunt) marries a bully who buys her such a hat: "she went away with a paper bag and the reddest of all the plushes and the bluest of all the feathers; . . . a hat for which no girl need have hesitated to sell her soul."[13] The heroine does trade soul and body for a vulgar, presumably synthetically dyed blue-trimmed scarlet hat. The moral of Lizerunt's misplaced bourgeois aspirations could not be more clear: after her marriage the husband who bought the hat beats her and eventually turns the young mother out into the streets to earn her living as a prostitute.

Millinery was a particularly classed aspect of female attire and a marker of taste. In *The Art of Beauty* Mrs. Hugh Reginald Haweis cautions her readers to be wary of the vulgar sensibilities of milliners: "With regard to the milliner, ladies should remember that by trusting a milliner's 'taste'(?) they are merely playing into the hands of various tradesmen whose interest is to sell their goods, be they good or bad."[14] The link between "bad" colors, such as Lizerunt's wild scarlet, and the rampant consumerism of the lower classes is a hallmark of the pseudoscience of physiological aesthetics. Grant Allen's description of red's irresistible appeal to "primitive tribes, the young and coarse-natured" in his 1892 book *The Colour-Sense* is a case in point: "Of course, we must further remember that red forms the favourite color, not only of primitive tribes, but also of the young and coarse-natured among our European nations. The Central African is bribed with yards of red calico . . . the baby in its cradle jumps at a bunch of red rags; the London serving-maid trims her cap with scarlet ribbons, and admires the soldier's coat as the most beautiful of human costumes."[15] Allen naturalizes the choice of red as the favorite color of the central African, the baby, and the London serving maid. However, he does not mention that the yards of red calico, bunches of rags, and scarlet ribbons they admire and jump at are cheap fabrics dyed with aniline colors. While the baby and primitive are lumped together for their unreflexive, physiological response to bright colors, the London serving maid, like Lizerunt, is criticized for mimicking her social betters. Like elaborate hats, ribbons were expensive, and their color and arrangement became a marker of sartorial refinement. Though the maid could not afford to trim her cap with truly tasteful ribbons, she still invested in ladylike attire. The synthetically tinted ribbons were probably the only trimmings within reach of the servant's pocketbook, not simply the ones that gratified her "coarse" desires for finery.

The maid's admiration of the soldier's red coat is explicitly classed, and military men's pretensions to finery are satirized in William S. Gilbert and Arthur Sullivan's operetta *Patience* (1881). Contrary to the expectations of the queen's soldiers, the aesthetic ladies Ella, Angela, and Saphir turn up their noses at the officers' bright uniforms and Hessian boots. The only emotion the military men arouse is scorn. In the song "When I first put this uniform on," the soldiers complain of the inefficacy of their "freely gold-laced" outfits:

> I said, when I first put it on,
> "It is plain to the veriest dunce, that every beauty
> Will feel it her duty
> To yield to its glamour at once."[16]

When the women fail to swoon before their splendid uniforms, the soldiers attract their attention by donning aesthetic garb and posing in uncomfortable "stained-glass attitudes."[17] The ladies immediately find them "perceptively intense and consummately utter" and resolve to marry them. Due to the sophisticated tastes of the aesthetic ladies, the soldiers are unable to find mates until they shed their scarlet plumage and adopt the "tasteful" and subdued colors of aesthetic dress.

Though Ella, Angela, and Saphir are parodied as sophisticated enough consumers on the marriage market to reject the glaring red of the officers' Hessians, not all classes were thought to possess even these limited powers of discrimination. According to physiological theories, the vulgar mass of humanity lacked not only the nervous constitution to distinguish and appreciate subtle variations of hue but the vocabulary with which to name them. Allen stated that the average person can neither recognize nor describe many shades: "Six colours are commonly recognized by the popular mind — black and white, red and blue, green and yellow. . . . Even the educated only speak of scarlet, crimson, lilac and purple under exceptional circumstances, as in literary composition or for technical purposes; but to the mass of mankind these lesser distinctions of language are wholly unknown."[18] At a time when more and more women were becoming mass-market consumers, such a statement was both fundamentally illogical and patently untrue. Nowhere is female appropriation of a sophisticated color vocabulary more apparent than in fashion publications, where nuances of hue and fabric are discussed at length. A whole genre of fashion manuals arose in order to help women coordinate their wardrobes. For example, the book *Dress as a Fine Art* (1854) was written by Mrs. Mary Merrifield, an art expert and polymath who translated medieval and Renaissance texts on painting, dyeing, and preparing colors and wrote several practical artistic guides. Yet women's discussions of color, expert as they were, were no more exempt from class rhetoric than Allen's physiological aesthetics. Aniline mauve and magenta, the first synthetic pigments available commercially in England, provide an index for shifting attitudes toward color in female dress from the high Victorian era to the fin de siècle.

When mauve was introduced as a synthetic color in 1856, the natural vegetable color called mauve, derived from the mauve flower, was already popular in France. In 1857 it was "the rage of Paris, where it [was] an especial favourite of the Empress Eugenie."[19] The *Illustrated London News* of 3 April 1858 noted that Queen Victoria wore this highly fashionable and "beautiful hue on the occasion of the marriage of the Princess Royal, and at the last levee her Majesty's train was of mauve velvet."[20] The Perkin firm that developed the synthetic dye was quick to capitalize on purple's aristocratic connotations and the natural mauve dye's popularity with French and English royalty. It marketed cheap aniline mauve under the trade name Tyrian Purple, a costly dye derived from the murex shell and used for the togas of Roman emperors. Despite the firm's pretentious appellation for the color, purple could no longer lay claim to its status as a color of royal privilege: everyone could afford to wear the new synthetic mauve, and for several years it became all the rage in London.

In 1863 the *Englishwoman's Domestic Magazine* celebrated the introduction of "splendid" synthetic hues and advertised a ball toilet of "magenta silk, trimmed with puffed tulle or tarlatane at the bottom, dotted at regular intervals with magenta roses . . . [with] the skirt being edged with magenta ribbon" as the height of fashion.[21] Yet fifteen years later, in her aesthetic guide to fashion and furnishings, Mrs. Haweis advises women to "carefully eschew" magenta, "as it ruins the complexion and will not amalgamate with surrounding colors."[22] In her desire to avoid clashing color combinations, Mrs. Haweis emphasizes the antagonism between synthetic and natural dyes, describing magenta and mauve as "members of an alien tribe that refuse to hold any intercourse with strangers."[23]

In her characterization of these colors as members of different tribes Mrs. Haweis uses a racial metaphor to gloss over the class dynamics operating in women's selection of fashionable shades. However, George Du Maurier's *Punch* cartoon "True Artistic Refinement" of 1877 reveals and satirizes aestheticism's coloristic snobbery. As the subtitle puns, the male protagonist has "died of a colour, in aesthetic pain." Du Maurier's image represents one of a series of caricatures of the aesthetic movement, featuring such fictional aesthetes as Jellaby Postlethwaite and the painter Maudle. Small visual cues, such as the painting of a Venetian canal and gondola hanging on the wall, mark this household as superficially fashionable and refined. The hostess accosts Mr. Mirabel, a young aesthete, in order to introduce him to one of her female guests. He foils her attempts by refusing to go down to dinner with anyone wearing "Mauve Twimmings in her skirt and Magenta Wibbons in her hair." Du Maurier emphasizes the aesthete's alienation: the woman is centrally positioned, while the monocled aesthete assumes a marginal stance at the far right of the image. The aloof young man maintains both a physical and social distance from a woman whose color choices and fashion sense, as the caption makes clear, cause him aesthetic pain. Du Maurier ridicules Mr. Mirabel's pretensions to coloristic superiority. The aesthete feels as entitled to pass judgment on a woman's color sense as he would on a painting, even though the selection of his own smart black and white evening attire did not require a similar talent.

As the snubs against mauve and magenta made by Mrs. Haweis and Du Maurier's Mr. Mirabel demonstrate, both genders were implicated in the coloristic elitism of aestheticism. In the face of color's increased accessibility to all classes, male and female aesthetes alike rejected the gaudy cheapness of synthetic hues. That even working-class women were beginning to encroach on aesthetic territory forced the connoisseur to retrench and reclaim coloristic expertise as a personal preserve. He or she accomplished this end by proving his or her ability to distinguish between the finest nuances of color in language or pigment. Scientific theories reinforced the aesthete's sense of superiority, for they made the capacity to discriminate between subtle shades a mark of the highest intelligence. For

George Du Maurier, "True Artistic Refinement," *Punch,* 1877.
Reprinted in *Society Pictures* (London: Bradbury, Agnew, 1877).
Courtesy of Stanford University Art Library.

example, the Victorian psychologist Alexander Bain wrote: "The basis, or fundamental peculiarity of the intellect is the discrimination, or the feeling of difference between consecutive, or co-existing impressions. Nothing more fundamental can possibly be assigned as the defining mark of intelligence."[24] He adds: "To feel distinctly a faint transition, *as of a slight gradation of tint,* or a small alteration of the pitch of a sound, is the mark of a brain discriminative by nature."[25] While the governess admired the latest shade of Violet de Paris in *Godey's Ladies Book,* the aesthete cultivated the more artistic connotations of sanguine and verdigris in poetry, prose, or painting.

Though aesthetes scorned the indiscriminate consumerism and gaudy tastes of the lower classes, aestheticism itself was but an elite form of consumerism, though it attempted to conceal the agency of the buyer. Aestheticism's commodification of color becomes clear when the aesthetic lady is given practical shopping advice, as in Mrs. Haweis's *Art of Dress.* Artistic colors are deliberately divested of their material connotations and prized for their effects on the soul rather than their drain on the pocketbook (although their relative costliness is acknowledged by Haweis).[26] For women who are not naturally gifted with coloristic talent she suggests: "The best rule for selection is, shut your eyes when you see a staring colour — dazzling blue, pink, violet, green, scarlet, what not. But when you see a colour which is moderately dull in tone, and so far indescribable that you question whether it is blue or green, green or brown, red or yellow, grapple it to your *soul* with hooks of steel; *it is an artistic colour,* and will mix well with almost any other artistic colour" (italics mine).[27] Hence the tenets of aestheticism divorce something as material as a dyed item of clothing from both its linguistic referent (it is "indescribable") and consumerism: its status as a luxury good is concealed by aestheticist rhetoric. The aesthetic consumer does not leap at red ribbons or sell her soul for a plush hat. In a phrase that makes reference to Shakespearean language and assumes a highly literate female public, the aesthetic woman is instructed to clasp artistic colors to her soul, not her bosom. Unlike the unfortunate Lizerunt, the upper-class lady is able to remain unscathed by her desire for attractive finery, for her interest in color is ostensibly spiritual rather than self-centered.

However, according to Allen's theories, the taste for subtly hued clothing, no matter how artistic, was still a lower evolutionary form of aestheticism, slavishly tied to personal adornment. By contrast, female aesthetes such as Haweis wished to foster the idea of women's agency and even artistry in the pursuit of tasteful clothing. She suggested that women see dressing as an art form akin to painting: "If everybody who could hold a pencil were suddenly called upon to paint a picture, there would be only a few out of every score . . . who would betray any sense of grace, colour or design. What is true of painting is also true of dress. We need not all paint, but we have all got to dress, and the sooner dress is recognized by our women as an art product, the better . . . they will be able to apparel themselves."[28]

In the face of such assertions, late-Victorian critics tried to maintain their monopoly over the purchase and appreciation of painting, which represented a more disinterested level of aesthetic consumerism. Only the wealthiest citizens could afford to own significant painting collections, and their tastes are reflected in canvases such as Alfred Moore's *Sapphires.* These images attempt to assert both the coloristic sophistication of their owners and a renewed form of control over the female body. *Sapphires,* exhibited at the opening of the Grosvenor Gallery in 1877, is typical of the works enjoyed and purchased by this new breed of connoisseur. Like most of his works, Moore's painting presents a statuesque woman clothed in vaguely Grecian attire. This one sports a pale-blue gown, a pearl-and-sapphire necklace, and a blue-and-red turban. Unlike Haweis's female aesthete, this painted beauty is not an active agent but an object consumed, posing languidly in a subdued atmosphere of which she is barely conscious. The Sapphire is all form and no content, an ethereal and inhuman woman-jewel. Moore's choice of the gem sapphire for his title is revealing. Havelock Ellis, the sexologist, describes it in his 1896 lecture "The Colour-Sense in Literature" as not merely an "artistic" but a "metaphorical" color, counting it with "Emerald" and "Argent."[29] In more literal terms sapphires were the most expensive and rare of jewels.[30] By acquiring the Moore painting and hanging it in his home, its owner was able to assume the socioeconomic status conferred by the possession of sapphires, while asserting his coloristic sophistication and the abstract qualities of his dazzling gemlike work.

In *The Renaissance: Studies in Art and Poetry* Pater famously describes the attitude the aesthete ought to take toward life and art: "While all melts under our feet, we may well catch at any exquisite passion . . . or any stirring of the senses, strange dyes, strange colours and curious odours, or work of the artist's hand, or the face of one's friend."

Like the metaphoric orange blaze of Leighton's *Flaming June,* the glitter of strange dyes and strange colors in Moore's *Sapphires* is meant to stir the senses of the appreciative aesthete. The frozen beauty of the painting's jeweled hues is intended to induce a state of sensory ecstasy, to make viewers "burn always with [a] hard, gemlike flame," according to Pater's famous dictum for success in life.[31] Yet as I have argued throughout this article, in their concrete forms these metaphoric colors and gems carry unmistakable economic ramifications, as do texts, apparel, and art objects. Vernon Lee describes the crowds contemplating expensive gems at the 1900 Paris World's Fair: "I do not really hate all the various vulgar *divertissements* so long as anyone is diverted; and I can even hope that it is not merely horrid covetousness, but in some simple breasts a vague fairy-story wonder which gathers the sordid multitudes round the cases of diamonds and rubies and emeralds. People distil the poetry needful for healthy life out of many very different things, and most appeals to the imaginations are, after all, better than nothing."[32] Though Lee speaks from the vantage of one who disdains consumerist desires, she allows for the possibility of poetic feeling in all humankind. Despite her position among the ranks of the leisure classes, her hopes that these fascinated crowds are at least partially motivated by imaginative wonder are democratic in spirit at least.

The aesthetic movement set itself above the masses and marked class and gender divisions by its choice of arcane and poetic color vocabulary. Yet color's ascent into the realms of metaphoric immateriality also freed it to act as a powerful agent of erotic subversion. Contemporary debates over the materiality or immateriality of color and its relationship to language inflected the work of writers whose sexuality was "inverted" in liberatory ways. For the aesthetes Symonds and Lee, coloristic vocabulary provided a formal, seemingly neutral, and inherently sexless vehicle for inscribing homoerotic desire.[33] Symonds's writing on Venice is of especial interest, since the Renaissance school of Venetian painting is traditionally associated with sensuous color, while Roman and Florentine schools excelled at the more intellectual art of design. For Symonds the Venetians were able to produce works of such brilliant color precisely because of the *absence* of nature in Venice. In *The Renaissance in Italy,* published in 1886, Symonds states:

> There is colour in flowers. Gardens of tulips are radiant, and mountain valleys touch the soul with the beauty of their pure and gemlike hues. . . . But what are the purples and scarlets and blues of iris, anemone, or columbine, when compared with that melodrama of flame and gold and rose and orange and azure, which the skies and lagoons of Venice yield almost daily to the eyes? The Venetians *had no green fields and trees, no garden borders, no blossoming orchards,* to teach them the tender suggestiveness, the quaint poetry of isolated or contrasted tints. . . . It was in consequence of this that the Venetians conceived colour heroically, not as a matter of missal-margins or of subordinate decorations, but as a motive worthy in itself of sublime treatment.[34]

For Symonds natural color, exemplified by flowers, is inferior to the antinaturalism of Venetian color for color's sake. He elevates the Venetian school, repudiating its feminization by asserting that in Venice color was not "subordinate," decorative, or ornamental but "sublime," an adjective gendered masculine in Edmund Burke's eighteenth-century aesthetic theories. Symonds disdains the floral yields of feminine spaces, of garden borders and blooming pastures: from Venice's skies and waters he reaps not fertile crops but a more painterly harvest of gold and azure.

Symonds's rampant aestheticization of the Venetian landscape plays itself out more fully in his 1893 poem "In the Key of Blue."[35] The wealthy aesthete-poet, who pursued several relationships with less affluent men, objectifies and eroticizes a member of the Italian working class in verse form. The Venetian gondolier, traditionally clad in several shades of blue, becomes a spectacle for Symonds's enjoyment. The poet paints him in color words:

A symphony of black and blue —
Venice asleep, vast night, and you;
The skies were blurred with vapours dank:
The long canal stretched inky blank,
With lights on heaving water shed
From lamps that trembled overhead.
Pitch-dark! You were the one thing blue;
Four tints of pure celestial hue:
The larkspur blouse by tones degraded
Through silken sash of sapphire faded,
The faintly floating violet tie,
The hose of lapis-lazuli.

Symonds's selection of blue as the dominant key for his word painting was deliberate. Although blue has traditionally symbolized spirituality, as a material it carries distinct economic connotations. The natural blue pigment ultramarine was the most expensive available to both Renaissance and Victorian artists. Symonds makes this association clear when he uses the Latin name of the priceless blue stone ground up to form ultramarine to describe the gondolier's "hose of lapis-lazuli." By calling his poem a symphony in blue and richly embellishing it with a vocabulary laden with precious stuffs and colors, he makes his creation as costly and rare as the pigments and sapphires he versifies. The poet seems to be inverting the traditional symbolic associations of blue as a color of the spirit. For Symonds, whose antinaturalism was a statement about his Uranian sexuality, blue, not red, becomes the color of desire. Blue would also seem a natural color for a Uranian poet, since the appellation is derived from the Greek *Ouranos,* or sky.

In its artful selection of colors and deprivileging of the working-class subject portrayed, "In the Key of Blue" is the verbal equivalent of a Whistler painting.[36] The same structures are apparent in Whistler's depictions of women. For example, his famous portrait of his mother is titled

Arrangement in Black and Gray and only subtitled *The Artist's Mother.* One critic at the time censured the artist for considering his mother "merely prismatically."[37] Symonds's poem effects a similar transformation on the gondolier: he becomes little more than a static ivory figurine encrusted with jet and turquoise:

> The *ivory* of your brows, the glow
> Of those large orbs that are your eyes:
> Those starry orbs of lustrous *jet*
> In clear *enamelled turquoise* set.

The economic implications of an aesthete's rendition of the landscape culminate in Symonds's stanza about the dyers of Venice:

> A symphony of blues and green
> Swart indigo and eau-marine.
> Stripped to the waist two dyers kneel
> On grey steps strewn with orange peel. . . .
> The men wring cloth that drips and takes
> Verditer hues of water-snakes,
> While pali paled by sun and seas
> Repeat the tint in verdigris.
> Those brows, nude breasts, and arms of might,
> The pride of youth and manhood white,
> Now smirched with woad, proclaim the doom
> Of labour and its life-long gloom.

The workers are literally immersed in vats of dye. Color is a part of their daily labor: they are blind to its beauties, since they do not have the leisure to enjoy the verditer and verdigris hues of the cloth they dye. For the author the dyers have become one more blue element of the symphony in blue that is Venice. In observing the spectacle that the young, muscular dyers present to his appreciative eye, the poet remains untainted. His labor does not involve dirtying his hands. The aesthete stands one step removed, able to take pleasure in the scene and all its subtle variegations of hue from his lofty vantage. Unlike the dyers, who are tied to the site of their labor, Symonds is free to roam the canals of Venice, recording the intensity of his visual sensations and weaving them into a poem. His social commentary is limited to remarking on the doom of labor and its lifelong gloom, a colorless existence from which he is exempt.[38]

As Lee wanders through a foreign landscape, her rhetoric recalls that of

Symonds. Though she writes in prose vignettes rather than verse, Lee also aestheticizes the working-class landscape of Paris. In the essay "Of Paris and the Exhibition," she uses the language of labor to affirm that on the third day of her visit she "simply struck, refused point blank to enter the Exhibition." She shuns the site of mass display, avoids the tourists, and takes a cab to a less commercialized part of the city. Like Symonds, who encounters the Venetian dyers as his gondola passes through "a narrow Rio," Lee records her fleeting glimpses of the daily activities of Parisian workers as she strolls along. Her aesthete's eye transforms the menial tasks of ironers, cooks, and housepainters into a vibrantly sketched verbal tableau: "Behind the windows, the meagre geraniums, young women were ironing print frocks . . . and white house-painters, and whiter cook-boys like Watteau Pierrots, . . . were all a leisurely bustle in the greyish-blue atmosphere, against that greyish-white background, touched with the vivid orange and cobalt of posters, which all of it means Paris. Means it at least to me, and, I should think, to everyone who cares for real places and hates shams, and — well, and exhibitions."[39] Though she describes working-class Paris as a real place, her comparison of the flour-smeared cook boys with Watteau Pierrots is erudite and painterly. It enlists these working men and women as actors in a private production of the commedia dell'arte performed for her express pleasure. Lee surveys the bustle of the workers' daily tasks and leisurely activities with the same admiring, entertained gaze she would bring to an exhibition of eighteenth-century paintings in the Louvre.

Whereas in this passage Lee paints a canvas of working-class Paris rather than same-sex desire, in *Miss Brown* the homoeroticism of her language is thinly veiled in her description of the heroine's "diaphanous pallor" in the Italian church. The sensuality of Lee's rhetoric, doubly concealed behind a male pseudonym and a male narrator, Hamlin, reads remarkably like Symonds's description of the gondolier Augusto. When Hamlin first catches sight of Anne, he describes her thus: "The complexion was of a uniform opaque pallor, more like a certain old marble than ivory; indeed you might almost imagine, as she sat motionless at the head of the table, that this was no living creature, but some sort of strange statue — cheek and chin and forehead of Parian marble, scarcely stained a dull red in the lips, and hair of dull wrought iron, and eyes of some mysterious greyish-blue, slate-tinted onyx: a beautiful and sombre idol of the heathen."[40] The sculptural metaphors Lee summons to evoke Anne's Parian marble complexion and eyes of slate-tinted onyx recall Symonds's loving description of the ivory of Augusto's brows, his gemlike eyes, "[t]hose starry orbs of lustrous *jet.*" With the aid of an elaborate, recondite color vocabulary, Lee and Symonds safely immobilized and aestheticized the objects of their desire.

Like the canvases by Lord Leighton and Moore, Symonds's and Lee's word paintings use the language of color and aestheticism to conceal inequalities of class and gender. The technological divorce between natural and synthetic pigments and women's increased visual and verbal command over the selection of fashionable hues resulted in concerted attempts to relocate the sphere of color consumerism and connoisseurship on a higher, ostensibly artistic level. Yet aestheticism's very efforts to free color from its material, economic, and erotic connotations also created new codes and possibilities for female and homosexual writers. In the language of color, desire was free to speak its name.

Notes

Themes introduced in this essay are part of a larger thesis project on gender, fashion, and colonialism in mid-nineteenth-century France and England and will be explored in greater depth therein. I would like to thank Regenia Gagnier, Jennifer Shaw, Sally Stein, Michael Marrinan, Jordanna Bailkin, Susana Sosa, Kristin Schwain, Carrie Lambert, and the Victorian reading group at Stanford University for their careful reading of this essay and useful suggestions.

1. For color illustrations of *Flaming June,* see the cover and color plate 78 of Robert Rosenblum and H. W. Janson, *Nineteenth-Century Art* (New York: Abrams, 1984). Many posters of the work have appeared in recent years, once again circulating and commodifying Leighton's aestheticization of the female body.

2. Walter Pater, "The School of Giorgione," in *Selected Writings of Walter Pater,* ed. Harold Bloom (New York: New American Library, 1974), 53–54.

3. Vernon Lee, *Miss Brown* (1884; reprint, New York: Garland, 1978), 305–6.

4. Ibid., 309–10.

5. Ibid., 83–84.

6. Jonathan Crary, *Techniques of the Observer* (Cambridge, Mass.: MIT Press, 1990), 71.

7. Ibid., 68–69. The treatise was translated into English in 1840 by Charles Eastlake.

8. Aniline dyes were derived by chemists from the by-products of coal processing.

9. Though the issue of aniline dyes in colonial expansion and trade is too complex to treat here, the imperialist intent of the chemists who created them was clear in their writings. August Wilhelm von Hofmann, Perkin's teacher at the Royal College of Chemistry, declared in 1862, "England will, beyond question, at no distant day, become herself the greatest colour-producing country in the world, nay, by the strangest of revolutions, she may, ere long, send her coal-derived blue to indigo-growing India, her tar-distilled crimson to cochineal-producing Mexico and her fossil substitutes for quercitron and safflower to China and Japan" (*Perkin Centenary London: 100 Years of Synthetic Dyestuffs* [London: Pergamon, 1958], 21).

10. The market for synthetic artists' pigments was smaller than the commercial dye industry's need for textile dyes. However, with the popularization of watercolor painting among amateur artists across a broad social spectrum came a demand for less expensive pigments (John Gage, *George Field and His Circle* [London: Christie's, 1989], 7).

11. Pure ultramarine, derived from Turkish lapis lazuli, was the most expensive pigment available to nineteenth-century artists. The most brilliant hue of blue, it was so precious and costly that it was often sold in grades usually reserved for measuring the quality of gold: the interested and prosperous artist could purchase it in three-, six-, and twelve-carat qualities. The colorist George Field's assistant Harry once spent 117 days grinding one stone (Ibid., 36).

12. Arthur Morrison, "Lizerunt," in *Working-Class Stories of the 1890s*, ed. P. J. Keating (London: Routledge and K. Paul, 1971), 30–31.

13. Ibid., 33.

14. Mrs. Hugh Reginald Haweis, *The Art of Dress* (London: Chatto and Windus, 1879), 15.

15. Grant Allen, *The Colour-Sense,* 2d ed. (London: Kegan Paul, Trench, Trubner, 1892), 229.

16. Sir Arthur Sullivan, *Patience, or, Bunthorne's Bride* (1881; reprint, New York: G. Schirmer, 1950), 49.

17. The stage directions read: "(Enter Duke, Colonel, and Major R. They have *abandoned their uniforms,* and are *dressed and made up in imitation of Aesthetics.* They have long hair, and other signs of attachment to the brotherhood. As they sing they walk in stiff, constrained, and angular attitudes — a grotesque exaggeration of the attitudes adopted by Bunthorne and the young Ladies in Act I)" (italics mine) (Ibid., 158).

18. Allen, 259.

19. Anthony Travis, *The Rainbow-Makers: The Origins of the Synthetic Dyestuffs Industry in Western Europe* (Bethlehem, Pa.: Lehigh University Press, 1993), 46.

20. Ibid., 48.

21. *Englishwoman's Domestic Magazine* 8 (1863): 191.

22. Haweis, 192.

23. Ibid., 187.

24. Alexander Bain, *The Emotions and the Will* (Washington, D.C.: University Publications of America, 1859), 614.

25. Ibid., 623.

26. "There are a few London firms which make a specialty of artistic shades. These materials are generally costly to purchase . . . but have the nearly extinct quality of wearing remarkably well" (Haweis, 113).

27. Ibid.

28. Ibid., 110.

29. In the lecture, which was published in *Contemporary Review* (May 1896), Ellis enumerated instances of color terms in poets from Homer to his day (reprinted as Havelock Ellis, *The Colour-Sense in Literature* [London: Ulysses Book Shop, 1931], 7–8).

30. Even Huysmans's consummate aesthete figure, Des Esseintes, who disdains emeralds and rubies since they remind him of the red and green lights of the common omnibus, loves and acquires sapphires: "seul, parmi ces pierres, le saphir a gardé des feux inviolés par la sottise industrielle et pécuniaire" (Joris-Karl Huysmans, *À rebours* [1881; reprint, Paris: Gallimard, 1977], 130).

31. Walter Pater, "The Renaissance," in *Selected Writings,* 60.

32. Vernon Lee, "Of Paris and the Exhibition," in *The Enchanted Woods* (London: J. Lane, 1905), 77.

33. Pater's painterly description of the young Christian soldier beloved by Marius in his novel *Marius the Epicurean* is another case in point.

34. John Addington Symonds, *The Renaissance in Italy* (1886; reprint, London: J. Murray, 1920–21), 3:256.

35. John Addington Symonds, *In the Key of Blue* (London: Elkin Matthews and John Lane, 1893).

36. Whistler's description of the artist's mission could equally apply to Symonds. The painter's "Ten O'clock Lecture" (1885) opens with this statement: "Nature contains the elements, in colour and form, of all pictures, as the keyboard contains the notes of all music. But the artist is born to pick, and choose, and group with science, these elements, that the result may be beautiful — as the musician gathers his notes, and forms his chords, until he bring forth from chaos glorious harmony. To say to the painter, that Nature is to be taken as she is, is to say to the player, that he may sit on the piano" (James McNeill Whistler, "The Ten O'clock Lecture," in *Symbolist Art Theories,* ed. Henri Dorra [Berkeley: University of California Press, 1994], 65–70).

37. Richard Le Gallienne, cited in Karl Beckson, *London in the 1890s: A Cultural History* (New York: Norton, 1993), 60.

38. *In the Skin of a Lion,* Ondaatje's novel about working-class immigrants in early-twentieth-century Toronto, describes the effects of leather dyeing on the health of workers: "Dye work took place in the courtyards next to the warehouse.

Circular pools had been cut into the stone — into which the men leapt waist-deep within the reds and ochres and greens, leapt in embracing the skins of recently slaughtered animals . . . and the men stepped out in colours up to their necks, pulling wet hides out after them so it appeared they had removed the skin from their own bodies. . . . They had consumed the most evil smell in history, they were consuming it now, flesh death . . . and even if they never stepped into this pit again — a year from now they would burp up that odour. That they would die of consumption and they did not know it. . . . They were paid one dollar a day. Nobody could last in that job more than six months and only the desperate took it" (Michael Ondaatje, *In the Skin of a Lion* [Toronto: McClelland and Stewart, 1987], 130–31).

39. Lee, "Of Paris," 74–75.

40. Lee, *Miss Brown,* 24.

Chapter 10

MARGARET DEBELIUS

Countering a Counterpoetics

Ada Leverson and Oscar Wilde

O, Gilded Sphinx,
Part prophetess, and part conspirator,
Swirling your seven cloaks around you,
What do you plot?

To restore the rule of Isis, Ibis
And the Sacred Cat?
No, I will tell your secret!

Great loyalty, great wit:
(Each strives against the other)
Both win: both lose; both benefit
In laughter none can smother.

Essential wisdom shows.
Alone, you know it is not silly
To scent the tuberose
And gild the lily.
— Osbert Sitwell on Ada Leverson

"NOTHING spoils a romance more than a sense of humor in a woman," sighs Lord Illingworth in Oscar Wilde's *A Woman of No Importance.* "Or the lack of it in a man," replies Mrs. Allonby. Although the epigrammatic logic sounds purely Wildean, Philippe Julian, one of Wilde's biographers, attributes the original remark to Wilde's close friend Ada Leverson.[1] Regardless of who said it first, the sentence highlights how a sense of humor is perceived to be more appropriate in a man than in a woman. By 1893, when the play premiered, decadent males like Wilde had earned a reputation for their linguistic exuberance and parodic challenges to Victorian social norms, creating what critics have since labeled a "counterdiscourse."[2] In contrast, the periodical press had dismissed the decadent's female counterpart, the New Woman, as a humorless bore. Leverson, however, recognized by Osbert Sitwell and many others as a "great wit," toppled the stereotype of the overly serious female by penning some of the era's funniest and most suggestive parodies of Wilde and other male aesthetes.

Whereas several critics interested in the complex relation between gender and decadence have examined the parodic strategies of male writers, most have ignored parody as a tool for feminist subversion. Considering parodies by women, specifically Leverson's parodies of Wilde, sheds light on fin-de-siècle women writers' ambivalent and often contradictory attitude toward literary and cultural decadence. In Leverson's case parody worked as a double-edged sword that allowed her both to express her great loyalty to Wilde and to use her great wit to distance herself from those aspects of aestheticism she found distasteful. As Elaine Showalter argues in her introduction to *Daughters of Decadence,* "New Women writers needed to purge aestheticism and decadence of their misogyny and to rewrite the myths of art that denigrated women."[3] Yet even while rewriting aestheticism, many women writers like Leverson identified with an aesthetic sensibility that elevated art over nature. It is precisely through parody that Leverson defined herself as a writer sympathetic to aspects of aestheticism while still critiquing its masculinist politics. Using parody to revise misogynist codes, she created her own counterpoetics, a sort of counter-counterdiscourse.

Today Leverson is best remembered for having sheltered Wilde in her attic nursery between his trials when no London hotel would admit him, but in her own time she was hailed as a talented writer and raconteur, renowned for her quick repartee. The publisher Grant Richards called her "the Egeria of the whole 'nineties movement,' the woman whose wit provoked wit in others, whose intelligence helped so much to leaven the dullness of her period."[4] When a guest once excused himself from one of her parties, explaining that he had to get to bed early in order to keep his youth, she smiled and responded slyly, "I didn't know that you were keeping a youth."[5] And when Wilde boasted to her of an Apache in Paris who was so devoted that he followed Wilde everywhere with a knife in one hand, it was typical of Leverson to reply, "I'm sure he had a fork in the other!"[6] Her skits, satirical letters, and dialogues for *Punch,* the *Sketch, Black and White,* and other periodicals parody friends and acquaintances, aesthetes like Aubrey Beardsley ("Weirdsley"), Arthur Symons ("Simple Symons"), Max Beerbohm ("Mereboom"), Henry James, and others.

But it is her parodies of Wilde that best express her brilliance and highly developed sense of the ridiculous — as well as her feminist perspective on aestheticism. In a succession of *Punch* sketches, including "An Afternoon Tea Party," "The Minx — A Poem in Prose," "Overheard Fragment of a Dialogue," and "The Advisability of Not Being Brought Up in a Handbag," she revealed the machinery behind the elaborate facade of Wildean decadence, often to hilarious effect.[7] It seems unusual that Wilde's friend would also be his parodist and publish in, of all hostile places, *Punch,* the comic magazine devoted to ridiculing not only Wilde (most notably as the poet Maudle in George Du Maurier's cartoon series) but also women writers.[8] Leverson, however, quietly subverted *Punch*'s attitude by anonymously publishing her humorous sketches sympathetic to both Wilde and women.

Born Ada Beddington in 1862 to a wealthy Jewish family, she married Ernest Leverson, a London diamond merchant, in 1881.[9] (They separated in 1902; theirs seems to have been a romance spoiled in large part by her own sense of humor and her husband's lack thereof.) Her biographers disagree about the precise origin of her friendship with Wilde. According to her own recollections, she met him in 1892 at a party celebrating the opening of *Lady Windermere's Fan.*[10] Yet Sitwell recalls Leverson describing her first meeting with Wilde taking place nearly a year later; in Sitwell's version the introduction becomes a story about humor and gendered expectations. Wilde so enjoyed an anonymous *Punch* parody of *The Picture of Dorian Gray* (1891) that he arranged to meet its author, and, recalls Sitwell, "when this meeting took place Wilde was amazed to find a woman who entered the room."[11] However they met, the two became fast friends, finding common ground in their shared love of conversation and the absurd.

Early on, Wilde dubbed Leverson "Sphinx," a sobriquet she kept until her death in 1933. "The author of 'The Sphinx' will on Wednesday at two eat pomegranates with the Sphinx of Modern Life," reads a 28 July 1893 telegram from him to her. Soon after this telegram he published "The Sphinx," an exotic verse reverie in which the title character appears first as a "half woman / and half animal" and later as a "loathsome mystery." As Sally Beauman has noted, it seems "[o]dd, after such a poem to apply the term 'Sphinx' to a friend."[12] Indeed, critics have usually interpreted the devouring Sphinx of Greek myth as one of the many incarnations of the feminine threat to civilization, as alarming as the Judiths and Salomes portrayed on so many symbolist canvases.[13] One reason the Sphinx figures so prominently in the decadent imagination is its capacity to symbolize both of women's roles; as perceived by many male aesthetes, women were either objects of aesthetic valuation (like the Egyptian Great Sphinx at Giza) or femme fatales (like the Sphinx of Greek myth).

Leverson, however, was a sphinx of a different color. Rather than ingesting her interlocutors like the Greek Sphinx, she kept them in stitches with her riddles. As a writer and humorist, she resisted the role of both aesthetic object and devouring woman, adopting instead the stance of cultural critic. Her parodies carve out a place for women in the aesthetic movement by repeatedly deconstructing what it means to be a sphinx.

The Politics of Parody

How was Leverson able to walk the tightrope between identifying with aesthetes and critiquing them? How can she, in Sitwell's words, balance great loyalty with great wit? The answer lies with her chosen genre, parody. Notoriously difficult to define, parody eludes easy classification. In the most limited sense it is the imitation or quotation of a style, often with comic intent. But discussions of parody soon become untidy, expanding to include close relatives: pastiche, allusion, satire, burlesque, and irony. As Lawrence Danson has complained, even "definitions of parodies tend to sound like parodies."[14] Margaret Rose, more lucid than many, has suggested that parody is "a literary work perceived by the reader as juxtaposing performed language material with other linguistic or literary material in an incongruous manner in a new context, to produce a comic effect."[15]

Like Leverson herself, parody walks a tightrope; critical communities have alternately dismissed and embraced it. F. R. Leavis, one of the form's best-known detractors, denounced it as an enemy of creative genius.[16] His objection points to a prevalent critique, namely that parody acts as a sort of aesthetic police force that arrests works of real, presumably original, genius by mocking them. On the other hand, Wilde declared parody a form of homage. In an 1889 letter to the critic Oscar Hamilton, Wilde wrote, "Parody, which is the Muse with her tongue in her cheek, has always amused me; but it requires a light touch . . . and oddly enough a love of the poet whom it caricatures. One's disciples can parody one — nobody else."[17]

More recent critics have celebrated parody precisely for its slippery doubleness, for its ability to be both loving, as Wilde suggested, and aggressive, as Leavis implied. For Linda Hutcheon parody is a "repetition with a critical distance." The ideological status of parody is a subtle one, implying, "at one and the same time, authority and transgression." She has described the "textual doubling of parody," citing the "double etymology of the prefix 'para' that can mean both 'counter' and 'beside.'"[18]

Parodically rewriting Wilde allowed Leverson both to stand beside her friend and to stand counter to him. For all that her parodies grew out of a sincere affection for Wilde, they also display a revisionary impulse. Wilde might imagine her parodies as "the Muse with her tongue in her cheek," but this muse also has teeth. When one of Leverson's biographers dismissed her parodies as "cool, harmless, funny skits," he ignored the way in which they allowed her to critique aestheticism from a feminine perspective.[19] Leverson loved Wilde enough to repeat him convincingly, but it was a repetition with a difference. And this difference carries the power of subversion.

Parody, the New Woman, and the Decadent

Although several theorists have considered parody in their analyses of gender and decadence in the fin de siècle, most have seen parody as the prerogative of the male decadent writer. Both Linda Dowling and Rita Felski use parody to assess the relationship between the New Woman and the decadent male, but both offer incomplete pictures by focusing exclusively on the decadent side of the equation. Dowling has argued that contemporary periodicals (like *Punch*) linked aesthetes and New Women in an unholy alliance, identifying both as profound threats to established culture. "To most late Victorians the decadent was new and the New Woman decadent," she contends. She cites extensive evidence of a union between the two camps, including Ernest Dowson's supposedly satirical annotations of Olive Schreiner's *Story of an African Farm* (1883). Dowling argues, however, that there is "little satire" in Dowson's work. Instead she reads his parodic commentary as a sign that he actually "admired Schreiner's work profoundly" and concludes that the apparent rivalry between New Women and decadents is illusory.[20]

Felski also looked to parody when she challenged Dowling's view of an alliance between revolutionaries in "The Counterdiscourse of the Feminine in Three Texts by Wilde, Huysmans, and Sacher-Masoch." In this article Felski investigates how these three male writers appropriated an imaginary femininity through the "parodistic citation of gender codes." However, she goes on to suggest that the aesthete's "appropriation of metaphors of femininity" was opposed to, rather than aligned with, a feminist project that sought to question traditional gender roles. Overturning gender categories actually served to strengthen them, she contends, explaining, "the male aesthete's playful subversion of gender norms, his adoption of feminine traits, paradoxically reinforces his distance from and elevation above women, who are by nature incapable of such intellectual mobility and aesthetic sophistication."[21]

As evidence of the decadent artist's disdain for women, Felski cites Lord Henry Wotton's definition of women from *The Picture of Dorian Gray.* "Women are 'sphinxes without secrets' in the words of Wilde, their enigmatic aura purely superficial, exemplifying conventionality without aesthetic self-consciousness," Felski explains.[22] Picking up where Felski's groundbreaking study leaves off, I will ask what happens when Leverson gets hold of Wilde's remark and decides to parody the parodist. Rather than indicating either an alliance or a battle between male aesthetes and women artists, Leverson's work suggests a blend of both. Our impression of parody and aestheticism changes when we consider female parodists of the period such as Leverson, who were, despite impressions to the contrary, extremely capable of intellectual mobility, aesthetic sophistication, self-consciousness, and laughter.

Wonderful Sphinx

In "An Afternoon Tea Party," Leverson's first and one of her funniest parodies of Wilde, she rewrote Wotton's aperçu; in her version Lord Illingworth explains to Lord Henry, "Women are secrets, not sphinxes." In a stroke Leverson returned to women the sense of ironic self-consciousness and interiority — the secrets — that aestheticism had threatened to take away by positioning women as art objects. In this and other parodies Leverson rewrote the role of sphinx to revise aestheticism's vexed relationship to both women and popular culture, a relationship that hinged on both debt and disavowal. Tracing the dizzying train of associations that Wilde and Leverson traded about sphinxes illustrates in brief just how she used parody both to echo and to revise the decadent creed. When Leverson parodied Wilde's remark about sphinxes without secrets, she was well aware that he had used it several times, as the title of the short story "The Sphinx without a Secret" (1887), as Lord Illingworth's definition of the female sex to Mrs. Allonby in *A Woman of No Importance* (1893), and as Lord Henry's view of women in *The Picture of Dorian Gray* (1891). (Poking fun at Wilde's well-known penchant for recycling his own jokes, Leverson's Lord Henry gleefully shouts, "Mine again!" in response to her Lord Illingworth's definition of women as "secrets, not sphinxes.")

Leverson might have guessed that Wilde lifted the canard about women being sphinxes without secrets from Charles Baudelaire.[23] In an essay on Edgar Allan Poe, the French writer had called public opinion "ce sphinx sans enigme." Wilde's transformation of Baudelaire's words from a reference to public opinion into a reference to women demonstrates the way in which the popular and women were conflated at the turn of the century.[24] Recent studies of Wilde are divided on his notoriously contradictory attitude toward the popular and women. Some critics, like Felski, have insisted on Wilde's misogyny, arguing that his work relies on a "logic of exclusion" in which the excluded terms are the masses and women, the "twin symbols of the democratizing mediocrity of modern life, embodying a murky threat to the precarious status and identity of the artist."[25] Other critics, such as Sos Eltis, have argued that Wilde was a "consistent champion of women's rights both in his life and work, supporting all the primary demands of late-nineteenth century feminism."[26] Leverson's parodies suggest that Wilde's attitudes toward the popular and women were more complicated than either of these critical positions allows — and that, regardless of his attitude, his works owe a substantial debt to both popular culture and women.

Several critics have noted how decadence defined itself against the feminine and the biological creativity of women. Antinaturalism, as Jean Pierrot explains in *The Decadent Imagination,* leads directly to antifeminism; women were seen as closer to nature and the body, while men were aligned with art and the intellect.[27] In the words of Wilde's Wotton, women represent the "triumph of matter over mind." The most brutal version of this misogyny comes from Baudelaire, who described women as being entirely governed by their biological and physical impulses. "Woman is *natural,* that is to say abominable. Also, she is always vulgar, that is to say the contrary of the dandy."[28] As the linking of "natural" and "vulgar" suggests, the rejection of the feminine in decadent texts involves a corresponding disavowal of the popular. Wotton, for example, couples his dislike for women with a hatred of the popular, lamenting the state of "an age so limited and vulgar as our own." In particular he cringes at art for the masses, expressing his distaste for "vulgar realism in literature."

While the facts of Wilde's biography (including his work as editor of the *Woman's World*) suggest that his own position on women and popular culture is rather more complex than either Wotton's or Baudelaire's, many of his characters nonetheless make overtly misogynistic remarks. It is these remarks that Leverson chose to revise, embracing an aesthetic that rejected the natural without devaluing the feminine or the popular. She shared Wilde's delight in artifice: "Though not affected myself, I like other people to be," she observed on more than one occasion. And she was quick to advise Sitwell, "It's not *natural* for a writer to be natural, that's what I say!"[29] She also enjoyed recounting how Beardsley once asked her to come to a party an hour early to help him prepare the flowers. On arriving she found him spraying the gardenias and tuberoses with opopanax; he presented her with a spray of frangipani for the stephanotis (hence Sitwell's tribute, "Alone, you know it is not silly / To scent the tuberose / And gild the lily"). Devoted to surface and fashion, she incurred exorbitant bills at expensive dressmakers, including Worth, Paquin, and Madame Poutz. Even her commitment to parody, which imitates art rather than nature, underscores her interest in artifice.

Unlike some of her male colleagues, however, Leverson maintained a commitment to artifice without devaluing the popular. One very literal way in which she embraced the popular was to introduce aestheticism to a large audience by publishing parodies of Wilde in *Punch,* the widely circulated defender of middle-class life. "An Afternoon Tea Party" features a variety of guests from the contemporary stage, the most prominent of whom is Wilde's Salome. Although Wilde's society comedies enjoyed popular acclaim, *Salome* remained virtually unseen. Banned by the censor for its profane treatment of a biblical subject in 1892, the play was published by the Bodley Head and the avant-garde Librairie de L'Art Indépendant in 1893 in French in a limited edition of six hundred copies (five hundred for sale). Writing for a humor magazine whose circulation exceeded thirty thousand per week, Leverson thus introduced *Salome* — and aspects of aestheticism — to a wide popular audience.[30] As Hutcheon has argued, parody is often charged with elitism, since its readers must "meet certain requisite conditions" to understand the references to earlier texts.[31] But "An Afternoon Tea Party," rather than being elitist, serves a democratizing function by exposing Wilde's expensive limited-edition work to general examination. Bugs Bunny cartoons work the same way — by introducing viewers to generic conventions long before they see their first opera.

Leverson not only published "An Afternoon Tea Party" in a popular magazine, she also used the occasion to suggest how even Wilde's most rarefied work owed a debt to popular culture. Wilde, who dodged accusations of plagiarism throughout his career, always insisted that his plays, though popular successes, were undervalued. He became irate when critics dubbed him "the English Sardou." Particularly sensitive to such accusations, Wilde declared indignantly to a reporter, "My works are dominated by myself," and added that no dramatist of the nineteenth century had influenced him even "in the smallest degree."[32] (Of course, his well-known penchant for paradox meant that he courted public opinion even as he disdained it. Regenia Gagnier has shown in *Idylls of the Marketplace* how he was, above all, an engaged playwright.) In "An Afternoon Tea Party" Leverson introduced several of Wilde's characters to a star-studded collection of guests from the contemporary stage, including Nora from Henrik Ibsen's *A Doll's House* and Hilda Wangel from his *The Master Builder,* Dora from Victorien Sardou's *Dora,* Madame Santuzza from Pietro Mascagni's *Cavalleria rusticana,* Charley's Aunt from Brandon Thomas's play of the same name, and Mrs. Tanqueray from Arthur Pinero's *The Second Mrs. Tanqueray.* These guests were not only popular stage figures, they were also the very characters that critics have claimed Wilde had cribbed to create his own dramas. Kerry Powell has noted, for example, how Sardou influenced *Salome,* calling Salome "a Sarah Bernhardt character in the mold of Fedora, Floria, and Theodora."[33] (Even Bernhardt's Salome costume was borrowed from the wardrobe of Sardou's *Cleopatra.*) And, as Jane Marcus has argued, Salome's sensuous dance of the seven veils "exactly parallels Nora's tarantella in *A Doll's House* which London audiences had first seen performed only a few years earlier."[34]

By juxtaposing Wilde's characters with these well-known figures of the 1890s, Leverson exposed his debt to his peers. Just as Wilde denied the mantle of authorial influence, so Leverson's Princess Salome causes a scuffle in the cloakroom when she hotly denies having taken a shawl from Charley's Aunt: "I don't want your shawl. Your shawl is hideous. It is covered with dust. It is a tartan shawl. It is like the shawl worn in melodrama by the injured heroine who is about to throw herself over the bridge by moonlight. It is the shawl of a betrayed heroine in melodrama. There never was anything so hideous as your shawl." The passage recalls Salome's rejection of Iokanaan's hair and body in *Salome* ("Thy body is hideous. It is like the body of a leper. It is like a plastered wall, where vipers have crawled; like a plastered wall where scorpions have made their nest"), but Leverson recast the speech as a dispute over a dusty tartan shawl to suggest Wilde's denial of his literary and melodramatic relatives.[35] Much of the humor of the passage derives from an image of Salome, whom critics have identified as everything from an avatar of the New Woman to an image of Wilde himself, haranguing Charley's Aunt, a man in drag.[36]

If, as seems likely, Leverson either purchased or received a presentation copy of the 1893 *Salome,* she might have noticed a curious device on the frontispiece. Less well known than Beardsley's illustrations for the 1894 English-language edition, Felicien Rops's design for the 1893 title page features not Salome but an angry sphinx. Even more threatening than Salome, who desires only the head of Iokanaan, this angry winged sphinx sits triumphant over a dismembered male body. The Latin epigram beneath the device comes from Martial; translated, it reads, "This is not a fish you're eating, you're eating a man." Leverson's parody, however, defused the threat of the devouring Salome-sphinx figure by portraying her Salome at the buffet line:

> "Is that mayonnaise?" asked the Princess Salome of Captain Coddington, who had taken her to the buffet. "I think it is mayonnaise. I am sure it is mayonnaise. It is mayonnaise of salmon, pink as a branch of coral which fisherman may find in the twilight of the sea, and which they keep for the King. It is pinker than the pink roses that bloom in the Queen's garden. The pink roses that bloom in the garden of the Queen of Arabia are not so pink."

Leverson here inverted Wilde by making his metaphor literal; his vehicle became her tenor. The original Salome's tribute to Iokanaan reads like a menu from an exotic restaurant: his "hair is like a cluster of grapes," his mouth "like a pomegranate cut in twain with a knife of ivory" or like the red "feet of those who tread the wine in the wine-press."[37] These gastronomic images prefigure the sensual way in which Salome wants to devour her captive — and connect her to Rops's frontispiece image of a sphinx licking her chops. Leverson's parody, however, pokes fun at the imagined threat of the insatiable woman by suggesting that Princess Salome is more interested in eating a condiment than a man's head. (Even when the man in question, the absurdly named Captain Coddington, could quite easily be mistaken for the fish course.)

Leverson continued her dialogue with Wilde about sphinxes in "The Minx — A Poem in Prose," which parodies Wilde's 1894 poem "The Sphinx." Although Wilde's dramatic comedies enjoyed large audiences, his poetry remained in limited circulation. "My first idea was to print only three copies, one for myself, one for the British Museum, and one for Heaven. I had some doubts about the British Museum," he is reported to have said of the poem.[38] Ultimately only two hundred copies were published by the Bodley Head (with an elaborate gilded cover design and illustrations by Charles Ricketts), making "The Sphinx" a rare commodity indeed. In a letter to John Lane, Wilde asserted his desire to maintain the poem's exclusivity, refusing to have it reviewed ("A book of this kind — very rare and curious — must not be thrown into the gutter of English journalism"), and insisted that "no new edition is to be brought out without my sanction: I mean no such thing as a cheap or popular edition is to be brought out."[39] Leverson's "The Minx," published in a widely circulated humor magazine, becomes the cheap or popular edition that Wilde feared.

Wilde's poem works as a hymn to the exotic, revolving around a student interrogating a silent Sphinx about her "thousand weary centuries" of past lovers. The Sphinx, a symbol of empire and all things foreign, suggests to the student the sensual pleasures associated with crossing racial, sexual, and national boundaries — he conjures up a "brown Sidonian," merchants from Kurdistan, a "swarthy Ethiop whose body was of polished jet," "Memphian Lords," and "bearded Bedouins." "Who were your lovers? who were they who wrestled for you in the dust?" the student insists. His imagination grows bold as he envisions the Sphinx committing lesbian incest (with her sister the "horrible Chimaera") and necrophilia (using a "black sarcophagus" as her "lupanar" or brothel).

Like Dante Gabriel Rossetti's Jenny, the Sphinx of Wilde's poem remains "beautiful and silent" while the narrator engages in his transgressive fantasies of border crossing. But Wilde's real-life sphinx — Leverson — talks back. In "The Minx" she restaged all that was strange and foreign about the form and content of Wilde's poem as something local and familiar. Rather than mimic Wilde's elaborate diction and rhyme scheme, she rewrote the scene in a more everyday genre — as a society-page newspaper interview between an unnamed poet and a glib sphinx. The interview format alludes to (or parodies) some of the interviews that Wilde gave to the newspapers and through which the public knew him:

> Poet: You knew AMMON very well I believe?
>
> Sphinx (frankly): AMMON and I were great pals. I used to see a good deal of him. He came in to tea very often — he was quite interesting. But I have not seen him for a long time. He had one fault — he would smoke in the drawing room.

The once threatening Sphinx, symbol of empire, devouring femininity, and perverse sexuality, becomes an utterly conventional drawing-room hostess who objects to Ammon, the Libyan Jupiter, smoking cigarettes indoors. Her chatty comments about making Cleopatra jealous by going "tunny fishing" with Antony stand in marked contrast to the solemn passion and richly imagined pleasures of Wilde's creature. By defusing the threat of the femme fatale in Wilde's poem, Leverson revised the role of sphinx to suggest that femininity is much less strange and dangerous than decadent poets imagine.

Leverson's parody, however, works on another level as well by highlighting a truth about "The Sphinx" that seems to have eluded many contemporary readers. When Wilde's poem appeared, literal-minded critics ridiculed him for casting himself as a student who had hardly seen "some twenty summers." Yet as Gagnier has argued, the student in the poem likely represents the young French symbolist poet Marcel Schwob, to whom the poem was dedicated in "friendship and admiration," while Wilde himself plays the part of the sphinx: "In writing the poem, Wilde the seducer/Sphinx confronted the reticent student/Schwob with Schwob's own thinly repressed desires."[40] While sphinxes are usually interpreted as female, it seems more accurate to interpret the creature — at least in this poem — as of indeterminate gender and ambiguous sexuality. Although the Greek Sphinx is female, the Egyptian Sphinx is usually male; Wilde combines both traditions in his poem, inventing a sphinx who lives both by the Nile and near the "Theban gate." Thus for Wilde the sphinx becomes a borderline creature, appealing precisely because of its shifting origin, gender, and sexuality.

The concluding lines of Leverson's parody suggest her understanding of the poem as a Wildean seduction. In Wilde's poem the poet at last rejects the Sphinx: "Get hence! I weary of your sullen ways, / . . . False Sphinx! False Sphinx!" Leverson's kiss-and-tell newspaper interview ends with the following rejection:

> Poet: In my opinion, you are not a sphinx at all.
> Sphinx (indignantly): What am I then?
> Poet: A Minx.

Just as her sphinx becomes a minx, Leverson suggests that Wilde's poem "The Sphinx," beneath its overblown syntax and labored rhymes, is really just an elaborate pickup line. Leverson's version delighted Wilde; as soon as "The Minx" appeared, he sent her a note congratulating her on the effort: "*Punch* is delightful and the drawing a masterpiece of clever caricature. I am afraid she was really a minx after all. You are the only Sphinx."[41]

This is where the sexual politics of Leverson's parody become positively vertiginous, where the counter-counterdiscourse gets complicated. Wilde had appropriated traditional metaphors of femininity to become a sphinx — what Felski might call the "counterdiscourse of the feminine" or the "parodistic citation of gender norms." But the game does not stop here: in her parody Leverson countered Wilde's counterdiscourse by unmasking him as a flirt; he is the sphinx/minx in pursuit of Schwob. Wilde responded with a congratulatory note conferring on Leverson the title of true Sphinx, who, presumably, maintains her secrets.

Leverson showed her teeth again when she returned to the sexual politics of the aesthete in "Overheard Fragment of a Dialogue." After attending a first-night performance of Wilde's *An Ideal Husband* at the Haymarket on 3 January 1895, Leverson penned this sketch featuring two of Wilde's best-known dandies, Lord Illingworth and Lord Goring. In her version they debate the role of women:

> Lord Illingworth: My dear Goring, I assure you that a well-tied tie is the first serious step in life.
>
> Lord Goring: My dear Illingworth, five well-made buttonholes a day are far more essential. They please women, and women rule society.
>
> Lord Illingworth: I understood you considered women of no importance?
>
> Lord Goring: My dear GEORGE, a man's life revolves on curves of intellect. It is on the hard lines of the emotions that a woman's life progresses. Both revolve in cycles of masterpieces. They should revolve on bi-cycles; built, if possible, for two. But I am keeping you?

As usual, Leverson's humor works on many levels. She skewered the dandy for his misogyny by troping on the title of Wilde's earlier play to suggest that Lord Goring considers all "women of no importance." In addition, she altered Lord Goring's final-act assertion to Lady Chiltern in *An Ideal Husband* about the proper spheres for men and women. Wilde's original version established rigid and traditional gender roles:

> Lord Goring: . . . A man's life is of more value than a woman's. It has larger issues, wider scope, greater ambitions. A woman's life revolves around curves of emotions. It is upon lines of intellect that a man's life progresses.[42]

Critics have puzzled over the way the speech reinscribes strict binaries (male lines and female curves, male intellect and female emotion, questions of value), the very binaries that Wilde sought to topple elsewhere in his plays. While it must be remembered that the speech is delivered by Lord Goring, himself a figure of social androgyny, the words remain troubling. As Eltis has explained, "It may be fairly assumed that the speech stands in relation to Wilde's other writings as Kate's final speech in *The Taming of the Shrew* does to Shakespeare's: both seem to contradict the strong position usually allotted to women in other plays, and both are unusual in their conservative didacticism."[43] And just as some Shakespeare scholars have read Kate's lines as potentially ironic, critics such as Peter Raby have read a potential for resistance in Lady Chiltern's repetition of Goring's speech: "Wilde ensures that her expression of it has an ironical gloss by making her repeat the lesson she has learned from Lord Goring like a parrot."[44]

Lady Chiltern's repetition of the speech, however, is just as likely to reinscribe traditional gender roles as to subvert them. But when Leverson repeated the lines with a difference — "a repetition with a critical distance," in Hutcheon's terms — she opened up a space for resistance. She substituted androgyny for Wilde's misogyny and threw biological determinism out the window by rendering curves masculine and hard lines feminine. In addition, she playfully invoked the bicycle, a new machine of the fin de siècle that seemed destined to subvert the conventions of sexual difference. Invented in 1885, the safety bicycle was a democratic form of transport that came to be associated with London's freethinkers (early devotees included H. G. Wells and George Bernard Shaw). *Punch* readers would also recognize the bicycle as one of the trappings of the New Woman, as much a symbol of liberation as the latchkey and the cigarette. By 1895 the novelist Victor Joze was attacking the bicycle on the pages of the French magazine *La Plume,* arguing that it "necessitates an androgynous outfit . . . worn by its adepts of the weaker sex."[45] By invoking a symbol of progress and androgyny, Leverson challenged the notion that the intellect and emotions belong to separate spheres, arguing instead that both are necessary and desirable.

Leverson's final *Punch* parody of Wilde, "The Advisability of Not Being Brought Up in a Handbag," appeared just one day after he had brought the marquess of Queensberry to the Marlborough Police Court on a charge of libel. Rewriting Wilde's subtitle to *The Importance of Being Earnest,* "A Trivial Comedy for Serious People," Leverson's subtitle, "A Trivial Tragedy for Wonderful People," suggests her suspicion that the Queensberry ordeal could only end tragically for London's greatest comic playwright. The sketch highlights the deadly serious nature of Wilde's farce (just as her parody of *Salome* underscores how Wilde's most ponderous drama borders on the comic). In this parody Leverson introduced her characters Aunt Augusta, Cousin Cicely, and Algy to Dorian Gray. Making the strange familiar, Leverson has Dorian show up in Aunt Augusta's garden to arrange a concert with "brown Algerians who beat monotonously on copper drums."[46] But the bunburying, anarchical, free-playing world of Wilde's triumphant comedy is interrupted by the dark shadow of the duke of Berwick, the character from *The Picture of Dorian Gray* who "got up in a marked manner and went out" in protest when Dorian entered the smoking room of the Churchill. So likewise Leverson included a duke of Berwick, who "rises in a marked manner, and leaves the garden" when her Dorian spouts a Wildean maxim. In Leverson's version Dorian announces, "To be really modern one should have no soul. To be really medieval one should have no cigarettes. To be really Greek — ." Wilde's version ends, "one should have no clothes," but Leverson hardly needed to include the final words. By leaving the sentence unfinished she left the interpretation open; a select group of readers would understand that Greece was associated with same-sex male desire and thus why the duke leaves in so marked and ominous a manner.

A secret sharer in Wilde's life and work, Leverson left ample evidence of her qualification for admission into what has previously been seen as a stag club of parodists. In addition to her parodies, she wrote similarly double-edged short stories that place her both within and outside aesthetic circles. Her "Suggestion" appeared in the *Yellow Book,* that perceived citadel of decadence, in 1895, soon after Wilde's imprisonment. The story dissects the cruelty and narcissism of its decadent narrator, an effeminate young man who speaks in phrases borrowed straight from *The Picture of Dorian Gray.* Cissy Carrington shares both Dorian's intense personal vanity and his desire for an onyx-paved bath room. One night at dinner Cissy contemplates at length "the waking wonder of my face," virtually the same words Lord Henry uses to describe Dorian.[47] But by placing the words in Cissy's mouth, Leverson drew attention to the narcissism that characterized so many members of the high aesthetic band.

It would be easy to dismiss Leverson's parodies as marginal, nothing more than footnotes to the life and works of Wilde. Although she went on to become a successful novelist in the early years of the twentieth century, her output during the 1890s was admittedly small. Not only her status as a female aesthete but also her chosen mode — parody — consigns her to the edges, since the form itself has been dismissed as a marginal art. But Leverson realized that to be marginal at the turn of the century was to be central. As she recalled of the era, "There was more margin: margin in every sense was in demand." (Indeed, by countering a counterpoetics she seems by definition to place herself in a doubly marginalized position.) She even suggested to Wilde that he "publish a book all margin; full of beautiful unwritten thoughts, and have this blank volume bound in some Nile-green skin powdered with gilt neuphars and smoothed with hard ivory, decorated with gold by Ricketts (if not Shannon) and printed on Japanese paper." Enchanted as always, Wilde agreed, promising to commission Beardsley to do the unwritten text and dedicate the volume to the Sphinx herself. Ever suspicious of creating art to please the public taste, he added, "There must be five hundred signed copies for particular friends, six for the general public, and one for America."[48]

To deny fin-de-siècle women a place in a discussion of parody is to risk reinforcing the timeworn fallacy that women have no sense of humor and the decadent misconception that women have no sense of art. Leverson was by no means the only turn-of-the-century woman with a talent for parody: Eleanor Marx and Florence Bell parodied Ibsen, while Vernon Lee skewered Henry James.[49] They, like Leverson, blended tribute and transgression to reveal an attitude toward avant-garde men that was one neither of easy camaraderie, as envisioned by Dowling, nor of unmitigated aggression, as imagined by Felski. Listening to female aesthetes who countered the counterpoetics (or parodied the parodists) provides a fresh perspective on British aestheticism and enhances our understanding of the term. William Butler Yeats once said of Ibsen that they may not have had the same friends, but they shared the same enemies.[50] The same is true of crusading male and female artists of the 1890s who may not have seen eye to eye, especially on issues of gender politics, but were united in their opposition to crumbling Victorian norms.

Notes

For crucial advice at various stages of composition, I would like to thank Elaine Showalter, Deborah Nord, Margaret Stetz, Larry Danson, Talia Schaffer, and Kathy Psomiades. An earlier version of this paper was delivered at the 1996 convention of the Modern Language Association in Washington, D.C., as part of a session titled "Race, Gender, and Decadence: The Woman's Story."

1. Philippe Julian, *Oscar Wilde,* trans. Violet Wyndham (London: Constable, 1969), 198.

2. The word "counterdiscourse" comes to me from Richard Terdiman by way of Rita Felski, "The Counterdiscourse of the Feminine in Three Texts by Wilde, Huysmans, and Sacher-Masoch," *PMLA* 106, no. 5 (1991): 1094–1105.

3. Elaine Showalter, introduction to *Daughters of Decadence: Women Writers of the Fin de Siècle* (New Brunswick, N.J.: Rutgers University Press, 1993), xi.

4. Quoted in Julie Speedie, *Wonderful Sphinx: The Biography of Ada Leverson* (London: Virago, 1993), 45.

5. Quoted in ibid., 35.

6. Quoted in Violet Wyndham, *The Sphinx and Her Circle* (London: Andre Deutsch, 1963), 24.

7. The sketches are found respectively in *Punch,* 15 July 1893, 13; *Punch,* 21 July 1894, 33; *Punch,* 13 January 1895, 24; and *Punch,* 2 March 1895, 107. All further citations refer to these issues.

8. In *The History of Punch* M. H. Spielman revealed the magazine's editorial attitude toward its few "lady literary contributors" as follows: "Women, as a rule, are humorists neither born nor made . . . at any rate they are usually out of their element in the comic arena" (M. H. Spielman, *The History of Punch* [1895; reprint, New York: Greenwood, 1969], 392). The magazine's numerous doggerel verses about New Women and cartoons of frowning, bespectacled, seemingly overeducated females serve to reinforce the stereotype.

9. Wyndham, 17.

10. Ibid., 24, and *Selected Letters of Oscar Wilde,* ed. Rupert Hart-Davis (London: Oxford University Press, 1979), 342.

11. Osbert Sitwell, *Noble Essences: A Book of Characters* (Boston: Little, Brown, 1950), 154.

12. Sally Beauman, introduction to *The Little Ottleys,* by Ada Leverson (New York: Dial, 1982), viii.

13. For an extended discussion of the sphinx as a symbol of feminine evil, see Bram Dijkstra, *Idols of Perversity: Fantasies of Feminine Evil in Fin-de-Siècle Culture* (New York: Oxford University Press, 1986), 324–32.

14. Lawrence Danson, *Max Beerbohm and the Act of Writing* (Oxford: Clarendon, 1989), 146.

15. Margaret Rose, *Parody: Ancient, Modern, and Post-modern* (Cambridge: Cambridge University Press, 1993), 79.

16. Cited in Linda Hutcheon, *A Theory of Parody* (New York: Routledge, 1985), 4.

17. Speedie, 63.

18. Hutcheon, 6, 69, 14.

19. Charles Burkhart, *Ada Leverson* (New York: Twayne, 1973), 22.

20. Linda Dowling, "The Decadent and the New Woman in the 1890's," *Nineteenth Century Fiction* 33, no. 4 (1979): 435–36.

21. Felski, 1100, 1104.

22. Ibid., 1104.

23. Isobel Murray, *Oscar Wilde: A Critical Edition of the Major Works* (New York: Oxford University Press), 585.

24. On the conflation of the popular and women at the end of the nineteenth century, see Andreas Huyssen, "Mass Culture as Women: Modernism's Other," in *After the Great Divide: Modernism, Mass Culture, and Postmodernism* (Bloomington: Indiana University Press, 1986), and Rita Felski, *The Gender of Modernity* (Cambridge, Mass.: Harvard University Press, 1995).

25. Felski, *Gender of Modernity,* 106.

26. Sos Eltis, *Revising Wilde: Society and Subversion in the Plays of Oscar Wilde* (Oxford: Clarendon, 1996), 107.

27. Jean Pierrot, *The Decadent Imagination, 1880–1900,* trans. Derek Coltman (Chicago: University of Chicago Press, 1981), 10.

28. Quoted in Felski, *Gender of Modernity,* 112.

29. Sitwell, 154.

30. Spielman, 49.

31. Hutcheon, 93.

32. Quoted from an interview with Wilde in the *St. James Gazette,* 18 January 1895, 4–5; reprinted in *Oscar Wilde: Interviews and Recollections,* ed. E. H. Mikhail (London: Macmillan, 1979), 1:249.

33. Kerry Powell, *Oscar Wilde and the Theatre of the 1890s* (Cambridge: Cambridge University Press, 1990), 13.

34. Jane Marcus, "Salome: The Jewish Princess Was a New Woman," *Bulletin of the New York Public Library* 78 (1974): 100.

35. Oscar Wilde, *Salome,* in *The Oxford Authors: Oscar Wilde,* ed. Isobel Murray (New York: Oxford University Press, 1989), 309.

36. For summaries of varying interpretations of Salome, see Richard Dellamora, "Traversing the Feminine in Oscar Wilde's Salome," in *Victorian Sages and Cultural Discourse,* ed. Thaïs Morgan (New Brunswick, N.J.: Rutgers University Press, 1990), 246–64, and Elaine Showalter, *Sexual Anarchy: Gender and Culture at the Fin de Siècle* (New York: Penguin, 1990), 150–52.

37. Wilde, *Salome,* 310.

38. Quoted in Margaret Stetz and Mark Samuels Lasner, *England in the 1890s: Literary Publishing at the Bodley Head* (Washington, D.C.: Georgetown University Press, 1990), 13.

39. *Letters of Oscar Wilde,* 319.

40. Regenia Gagnier, *Idylls of the Marketplace: Oscar Wilde and the Victorian Public* (Stanford, Calif.: Stanford University Press, 1986), 45.

41. Quoted in Speedie, 67.

42. Oscar Wilde, *An Ideal Husband,* in *The Oxford Authors: Oscar Wilde,* ed. Isobel Murray (New York: Oxford University Press, 1989), 159.

43. Eltis, 160 n.

44. Peter Raby, *Oscar Wilde* (New York: Cambridge University Press, 1988), 97.

45. Quoted in Debora L. Silverman, *Art Nouveau in Fin-de-Siècle France* (Berkeley: University of California Press, 1989), 72.

46. On 16 January, Wilde had sent Leverson a note announcing his departure with Lord Alfred Douglas for Algiers in the middle of rehearsals for *Earnest.* The most famous story (recounted by Richard Ellmann and others) from the trip concerns Wilde's meeting André Gide and, upon seeing an Arab boy playing the flute outside a café, asking Gide, "Do you want the little musician?" Although Leverson would not have heard this remark, the reference seems nonetheless knowing since Algiers was a well-known site on the gay man's grand tour.

47. Leverson, "Suggestion," in Showalter, *Daughters of Decadence,* 40.

48. Quoted in Wyndham, 105.

49. Eleanor Marx Aveling and Israel Zangwill parodied Ibsen and his critics in "The Doll's House Repaired," *Time,* March 1891, 5–8. Powell discusses Florence Bell's "Jerry Builder Solness," an unpublished parody of *The Master Builder* (76). Vernon Lee satirized Henry James in her short story "Lady Tal," in *Vanities* (London: Heinemann, 1896).

50. Michael Meyer, *Ibsen: A Biography* (New York: Doubleday, 1971), 608.

Chapter 11

DIANA MALTZ

Engaging "Delicate Brains"

From Working-Class Enculturation to Upper-Class Lesbian Liberation in Vernon Lee and Kit Anstruther-Thomson's Psychological Aesthetics

THE YEAR is 1896. A young woman stands before an ancient Greek vase in a gallery of the British Museum and begins to describe the vase's influence on her body to a small audience. The neck of the vase, she says, forces her unconsciously to stretch her back and arch her neck higher. The squat base gives her an agreeable sense of "rootedness" to the ground. The roundness of the vase drives her to widen her chest, so that while she sustains the air in her lungs she gains a sense of buoyancy. The designs on the surface of the vase seem to struggle against its confining three-dimensional shape, and she in response feels a swaying motion from the belly, which pleasantly resolves itself as she discovers her point of equilibrium. This movement also encourages her to "assimilate" the shape of the vase into her own body, so that she loses her sense of distance from the object and gains comfort, confidence, and security. This young woman, Clementina "Kit" Anstruther-Thomson, pauses to gaze at one particularly enthralled female listener, and then casts a meaningful glance across the room at her mentor and lover, Vernon Lee.

From the 1890s through the 1910s Vernon Lee (Violet Paget; 1856–1935), a renowned historian of Renaissance art and an author of fiction, drama, travel essays, and studies of eighteenth-century music and philosophy, turned her focus away from the art object in isolation to pursue "psychological aesthetics," which she defined as the study of the "particular group of mental activities and habits" art evokes in its beholders.[1] She believed herself to have found in her lover and collaborator in aesthetic theory, Kit Anstruther-Thomson (1857–1921), an ideal body so sensitive to art that it experienced aesthetic pleasure through heightened respiration, acute shifts in balance, and changes in temperature. The two observed a strict regimen of "gallery experiments," wherein Anstruther-Thomson monitored her bodily responses to paintings, architecture, and sculpture and Lee theorized their significance.

To tell the story of psychological aesthetics is to tell a love story. "Kit talked of art in terms of what one might call energetic elements, movement, spring, poise, etc., which were native to her," their friend Irene Cooper Willis recalled. "Then when she found out how electrifying such talk was upon Vernon Lee she went a step further and proceeded to believe that she actually felt art in those energetic terms . . . partly, probably, in response to Vernon Lee's probing, searching interest and admiration."[2] Willis, like many of their associates, doubted the legitimacy of Lee and Anstruther-Thomson's investigations, concluding that Lee's emotional investment in Anstruther-Thomson's genius amounted to an adulation of her. As early as their first vacation together in Scotland in 1887, Anstruther-Thomson encouraged this belief in her clairvoyance through dramatic and veiled language: before a twilight seascape, she had observed mysteriously, "Now we have become mere intruders. Now it is They who are in possession."[3] Lee continued to attribute a mysticism to Anstruther-Thomson's "brief and hushed moments" before landscapes and art: "[T]o see what it was all about. That was Kit's homely but mysterious phrase, often accompanied by a hand laid on one's arm, or a twitch at one's sleeve, as after a long, silent pause in front of whatever might happen to be the It under discussion, she turned round, too absorbed, however, to notice the frequent vacuity in her listener's face: 'Now don't you see what It is doing?' And without waiting for my perfunctory answer, she would begin to analyze what it was she had seen."[4] "It" might be the roots of a tree pressing into the ground, or the angle of a waterfall's spray, or the shadow cast on a statue's flank. Lee's belief in Anstruther-Thomson's ethereality sustained not only their professional collaboration but the erotic pull of their relationship.

Since the opening of the Vernon Lee Collection at Colby College, in Waterville, Maine, in 1980, the only published article on the collaboration between Lee and Anstruther-Thomson has celebrated it as an "equal partnership in love and work." Using their correspondence, Phyllis Mannocchi has judged the women's affectionate relationship, sustained by a shared intellectual pursuit, in the context of exemplary "romantic friendships" of the fin de siècle, such as those of Edith Somerville and Violet

Martin (who published fiction jointly under the names E. O. Somerville and Martin Ross) and of Katherine Bradley and Edith Cooper (whose friends called them by their pen name, Michael Field).[5] Yet, initially fashioning psychological aesthetics as a mission to the poor, Lee modeled her collaboration with Anstruther-Thomson not only on these literary partnerships of the 1890s but on an earlier generation of female philanthropists. In the 1870s women such as settlement founder Jane Addams had publicly sanitized their own "Boston marriages" through a lifelong commitment to social reform, defining them as expedient situations for female magnanimity.[6] Lee's adherence to this model produced unusual stresses within psychological aesthetics. Bent on enabling others to revere Anstruther-Thomson's sentient body as she did, Lee stifled her original social-reform imperative. In the spirit of the fin de siècle, Anstruther-Thomson used her decadent focus on bodily sensations to subvert Lee's social and educational agendas, in effect producing a new version of psychological aesthetics, one in which social service was subordinated to sexuality. The museum gallery was in fact a social arena where Anstruther-Thomson used her body to titillate an audience of female, upper-class devotees. Even as it aspired to scientific legitimacy, psychological aesthetics in practice was the stuff of decadent high comedy. In Anstruther-Thomson's hands, this program, originally designed as a means of enhancing the lives of the poor, became instead a lively, liberatory forum for an aristocratic lesbian elite.

The Growth of a Romance and a Theory

An amateur painter of Scottish descent, Anstruther-Thomson met Lee in England in 1887 and visited her in Florence the following year. This courtship, which coincided with a period of physical recuperation for Lee (who suffered from chronic neuralgia), included daily drives in the environs of Florence to humor the invalid and Anstruther-Thomson's introduction to political economy under Lee's guidance. After reading John Ruskin and John Stuart Mill, Anstruther-Thomson forsook painting and underwent an independent study of art with the intent of eventually guiding East Enders through London art galleries. Such a course of study must have been something of a revelation to Anstruther-Thomson, who had enjoyed an aristocratic childhood that Matthew Arnold would have called quintessentially "Barbarian": her family's interests were overwhelmingly equestrian, and her formal education had been "left to the stud groom."[7] Between 1884 and 1889 she studied modern painting at the South Kensington, the Slade, and the studio of Carolus Duran in Paris;[8] she asserted her authority as a practical artist, claiming later, when Lee was preparing a lecture in 1892 on Renaissance sculpture, "I helped her with the technical and anatomical reasons of various things."[9] It was only on embracing art philanthropy that she began to compensate for her inadequate learning.[10] Lee's accounts and Anstruther-Thomson's letters offer evidence that during the 1890s Anstruther-Thomson read on political economy, Gothic architecture, and seventeenth-century painting, attended lectures on sculpture given by the archaeologist Eugenie Sellars, and briefly studied illuminated twelfth-century missals under Emery Walker.[11] Still, Anstruther-Thomson limited herself largely to a firsthand exploration of composition as constituted by lines and masses against one another in a constant play of spatial pressures. Her description of a jumping hare is typical: "The palm leaf at the stop swings him forward, but the big spiral behind him collects itself and holds back."[12]

During a gallery visit in March 1894, Anstruther-Thomson noticed that her breathing altered in response to different paintings. Lee seized on the discovery delightedly; here was proof of art's benefit to the body. From there it was a short step to asserting that the body gained vitality by literally echoing the "pulls forward" and "lifts up" the eye perceived. While Anstruther-Thomson continued to monitor her own sensations before art objects, Lee immersed herself in the literature of psychology.[13] She discovered a theoretical foundation for Anstruther-Thomson's responses in William James's *Principles of Psychology* (1890). Here James had argued that bodily changes do not follow an emotion but themselves constitute that emotion: in Lee's words, "a man does not weep because he feels sad, but feels sad because he weeps."[14] From this, Lee arrived at the theory of aesthetic empathy: the idea that contemplation of a beautiful object elicits hidden motor adjustments in the viewer, an unconscious imitation of the form one sees and a projection of one's bodily movements back onto it. We acknowledge shapes or scenes as beautiful when the lines within them fulfill our vital needs for balance, rhythm, and weight.

In an age that valued scientific objectivity, Lee sought to tabulate minute data about the body's reactions to particular phenomena as a means of arriving at general physiological laws. But unlike social scientists such as Charles Booth who used demographic statistics to reach their conclusions, she focused only on Anstruther-Thomson. Lee posited that nature had endowed Anstruther-Thomson with an extraordinary "bodily organization," enabling her to see in art what others overlooked. Lee made a cult of the vigor she envied and adored in her lover, projecting those properties of ease and health onto "good" art when she described it as "resilient," "vital," "restorative," "braced."

In their essay "Beauty and Ugliness" (1897) Lee cited Anstruther-Thomson's response to the facade of the Santa Maria Novella church in Florence as the epitome of a viewer's physiological act of "miming." Anstruther-Thomson wrote in her gallery journal:

> [T]he facade . . . is planted solidly on the ground, and the perception of this fact involves a sense of weight and lifting up in ourselves; we feel a faint desire to enclose the form between the pressure of our feet on the ground and the very slight downward pressure of the head, and the two pressures result in resisting gravitation. They can be tracked to the perception of the grip of the ground of the facade's base and the downward pressure of the mouldings and cornices. On the other hand, the arches and upswinging lines produce sensations of easy liftings up and of pleasant activity which more than counter-balance these downward pressures, so that the main impression is one of light-heartedness.[15]

With terms like "easy," "pleasant," and "light-heartedness" Lee and Anstruther-Thomson justified the social value of aesthetic empathy by claiming that a deeper attention to art would prompt the viewer to feel invigorating muscular sensations and hence increased happiness. Just as Ruskin had defended the morality of beauty on the basis of the worker's decent conditions of art production they posited a "beauty of health" contingent on their belief that a work of art exists to improve the viewer's physical experience of life.

So then, from the start a strong social-reform ethic pervaded the women's relationship and project. As her letters indicate, Anstruther-Thomson took a strong interest in modern class struggles, such as the rights of exploited match girls and London dockworkers and the lobby for the London School Board to provide school lunches for children. She lectured on aesthetics at Toynbee Hall and joined Lee as a docent for "Toynbee Travellers," visiting Florence and Rome.[16] According to Lee, Anstruther-Thomson would have devoted her life to "nursing, doctoring, or some sort of social organizing" if she had not "persuaded herself that the accumulated treasures of art must be made accessible to the less privileged classes, and that this could be compassed by explaining the manner in which art works upon our spirit."[17]

Yet in the act of explaining how the Santa Maria Novella facade "works upon our spirit," Anstruther-Thomson relied on assumptions attributable to Walter Pater, not Ruskin. Asking the very questions that Pater had posed in his introduction to *The Renaissance: Studies in Art and Poetry* — "What is this song or picture . . . to me? . . . How is my nature modified by its presence, and under its influence?" — Anstruther-Thomson, as we have seen, judged an object's aesthetic value by its capacity to evoke pleasant physical sensations, whether of temperature, respiration, or, most crucially, the push and pull of its external shape and interior lines.[18] In this way she confirmed the legitimacy of the individual's own impressions. Lee, after years of painstaking historical research on the arts, found this faith in one's instincts liberating. As a travel writer, she had long responded to landscape through artful reveries that paid homage to Pater's style. It was only under the guidance of Anstruther-Thomson in the 1890s that Lee sought sensory impressions within the gallery site itself: Anstruther-Thomson "was always seeing, asking herself what, or rather, how, she saw. And, becoming aware that, in her sense of seeing, I saw half nothing, I tried to learn to see by looking at her way of looking at things. This, when it was successful, meant that I was learning to see a little with my own eyes and my own reactions."[19] Once initiated, Lee berated art critics for their "unconscious[ness] of the changes [art] might work in your being" and asserted that "to appreciate any kind of art means, after all, not to appreciate its relations to other kinds of art, but to feel its relations with ourselves."[20]

As her "gallery jottings" demonstrate, Anstruther-Thomson was steered by her Paterian predilections. Like Lee, she maintained that the literary meaning and/or verisimilitude of a work of art did not matter as much as the arrangement of its formal components. But what lends interest to Anstruther-Thomson's critiques of sculpture is that she often attributes the formal tensions in the figure to the literary evocations of the sculpture's theme, re-creating the instant in which the figure has been frozen (for example, winged Mercury is unevenly balanced, hence poised to fly). Anstruther-Thomson's prose has its "Gioconda-like" moments, for instance in her description of Michelangelo's sculpture of the goddess Night, which

> has shaken off the garish mask of day and seems to be leaving it behind as she comes sinking down through the dusk. She might go sweeping downwards for ever if the movement were not stopped by her upraised foot which steadies and checks it. Her foot, all shining and luminous, rests on the fruits of the earth (one makes them out with difficulty, for they are rough hewn and there-

> fore arrest the eye); apples and corn asleep under the gleam of the moon. Night, too, is asleep, her head drooping; only the star in her hair and the young moon looking upwards; everything else suggesting the hush of the world and the sinking down of the darkness into its sleep. Only the owl is awake, the bird of night who stands by her vigilant like a warrior in his armour. We were meant to notice his presence, for he is very carefully worked; his surface is left rough (the moonlight does not touch him); his plumage is most carefully rendered. His eyes seem to pierce rather than merely to see. Perhaps he is looking back, while the evil world sleeps through the centuries, at the happier things which were first shown him by his first mistress, Athena; erect and vigilant, he keeps guard.[21]

Anstruther-Thomson's customary attention to unity in composition and weight in equilibrium (the upraised foot balancing the figure's downward motion, the stars and moon lifting up against the drooping head) is evident in this passage, as is her sensitivity to the effect of texture, which sets the pace of the viewer's eye, either giving it something to grip or eluding it and requiring a succession of glances, just as a slippery surface in shadow does elsewhere in the statue. But at times Anstruther-Thomson leaves the vocabulary of push and pull to build a narrative from the figure's literary symbolism. She re-creates the moment itself ("she comes sinking," "he keeps guard"), while dramatizing the sculpture's formal tensions through a conditional future ("she might go sweeping downwards"). Anstruther-Thomson characteristically uses a figure's eyes or hair as a point of departure for her most Paterian criticism: open lids or protruding curls over the eyes substantiate her later observation that "it looks ahead" and enable her to imagine what it sees. From the owl's piercing eyes, she glimpses his vision of an "evil world [sleeping] through the centuries," reminiscent of La Gioconda's Borgias and vampires.

Fascinated with her own muscular judgments on art, Anstruther-Thomson ignored her new studies of traditional art criticism and history while in the gallery. For instance, after reading up on Flemish paintings, she concluded, characteristically, "The Flemish art has a slightly petrifying action on one's vitals which I struggled under the whole time. . . . I believe it is a tense, unserene art isn't it making me breathe high up as in a Gothic church, and giving one a semi-lump in one's throat in consequence it's an emotional strain."[22] In 1894 Anstruther-Thomson took lessons in connoisseurship from Bernard Berenson: not only did she find these incomprehensible, but as her notes convey, she ignored his directives in the hours she devoted to the private study of art.[23] Instead, she adopted methods so literal that they strike the reader as comical in their physicality. To test a new theory that we best perceive sculpture under cold conditions, Anstruther-Thomson took off her gloves and put them on again. She arrived at the triumphant conclusion that "you can only see/feel the third dimension with one foot out in front of you."[24] Smiling, which Anstruther-Thomson defined as a "lifting up of the weight of the diaphragm," "comes naturally with one's hands on one's ribs, but it can be done if you carry a full gladstone bag in each hand."[25]

The Loss of Ethical Criteria in Psychological Aesthetics

Avid in her search for physiological proofs, Anstruther-Thomson did not confine her focus on her own body to her notebook but exercised her penchant for performing before others. As she designed her gallery tours, she did not attempt to turn her viewers into better, more responsible people, just into people more sensitive to art. She thus altered the character of psychological aesthetics in practice, unwittingly obscuring its long-term social objectives.

After 1900 Lee revised her original thesis that one physically mimed the lines of a work of art and now claimed that the sensation of miming merely occurred in the viewer's mind through internal acts of memory and association. With this Lee intensified art's ethical imperative: she located the viewer's physical discomfort and enervation when contemplating a work of art in the distasteful stored associations art could awaken. She tested this idea of storage in her fictional dialogues on "aspirations and duties," *Baldwin* (1886) and its sequel, *Althea* (1894).[26]

The aristocratic aesthetes who populate *Baldwin* and *Althea* experience an aesthetic "keenness" that regulates their social relations. Lee suggests in these texts that one can only feel enjoyment in entertainment if it evokes reverberations of the morally good: one character remarks wonderingly of a musical solo, "it made me think of all the good people I knew."[27] In lectures of the 1890s, Lee proposes a process wherein "the desire for [formal] congruity [in art] . . . may expand and develop into such love of harmony between ourselves and the ways of the universe as shall make us wince at other folks' loss united to our gain, at their deterioration united to our pleasure, even as we wince at a false note or a discordant arrangement of colours."[28] The degradation of the poor pains Lee's aesthete Lady Althea, because it offends this morally endowed aesthetic sense. She endures a "sort of semi-aesthetic sensitiveness of fibre which also made . . . the thought of concrete evil as intolerable as a series of false notes or a disgusting smell."[29]

Because Lee believed a harmonious life was contingent on conscientious consumer choices, she used the rhetoric of political economy to contrast the aesthete's ethical discrimination with the decadent's focus on bodily and spiritual pleasures.[30] The "intrusion of baser things" will "make holes in [the] soul, and let . . . pleasure, serenity, ooze and leak out and be wasted."[31] Not only do the decadent's "rapture" and "excess" produce his own restlessness and lassitude, but they harm others. When he justifies having strawberries in January "because it contributes to raise the standard of refined and exquisite living," he requires more work out of already exhausted laborers.[32] Baldwin reprimands him: "What right have you to a diminution of the pain mixed up with your pleasure by a diminution of the pleasure mixed up with your neighbor's pain?"[33] Through such wasteful caprices, the wealthy decadent also mocks his responsibility to act as an ethical model and spiritual prophet to the masses. Baldwin challenges him, "What right have you to curtain out the intellectual light from eyes which are required to see for others as well as for yourself?"[34]

Baldwin and his friends not only prophesy but also embody Lee's dual vision of evolutionary refinement and communal harmony. She imagined that everyone could acquire a refined aesthetic sensibility that would prompt a more astute sense of sympathy and social responsibility, resulting in a voluntary, gradual, cooperative social reorganization that would include a redistribution of capital and labor. Her desire for a consolidation of aesthetic and moral senses led Lee to endow the exemplary character of Althea, Lee's loving fictionalization of Anstruther-Thomson, with exceptional virtue as well as aesthetic acuteness. This is ironic, because Anstruther-Thomson failed to grasp Lee's new emphasis on the interplay of personal memories during the moment of aesthetic appreciation; in gallery tours she continued to advance their original concept of psychological aesthetics as a science of miming the art object. This meant that Anstruther-Thomson's tours promoted a shallow "art for sensation's sake," relieved of the imperative of judging one's impressions as moral or immoral.

By focusing on the immediate and sensory, Anstruther-Thomson divested Lee's psychological aesthetics not only of its moral intent but of its academic pretenses. Lee's striving for scholarly legitimacy prompted her to use a jargon-laden, circular prose in her explanations of Anstruther-

Thomson's gallery notes in "Beauty and Ugliness." In contrast, Anstruther-Thomson's prose stands out for its raw, practical vocabulary, what Lee called a "very homely language."[35]

Throughout her writings Anstruther-Thomson resisted the dry, academic language preferred by Lee. She described her studies of art's impact on her body as "taking things to bits," "what it is all about," looking for "what it all hitches on to."[36] When she and Lee tested the impact of sound on the visual reception of art, she characterized the loss of vividness when rhythms ceased as "the statue dropping to pieces."[37] As if aware that her word choices were inadequate, she fell back on italics as a means of pressing the reader into understanding, for example, "trying to find out what *It* is doing."[38] But awkward invented nouns like "overheadness" and "underfootness," "the lifts up" and "the pressures down" convey her meaning with immediacy. Like Lee, she knew that borrowing from medical terminology to describe conditions of sight, hearing, and respiration would lend her writing credence. While in London in 1896, she visited the medical college to view models of eyes and ears.[39] But her study appears to have been cursory, and in her notes she uses scientific words like "fovea" to launch flights of fancy ("how it feels") rather than to describe physiological processes. "The reason we see so widely now is that the aisles [of the church] have caught the outside of our eyes, and we seem to see with the whole of both eyes instead of only with the fovea. . . . [W]e seem to follow the aisles . . . by some unconscious movements of our ears . . . and this sensation sideways gives us the curious sense of living sideways as well as living to the front."[40] Anstruther-Thomson was more concerned to speculate on her impressions than to prove them, and her notes capture this spirit of subjective inquiry: she dots her prose with exclamation points at moments of excited discovery. Feeling that her lively notions were deadened and betrayed by Lee's pedantry, she advised a friend against reading "Beauty and Ugliness" in full.

Resistant to abstraction as a rule, Anstruther-Thomson eventually turned away from art history: after briefly "dipping into" some French works on the philosophy of beauty, she notoriously dismissed aesthetic scholarship altogether ("Le Bô").[41] Bernard Berenson referred to Anstruther-Thomson as "bovine" in her sensibilities and only retracted his claim that she had absolutely no memory for art in 1897, when, on reading "Beauty and Ugliness," he accused her and Lee of plagiarizing his ideas.[42] At this point Anstruther-Thomson had already suffered a mental breakdown from overwork while trying to revise the notes of her experiments into book form.[43] Intent on refuting Berenson's allegations, an exhausted Anstruther-Thomson returned to her notebooks to cite the dates and locations of her independent discoveries. At least one critic has argued that, while retracing her development, she realized exactly how much her theory owed to Berenson's docentship.[44] Whatever the case, Anstruther-Thomson withdrew from the revisions of "Beauty and Ugliness" and from the greater book project that was to have grown from the essay.

But did this end her participation in psychological aesthetics? While she freed herself from the rigors of formal study, Anstruther-Thomson continued to claim the role of seer that psychological aesthetics had afforded her in social circles. If Lee had exploited the impersonal voice of nineteenth-century science as a means of gaining authority among the elite aestheticians whom she saw as her peers, Anstruther-Thomson too sought authority but had another audience in view.

From Proof to Practice: Lesbian Exhibition in Anstruther-Thomson's Gallery Tours

Writing to Lee in 1894, Anstruther-Thomson enthusiastically described a performance of Hungarian musicians she had witnessed at a party the night before: "presently it came home to me that it didn't matter what rubbish they played what they were really playing was us. They were flattening us down between the boards & then blowing life into us, and chucking us aloft sometimes bringing us down with a tearing rush like a toboggan ride, & sometimes in little tosses like a feather with suspensions in between when nothing happened except anxiety."[45] This trope of being played upon is familiar to readers of decadent fiction: Lord Henry Wotton, for instance, relishes his influence over Dorian Gray, "Talking to him was like playing upon an exquisite violin. He answered to every thrill and touch of the bow."[46] In Lee's own *Miss Brown,* Walter Hamlin "enjoy[s] playing upon a living soul . . . slow to respond to his touch, with low and long-sustained vibrations, like those of a deep-toned instrument."[47] We can judge Anstruther-Thomson's gallery tours in the context of decadent novels in which protagonists endure painful self-revelations as they abandon their bodies and wills to their own experiments or yield to the pseudoscientific machinations of others. Lee had recognized aesthetic schooling as a potential site of domination and impure influence. In a crucial teaching scenario in *Miss Brown,* the pernicious Edmund Lewis spreads before the vicar's daughters a portfolio of nudes: throwing collusive looks at his fellow painter, Hamlin, he seems to anticipate his young subjects' titillation and hopes to encourage it. This scene ironically anticipates the decadent direction of psychological aesthetics in practice.

The galleries provided Anstruther-Thomson and Lee with a forum where, one coyly, the other subconsciously, they could resurrect the influence of *Miss Brown*'s Edmund Lewis — here, on an eager audience of onlookers. According to Burdett Gardner, "Vernon Lee gathered around her a whole flock of young girls, who experienced a kind of redemption under her aegis and wrote to her in ecstatic and glassy eyed gratitude."[48] Lee sought a strange, vicarious gratification by eliciting her protégées' physical excitement through her descriptions of art. Anstruther-Thomson acted as a kind of procurer, endorsing a rebounding titillation by recounting other women's admiration for Lee in physical terms, "I think she thinks about you with bated breath 'that wonderful woman' she says when she asks what you think about things."[49] "I met a girl today at Mrs. Humphry Ward [*sic*]. I don't know who she was but she said, 'I went to Vernon Lee's lecture and it was like a new world to me. It has made things look quite different' this with a little gasp of enthusiasm. I think this is what you wanted to do isn't it."[50] This trademark "gasp" occurs more than once in Anstruther-Thomson's letters to Lee; we can read it as a sign of sexual passion projected onto the art object. In the letters themselves it is a metaphor, a fragment of a coded language about sex and sensibility within this social milieu, where romantic friendships informed intellectual endeavors. The women who allegedly fell under Lee's spell often thanked her for the discriminating, assiduous direction of their learning and begged for her attentions in greedy, desperate tones: "I want more lessons from you badly!"[51]

As resident "motor-type," Anstruther-Thomson too prompted not only her viewers' vicarious experience of heightened respiration but their breathless admiration for her. As she advised fellow upper-class women to imagine how her body felt and to imitate her postures, she constructed a theater for female eroticism. Certainly, nowhere else short of the opera house were women prone to same-sex romances and idolatries given license (here, prescribed) to observe the body of another woman, her gestures, her vocal inflections, so attentively.[52] But even more, Anstruther-Thomson brought to the gallery floor the supernatural airs that Lee had admired in the late 1880s, endowing the project with mystery and herself with second sight. She conducted aesthetic empathy as more of a parlor game than a science. Dame Ethel Smyth described a performance by Anstruther-Thomson that clearly surpassed the miming of lines in art:

> To give an illustration of Vernon's method of eliciting pronouncements from her oracle, some few years ago I had gone with her and Kit to the Vatican, when, pulling up before what Baedeker rather unnecessarily described as a Roman copy of a Greek bust of Apollo, but which Il Palmerino [Vernon Lee] had decided was a Greek original, Vernon suddenly said, "Kit! show us that bust!" Kit's proceedings were remarkable; in dead silence she advanced, then retreated, shaded her eyes, and then ejaculated, "Look at that Johnny! how he sings! . . . how he sings!" Various technical details were then pointed out as proving their contention, though Vernon considered these less important than the singing quality discovered by her friend. And afterwards, when I privately expressed my opinion of this style of Art Criticism, Vernon was very angry and begged me not to "expose" myself.[53]

The scene resembles one out of *The Bostonians* not merely for the subtext of a power dynamic within a sexually charged same-sex relationship (Lee demands an explication from Anstruther-Thomson, who surpasses her in "sight") but also for the bizarre mysticism of Anstruther-Thomson's performance, which emulates a séance through its "dead silence," dramatic motions, including the shading of the eyes, and unexpected burst of words as impenetrable as any parable.

Submissive to the alleged influences of art, masterful as a performer and director, Anstruther-Thomson transformed Lee's aesthetic mission into a decadent amusement. It is no wonder, following this giddy period of proud spectacle, that Anstruther-Thomson, having deserted Lee and the task of revising "Beauty and Ugliness," continued to act as a prophet to young women into the 1910s, escorting them through galleries, judging the paintings before them in terms of push and pull, and eliciting their wonder and admiration. Radiantly attired in patent-leather shoes and white kid gloves ("she was the height of a Guardsman," Irene Cooper Willis commented), she delighted in her influence.[54]

In Italy, Anstruther-Thomson may have been the model of studious, solitary industry for which Lee venerated her, but in London her gallery experiments were social tête-à-têtes, often devolving into giggles. After these experiments she would revere her friends for their aesthetic sensibility in letters to Lee. She wondered why an acquaintance who likes the "right pictures" does not "turn into an expert." Another companion "sometimes says quite luminous things about Renaissance sculptures." Seeking proof of talent, Anstruther-Thomson could be equally trenchant about others' aesthetic callousness. In correspondence she ridiculed acquaintances whose pronouncements on art failed to convince her:

"blighted sort of manner of hers, you know & a little gasp! — in the middle of a banal sentence." Ultimately, in her own ranks psychological aesthetics was about performance, authority, and exclusion. Those who earned Anstruther-Thomson's approbation, however, delighted in the sexually charged rituals of her gallery tours.

In an 1896 letter to Lee, Anstruther-Thomson playfully coined the phrase "delicate brains" as a code word for lesbianism, implying that a sharpened aesthetic sensibility originated in one's sexual orientation. Perhaps, in the galleries, she appealed to her fellow female aristocrats by imbuing her revelations with the innuendos of a shared upper-class lesbian subculture. But there is one obstacle to this thesis. Unlike, say, modern-day dramas by New York City's WOW Café, which address a lesbian audience through subcultural in-jokes,[55] Anstruther-Thomson's performances before these women may not have contained particular innuendo; we have no transcripts of them besides that in Smyth's memoir and no evidence that they differed from the tours she offered to working people.[56] It is only retrospectively in letters to Lee that Anstruther-Thomson clearly eroticized their relationship to upper-class devotees. If, in gallery tours for the working classes, Anstruther-Thomson continued to draw attention to her body and to demonstrate the same pushings up and pressures down, in her letters following these art tours she expunged her performances of their potential eroticism.

But What of the Poor? Oversights in Psychological Aesthetics

If "delicate brains" were essentially the province of a lesbian aristocratic elite, why try to disseminate them at all? Here is the crux of Anstruther-Thomson's joyful, carefree social invention of the 1890s in relation to her reformist imperative. Convinced that she had to live a life of aristocratic female philanthropy, Anstruther-Thomson took the talent with which Lee had subjectively endowed her, her alleged muscular keenness to art, and contrived it into a gift to the poor. But for aesthetic empathy to be recognized as a philanthropic practice, it had to conform to — and be regulated by — the still-prevailing discourse of 1870s missionary aestheticism. In letters about her lectures to the working classes, Anstruther-Thomson recasts herself as a bourgeoise who undertakes docent work for the usual reasons: she laments (in the tradition of Ruskin and William Morris) the loss of handicraft and the ensuing alienation of people from art and asserts (in the tradition of the Sunday Society, to which she belonged) that one might be as starved for art as for bread. "I see for certain that one must show people things there is a regular gulf fixed isn't there between the producer and the consumer. Like wheat waiting for ships at Odessa and shipless people waiting for it."[57] Gone are the allusions to little gasps.

Anstruther-Thomson's recorded responses to laborers convey her enthusiasm and energy, but they are maddeningly vague about the lessons themselves. On one occasion early in 1893, she wrote to Lee, "I've had to throw over all my artisan and factory women that I was going to show museums to. They are such nice people. & so interested its simply impossible to send them to sleep when one tells them about things. They are so ready and they remember every thing."[58] Elsewhere she wrote, "I find I am shifted into the appalling predicament of having to take 30 youths from Waterloo Bridge Road through Praxeletes & [indiscernible] on the way! When I think of it I wish I were dead, but I wished I was dead last Sat when I had to take some East End girls round but when the time came I liked it very much they were so clever & delightful so perhaps it won't be so bad."[59] As a performer, Anstruther-Thomson demands an attentive audience: she "tells them about things"; they are "nice" because they listen, understand, and remember it all. It seems that she does let them critique the art themselves, since the women are "clever," but presumably they are acting in compliance with her method, and this is why she is pleased. Rather than seeking a Pygmalion among the novices (for she remembers no working people by name, nor even individually in the letters), she is intent on demonstrating her insight to them, just as she had among her aristocratic friends. She permits herself an expression of class condescension when complaining of the weariness of her "business," but one cannot tell if it was merely the size of the crowd that appalled her or an unspoken embarrassment at their noise or demeanor.

Had Anstruther-Thomson thought more about it, their difference in class might have provoked her to question her presumed equation between her body and their bodies. Her body had rested in English country houses and luxurious Italian villas and had exercised on their grounds; her eyes had witnessed cathedrals on the Continent. But their bodies, strapped by the need to work and lack of money, were bound within the sphere of East End streets and sweatshops, had encountered nature only rarely, and had had little access to travel. Following her style of sanctioning the personal associations art objects evoked in her, how were these men and women to comprehend her declaration that the Venus de Milo "moves like a sailing yacht?"[60] This oversight was Lee's as well. In essays Lee had cursed aristocrats' hiding art from the poor.[61] But in psychological aesthetics, when she cited Anstruther-Thomson's body as a model to be imitated and urged "everyone" to give themselves voluntarily to a work of art for health's sake, to "meet [art] more than half-way," she overlooked their lack of leisure to visit and revisit an exhibit.[62]

At one point in an 1896 letter to Lee, Anstruther-Thomson, echoing Lee's Ruskinian essays, acknowledged that exposure to art is difficult under capitalism: "nobody can see a Botticelli if they are trying to catch a train, and nobody can see discord in life if they are wrastling after advantage at high pressure." Yet what solutions did she offer the laborer who had no choice but to "desire things," to struggle for a livelihood, to catch trains? None: however "socialistically-inclined," she shied from advocating revolution.[63] Instead, she censured "practical people" whose "anxiety" and "desiring things" deceive them into feeling "as if [life] were leaning forward before a work of art." She concluded, "Getting an eye for life-as-it-may-be is just like getting an eye for genuine Botticellis. After a bit, people couldn't do with coarse things or discordant things."[64] Promoting the gallery tour as a catalyst for sharpening universal aesthetic sensibility, Anstruther-Thomson hardly alluded to the denouement that was Lee's primary objective: a more just civilization arising from a correspondent evolution of human sympathy. As she transformed the gallery space into a zone for the disclosure of mutual appeal, Anstruther-Thomson ultimately focused on the erotic emancipation of her own kind — moneyed, independent women.

Notes

I am grateful to Colby College's librarian of special collections, Nancy Reinhart, for her generous assistance and to Regenia Gagnier, Joss Marsh, Seth Koven, and the Stanford University Victorian reading group for critiquing earlier drafts of this essay.

1. Vernon Lee, *The Beautiful: An Introduction to Psychological Aesthetics* (Cambridge: Cambridge University Press, 1913), 1.

2. Irene Cooper Willis, Vernon Lee notes, 1950, Vernon Lee Collection, Colby College Library, Waterville, Maine, 14.

3. Vernon Lee, introduction to *Art and Man: Essays and Fragments,* by Clementina Anstruther-Thomson (London: John Lane, The Bodley Head, 1924), 12.

4. Ibid., 30.

5. Phyllis Mannocchi, "Vernon Lee and Kit Anstruther-Thomson: A Study of Love and Collaboration between Friends," *Women's Studies* 12 (1986): 130–31.

6. Lillian Faderman, *Odd Girls and Twilight Lovers* (New York: Columbia University Press, 1991), 23–24; Esther Newton, "The Mythic, Mannish Lesbian: Radclyffe Hall and the New Woman," *Signs* 9, no. 4 (1984): 561.

7. Lee, introduction to *Art and Man,* 9.

8. For a glimpse of Duran's atelier and the Slade as a center for popular "greenery-yallery" aestheticism, see Stuart Macdonald, *The History and Philosophy of Art Education* (London: University of London, 1970), 146–48.

9. Clementina Anstruther-Thomson, "Statement Describing the Writing of Beauty and Ugliness," 1898, Vernon Lee Collection.

10. Lee, introduction to *Art and Man,* 27.

11. Ibid.; Anstruther-Thomson, "Statement"; Clementina Anstruther-Thomson to Vernon Lee, n.d., Vernon Lee Collection. Anstruther-Thomson did not customarily date her letters. Archivists of the Vernon Lee Collection have divided her letters to Vernon Lee into four consecutive folders.

12. Anstruther-Thomson, *Art and Man,* 119.

13. René Wellek, "Vernon Lee, Bernard Berenson, and Aesthetics," in *Discriminations: Further Concepts of Criticism* (New Haven, Conn.: Yale University Press, 1970), 169–70.

14. Lee, introduction to *Art and Man,* 47.

15. Vernon Lee, *Beauty and Ugliness and Other Studies in Psychological Aesthetics* (London: John Lane, The Bodley Head, 1912), 188.

16. Lee, introduction to *Art and Man,* 26.

17. Ibid., 27. Lee alternated between advocating an aesthetic of social conscience and recoiling from it in defense of the formal values of art; she thus isolated herself from social-reform missionary aesthetes who had established societies to "elevate" the poor through gifts of beauty. See Vineta Colby, "The Puritan Aesthete: Vernon Lee," in *The Singular Anomaly: Women Novelists of the Nineteenth Century* (New York: New York University Press, 1970), 238. On missionary aestheticism, see Diana Maltz, "Lessons in Sensuous Discontent: The Aesthetic Mission to the British Working Classes, 1869–1914" (Ph.D. diss., Stanford University, 1997).

18. Walter Pater, *Selected Writings of Walter Pater,* ed. Harold Bloom (New York: Columbia University Press, 1974), 17.

19. Lee, introduction to *Art and Man,* 30.

20. Vernon Lee, *Laurus Nobilis: Chapters on Life and Art* (London: John Lane, The Bodley Head, 1909), 164–65.

21. Anstruther-Thomson, *Art and Man,* 306.

22. Anstruther-Thomson to Lee, Vernon Lee Collection.

23. Anstruther-Thomson, "Statement."

24. Anstruther-Thomson to Lee, Vernon Lee Collection.

25. Ibid.

26. While *Baldwin* (London: Unwin, 1886) predates Lee's discovery of psychological aesthetics in the 1890s, it charts her vision that art must be disseminated by an elite and her faith that a universally refined aesthetic sensibility would prompt a more astute sense of social responsibility.

27. Vernon Lee, *Althea: A Second Book of Dialogues on Aspirations and Duties* (London: Osgood, McIlvaney, 1894), 87–88.

28. Lee, *Laurus,* 105.

29. Lee, *Althea,* 352.

30. Lee, *Laurus,* 63. In *Physiological Aesthetics* (London: H. S. King, 1877), Grant Allen posited pleasure and pain as bodily gains and losses and the beautiful as a "filter or disinfectant" protecting the body from the ravages of daily life. Lee applied Allen's paradigm of pleasure and pain to the social organism, weighing "the constant reaction of one creature upon the other"; see *Baldwin,* 333–34.

31. Vernon Lee, *Juvenilia: Being a Second Series of Essays on Sundry Aesthetical Questions* (London: Unwin, 1887), 210.

32. Lee, *Althea,* 174.

33. Lee, *Baldwin,* 158.

34. Ibid., 40.

35. Lee, introduction to *Art and Man,* 92.

36. Ibid., 30, 46, 47.

37. Ibid., 36.

38. Ibid., 46.

39. Anstruther-Thomson to Lee, Vernon Lee Collection.

40. Anstruther-Thomson, *Art and Man,* 188–89.

41. Lee, introduction to *Art and Man,* 65.

42. *Selected Letters of Bernard Berenson,* ed. A. K. McComb (Boston: Houghton Mifflin, 1964), 15, 55.

43. Lee, introduction to *Art and Man,* 51.

44. Burdett Gardner, *The Lesbian Imagination (Victorian Style): A Psychological and Critical Study of "Vernon Lee"* (New York: Garland, 1987), 248, a facsimile of Gardner's Ph.D. dissertation (Harvard University, 1954).

45. Anstruther-Thomson to Lee, Vernon Lee Collection.

46. Oscar Wilde, *The Picture of Dorian Gray* (1891; reprint, Harmondsworth, U.K.: Penguin, 1985), 60.

47. Vernon Lee, *Miss Brown* (1884; reprint, New York: Garland, 1977), 2:56.

48. Gardner, 217. While valuable for its extensive quotes from interviews and unpublished manuscripts, Gardner's 1954 study of Lee classifies lesbianism as a pathological illness. He calls her popularity as a seer among young women "a focal point for aestheticism in its decline" (217). His discomfort with Lee's sexuality echoes that of her contemporaries; see Colby, 303 n. 67.

49. Anstruther-Thomson to Lee, Vernon Lee Collection.

50. Ibid.

51. Gardner, 301.

52. Terry Castle, *The Apparitional Lesbian* (New York: Columbia University Press, 1993), 202.

53. Dame Ethel Smyth, *What Happened Next* (London: Longmans, Green, 1940), 160.

54. Willis, 10.

55. Kate Davy, "Constructing the Spectator: Reception, Context, and Address in Lesbian Performance," *Performing Arts Journal* 10, no. 2 (1986): 46.

56. Assuming that Anstruther-Thomson's performance did not shift based on the economic class of her audience, we might consider whether lesbian content exists in the eye of the beholder. See Marilyn Frye, *The Politics of Reality* (Trumansburg, N.Y.: Crossing, 1983), 166–73; Bonnie Zimmerman, "'Perverse Reading': The Lesbian Appropriation of Literature," in *Sexual Practice, Textual Theory: Lesbian Cultural Criticism,* ed. Susan J. Wolfe and Julia Penelope (Oxford: Blackwell, 1993), 135–49.

57. Anstruther-Thomson to Lee, Vernon Lee Collection.

58. Ibid.

59. Ibid.

60. Anstruther-Thomson, *Art and Man,* 96.

61. Lee, *Laurus,* 53, 250.

62. Lee, *Beautiful,* 133.

63. Willis, 9.

64. Anstruther-Thomson to Lee, Vernon Lee Collection.

PART IV

Aestheticism into the Modern

Chapter 12

ANN ARDIS

Netta Syrett's Aestheticization of Everyday Life

Countering the Counterdiscourse of Aestheticism

> Fie on sinful fantasy!
> Fie on lust and luxury!
> Lust is but a bloody fire,
> Kindled by unchaste desire,
> Fed in heart, whose flames aspire,
> As thoughts do blow them, higher and higher.
> Pinch him, fairies, mutually;
> Pinch him for his villainy;
> Pinch him, and burn him, and turn him about,
> Till candles and starlight and moonshine be out.
> — *The Merry Wives of Windsor*

RECENT CRITICISM on the fin de siècle often emphasizes one of the following: the sexual politics of aestheticism, the New Woman's rebellion against Victorian gender ideology, or the homosocial subculture that flourished in the 1880s and early 1890s until Oscar Wilde's trials in 1895 again tipped the social scales in favor of cultural conservatism. Interest in these expressions of "sexual anarchy" has been a major impetus behind efforts to reconceptualize the period, to claim for the fin de siècle an epistemic integrity that it never has when annexed to either Victorianism or early modernism.[1]

Given current interests in and characterizations of the 1890s, it might seem curious that a woman writer who lived through the period, Netta Syrett, is silent on all such instances of "gender trouble" in her autobiography, *The Sheltering Tree* (1939).[2] As someone who made her debut as a writer in the 1890s through the stewardship of Grant Allen and who forged lasting friendships at that time with Mabel Beardsley, Richard Le

Gallienne, Ella D'Arcy, the Henry Harlands, May Sinclair, and Violet Hunt, she presumably would have had something to say about the scandal surrounding Wilde's trials, for example, or the controversy over Allen's *The Woman Who Did.* Instead, Syrett jokes briefly in *The Sheltering Tree* about having almost met Wilde at a party that he left shortly before her arrival; and she presents Allen as a kindly father figure and mentor whose respectable middle-class home provided a safe haven for her in the heady days of her arrival on the London scene. Prompted to write her autobiography in the late 1930s by a recent crop of novels "dealing with the terribly restricted life" of women at the end of the nineteenth century, she objects to characterizations of the 1890s as either "the naughty nineties" or an era of continued Victorian repression. "[T]here was no untidy Bohemianism about the *Yellow Book* set," she insists. "[E]ven in the 'eighties, so long as a girl was working at some art, profession, or business, she was perfectly free . . . [to] go about her lawful occupations without censure — even from the censorious."[3]

Syrett's experience somewhat disproves this last assertion: her promising career as a playwright ended abruptly in 1902, when a review of the opening-night performance of her first play, *The Finding of Nancy,* suggested that its depiction of extramarital sexuality was autobiographical.[4] Nonetheless, Syrett maintains a view of the 1890s in *The Sheltering Tree* quite different from that offered in recent critical studies such as Richard Dellamora's *Masculine Desire,* Rita Kranidis's *Subversive Discourse,* and Ed Cohen's *Talk on the Wilde Side.*[5]

What are we to make of this difference?

I would like to suggest in this essay that Syrett's tamer, more respectable version of life among the *Yellow Book* set represents an attempt to sever the chain of associations forged in the 1890s between aestheticism and effeminacy (read homosexuality), New Hellenism, and aristocratic degeneracy. As Dellamora, Cohen, and others have suggested, Wilde's trials in 1895 were a defining moment for aestheticism as well as for a modern conceptualization of homosexuality.[6] After the trials the fluidity (and ambiguity) of categories such as Uranianism, sexual inversion, and manly love was contained through a new and increasingly scientific vocabulary of gender opposition. After the trials aestheticism was commonly equated with homosexuality: in the bourgeois public's eye aestheticism *was* Oscar Wilde, *was* the scandal of his affair with Lord Alfred Douglas and his character's "Dorian" sensibility. As evidenced by disparaging references to the "softness of the 'nineties'" as much as twenty years later in modernist manifestos, this chain of associations endured well into the twentieth century.[7] Only the hypermasculinity of male modernism could, it seems, rescue either British aestheticism or masculinity from the scandal of effeminacy.

Such at least has been the standard line of argument about how aestheticism "traveled" — in Edward Said's sense of this term — into the twentieth century.[8] A close reading of Netta Syrett's *Anne Page* (1909), as well as a brief discussion of her *Strange Marriage* (1930) for the light it sheds on the earlier novel, however, suggests possibilities for a different mapping of aestheticism's legacies to the twentieth century.

Allusions in Syrett's novels to works such as Théophile Gautier's *Mademoiselle de Maupin* (1835), Joris-Karl Huysmans's *À rebours* (1884), and Max Beerbohm's *The Happy Hypocrite* (1897) indicate her familiarity with the most important manifestos of French and British aestheticism. But they also evidence her rejection of the major tenets of what Linda Hughes has termed "dominant 'masculine' aestheticism": self-differentiation from bourgeois culture; appropriation of femininity and feminine artifice as symbols of art's autonomy from nature; and association of the material (female) body with corruption, decay, and degeneration.[9] Although Syrett offers no commentary in her autobiography on the sexual politics of aestheticism and the homosociality of the 1890s, novels such as *Anne Page* and *Strange Marriage* register her critical response to both.

In *Masculine Desire* Dellamora has suggested that the "crises of sexual identity and male privilege" that precipitated the sexual scandals of the 1890s ultimately "issued in the reaffirmation of the naturalness of gender norms, of manly men and womanly women, of marriage, of the return of middle-class women to the home, and of the primacy of mothering."[10] As I hope to show here, Syrett's work begins to propose a feminist alternative to this yo-yo cycle of defiance and containment. Even though her female aesthetes readily acknowledge that "a sense of the Beautiful" remains beyond the reach of "normal humanity," Syrett refused masculine aestheticism's antagonistic self-differentiation from bourgeois culture.[11] She rejected the movement's bipolar figurations of femininity while savoring its aestheticization of everyday life. While direct references to sexual-identity crises and male privilege may be rare in Syrett's work, ample evidence of her response to the "counterdiscourse" of aestheticism exists nonetheless.[12]

In many regards the eponymous heroine of *Anne Page* is the antithesis of woman as figured by British and French aesthetes. She is not an androgynous ingenue onto whom a male aesthete can project all of his idealizing, and often homoerotic, fantasies of Beauty and Truth. Nor is she a femme fatale, one of those "connoisseurs of bestiality and serpentine delights" who will initiate him into the worldly pleasures of the flesh.[13] She is not a New Woman, compromising her femininity and her capacity to symbolize woman through her struggles for economic and emotional independence. Nor is she a figure of the anti-Platonic, anti-Hellenistic degeneracy of the modern world: unlike Rider Haggard's She, Anne Page ages into beauty, health, and vibrancy rather than withering away and shriveling up into a horrifyingly apelike corpse. A woman in her late fifties, she lives the life of an aesthete in the quiet Warwickshire village of Dymfield, having turned herself as well as her house and gardens into an object of art. At thirty-five she was on the verge of becoming an old maid. At fifty-nine she resembles more and more, as her sister-in-law notes, one of Joshua Reynolds's elegant eighteenth-century portraits.

In spite of occasional references to eighteenth-century standards of female beauty, however, *Anne Page* is grounded primarily in turn-of-the-century aesthetic discourses. Its treatment of French artists in the 1860s offers a carefully displaced commentary on British artistic, sexual, and identity issues in the 1890s.[14] One way to understand Syrett's take on these issues, and her decision to displace them to an earlier time period, is to examine the allusions to Shakespeare in *Anne Page* and to explore how Syrett treated aestheticism in her later novel *Strange Marriage.* Therefore, before discussing *Anne Page* at length I will look briefly at the changing uses to which Shakespeare's name was put in the 1890s and at allusions to Wilde and aestheticism in *Strange Marriage.*

The authority of Shakespeare's name was invoked for very different reasons in discussions of the cultural work of English literature before and after Wilde's trials.[15] In forums such as the *New Review*'s 1890 symposium on candor in English fiction, Shakespeare's representations of human sexuality were admired for being more "candid" than the contemporary British novelist's could be, given the circulating libraries' stranglehold on the literary marketplace. After the trials efforts were made to rescue "Shakespeare" from the taint of decadence, and he was cast as the antithesis of the "erotomania" of the early 1890s. Intent on promulgating a great national tradition that would lift literature above the "socio-literary portents" of "anarchy" wracking British culture in 1895, reviewers and publishers lauded Shakespeare and the classics in an effort to contain and counter the licensing of greater candor in English fiction. Most pertinent to this discussion of *Anne Page,* however, is Shakespeare's cameo appearance in Wilde's trials as a New Hellenist: a man of intense homoerotic and homosocial attachments; a man who loved Willie Hughes *and* the dark lady of the sonnets. This third "Shakespeare" was of course familiar to Victorians long before Edward Carson cross-examined Wilde regarding "The Portrait of Mr. W. H."[16] As one of the literary texts used to indict Wilde, though, this essay epitomizes the association of aestheticism with homosexuality that was forged in the trials, with such negative consequences for English culture for decades.

The one overt allusion to Wilde's trials in a Syrett novel comes very late in *Strange Marriage,* her novel about the 1890s. Reminiscing with a friend about their lives ten years earlier when she sees a number of their old *Yellow Book* crowd in a theater audience, the protagonist notes:

> [I]n spite of all the superfluous nonsense the Yellow Book period *was* exciting, wasn't it? When all's said and done, there was lots of enthusiasm going. People were really thrilled by new experiments in art and life. It was a kind of expansion, a Renaissance on a small scale. And now it's all over. Smashed — (ridiculously, as I think) — by the Oscar Wilde affair, and all that! People have got stodgy again, and talk and behave as though stodginess is the only preservation of virtue. (255)

This quiet aside may be read as a refusal to condone the homophobic panic generated by and orchestrated through Wilde's trials. Notably, Syrett's references to homosexuality in *Strange Marriage* are carefully indirect — a fact that may have had as much to do with events contemporaneous with the writing of this novel (for example, the obscenity trial of Radclyffe Hall's *The Well of Loneliness [1928]*) as with Syrett's impatience with characterizations of the naughtiness of the 1890s.[17] By setting the first part of her story about the *Yellow Book* crowd in the first half of the 1890s Syrett downplays the association of aestheticism with effeminacy and oppositional sexual politics. Although any number of elegantly dressed aesthetes move languidly through the London drawing rooms in which her naive young country-born heroine, Jenny Ferris, must learn to make her way after her marriage, Syrett chose not to characterize them as socially deviant in any way. Unlike Wilde's Dorian Gray, for example, they do not participate in the life of the London underworld: they do not visit opium dens near the docks, fraternize with working-class boys, inspire once handsome and respectable young gentlemen to commit suicide. Instead, Syrett stresses only that they delight Jenny with their witty conversation and artistic gifts. Aware of other people's concern about their respectability,

Jenny is initially clueless about why this might be the case. When an older woman friend, Mrs. Lenster, hints that Jenny's reputation might be adversely affected by her association with this group of men (mainly) and women who would not be admitted to the best London homes, Jenny responds by suggesting that dull respectable people are simply jealous of their brilliance. Although Mrs. Lenster dismisses Jenny's comment initially, she is forced to concede her point in the end. When she hears a famous composer sing at a "decadent" soiree, she recognizes how his "affectations and obvious insincerities" drop from him when he performs, "leaving only the artist and his perfect achievement" (131). Contrasting the "titillating notoriety" of the crowd in front of her with the more discreetly filled drawing rooms in which she normally socializes (and to which she would like Jenny to restrict herself), Mrs. Lenster "found herself wishing that . . . the Good and True in normal humanity more often included a sense of the Beautiful" (127, 131).

Although Syrett refuses to condone the conservative backlash against effeminacy in *Strange Marriage,* she does not endorse nonheterosexual sexual experimentation. Her critique of both the homosociality and the femina-phobia of the New Hellenism is strong in this novel; and she offers no positive representations of what we would now term lesbianism in any of her novels, though emotional intimacy between women figures significantly in all of her work. Instead, Syrett might best be described as an advocate of nonnormative heterosexuality. In *Strange Marriage,* for example, just prior to the sequence of events that culminates in the birth of Jenny's illegitimate son, the consummation of her marriage to an inhumanly ascetic aesthete, and her successful artistic collaboration with her husband, the narrator notes the following about Jenny Ferris's exposure to the *Yellow Book* set:

> It is inevitable . . . that she should have learnt more than an appreciation of art from the sophisticated group of men and women to which she had been drawn.
>
> The atmosphere of eroticism that permeated it, the talk of love affairs (to which the fact of matrimony appeared no bar), the hints at further mysteries to which, though till recently she had no key, the passionate music of Wagner, the no less passionate modern verse which she now devoured, had had its effect in transforming the unawakened girl into the present Jenny, a woman unfulfilled, eager for personal experience, thirsting for her share in the more glowing gifts of life.
>
> The danger point for Jenny had been reached. (157)

When Jenny reaches this danger point — as is the case in so many of Syrett's novels — she chooses to satisfy herself. Syrett's female characters may or may not be sexually experienced, may or may not be married. What matters to Syrett is that they treat their sexuality as one of life's "glowing gifts" (to borrow the Paterian language of the passage above). In Jenny's case this will entail: having an affair, bearing an illegitimate child, asking her aesthete husband to consummate their marriage four years after their wedding, and entering into a successful artistic partnership with him. The Ferrises' "strange marriage" is ultimately fecund — though not in ways that either "Mrs. Grundy" or the homosocial coterie of avant-gardists with whom Niel Ferris once associated might approve. For it will feature a joyous heterosexuality unmarked by homophobia, shelter Jenny's illegitimate child, and foster the artistic creativity of both partners. Rewriting *The Picture of Dorian Gray,* George Bernard Shaw's *Pygmalion,* and Max Beerbohm's *The Happy Hypocrite,* Syrett makes *Strange Marriage* a celebration of nonnormative heterosexuality: a story about a woman who saves her aesthete husband's life through the discovery of her own as well as his heterosexuality *and* artistic creativity.[18]

Knowing even this much about *Strange Marriage* makes it easier to appreciate Syrett's subtle but nonetheless striking dissociation of "Shakespeare" from fin-de-siècle "effeminacy" in *Anne Page,* her story of a female aesthete's life in a "really beautiful English village" that is as narrow-minded morally and aesthetically as its thatched roofs and cottage gardens are stereotypically English.[19]

Syrett's protagonist's name is borrowed, of course, from *The Merry Wives of Windsor.* Like Shakespeare's Anne Page, Syrett's is sweet, shy, "has brown hair and speaks small, like a woman" (126). When the French artists who are to figure so significantly in her life first meet her, she is carrying a great sheaf of lilac and hawthorn branches in from the garden she has spent five years restoring on the Warwickshire estate of her invalid patron, and they admire her as "something between a Botticelli Madonna and . . . [the] pagan goddess" Flora, while also noting that "Warwickshire is Shakespeare's country, and Anne Page is one of Shakespeare's women" (132, 129). These artists' appreciation of her simple and natural beauty contrasts sharply with her own sense that she is "desperately plain," having been "considered hideous all her life" (132). After her mother died and her brother left for Australia to seek his fortune, Anne lived for thirteen years with her father, "anxiously counting her weekly allowance for fear that with all her pains, both ends could not be made to meet" (115). When her father became a "hopeless invalid," she nursed him single-handedly and "tried to bear his exacting temper with patience" (115). After his death, when she was thirty, she was invited to live with friends of his who had met her once as a child and taken pity on her. In their well-stocked library and weed-ridden garden she spent the next five years of her life, reading English and French literature voraciously and through it imaginatively "enter[ing] into the life of the great world outside her country home" — all the while remaining "as ignorant" of "actual individual experience" "as she had been all through her quiet existence" (98).

This situation changes when René Dampierre comes to pay his respects to Anne's patron, an old friend of his family's, and he and his three young artist friends befriend Anne, who has never before been the center of attention or enjoyed the luxury of intellectual companionship. In the company of these sophisticated Frenchmen she blossoms, and their return to Paris at the end of the summer, Anne fears, represents the end of her short reprieve from "the stagnant peacefulness" of the village and "the isolation, [and] . . . narrowness of her life" (170, 155). When her patron dies and leaves her entire estate to Anne, however, she suddenly has an opportunity to do something she never would have imagined possible: travel to Paris and offer to live with Dampierre as his mistress.

This plot development deserves further explanation before I can pursue my point about Syrett's dissociation of aestheticism from "effeminacy" and oppositional sexual politics through her characterization of Anne and Anne's garden "in which only Shakespeare's flowers should grow" (159).

Before the French artists leave Dymfield at the end of that magical summer of Anne's transformation from a "Dead Sea Fruit" into a woman who is "dangerous" to men (202, 180), Anne has a long conversation with François Fontenelle about love, artists, and the talent of their mutual friend René Dampierre. René, François tells Anne, "has genius" (173). "He will be great, as Corot, as Daubigny are great. He is the coming man. . . . In ten years time, he will be a leader, the founder of a new school of painting" (173). "Unless, of course," he adds ominously, "he plays the [sentimental] fool" and marries (173). Why should that pose a problem, Anne asks in response, suggesting that "[h]e might find the right wife" (175). François smiles at what he considers her naïveté and treats her to a predictable late-nineteenth-century male aesthete's peroration on men, women, and art, in which he claims that love is a woman's "whole existence" while a male artist needs to be free of all "absorbing passions" lest his work "go to pot" when his life is "merged in the life of one woman"

(176). (Anne does not know this, but François subsequently reminds René that "the art of life . . . is to manage one's episodes carefully. And to see that they remain episodes" [197].) Rather than argue with him, Anne simply sighs and notes that "art is very cruel" (177). But she remembers Fontenelle's words when René comes to say good-bye the night before he is to leave for Paris. And remembering, she stops him before he can declare his love for her.

When she learns of her inheritance, however, Anne realizes that her new wealth makes it possible "to take a step the very existence of which, till [then], she had not perceived" (205). As an elderly woman's "penniless companion," Anne had allowed Fontenelle to convince her that René needed to remain free of all deep emotional attachments for the sake of his artistic genius (206). As "a lady of great means," though, and as "a woman who is leaving her youth behind," she realizes that "a great if brief happiness [is] within her reach" if she has the "courage to take it" (207, 206).

> René Dampierre was young. Naturally, inevitably, sooner or later, he would turn to youth for love, and she must not stand in his way.
>
> But because of this, could she not even for a little while know the joy which was every woman's birthright?
>
> If she were willing to pay for it, why not? Whatever happened, whatever misery was in store, at least she paid alone. She involved no one in her debt . . . It was only courage that was necessary. Courage to stake high, and not to shrink when sooner or later the odds should turn against her. (205-6)

When René proposes to her after her arrival in Paris, she lets him make his declaration of love. But her response shocks him: "I won't marry you, dear, because I'm too old for you. I will never marry you. But if you want me, I will stay" (213). She explains further: "Two months ago I was prepared never to see you again. But things have altered. . . . I'm a rich woman now, and my life is my own, to do what I like with it. And because I love you, I propose to give it to you, for a little while at least. As long as you want me" (214). When he protests that she does not know what she is saying, "You will marry me of course, because we love each other, because — " she interrupts him to repeat her words: "I will never marry you. . . . If you won't consent to let me stay as I suggest, I shall say goodbye to you now, and I will not see you again" (214–15). "If I stay," she continues, "we both have perfect freedom. I am old enough to do what I please with my life. And I please to do this. . . . Don't you see how simple it is? . . . I'm rich now, so I can stay as long as you — as long as I please"

(214–15).[20] She stays with René for three years, leaving before he even realizes that he is attracted to the woman whose portrait he is painting. Subsequently, she travels through Europe for ten years before returning to Dymfield to complete the work of restoring her house and its gardens.

This account of Anne's initial encounter with the Frenchmen and her time in France and Europe comes out only through Anne's and Fontenelle's retrospective musings. When the reader is introduced to Anne, twenty years have passed since she first met René, and she is hosting a dinner party at her Dymfield estate, at which she introduces her old friend Fontenelle to some of her neighbors: the rector and the doctor and their wives. The women are very surprised to learn that this famous Parisian artist is an old friend of Anne's, surprised too to realize that she is a "brilliant conversationalist," capable of holding her own in "the sort of conversation [about literature and art] to which Dymfield was unaccustomed" (13). As the doctor's wife notes, it is difficult to reconcile this "new view of her hostess" with the "Miss Page who would spend hours in discussing the organization of a mother's meeting, of a local flower show, of a Church bazaar" (14). As the doctor notes on another occasion, she is a "curious anomaly": she is capable of both maintaining friendly relations with Carfax, the archetypally closed-minded village rector, and making reference to Huysmans's *À rebours* when characterizing a color scheme in her garden. "Huysmans, and a country practice, and Carfax — and you! It's an amazing world. I hope some intelligent Being doesn't miss the exquisite humour of many human juxtapositions," he adds (81–82).

Anne changes the subject abruptly rather than respond to the doctor's comment, and the narrator does not interject to confirm or deny his observations. But Syrett's point is made nonetheless: at fifty-seven Anne Page is a worldly aesthete who lives comfortably among the stolid, unworldly gentry of Dymfield. She is capable of speaking intelligently about both current French art and mundane village affairs. She has a past that would be scandalous if it were known, yet she leads the life of a Victorian Lady Bountiful, beloved of everyone in Dymfield and sought after to solve every personal and social problem that arises. Rather than defiantly differentiating herself from bourgeois values — by flaunting her past or present ties to a world of art and culture far from Dymfield — she seems to live in accordance with the village's precepts. Her garden may remind her of "an elaborately arranged 'sensation' scheme, planned by that madman in *A Rebours.*" But she reserves this observation for the one man in her immediate circle who can appreciate it, Dr. Dakin. And she explains the significance of this garden's having been planted in "homely natural flower[s]" that Huysmans's Des Esseintes "would have despised" to no one (81).

The narrator offers no explanation of the garden's design, either. But as the backdrop for the novel's main events, it is important to think about how the garden is characterized and why this might be significant. I would like to suggest that Syrett consciously sets up a contrast in *Anne Page* between a European aestheticism that is associated with bohemianism and decadence and an English aestheticism that values the "simple," "natural" beauty of English cottage garden flowers and that is fully compatible with life in a Warwickshire village.[21] Anne Page is well versed in decadent aestheticism: she has read Huysmans's *À rebours* and Gautier's *Mademoiselle de Maupin*; she has heard the standard antimarriage rhetoric of male avant-gardists; she has lived among the most important Parisian artists of the day; and she knows precisely how her life both does and does not echo that of Gautier's notorious gender-bending heroine.[22] But she and her garden, full of lilac and hawthorn "and sweet-Anne, too," epitomize English aestheticism: not the aestheticism of the London-based *Yellow Book* set, which was associated in the public's mind, through Wilde's trials, with the scandal of homosexuality; but a homegrown, country-based, "old-fashioned" English aestheticism that counters each of the major tenets of decadent aestheticism mentioned earlier.

As Rita Felski has noted, women have a characteristic double figuration in masculine aestheticism. On the one hand, they function as symbols of art's autonomy from nature. (Think of Wilde's claim in "The Decay of Lying" that art "has flowers that no forests know of, birds that no woodland possesses. She makes and unmakes many worlds, and can draw the moon from heaven with a scarlet thread."[23]) On the other hand, women epitomize the anti-Platonic, anti-Hellenistic degeneracy of the modern world and the impermanence of the flesh. They initiate the male aesthete into the worldly pleasures of the flesh — and threaten to suck him down permanently into "the vulgar reality of actual, prosaic facts."[24] Significantly, Syrett's female aesthete fails to conform to this standard pattern of associations. In fact, she inverts it. Art is figured in *Anne Page* as a collaboration with nature rather than an alternative to it: Anne's art *is* her garden, her house, and her elegantly aging self. And she cherishes the vulgar reality of actual, prosaic facts of life in Dymfield every bit as much as she cherishes the fine paintings and furniture she has collected and her memories of other places and another life. She lives simultaneously in the mundane world of church bazaars and village socials and in a world of ideas and artistic genius. That no one in her immediate social circle guesses the real value of the art hanging on her walls does not keep her from enjoying it. Moreover, far from being like the Cumaean sibyl, the prophetess who was granted eternal life but failed to ask for eternal youth invoked in T. S. Eliot's epigraph to *The Waste Land,* Anne ages not simply "gracefully" but beautifully, appearing more and more radiantly self-possessed to her old friend Fontenelle each time he visits her. In her dress of "grey-green and purple" that "might have been suggested by the lavender in the borders" of her Shakespearean garden in the novel's opening scene, she commands our attention as "an artist in life" (4). Having made "a perfect memory for herself," as well as for René, of their three-year love affair, she now lives in perfect visual and emotional harmony with her surroundings at Fairholme Court (231).

Throughout this essay, I have been using Hughes's term "dominant masculine aestheticism" to describe the aesthetic ideology most often associated with Wilde and Huysmans.[25] Generalizations about female aestheticism simply will not hold, of course. Most female aesthetes, for example, "followed hegemonic norms of aestheticism" in associating beauty with female youth. Syrett differs strikingly from contemporaries such as Graham R. Tomson and George Egerton in her aestheticization of aging women. What Syrett does share with other female aesthetes such as Rosamund Marriott Watson,[26] Gertrude Jekyll, and Vernon Lee, however, is an appreciation of the garden as a "place of artistic intentionality," a "place where large-scale vision could find one of its finest expressions," as Barbara Gates has suggested.[27] For Anne Page as well as for Syrett, good gardening "takes rank within the bounds of the fine arts. . . . [T]o plant well needs an artist of no mean capacity. . . . [H]is living picture must be right from all points, and in all lights."[28] Jekyll's comment in *Wood and Garden* (1899) helps us see how *Anne Page* "talks back" to Wilde's *Picture of Dorian Gray* through its characterization of gardening as portraiture while at the same time paying homage to the female aesthetic tradition of garden writing. René Dampierre's fame as an artist is based on his landscapes; François Fontenelle's best work is a painting of Anne. But the painting at the center of this novel is Anne's garden, the only appropriate backdrop for the work of art that is Anne herself.

To summarize, then: in novels such as *Anne Page* and *Strange Marriage* Syrett counters what Felski has so nicely termed the "counterdiscourse of aestheticism." Syrett associates aestheticism *with* bourgeois culture rather than setting it entirely apart from dominant culture or insisting on its opposition to bourgeois norms. In Syrett's view aestheticism is not completely compatible with bourgeois culture: Anne Page lives in the country, though she does not bury herself among the narrow-minded petite bourgeoisie of her aptly named village, Dymfield. Similarly, Jenny Ferris, the protagonist of *Strange Marriage,* falls in love with a handsome but ordinary young country gentleman and bears his child; yet she realizes she would be painfully lonely married to him, given his inability to share her intellectual and artistic passions. Even if these female aesthetes do not live their lives entirely in accordance with petit bourgeois standards of morality, they are not outspokenly critical of bourgeois culture either. Anne Page, for example, does not share the vicar's closed-mindedness; but she never challenges him directly. Indeed, her influence over him is all the more powerful for its invisibility to him. Jenny Ferris conceives a child out of wedlock, but she finds a way to shelter him within a traditional legal marriage, while also discovering her own as well as her husband's sexual and artistic creativity. In *Anne Page* and *Strange Marriage* scandal is avoided — not because Syrett's female aesthetes do not behave scandalously but because they do so without calling attention to their defiance of bourgeois social and sexual norms.

I suggested initially that Syrett's characterization of British life in the 1890s is tamer and more respectable than current criticism's. Insofar as the homosocial subculture of the *Yellow Book* set remains merely a backdrop in her novels and her female characters choose not to identify themselves as New Women rebelling openly against Victorian social norms, Syrett's version of the 1890s does seem tame and respectable in comparison with what we now think of as the sexual anarchy of the period. In other respects, however, Syrett's heroines are every bit as unconventional as Wilde's Dorian Gray or Beerbohm's Lord Hell. But they are quietly so.

In one regard this quietness functions as a tribute to Shakespeare's "sweet Anne Page." Without any of the bold fancifulness of Shakespeare's play (and without any help from an older generation of women, for Syrett's Anne plays the roles of both Mrs. Page *and* her daughter in this novel), Syrett's soft-spoken heroine manages to debunk the Falstaffs of her world. To borrow Shakespeare's language, she "pinch[es]" away at aestheticism's villainous misogyny — as expressed through the French artists' theories regarding bourgeois women and monogamy and as evidenced in Fontenelle's affair with the doctor's wife. But she is never oppositional.

Perhaps this stance needs to be understood, finally, not as a tribute to

Shakespeare's character, who was beloved by so many Victorians, but as an Edwardian woman writer's survival strategy. Given what happened to Syrett's promising career as a playwright in 1902, we need not be either surprised or overly critical of her refusal to play oppositional politics. We should instead appreciate the subtlety with which her middlebrow realist novels talk back to a high-culture discourse of aesthetics. Syrett was never a major player in the London literary scene, either in the 1890s or subsequently. She never enjoyed, or suffered, the kind of meteoric success and notoriety that Graham R. Tomson and George Egerton experienced — and that, thanks to John Lane, promoted the sale of their fiction. Syrett's long career — between 1890 and 1940 she published thirty-eight novels, twenty-seven short stories, four plays for children, and twenty books of fiction for children — does offer, however, a useful opportunity to rethink fin-de-siècle aestheticism's afterlife in the early twentieth century.[29]

Historians and literary critics such as Michael Foldy and Cassandra Laity have noted how the late-Victorian public's hostile reaction to Wilde's trials lingered for several generations after his death, fueling male modernists' attempts to erase the feminized "Aesthete from modern memory" and reinvent "a more acceptable sex/gender image of the poet and his poetics."[30] By considering Syrett's treatment of aestheticism in *Strange Marriage* and *Anne Page,* I have sought not only to recuperate some of this now forgotten writer's most interesting work but also to suggest a different way that aestheticism traveled into the twentieth century. Whereas Laity traces the positive and negative lineages of masculine aestheticism into high modernism, this essay has shown how Syrett presented female aestheticism to a middlebrow reading public: a reading public with a more sophisticated appreciation of aesthetics than modernist dismissals of realism might suggest.[31] Recent attempts to rethink the "great divide" between high and low culture have both enhanced and greatly altered our mappings of early-twentieth-century literary and cultural history.[32] But there is a great deal of work still to be done on this other public sphere: a cultural space that complicates our familiar, easy oppositions of modernist high and popular low culture and that is inhabited by aesthetes such Syrett, female artists who lived — not unlike her heroine Anne Page — with equal grace among the anti-intellectuals of Dymfield and the "great geniuses" of her day.

Notes

1. Elaine Showalter's phrasing in *Sexual Anarchy: Gender and Culture at the Fin de Siècle* (New York: Viking, 1990).

2. Judith Butler's phrasing in *Gender Trouble: Feminism and the Subversion of Identity* (New York: Routledge, 1990).

3. Netta Syrett, *The Sheltering Tree* (London: Bles, 1939), 5, 78, 78, 90.

4. See B. J. Robinson, "Netta Syrett," in *British Short-Fiction Writers, 1880–1914: The Realist Tradition,* ed. William B. Thesing (Detroit: Gale, 1994), 358; and Syrett, 138.

5. Richard Dellamora, *Masculine Desire: The Politics of Victorian Aestheticism* (Chapel Hill: University of North Carolina Press, 1990); Rita Kranidis, *Subversive Discourse: The Cultural Production of Late Victorian Novels* (New York: St. Martin's, 1995); Ed Cohen, *Talk on the Wilde Side: Toward a Genealogy of a Discourse on Male Sexualities* (New York: Routledge, 1993).

6. See also, for example, Jeffrey Weeks, *Coming Out: Homosexual Politics in Britain, from the Nineteenth Century to the Present* (London: Quartet, 1977); and Jonathan Dollimore, *Sexual Dissidence: Augustine to Wilde, Freud to Foucault* (Oxford: Oxford University Press, 1991).

7. Ezra Pound, "Lionel Johnson," 1915; reprinted in *Literary Essays of Ezra Pound,* ed. T. S. Eliot (New York: New Directions, 1935), 362. Another classic modernist outburst against 1890s aestheticism is T. E. Hulme's reference to late-nineteenth-century poetry as "the expression of sentimentality rather than of virile thought" ("A Lecture on Modern Poetry," in *Further Speculations,* ed. Sam Hynes [Lincoln: University of Nebraska Press, 1962], 69). Hostile representations of 1890s aestheticism also figure prominently in early-twentieth-century mass-market fiction; see, for example, the characterizations of Lord Greystoke in Edgar Rice Burroughs's *Tarzan* (1914) and Diana Mayo's dandy brother in E. M. Hull's *The Sheik* (1919). In *The Gender of Modernity* (Cambridge, Mass.: Harvard University Press, 1995), Rita Felski reminds us that the "effeminate aristocratic dandy was only one of the ways in which homosexuality was represented and represented itself in the fin-de-siècle; other influential 'traditions' of representation include the neoclassical ideal of heroic virility and sexology's conceptualization of sexual 'inversion' as an innate and predetermined condition" (105). In Britain, and in a literary context, however, the association of aestheticism with male homosexuality and aristocratic degeneracy was by far the dominant trope, as suggested by the persistence of these negative associations in high- and low-culture texts of the 1910s and early 1920s.

8. Edward Said, "Traveling Theory," in *The World, The Text, and the Critic* (Cambridge, Mass.: Harvard University Press, 1983), 226–47.

9. Linda Hughes, "A Female Aesthete at the Helm: *Sylvia's Journal* and 'Graham R. Tomson,' 1893–1894," *Victorian Periodicals Review* 29, no. 2 (1996): 182. In this

essay I will use *aestheticism* when referring most generally to both dominant and nonstandard instances of fin-de-siècle aesthetic ideology.

10. Dellamora, 216–17.

11. Netta Syrett, *Strange Marriage* (London: Bles, 1930), 131. All further citations will be noted parenthetically in the text and are taken from this edition.

12. Felski's term in *The Gender of Modernity*, 91–114.

13. Bram Dijkstra, *Idols of Perversity: Fantasies of Feminine Evil in Fin-de-Siècle Culture* (New York: Oxford University Press, 1990), 272.

14. In this respect *Anne Page* is not unlike George Du Maurier's *Trilby* (1894), which uses the setting of Paris in the 1850s to address contemporary aesthetic issues. See Jonathan Grossman's discussion of *Trilby* in these terms in "The Mythic Svengali: Anti-Aestheticism in *Trilby*," *Studies in the Novel* 28, no. 3 (1996): 525–40.

15. For a fuller treatment of these issues, see Ann Ardis, "'Shakespeare' and Mrs. Grundy: Modernizing Literary Values in the 1890s," in *Transforming Genres: New Approaches to British Fiction of the 1890s*, ed. Nikki Lee Manos and Meri-Jane Rochelson (New York: St. Martin's, 1994), 1–20.

16. As Joseph Bristow has noted, "the charge against the morality of Shakespeare's sonnets" was made "most memorably" by Henry Hallam in 1839, when he declared, "it is impossible not to wish that Shakespeare had never written them." See Bristow, *Effeminate England: Homoerotic Writing after 1885* (New York: Columbia University Press, 1995), 42.

17. As Bonnie Kime Scott has noted, *The Well of Loneliness* trial, along with the 1915 suppression of D. H. Lawrence's *The Rainbow* and the 1921 trial of Margaret Anderson and Jane Heap for publishing the "Nausicaa" episode of *Ulysses*, was "a watershed in [modern] cultural history" (*Refiguring Modernism: The Women of 1928* [Bloomington: Indiana University Press, 1995], 242). When writing this essay, I did not have access to the kind of biographical information that might offer insight into Syrett's reasons for writing about the 1890s in the wake of the controversy in 1928 surrounding Hall's representations of lesbian sexuality.

18. Jenny Ferris's dandy friend Jocko teases her mercilessly by referring to her as Jenny Mere, the female heroine of Beerbohm's *The Happy Hypocrite* (1906). But as the passage cited above might also suggest, another Jenny alluded to here is Dante Gabriel Rossetti's.

19. Netta Syrett, *Anne Page* (New York: John Lane, 1909), 130. All further citations will be noted parenthetically in the text and are taken from this edition.

20. Kathy Psomiades and Rita Felski recently have analyzed aestheticism's contradictory stance toward commodity culture. As Psomiades puts it most tellingly, "in [aestheticism's] doubled female figure[s], both pure and corrupt, it is possible simultaneously to recognize the economic status of the artwork and disavow that status by insisting on the artwork's symbolic value in a non-economic system of exchange" (Psomiades, "Beauty's Body: Gender Ideology and British Aestheti-

cism," *Victorian Studies* 36, no. 1 [1992]: 50); see also Felski, 91–114). Anne Page's straightforward acknowledgment of the cost of good taste *and* sexual liberty needs to be understood in the context of these larger arguments about the central contradictions in aestheticism: as Anne knows, her inheritance allows her to cultivate an exquisite aesthetic sensibility and gives her the wherewithal to travel — to escape Dymfield's Grundyism. Rather than conceptualizing art as antithetical to the "praxis of everyday life" (Peter Bürger, *Theory of the Avant-Garde* [Minneapolis: University of Minnesota Press, 1984], 27), Anne never denies that René's paintings have a monetary value, that her fine clothes cost a great deal of money, and that it takes money as well as time and skill to create a beautiful garden. In other words money has use value for Syrett's heroines; it enables them to buy art and to make themselves and their houses and gardens beautiful. In this regard, Syrett rejected outright masculine aestheticism's contradictory stance toward commodity culture. Anne participates gratefully in commodity culture — without, of course, having had to earn her income. For a similar treatment of domestic fine arts, see Syrett's novel *Three Women* (1912); in this later novel, however, the heroines earn a living on the basis of their good taste: they have an antique business and buy furnishings and paintings at estate auctions, which they resell to the nouveau riche.

21. As Jonathan Grossman has suggested in "The Mythic Svengali," "by the time of the Wilde trials . . . , bohemia was not simply a foreign artist's colony, but part of [British] culture's emerging concept of homosexuality" (531). Although set in Paris in 1856–57, George Du Maurier's *Trilby* collapses "the older artistic sense of bohemia into its newer sexual meanings" (531), functioning thereby as a historically and temporally displaced commentary on artistic, sexual, and identity issues of the 1890s. Like Du Maurier, Syrett writes about the 1890s by situating her narrative in a different time period, writing about Anne Page's life with French artists in Paris in the 1860s, and seeks to contrast English purity and European decadence. Unlike Du Maurier, however, Syrett preserves the older artistic sense of bohemia, not its newer sexual meanings, in her characterization of Anne's Parisian interlude.

22. Anne herself invokes *Mademoiselle de Maupin* in a conversation with her friend Fontenelle just before she leaves René. Reminding him that he loaned her the book three years earlier (the summer they spent in England), she notes, "It's very different from my story, isn't it? But the way she found, I had already discovered for myself before I read the book. It's the right way. In my case, the only way" (252). Unlike Jenny Ferris in *Strange Marriage* — who does not understand why her friend Jocko calls her Jenny Mere — Anne is an educated rather than a natural aesthete.

23. Oscar Wilde, "The Decay of Lying," in *The Modern Tradition,* ed. Richard Ellmann (New York: Oxford University Press, 65), 20.

24. J.-K. Huysmans, *Against the Grain,* as quoted in Felski, 104.

25. Linda Hughes, "A *Fin-de-Siècle* Beauty and the Beast: Configuring the Body in Works by 'Graham R. Tomson' (Rosamund Marriott Watson)," *Tulsa Studies in Women's Literature* 14, no. 1 (1995): 101.

26. Here I am using the second of Graham R. Tomson's names to refer to her as the author of gardening books such as *The Heart of the Garden* (1906).

27. Barbara Gates, "The Aesthetic in the Natural: Gertrude Jekyll's Garden Writing," chap. 8 in this volume.

28. Gertrude Jekyll, as quoted by Gates.

29. For further discussion of her career, see Jill Owens, "Netta Syrett: A Chronological, Annotated Bibliography of Her Works, 1890–1940," *Bulletin of Bibliography* 45 (1988): 8–14; and Robinson, 351–61.

30. Michael S. Foldy, *The Trials of Oscar Wilde: Deviance, Morality, and Late-Victorian Society* (New Haven, Conn.: Yale University Press, 1997), xi; Cassandra Laity, *H. D. and the Victorian Fin de Siècle* (New York: Cambridge University Press, 1996), 2.

31. For a more detailed but still exploratory discussion of these issues, see Ann Ardis, "Toward a Redefinition of 'Experimental Writing': Netta Syrett's Realism, 1908–12," in *Famous Last Words: Changes in Gender and Narrative Closure,* ed. Alison Booth (Charlottesville: University Press of Virginia, 1993), 259–80.

32. The term "great divide" is Andreas Huyssen's, used first in *After the Great Divide: Modernism, Mass Culture, Postmodernism* (Bloomington: Indiana University Press, 1986).

DENNIS DENISOFF

The Forest beyond the Frame

Picturing Women's Desires in Vernon Lee and Virginia Woolf

WHEN IT comes to notions of desire, late-Victorian portraiture and aestheticism make odd bedfellows. Over the centuries portrait conventions had ossified into reinforcements of the historical and biological status quo, discouraging the depiction of uncommon desires, which would have been seen as contaminating. The genre therefore lacked the creative flexibility necessary to accommodate aestheticism's interrogation of heterosexual models of identity. Recognizing the artistic and political values that intersect in portraiture, however, aestheticism turned this rigidity into a means of contesting the very ideals that the genre had conventionally enforced. Both Vernon Lee, in her story "Oke of Okehurst" (1892), and Virginia Woolf, in her post-Victorian novel *Orlando* (1928), took advantage of portraiture's inflexibility for gender- and sex-based political purposes. Efforts in Victorian literature to represent women whose main objects of attraction and desire are other women had generally resulted in depictions of friends engaged in sanitized nonsexual relationships or silent spinsters cowering in the shadowy leaves of secondary narratives before withering away like the spindly branches of otherwise vibrant family trees.[1] Lee and Woolf, however, combined the visual genre with a feminist aestheticism most fully articulated in Lee's theoretical works. Doing so allowed them to take essentializing artistic conventions that hindered individual exploration and self-expression and reconfigure them into literary tools of contestation for women who wished to articulate their unsanctioned emotional needs and desires.

Aestheticism and Vernon Lee's Undying Empathy

It may be sticking one's neck out to argue that *Orlando*'s opening description of the young hero playing at decapitation is a reference to Lee's own childhood participation in historical charades of the beheading of Mary Queen of Scots and the Earl of Essex,[2] even if one of the decapitations that Woolf refers to is Mary's.[3] Nevertheless, Woolf had read much of Lee's work, and the Woolfs' Hogarth Press had even published Lee's appropriately ekphrastic treatise *The Poet's Eye* (1926) two years before *Orlando* hit the market. Woolf was also aware that their mutual acquaintance, Roger Fry, valued the older woman's views.[4] In fact, Fry's highly influential aesthetic theory, which bases the experience of beauty in "significant form" rather than in the things defined by forms, accords in a number of ways with the concepts of beauty and appreciation that Lee had begun articulating decades earlier.

Textual echoes of Lee's works are also scattered throughout Woolf's novel, from the arboreal titles of Lee's "Oke of Okehurst" and Orlando's poem "The Oak," to the sexually ambiguous Russian woman in both Lee's *Miss Brown* (1884) and *Orlando* (named Sacha and Sasha, respectively), to the general setting of "Oke of Okehurst" and *Orlando* in Kentish manor houses stuffed with history, mystery, and portrait galleries.[5] *Orlando* also follows *Miss Brown* in its abundance of portraits and lopped-off heads. Orlando's time travel brings to mind not only "Oke of Okehurst" but also Lee's first publication, *Les Aventures d'une pièce de monnaie* (1870), which depicts the adventures of a coin over hundreds of years, the coin itself being a portrait miniature. In addition to more intricate echoes, such as the representations of gender ambiguity and female-female attraction, one of the most complex elements found in both Lee's texts and *Orlando* is the use of portraiture to critique the male-privileging, heterosexual conventions of aesthetics, inheritance, and affection.

Lee's claim that aestheticism was dead in London as early as 1881 notwithstanding,[6] her later discussions of beauty are aligned with the more popular theories of aestheticism, such as those of Walter Pater, in their attention to amorality and sensual pleasure. As Lee argued in her study *The Beautiful: An Introduction to Psychological Aesthetics,* beauty is amoral because it is the product of a person's psychological response not to an object but to its formal qualities. Despite the formalist slant of her argument, Lee refers to this experience of beauty as "empathy" (from the German *Einfühlung*), the element of perception to which "we probably owe the bulk of whatever satisfaction we connect with the word Beautiful." This empathy occurs when a person is stimulated to project sensations of movement onto the object whose form is being appreciated. Each experience of beauty, moreover, operates in combination with a person's accumulated and averaged past experience of movements of the same kind.[7] Beauty is the product not of an isolated fleeting impression but of this impression in combination with one's memory (or some other mode of retention) of previous comparable experiences, as well as the cumulative history of such experiences. An atemporal social bond is reinforced by each experience of the beautiful because, regardless of its transitoriness, it is part of an ongoing empathy — a historical repetition of an emotional experience that knows no origin. History, in other words, is enlivened and made immediate through such an experience. The sense of "being companioned by the past, of being in a place warmed for our living by the lives of others," arises whenever someone enjoys this form of pleasure, whether it be while viewing the Italian countryside, a Gothic arch, or a human being.[8]

By defining empathy as the appreciation of transhistorical beauty, Lee also constructed a safer context for exploring in words her love and affection for other women, such as Mary Robinson and Kit Anstruther-Thomson. The conceptual distance that most scholars at this time saw as necessary for aesthetic appreciation assumed a separation of the admirer from the object of admiration. The tendency would be to read erotically charged (albeit still covert) aesthetic discussions such as Lee's as disembodied and nonthreatening. Lee herself reflects this perception, appearing to have no difficulty addressing sensuality if it is positioned historically. She readily compares "this historic habit . . . to the capacity of deriving pleasure from nature, not merely through the eye, but through all the senses."[9] The erotics of her notion of empathy are apparent from the sensuality of her descriptions of the experience, as well as from her focus on emotions, movement, and vitality. In *The Beautiful,* for example, she described a landscape as being made up of "keenly thrusting, delicately yielding lines, meeting as purposefully as if they had all been alive and executing *some* great, intricate dance."[10] Elsewhere, she depicted her experience of empathy as an indescribable "kind of rapture . . . compounded of many and various elements, [with] its origin far down in mysterious depths of our nature; . . . it arises overwhelmingly from many springs, filling us with the throb of vague passions welling from our most vital parts." "Swept along the dark and gleaming whirlpools of the past," Lee's empathy is nothing less than an orgasmic submersion into a flowing, throbbing rapture.[11]

In "Oke of Okehurst" visual portraits function to fuse the sensuality of Lee's aestheticism with gender and sexual politics. Throughout Lee's life, portraiture reinforced the view of genealogy as an essential identificatory trait. Diane Gillespie has suggested that the genre also fulfilled such a role for some of Woolf's characters by recalling "family intimacy and identity, tradition and authority. . . . [T]he paintings help to characterize their owners."[12] Nevertheless, portraiture could not entirely alleviate contemporary concerns regarding the increasing influence of the nouveau riche. The genre still signified financial wealth, but it was no longer as likely to guarantee traditional upper-class values. Meanwhile, nonprofessional photographers were undermining portraiture's exclusionary values even further, frequently breaking the rules of the genre while making the end product available to more people from a broader range of classes.[13]

In addition to challenging portraiture's elitism, photographers were adding pressure to the painter's claim of capturing the essence of a subject. For hundreds of years western European culture has seen the visual arts in general as accessing a source of expression unavailable to the written word. If a person's "very essence" cannot be seized, laments the narrator of Lee's "Oke of Okehurst," by "the pencil and brush, imitating each line and tint, . . . how is it possible to give even the vaguest notion with mere wretched words — words possessing only a wretched abstract meaning, an impotent conventional association?"[14] Woolf's great-aunt, the photographer Julia Margaret Cameron, similarly concluded that "[b]eyond the mere portrayal of external form and feature, . . . the portraitist had a moral obligation to reveal the inner spiritual qualities that ennobled mind and soul."[15] Lee, however, contested the possibility of representing or defining such a phantasmal phenomenon. For her the portrait was "one of our most signal cravings after *the impossible:* an attempt to overcome space and baffle time; to imprison and use at pleasure *the most fleeting, intangible, and uncommunicable* of all mysterious essences, a human personality" (italics mine).[16] "Oke of Okehurst" depicts a portrait not entrapping a person's essence but allowing a person to transgress temporal boundaries through empathy, a transgression that also challenges barriers to unconventional desires.[17]

"Oke of Okehurst" is the story of a woman who, thanks to a portrait, develops an immense empathy for her ancestral namesake such that she adopts the dead woman's attitude, clothing, and often androgynous appearance: "the Alice Oke of the year 1626 was the caprice, the mania, the pose, the whatever you may call it, of the Alice Oke of 1880" (138). The narrator of the story criticizes the heroine for being "utterly incapable of understanding or sympathising with the feelings of other persons, [having] entered completely and passionately into the feelings of this woman" (153). Alice's husband, William, is also disturbed by her attachment, primarily because the ancestor is rumored to have committed adultery. Nor are his anxieties alleviated by the added legend that the seventeenth-century Alice, while dressed as a man, had helped her husband kill the adulterer. The heroine now keeps hidden from William a miniature portrait believed to be of the murdered Cavalier poet.

Because her affections are directed backward in time toward her namesake and the namesake's rumored lover, Alice is not bothered by the fact that she and her husband are childless, the end of a gnarled aristocratic family tree. For the same reason she does not follow her ancestor in committing adultery. Nevertheless, William's doubts get the best of him, and in a state of delusion he shoots his wife while thinking that he is shooting her male lover, an entity who does not in fact exist. Although this anxious attack seals the Okes' hereditary fate, it does nothing to keep the overwhelming empathy between the Alices from being inherited by some future individual through the aesthetic admiration of what has by now, due to Alice's adaptation of her ancestor's identity, become a painting of both women.

The narrator of this story is a man whom the Okes have hired to paint their likenesses. During his narrative he articulates principal elements of Lee's aestheticism. He brings to mind her sense of "being in a place warmed for our living by the lives of others," for example, when he comments that the "impressions of the past" that he feels in Okehurst Manor "seemed faded like the figures in the arras, but still warm like the embers in the fire-place, still sweet and subtle like the perfume of the dead rose-leaves and broken spices in the china bowls" (120). In accord with the historical component of Lee's aestheticism, he also recognizes that the essence always escapes the portrait because "real beauty is as much a thing in time — a thing like music, a succession, a series — as in space" (124). It is on their attitude toward gender, however, that the author and her male narrator diverge.

The painter's biases surface in his approach to the Okes both as subjects of his art and as members of society. He completes the likeness of William without a hitch, but that of Alice escapes him, remaining in the end "merely blocked in, and seem[ing] quite mad" (110). He cannot capture Alice's essence without understanding her desires, an experience that he claims is impeded by her mental instability but that comes across as being curtailed by his dependence on generic formulas. Lee contrasts the heroine's attraction to her ancestor with the painter's infatuation with the living Alice not as a person but as a collection of formal qualities, "a combination of lines, a system of movements, an outline, a gesture" (122). "I never thought about her as a body — bones, flesh, that sort of thing," he observes, "but merely as a wonderful series of lines, and a wonderful strangeness of personality" (122). The portraitist ultimately decides that, regardless of the ramifications, he must paint the woman in the exact same clothes, stance, and setting as those in which the dead Alice appears in *her* portrait. He fails to realize that such a venture could at best only reproduce the painting that already exists or — looking at it from another direction — that the Victorian Alice is already the closest thing to the living form, the "essence," of the portrait painted centuries ago, even as she is her own individual. The portraitist's unemotional aestheticization of the female body diverges from Lee's theory of empathy, which we find embodied in Alice Oke, a woman whose beauty and affections transgress time.

The force of the same-sex bond in "Oke of Okehurst" arises from the heroine's devotion to her namesake surpassing not only the portraitist's interest in the living Alice but also the dead Alice's dubious attachment to a lover who may have never existed and, if he did, whom she then helped murder. The incommensurability of Alice's main attraction, on the one hand, and generic and cultural conventions, on the other, causes a disjuncture that established social and textual narratives appear unable to reconcile without killing off the heroine. More precisely, Alice's murder is the result of her society's inability or unwillingness to accept her attachment to this woman from the past. William kills his wife not for her interest in another man but for her undying devotion to another woman. The narrator, meanwhile, concludes that the heroine's empathy is a "psychological peculiarity" that "might be summed up in an exorbitant and absorbing interest in herself — a Narcissus attitude" combined with "a perverse desire to surprise and shock" (127).[18] In an effort to cover up his own biases, the painter adds a coat of scientific discourse to reinforce his self-serving aestheticism.

The portraitist's description of Alice as both self-absorbed and desperate for social confirmation strongly echoes the accusations that the eponymous heroine of Lee's *Miss Brown,* roughly a decade earlier, directs against a community of male artists. The novel's depiction of late-Victorian aesthetes is, as many readers of the time argued, an oversimplified caricature. Nevertheless, within the reality of the novel itself, the heroine's critique is warranted by the men's shallowness, elitism, and misogyny. The narrator of "Oke of Okehurst," conversely, has a far flimsier basis for his medical prognosis, especially after he (it seems inadvertently) notes his own mental instability. In one scene he imagines that he sees the Cavalier poet and his dead horse in the middle of a room full of guests. He then quickly blames the hallucination on the other visitors and never mentions it again.

Yet the male painter's delusion adds a sort of validity to the patriarch's mental instability. He notes William's recurring "maniac-frown" and describes a number of occasions on which the husband claims to see the nonexistent Cavalier. The portraitist goes out of his way, however, to counter these signs of dementia by effusing over the man as a "perfectly conscientious young Englishman" (128), "a regular Kentish Tory" (128), a "serious, conscientious, slow-brained representative of English simplicity and honesty and thoroughness" (168). Recognizing that men like William are necessary to reinforce his society's dominant order, the painter shifts the responsibility for William's dementia onto the woman. He describes Alice not only as deranged but also as forcing her husband to suffer mental abuse by encouraging him to believe that the ghost of the Cavalier does exist. Reinforcing his essentializing discourses of portrait aesthetics and science, the painter makes Alice responsible for her own murder by describing her as a conniving maniac lacking English simplicity.

The heroine meanwhile, through her attraction to her namesake, has made it apparent that the appreciation of beauty does not require the idealization and disembodiment that men frequently impose on their female subjects. Admiration may be a formalist quality for Lee, but it is also vital, dynamic, and empathic. The author's aestheticist challenge to dehumanizing notions of beauty is paralleled by the threat that Alice's affections pose to the power hierarchy by which traditional notions of family and nation are secured. Woolf similarly takes advantage of portraiture's significatory richness, in *Orlando,* to interrogate how established notions of beauty, inheritance, gender, and desire reinforce one another.

The Desiring Narrative of Orlando's *Portrait*

Heads strung up by ropes, heads stuck on spears, heads tumbling through the streets — references to decapitation abound in Woolf's *Orlando.* The novel even opens with decapitation: "He — for there could be no doubt of his sex, though the fashion of the time did something to disguise it — was in the act of slicing at the head of a Moor which swung from the rafters" (15). This spill of heads is echoed by an equal proliferation of visual portraits whose figures, although conventionally intended to signify that the heads of the family and the nation remain securely in place, are often presented as severed by the picture frames, if not bodiless. Even the image of a privileged androgynous youth swinging a knife at a head hanging in an attic incorporates portraiture by bringing to mind the climactic scene of Oscar Wilde's *Picture of Dorian Gray,* in which the hero slices at his own likeness.

Orlando and Dorian could have been brothers. Both of the knife-wielding men are wealthy, handsome, and sexually unconventional, and both maintain a youthfulness far beyond the powers of any skin-care products of their time. The comic tone of Woolf's allusion to the earlier work suggests, however, that although she may have appreciated Wilde's complex inquiry into the relations between pose and identity she was also taking a jab at the aestheticist penchant for idealizing the human body, a practice that was anything but novel when directed at women. Although Woolf includes Pater among the humorously long list of friends whom she thanks in the preface to *Orlando* (vii), she also felt that literature "had grown a little sultry and scented with Oscar Wilde and Walter Pater."[19] To see Woolf's ambivalence toward the views and styles of these men as a reaction to all that aestheticism had to offer, however, is to ignore her adaptation of Lee's research and writing on the relation of beauty and humanity.[20]

One can detect Lee's aestheticism at various points in *Orlando.* Woolf's narrator questions the notion of a single identity, for example, by claiming that there are multiple "selves of which we are built up, one on top of another, . . . [with] attachments elsewhere, sympathies, little constitutions and rights of their own, call them what you will (and for many of these things there is no name), . . . and some are too wildly ridiculous to be mentioned in print at all" (277). This passage not only foregrounds nonnormative and often nameless "attachments elsewhere" but also acknowledges that the printed text imposes limits on the iteration of such attachments. The layering of identity described by *Orlando*'s narrator brings to mind Lee's definition of beauty as a building up of experiences of empathy that transgress time. Prevented from fully addressing her needs and desires in the present, Lee described "being companioned by the past," just as Orlando searches for signs of affection and empathy in ancestral portraits.[21] In a note to herself Woolf wrote that *Orlando* was to be based on the theory that "character goes on underground before we are born;

and leaves something afterwards also."[22] Thus Orlando asks, "how many different people are there not — Heaven help us — all having lodgment at one time or another in the human spirit?" (277). Orlando eventually finds solace in an elusive entity from the past — "something one trembles to pin through the body with a name and call beauty, for it has no body, is as a shadow without substance or quality of its own, yet has the power to change whatever it adds itself to" (289). Like Alice Oke, Orlando is both a person who looks to the past for empathy and emotional fulfillment and the omnitemporal embodiment that affirms that such a beautiful experience is possible.

Woolf often tried to conceive of her writing visually. She even referred to some of her own works as portraits and to her friends as "a gallery of little bright portraits hanging against the wall of my mind."[23] Invoking a central tenet of Cameron's portrait theory, Woolf experimented with styles of writing that might capture the character of her subject rather than simply offer a recognizable physical blazon. In her biography of Fry, for example, she incorporated some of his own writings because, as she explained (turning to a painterly metaphor), she "was certain he would shine by his own light better than through any painted shade of [hers]."[24] In *To the Lighthouse* (1927) the painter Lily Briscoe similarly voices the difficulty of capturing people's inner characters, of knowing "one thing or another thing about people, sealed as they were."[25] Gillespie, in an analysis of Woolf's representation of Lytton Strachey, has commented that the author turns to language suggestive of the visual arts in her effort to get at Strachey's "essential character."[26] These examples, however, suggest something less coherent than a frustration with writing's limitations when it comes to capturing a human essence. In her discussion of the Fry biography Woolf turns to painting as a metaphor for the *limits* of her insight, just as Lily has to struggle for much of *To the Lighthouse* before feeling that she has, as if by chance, captured a "vision" on canvas. As *Orlando* demonstrates, Woolf's interest in ekphrasis is not based on a preference for one art form over another, but reflects a more complex interpretation of her society's notions of essence.

As Talia Schaffer has demonstrated, Woolf used marked differences between *Orlando*'s visual and verbal portraits to depict what Judith Butler has analyzed as the performative element in identity formation.[27] The incorporation of visual portraits into *Orlando* offered Woolf not simply a second medium for constructing positive depictions of nonheterosexual emotions and desires but also a new significatory system arising from the dynamics between the sister arts. The portraits incite an ekphrastic discord that accentuates differences between the life stories that are culturally prescribed for women and a broader range of narratives from which Woolf felt that they had a right to choose.

The first published edition of *Orlando* is interspersed with painted and photographic portraits, most of which depict the eponymous character at different stages of life. The text opens with a full-length painting titled *Orlando as a Boy* depicting a confident, aristocratic youth during the reign of Queen Elizabeth. Throughout the Victorian and Edwardian periods (as in the Renaissance), male subjects of portraits were encouraged to adopt qualities that reflected not just their high social standing but also their natural worthiness of the position, a combination intended to reflect a nation's strength and valor. Orlando's pose in this figure — the feet apart, the stern facial expression, the sharp bend in the elbow, the extended right hand--conforms perfectly to these conventions.[28]

This portrait, which is the frontispiece to the novel, does not quite accord with the opening description of the boy "slicing at the head of a Moor which swung from the rafters." The whimsy of the written text effectively highlights the constructed quality of masculinity by deflating the youth's awkward pose of grandeur in the portrait and suggesting the broader implications of the male inheritance of authority. "Orlando's fathers," we are told, "had struck many heads of many colours off many shoulders, and brought them back to hang from the rafters. So too would Orlando, he vowed." This macabre little gallery is, like more conventional portrait galleries, both a national and a family heirloom: "Orlando's father, or perhaps his grandfather, had struck [the Moor's head] from the shoulders of a vast Pagan who had started up under the moon in the barbarian fields of Africa; and now it swung, gently, perpetually, in the breeze which never ceased blowing through the attic rooms of the gigantic house of the lord who had slain him" (15). In this passage Orlando's amateurish performance of masculinity undermines the naturalized ideal of authority personified by the father and reinforced by a rhetoric of national, religious, and class-based superiority, as suggested by phrases such as "barbarian fields," "vast Pagan," and "gigantic house of the lord." The head hanging for perpetuity in Orlando's attic is that of a person who traditionally does not warrant such portraiture-like recognition, but the paradox is resolved for Orlando's family because the body part is abused by the rightful heir to power. Yet this image offers the reader the added paradox of the British elite coming across as barbarians.

Orlando as a Boy.
Photograph supplied courtesy of the Doris Lewis Rare Books Room, Dana Porter Library, University of Waterloo.

Woolf emphasizes the politicized identity that inheritance stamps onto the young hero by turning, immediately after this opening, to a description of the boy standing in the light passing through "the stained glass of a vast coat of arms in the window," the symbol of Orlando's chivalric, "noble" fathers. While the boy's body is "decorated with various tints of heraldic light," his face is "lit solely by the sun itself" (16). He is both identified and physically painted by his lineage; as the narrator puts it (with cookie-cutter accuracy), Orlando is "cut out precisely" for a career of glory

(17). Only his head hovers separate from this influence, leaving the image open to ambiguous readings of either decapitation or independent thought, or possibly genealogical decapitation in retaliation for independent thought.

Although the inheritance painted onto both Orlando's portrait and his body offers him an identity, the generic conventions fail to address his interests and needs. The seemingly innumerable galleries scattered throughout the family home ensure that Orlando, the living embodiment of one extended lineage, remains as keenly aware of ancestry as Alice Oke does. Less fulfilled by such bonds than Alice, however, the heir spends an undefined period of despondency "pacing the long galleries and ballrooms with a taper in his hand, looking at picture after picture as if he sought the likeness of somebody whom he could not find" (67). The family portraits function only to sustain class and gendered privileges, without transferring any of the empathy and affection for which Orlando yearns. One gets a feeling of extreme isolation when the narrator describes the eponymous character wandering through the galleries while "the dark visage of this Lord Keeper, that Lord Chamberlain, among her ancestors" "loom down at her" (156). Near the close of the novel Orlando sits at the end of a gallery that "stretched far away to a point where the light almost failed. It was a tunnel bored deep into the past. As her eyes peered down it, she could see people laughing and talking" (287). As she looks back at her centuries of existence, Orlando feels only a melancholy isolation. This sense of exclusion brings to mind Woolf's lover Vita Sackville-West's emotional loss of the family home of Knole when her father died and the estate was passed on to the closest male heir. Moreover, it suggests Woolf's own lack of emotional and sexual fulfillment, or the medium with which to celebrate it.

As critics have noted, Woolf's depiction of lesbianism in *Orlando* is not explicit. This is not to say that Woolf never refers to same-sex female desire overtly. The narrator, for example, follows Mr. T. R.'s claim that "women are incapable of any feeling of affection for their own sex" (199) with the observation that Orlando "enjoyed the love of both sexes equally" (200). Despite such occasional directness, however, the playfulness of Woolf's novel encourages a not wholly serious attitude toward lesbianism. On the verge of having sex with Nell, a female prostitute, Orlando reveals herself to be a woman, and then, and then, . . . Nell breaks out in laughter and invites Orlando to a cup of punch and a story (197). Such sudden deflections occur more than once in the novel. Although one can argue that *Orlando* is often equally flippant regarding heterosexual affection and that it incorporates extensive gender ambiguities, the novel nevertheless offers far more depictions of heterosexual relationships, giving them a sense of primacy. Lillian Faderman has argued that the whimsy of the novel is used to obscure lesbianism specifically. Adam Parkes has developed this argument in his claim that Woolf intended *Orlando* not as a support of the dominant scientific and psychological defenses of lesbianism as purely innate but as a fantasy that would force readers to question any normalizing notions of gender and sexuality. Arguing in 1988 that *Orlando* is the "first positive, and still unsurpassed, sapphic portrait in literature," Sherron Knopp concluded that the allusiveness of the novel is not due simply to Woolf's concern about censorship and prosecution but a reflection of the absence of a language that allows a positive depiction of lesbianism.[29] Like Lee, Woolf attempts to establish such a language by pushing the limitations of the conventions surrounding portraiture and inheritance.

Orlando is a refreshingly open-minded character when it comes to alignments of sex and gender. On meeting someone of "extraordinary seductiveness" (36), the hero gives the person the androgynous nickname Sasha but, in accord with the rules of portraiture, still reads the person's physical strength as male. Yet when he discovers Sasha to be a woman, the attraction of the masculine qualities does not wane. He is similarly unruffled when, later in the novel, he wakes to find that his biological sex has miraculously changed. Turning to portraiture, the narrator notes, "The change of sex, though it altered their future, did nothing whatever to alter their identity. Their faces remained, as their portraits prove, practically the same" (127). The change of Orlando's sex is also not immediately coupled with a change in gender attributes. She maintains, for example, a masculine strength and self-determination, comically confirmed by her one-on-one combat during a life-threatening departure from Constantinople.

Orlando then falls into a rigorous life among a community of gypsies in which, the narrator makes a point of informing us, "the gipsy women, except in one or two important particulars, differ very little from the gipsy men" (140). In this section of the text the East appears to function for the hero as an orientalist liminal zone that permits gendered transfigurations that do not accord with mainstream British culture. Joseph Boone has noted that Western authors have often turned to the East as a space that permits a broader range of sex- and gender-based experiences.[30] While

Woolf does tap into this convention, *Orlando* also depicts such experiences as occurring in the West. In contrast to her brisk physical alteration, Orlando's passage through her own private Orient represents a gradual gender transition that disrupts the conflation of sex and gender. Qualities such as strength and stamina, which are traditionally defined as male in Woolf's society, are presented, among the gypsies, as traits defined by economic concerns; that is, in the gypsy culture's conception of physical power, a person's gender is secondary to his or her ability to meet the community's needs. By positioning Orlando's feminization within this context of non-British values, Woolf is not simply using a fantastic exoticism to protect herself from accusations of deviancy but emphasizing the impact of cultural perspective on gender norms. This allows her, in the next section of the novel, to highlight the forced conflation of gender and sex in British society.

Back in England, Orlando's gender ambiguity persists throughout the centuries. When she and Shelmerdine meet, each is pleasantly surprised by the other's "sympathy" and astonished "that a woman could be as tolerant and free-spoken as a man, and a man as strange and subtle as a woman" (232). It would appear that Orlando has finally found a kindred spirit, somebody who possesses a similar disposition and willingly ambiguous sexuality. Woolf, however, does not allow the narrative to sustain such escapism. The portraits of Orlando as a woman (actually photographs of Sackville-West) make it clear that such a blissful ambiguity is only part of the picture.

At one point in the novel Orlando recollects that, when she was a man, she "had insisted that women must be obedient, chaste, scented, and exquisitely apparelled" (143). No doubt she had attained some of these expectations from her family galleries, since portraiture dictated that the main characteristics of women to be communicated were modesty, chastity, and passivity.[31] Nor were women allowed any boldness of action or gesture. In many works the woman's neck and shoulders are exposed, but, signifying her modesty and chastity, she is virtually never depicted as recognizing her erotic appeal and often does not acknowledge the spectator. From the breasts down, the subject is frequently buried in a mass of folds, frills, and drapes, with this constriction of movement enhanced by the poses deemed appropriate for a woman to take. Unlike her male counterpart, a woman never poses with feet apart. Her hands, if they hold anything, do so in a feeble manner. More often, they just limply touch her cheek, chin, or cleavage. All else is smooth, rolling curves and turns that draw attention back to the woman's dignified yet passive (if not semiconscious) gaze.[32] In accord with these conventions the narrator of Woolf's novel notes, in a comparison of portraits of Orlando as a man and a woman, "The man has his hand free to seize his sword, the woman must use hers to keep the satins from slipping from her shoulders. The man looks the world full in the face, as if it were made for his uses and fashioned to his liking. The woman takes a sidelong glance at it, full of subtlety, even of suspicion" (171). In the portrait *Orlando on Her Return to England* we find an excellent example of the conventional feminine pose, with soft lines in the body, exposed flesh, awkward clothing, and a gentle gaze. The confident stance of the young boy in the frontispiece has been replaced by a passivity that looks almost dysfunctional in comparison. The full-length portrait of the young heir is supplanted by the severed image of Sackville-West, the disinherited female.

Although Orlando sees marriage as "the most desperate of remedies . . . much against her natural temperament" (219), she eventually accepts the traditional female role and briskly marries and has a son. While her husband is still free to partake in adventures on the high seas, "No longer could she stride through the garden with her dogs" (220). But Woolf is heavy-handed in her mockery of marriage, with both the husband and child disappearing from the narrative as soon as they are identified. "If one liked other people," asks the heroine, "was it marriage?" (238). Heterosexual ritual does little for Orlando but stop an irritating itch. As the novel's last photograph implies, Orlando's life narrative remains anybody's guess.

The final portrait in *Orlando* offers a more optimistic view than "Oke of Okehurst" regarding the potential benefit of empathy for women's agency. A photograph of Sackville-West titled *Orlando at the Present Time,* the picture reflects a moment in the written text when Orlando, having stared back through the time tunnel of her portrait gallery, suddenly breaks from traditional influence and, accompanied by her dogs, walks determinedly into the garden (288). A stroll in the yard is of course not as exciting as being an ambassador or living with gypsies. However, the final photograph encourages a reading of the gesture as a risky exploration into identities and affections that are either nameless or deemed unmentionable.

The aesthetic construction of the subject in the last portrait differs radically from that of *Orlando on Her Return to England.* Gone is the noose of pearls around Orlando's neck, the exposed, vulnerable flesh, the soft facial expression. In the penultimate portrait of Orlando, *Orlando about the*

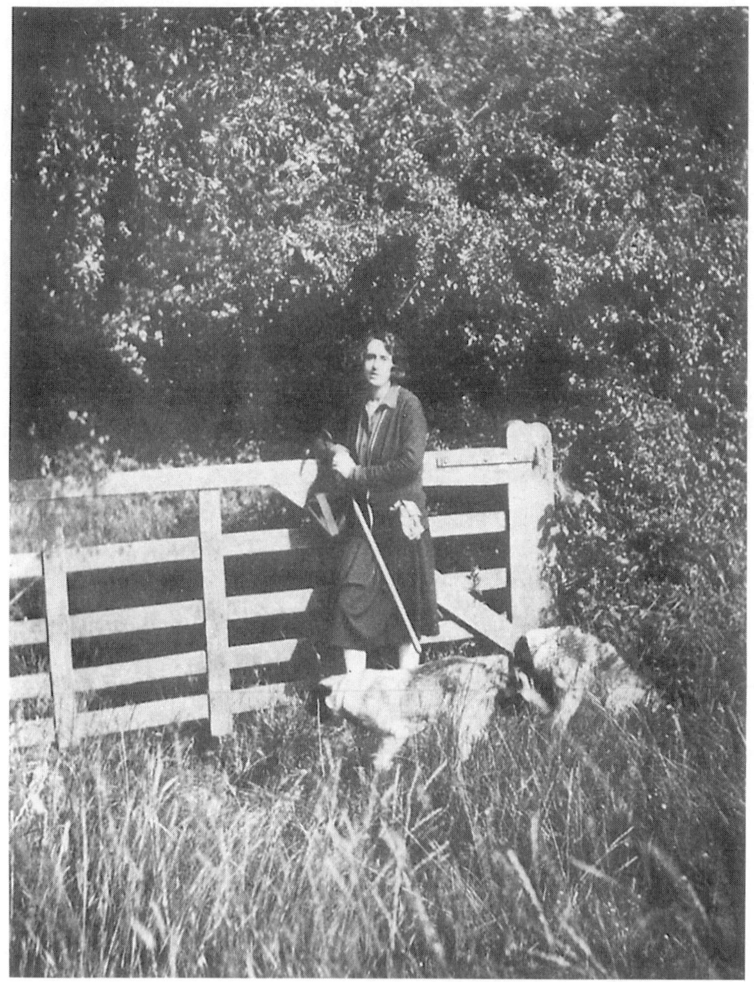

Orlando at the Present Time.

Photograph supplied courtesy of the Doris Lewis Rare Books Room, Dana Porter Library, University of Waterloo.

Year 1840, the heroine displays the satirically gaudy ring adorning her wedding finger, but the jewelry is absent from *Orlando at the Present Time.* Instead, we have a full-length shot of a woman confidently leaning against a fence out in the countryside, her two dogs vigorously scurrying about. Her general pose and her angle to the viewer repeat those of Orlando as a boy in the frontispiece, as does the confident gaze, the parted legs, and the masculine crook in the left elbow. The bend in her right leg and her walking stick connote a boldness and confidence that surpass the boy's. The male youth, confident of his inheritance of power and authority, is depicted as secure and comfortable within the family manor while the outside world exists only as a partial blur behind a heavy curtain. In contrast, *Orlando at the Present Time* actively explores this world beyond. Echoing Lee's struggle for lesbian iterability, Woolf conjoins aestheticism and portraiture to defend diverse desires, including those deemed illegitimate and, as the final portrait suggests, others not yet realized. We last see Orlando, having already experienced numerous sexual adventures, confidently poised to jump yet another fence and proceed into the forest beyond the frame.

Notes

For their comments and help with this article, I would like to thank Elana Gomel, Michael M. Holmes, Kathy Psomiades, and Talia Schaffer. The research for this article was funded in part by a Social Sciences and Humanities Research Council of Canada postdoctoral fellowship at Princeton University.

1. On representations of lesbianism in British literature, see Terry Castle, *The Apparitional Lesbian: Female Homosexuality and Modern Culture* (New York: Columbia University Press, 1993); Lillian Faderman, *Surpassing the Love of Men: Romantic Friendship and Love between Women from the Renaissance to the Present* (New York: Morrow, 1981); and Lisa L. Moore, *Dangerous Intimacies: Toward a Sapphic History of the British Novel* (Durham, N.C.: Duke University Press, 1997).

2. Peter Gunn, *Vernon Lee/Violet Paget, 1856–1935* (London: Oxford University Press, 1964), 33–34.

3. Virginia Woolf, *Orlando: A Biography* (London: Hogarth, 1928), 156–57. All further citations will be noted parenthetically in the text and are taken from this edition.

4. Gunn, 229.

5. Like much of the novel, the title of Orlando's poem was probably inspired by Vita Sackville-West, whose family estate of Knole is located in Sevenoaks, Kent, and, like Orlando's home, has "oak trees dotted here and there" (150). The Okes no doubt derived their family name from the "oak-dotted park-land" surrounding their manor house (Vernon Lee, "Oke of Okehurst," in *Hauntings: Fantastic Stories* [1892; reprint, London: John Lane, 1906], 187. All further citations will be noted parenthetically in the text and are taken from this edition.). Of equal importance to my discussion of inheritance, the oak has also appeared in numerous works over the centuries as a symbol of England's heritage and national vigor.

6. Gunn, 98.

7. Vernon Lee, *The Beautiful: An Introduction to Psychological Aesthetics* (Cambridge, U.K.: Cambridge University Press, 1913), 59, 65.

8. Vernon Lee, "The Sense of the Past," in *A Vernon Lee Anthology: Selections from the Earlier Works,* ed. Irene Cooper Willis (London: J. Lane, 1929), 168. Pater offers a similar notion of history's role in aesthetics in various works, including *Studies in the History of the Renaissance* (1873).

9. Lee, "Sense of the Past," 167.

10. Lee, *Beautiful,* 15.

11. Lee, "Sense of the Past," 173, 174.

12. Diane Gillespie, *The Sisters' Arts: The Writing and Painting of Virginia Woolf and Vanessa Bell* (Syracuse, N.Y.: Syracuse University Press, 1988), 205.

13. For an informative analysis of photography in *Orlando,* see Talia Schaffer, "Posing *Orlando,*" in *Genders: Sexual Artifice, Images, Politics,* ed. Ann Kibbey, Kayann Short, and Abuali Farmanfarmaian (New York: New York University Press, 1994), 26–63. A more general discussion of photography in Woolf's work can be found in Diane Gillespie, "'Her Kodak Pointed at His Head': Virginia Woolf and Photography," in *The Multiple Muses of Virginia Woolf,* ed. Diane Gillespie (Columbia: University of Missouri Press, 1993), 113–47.

14. Lee, "Oke of Okehurst," 124.

15. Quoted in Audrey Linkman, *The Victorians: Photographic Portraits* (London: Tauris Parke, 1993), 33.

16. Vernon Lee, "The Blame of Portraits," in *Hortus Vitae: Essays on the Gardening of Life* (London: John Lane, 1904), 140.

17. Besides "Oke of Okehurst," texts by Lee that use portraiture in their analysis of empathy and desire include the novel *Miss Brown* (1884) and "Amour Dure" (1890), a story about a man who, through portraits, falls in love with a dead woman.

18. Same-sex desire has frequently been psychologized in the twentieth century as a dysfunctional narcissism. Five years after Lee's parody of scientific authority, Havelock Ellis gave narcissism his scientific consideration, defining it as an autoerotic perversion (Havelock Ellis, *Studies in the Psychology of Sex,* 4 vols. [London: University Press, 1897], vol. 1).

19. Virginia Woolf, "The Narrow Bridge of Art," in *Collected Essays* (New York: Harcourt, Brace, 1967), 2:223.

20. Lee is of course not the sole influence on Woolf's interest in aesthetics. For discussions of Woolf's writing in relation to the visual arts, see, among other texts, Diane Gillespie's *Sisters' Arts* and Marianna Torgovnick, *Visual Arts, Pictorialism, and the Novel: James, Lawrence, and Woolf* (Princeton, N.J.: Princeton University Press, 1985).

21. Lee, "Sense of the Past," 168.

22. Quoted in J. J. Wilson, "Why is Orlando Difficult?" in *New Feminist Essays*

on Virginia Woolf, ed. Jane Marcus (Lincoln: University of Nebraska Press, 1981), 179.

23. Virginia Woolf, *Diary of Virginia Woolf,* ed. Anne Oliver Bell, vol. 2, *1920–1924* (New York: Harcourt Brace Jovanovich, 1978), 114, 156.

24. Virginia Woolf, *Letters of Virginia Woolf,* ed. Nigel Nicolson and Joanne Trautmann, vol. 6, *1936–1941* (New York: Harcourt Brace Jovanovich, 1980), 417.

25. Virginia Woolf, *To the Lighthouse* (1927; reprint, London: Collins, 1987), 79.

26. Gillespie, *Sisters' Arts,* 171.

27. Schaffer; Judith Butler, *Gender Trouble: Feminism and the Subversion of Identity* (New York: Routledge, 1990).

28. For an excellent summary of such conventions for both men and women, see Linkman.

29. Faderman, 392; Adam Parkes, "Lesbianism, History, and Censorship: *The Well of Loneliness* and the SUPPRESSED RANDINESS of Virginia Woolf's *Orlando,*" *Twentieth Century Literature* 40, no. 4 (1994): 434–60; Sherron E. Knopp, "'If I Saw You Would You Kiss Me?': Sapphism and the Subversiveness of Virginia Woolf's Orlando," *PMLA* 103, no. 1 (1988): 33.

30. Joseph A. Boone, "Vacation Cruises; or, The Homoerotics of Orientalism," *PMLA* 110, no. 1 (1995): 89–107.

31. Linkman, 137.

32. Certain exceptions to the convention of humility and sexual naïveté demonstrate the artifice of the pose and expression. In John Phillip's *Gypsy Sisters of Seville* (1854), for example, the two (non-British) women direct seductive gazes at the viewer while they stand extremely close together, the fronts of their bodies conceivably touching while their arms and clothing enwrap them. Michael Cohen offers an astute reading of Sir John Everett Millais's *Hearts Are Trump* (1872), a painting of three card-playing sisters in which one gazes at, and exposes her hand to, the viewer (who is the implied fourth in the card game) while another eyes the more active sister with a look suggesting an understanding of the romantic and erotic play (Michael Cohen, *Sisters: Relation and Rescue in Nineteenth-Century British Novels and Paintings* [Madison, N.J.: Fairleigh Dickinson University Press, 1995], 30–31).

Chapter 14

REGENIA GAGNIER

Productive Bodies, Pleasured Bodies

On Victorian Aesthetics

In a recent article in *ELT* titled "The Economies of Taste" the British Wilde scholar and cultural theorist Ian Small labeled a school of critics distinctively "American."[1] In contradistinction to the British tendency to emphasize production and producers, these critics have brought to the fore the institutions of the marketplace, the commodification of culture and artists, consumerism, and the psychology of desire for the goods and services of modernity. Small used my work in *Idylls of the Marketplace* and more recently on the histories of economics and aesthetics as examples, but he might have used any number of recent works on commodification, largely but not exclusively from the United States: Andrew Miller's work on the centrality of the commodity form in Victorian life, Anne McClintock's work on commodity racism, Rita Felski's work on feminine modernity as the erotics and aesthetics of the commodity, Kathy Psomiades's work on how the duality of femininity permitted aestheticism both to acknowledge and repress art's status as commodity, and Laurel Brake's work on the periodicals market.[2] Writing on Oscar Wilde, Richard Dellamora has recently used Georges Bataille to talk about "nonproductive expenditure."[3] In *The Ruling Passion* Christopher Lane has focused on exchange as a motive for empire, which would be nothing new except that he means the exchange of sexual desire among men rather than goods.[4] Talia Schaffer has shown how the respective commodifications of interior design and home decoration in the fin de siècle were gendered.[5]

Now, it is not surprising that this emphasis on markets, commodification, and consumption is more prominent in U.S. scholarship than in British. As early as the 1840s John Stuart Mill, Karl Marx, and other observers of the spirit of capitalism anticipated that the United States would go further than Europe in the unrestrained pursuit of markets, and it is a commonplace of political economy that U.S. consumer capitalism began to replace British industrial capitalism by the end of the nineteenth century. And Small is right to point out that there has been a shift in emphasis in U.S. scholarship away from an aesthetics of production to an aesthetics of consumption. This shift is evidently reconfiguring Victorian studies as a whole, once dominated by figures of industrial revolution and increasingly dominated by figures of speculation, finance, circulation, exchange, and desire in all its modern forms. This drift has entailed a new focus on the late-Victorian period. If gender, sexuality, race, and postcolonial studies have revitalized the entire field of Victorian studies, they have arguably shone with most brilliance as they have converged with commodity theory on the fin de siècle.

The political critique driving this scholarship often has identified productivism with masculinist marxism or heterosexism. It has been argued that male leftists blamed a decline in working-class consciousness on a feminine desire to consume and imitate the decadent leisure class, a betrayal that led to universal commodification and massification.[6] The feminist, gay, and multicultural responses to this masculine leftism were in defense of desire, especially the desire of the forgotten peoples of modernity for the goods and services of the world (including sexual goods and services). In my view this defense of desire is as justified as the earlier marxist defense of the value of labor. Yet some of the more sensational recent work on what Guy Debord called the society of the spectacle suggests that the emphasis on desire has become less a criticism of the limits of productivism (as in Jean Baudrillard's early *Mirror of Production* [1975]) than the concomitant of neoliberal, or market, society itself.

Theoretically, the gender implications of the shift from production to consumption are unstable and potentially volatile. It may be that marxism and other productivist analytics valued labor at the expense of desire; but inseparable from the centrality of labor was the centrality of the laboring body in social relations. Even if we were to grant a positive role to women as consumers in the liberation of desire, late-Victorian consumerism in the form of the economics of desire — theorized in marginal utility theory — is known precisely for its formalism and abstraction, qualities that have historically been associated with masculine, abstract individualism. This means that no gender absolutes can be derived from the shift from production to consumption. It is because neoliberalism, or consumer-driven market policy, is purely formal that it has been able to crow about growth and efficiency while occluding actual social relations. Arguments like Lawrence Birken's that, whereas the labor theory of value made work and property necessary to citizenship, modern mass consumption liberates all alike, especially women and children, might be called neoliberal scholarship.[7]

Now, surely a criticism that occludes human labor and creativity is as reductive as one that sees people as mere producers and reproducers. Surely people are *both* producers and consumers, workers and wanters, sociable and self-interested, vulnerable to pain but desirous of pleasure, longing for security but also taking pleasure in competition. If we add to these continua the fact that people may also be idle, apathetic, and unconscious of their motivations, we approach something like the grid of possibilities in modern market society. That is, people do not only identify themselves by what they consume, what they do in their leisure, what constitutes their pleasure, or, conversely, what they do not do, or do not have, in relation to others. They also identify themselves by whether they make nails, automobiles, books, contracts, breakfast, hotel beds, music, babies, or speeches.

The so-called decadents themselves expressed a range of emotions on modern market society. As early as 1863 Charles Baudelaire analyzed the dandy as a reaction against a productive and reproductive ethos of "work and money" and insisted that "the more a man cultivates the arts, the less often he gets an erection."[8] Attacking the socialist-feminist George Sand, he wrote, "Only the brute gets really good erections. Fucking is the lyricism of the masses."[9] He himself went on to explore the more voyeuristic, consuming pleasures of the flaneur. The dandy Barbey formulated the choices to Joris-Karl Huysmans between renunciation of worldly goods and total, self-destructive consumption. After *À rebours* Huysmans had only two options: "the foot of the cross or the muzzle of a pistol." *À rebours* itself proclaimed a weariness with both production and reproduction: Des Esseintes gives himself "a funeral banquet in memory of [his own] virility" and sets himself to consuming the exotica of the world.[10] George Moore's hero Mike Fletcher treats women like cigarettes, consuming and disposing of them in an insatiable search for stimulation: "More than ever did he seek women, urged by a nervous erithism which he could not explain or control. Married women and young girls came to him from drawing-rooms, actresses from theatres, shopgirls from the streets, and though seemingly all were as unimportant and accidental as the cigarettes he smoked, each was a drop in the ocean of the immense ennui accumulating in his soul."[11] Wilde's description of a cigarette also described the perfect commodity: cigarettes, Wilde said, were the perfect type of the perfect pleasure, because they left one unsatisfied.[12] The fin de siècle's basic stances toward the economy — boredom with production but love of comfort, insatiable desire for new sensation, and fear of falling behind the competition — culminated in Max Beerbohm's publication of his *Complete Works* at the age of twenty-four. "I shall write no more," he stated in the preface of 1896. "Already I feel myself to be a trifle outmoded. I belong to the Beardsley period. Younger men, with months of activity before them . . . have pressed forward since then. *Cedo junioribus.*" Beerbohm satirized the duality of aestheticizing and commodifying one's life in *Zuleika Dobson* (1911) in the double images of dandy and female superstar. Real women, like Mrs. (Mary Eliza) Haweis in her *Beautiful Houses* (1881), on the other hand, were packaging the world in moments of taste and connoisseurship and commodifying them for suburban effects. Indeed, in political economy it is the comfort of the suburban home, comfort increasingly — or illusorily — accessible to common folk, that won for consumption its status as the essence of modernity.[13] As I shall discuss below, other essays in this volume confirm the role of suburban consumption in the foundations of Victorian aestheticism.

I could easily multiply examples of late-Victorian self-awareness of the turn from production to consumption. But now I want to situate the basic stances toward the economy listed above in relation to moments in the history of aesthetics and cultural critique.

In the remainder of this essay I will discuss some nineteenth-century aesthetic epistemologies in relation to production and consumption and their correspondingly imagined bodies. The approach is pragmatic: to see what these aesthetics *did.* Ethical aesthetics arose with industrialism and was concerned with the creation of self-regulating subjects and autonomous works; aesthetics of production focused on producers or creators of work; aesthetics of taste or consumption, often with a physiological base, became dominant by the fin de siècle; and aesthetics of evaluation, best evoked today by the name of Matthew Arnold, were historically linked with the idea of national cultures and races (remembering the range of meanings these terms encompassed in nineteenth-century Britain). These aesthetics had a number of points of contact or overlap, but they were often promoted for very different purposes. Mill, like Immanuel Kant before him, was concerned with the moral good and the creation of the liberal, ethical individual who could be relied on to subjugate individual desires to the social good. Marx, John Ruskin, and William Morris wanted to provide the conditions for producers whose work would be emotionally, intellectually, and sensuously fulfilling and whose societies would be judged by their success in cultivating creators and creativity. Aesthetics of taste, deriving from David Hume and Edmund Burke, distinguished between objects of beauty and then distinguished between those who could and could not distinguish, often claiming that such capacities correlated to physiological or social stages of development. Finally, there were aesthetics of evaluation, like Arnold's, in which the point was to measure one object against another by standards of "truth" or "seriousness"; but the "tact" that was thus demonstrated in one's ability to discriminate was a matter less of physiology than of status, for Arnoldian evaluation was in the service of locating individuals in relation to class, class in relation to nation or culture, and nation or culture in relation to globe or "civilisation."

Thus some aesthetics were concerned with the human as ethical individual, and others with the human as creator fulfilling her role as producer of the world. Some aesthetics were concerned with the object produced or created, and others with the consumers of objects. Another way to put this: some were concerned with productive bodies, whose labor could be creative or alienated, while others were concerned with pleasured bodies, whose tastes established their identities. Granting overlap among these groups — for example, bodies that took pleasure in their labor — much confusion has nonetheless resulted from the reification of something called the Aesthetic and of something monolithic called Value, and this reification has only recently begun to be rectified, primarily through feminist scholarship.[14] In proposing a historical epistemology of aesthetic value*s*, I want to clarify our possibilities for aesthetics, value, and the contested development of these in market society. In accordance with the aims of this volume, I also explore the effect a focus on women has on our understanding of Victorian aesthetics.

For example, a number of essays in this collection confirm that the differences between production and consumption models are equally prominent when one considers high-Victorian aesthetic theory and popular forms of aestheticism. Although women aesthetes often sided with male counterdecadents in negating the decadent negation of bourgeois life, their work in country cottages (see that of Anne Page in Ann Ardis's essay), London suburbs (Marie Corelli in Annette R. Federico's essay), or the empire itself (Sarojini Naidu and Adela Nicolson in Edward Marx's essay) popularized aestheticism for broader audiences while simultaneously expressing the desires of subordinated groups for ideals beyond production and reproduction (see Alison Victoria Matthews's essay on the production of synthetic dyes). Thus Anne Page's "elegantly aging self" refuses the antibourgeois stance of Wilde and company but creates an aesthetic life in a Warwickshire garden untrammeled by husband or children. Marie Corelli resolved the conflict between the artistic value of autonomous literature and the cash value of literary commodities through a complex narrative trade between aestheticism and popular fiction. In Marx's accounts of Naidu and Nicolson (Laurence Hope) the popular demand for "exotic" literature created opportunities for women writers "who possessed direct knowledge of exotic places"; and Marx proposes a history of women's readership, or literary consumption, in our analyses of decadent exoticism.

In these essays aestheticism may function as "an elite form of consumerism" (Matthews) in which aesthetic rhetoric conceals inequalities of class, race, gender, and access to luxury goods. Yet in all of these cases consumption is also driving the production of women and other marginal writers. In Schaffer's reading, *The History of Sir Richard Calmady* by Lucas Malet (Mary St. Leger Kingsley Harrison) provides a highly self-conscious, literary critique of late-Victorian commodification and consumption in the character of a crippled, emasculated aristocrat who cannot engage in productive activity himself but who ultimately devotes his life to helping the victims of industrial casualties. It would seem that the women involved in aestheticism were consistently sensitive to the manifold politics of production and consumption. If they sometimes reinforced gender and heterosexual stereotypes while countering the excesses of male decadents or protecting women (see Lisa K. Hamilton's essay as well as Schaffer's), they also confronted their implication in commodity culture more directly than some of the male aesthetes (see especially my remarks on Morris in "The Productive Body" below). In what follows, I interrogate the aesthetic possibilities available to the Victorians from the perspective of women and gender.

The Self-Regulating Body

In Kant the moral good consists in acting autonomously, as one ought, rather than heteronomously, or from desire, emotion, or self-interest. This freedom to act autonomously can only be achieved by reason, but it can be prefigured by feeling, the feeling of freedom from desire or self-interest that we get when we perceive the beautiful object. When we perceive the beautiful object — which in Kant is typically a natural object theoretically accessible to all rather than a work of art, which, Kant says, may give rise to an element of ego or possessiveness — the disjunction between our perception and our concept creates an excess, a free play of imagination, that prefigures moral freedom, or freedom from desire and self-interest. It prefigures the reconciliation between individual and social life that the moral good entails, that is, to act according to duty rather than according to desire or self-interest, or to act in such a way that one's actions embody a universal principle for action.[15] In Kant's *Anthropology from a Pragmatic Point of View,* making a man of taste falls short of making a morally good man, but it prepares him for it by the effort he makes in society to please others.[16] This taste for freedom is thus (notoriously) a form of discipline.

In Kant a judgment of taste is neither simply subjective, relating to the consumer, nor objective, relating to the object. It begins with the harmonious workings of the faculties when a perceiver is confronted with certain objects. At first this aesthetic feeling is subjective and phenomenal. In the disinterested pleasure that comes to me without the element of desire or self-interest, I do not transcend the phenomenal sphere (see "Analytic of Aesthetic Judgment" in *Critique of Judgment*). But Kant insisted, for purposes of the logic of his entire system, that judgments of taste were also objective. When we say that the beautiful object ought to please others also, we bring in rational and objective elements. Recognizing something in us that is common to the species, and something in each member of the species that is not owned but is universal property, we are freed from our former confinement and limitations (see "Dialectic of Aesthetic Judgment"). Many people, of course, who are persuaded by Kant's phenomenology of aesthetic feeling — the free play of imagination synthesizing perception and concept — are not persuaded by his rationalizing or universalizing of it to make it a symbol of the moral good, or freedom.[17]

Without Kant's metaphysic Mill's aesthetic also functioned as a discipline. In his two major essays on poetry of 1833, Mill distinguished poetry from mere eloquence by its discipline and autonomy: poetry is overheard whereas eloquence is heard; poetry is unconscious of listeners whereas eloquence is directed toward an audience; poetry is an end in itself whereas eloquence is a means toward an end; poetry is thought tinged by feeling whereas in eloquence feelings pour themselves out to other minds; poetry is feeling unconscious of being watched whereas eloquence is found in attitudinizers showing themselves off before spectators.[18] For Mill the French — social, vain, and dependent on others — are eloquent but not poetic, subject to law or external constraint but not self-disciplined. Autonomous, disciplined lovers of poetry are also distinguished from primitive peoples (or vulgar people in advanced societies), who prefer stories (or novels), as those who prefer "a state of sensibility" are distinguished from those drawn to "mere outward circumstance." Obviously Mill's lover of poetry in these early essays prefigures his lover of liberty in *On Liberty* of 1859, who acts freely without inhibiting the freedom of others. Because the poet is a disciplined, ethical exemplar, poetry is disciplined feeling, and the lover of poetry is the autonomous, self-disciplined feeler. The poem embodies the process that will educate the readers in how to be autonomous (rational, self-reflective) themselves.[19] For Mill aesthetics partakes of rational self-reflection in the service of progressive individuals.

We see a recent treatment of aesthetics as ethics inscribed in the senses or emotions in the last years of Michel Foucault, from the posthumously published *The Use of Pleasure* (1984) and *The Care of the Self* (1984), volumes two and three of *The History of Sexuality,* to his last interviews, in which he spoke of social practices amounting to ascesis, or self-discipline.[20] Kant's ethics derived from the systematic relations among the good, the true, and the beautiful; Mill's and Foucault's, respectively, from education and a system of social practices; but they all share an idea of the aesthetic creation of an ethical being. Two critics strongly influenced by Foucault have emphasized this aesthetic as ethic, although, I think, by overemphasizing the institutional aspect of Foucault (in, for example, *Discipline and Punish*) at the expense of the creative or aesthetic aspect (evident in his work on the Greeks). In *Outside Literature* Tony Bennett claimed that philosophical aesthetics has always posited a "universalized valuing subject."[21] He concluded in full neo-Foucauldian declamatory style that aesthetics "is part of a technology of person formation whose effects are assessed as positive and productive in serving as a means of normalising the attributes of extended populations as a part of the more general procedures and apparatuses of government through which, in Foucault's conception, the attributes of modern citizenries have been shaped into being."[22] Like Bennett, Ian Hunter sees the mapping of aesthetics and ethics as a hegemony: aesthetics "are the instruments and objects of a special practice of the self, deployed for essentially ethical purposes. They are the phenomena whose systematically polarized structure is symptomatic of their systemic use as reflexive instruments of self-problematization and self-modification."[23]

Yet Foucault distinguished between a care of the self — practiced, he thought, by elites in ancient Greece and the Renaissance and by nineteenth-century dandies and amounting to the ethical construction of an aesthetic life — and the institutional practices that disciplined individuals in mass society. His characterization of the Greek citizen as mastering his desires resonates with Kant's distinction between autonomy and heteronomy but does not partake of Kantian universality. Yet although Foucault saw the care of the self as potentially liberating and potentially an alternative to the disciplinary structures of modern institutions, he and Kant shared the idea of the centrality of the monitored self, whether self-mastered or institutionally disciplined. The care of the self represented the creation of an ethical being in pursuit of the aesthetic or beautiful life. This notion of aesthetics as ethics, of self-regulation in a disciplined society, has been the dominant one among Foucauldians and New Historicists, who have focused on bourgeois hegemony; but this notion's assumptions of constraint, self-restraint, and internal regulation render it inadequate to analyze the hedonics of modern consumer culture. (More on hedonics below.) What is relevant here is that the figure connecting them all — whether Kant's moral agent, Mill's poet, or Foucault's self-fashioning ascetic — is an autonomous, self-regulating male. To this extent the ethical aesthetic is a liberal aesthetic and carries with it the masculine appurtenances of liberal autonomy. When middle-class women, like Netta Syrett's Anne Page, cultivated such an aesthetic, for instance when Anne, in a gesture toward an aesthetic life, renounces her young lover, they participated in similar designs of autonomy. Such autonomy, whether in Syrett's Anne Page or Foucault's Greek, was typically the property of elites untrammeled by labor and production (if male) or by reproduction (if female).

The Productive Body

The movement that Ruskin called the political economy of art focused less on the spectator or consumer than on the producer of the work and the conditions of production: this was Ruskin's aesthetic, Morris's after him, and, of course, Marx's and generations of marxists' (although marxist aesthetics has typically included a critique of ideology with its critique of production). Contrary to an aesthetics located in the object (Plato's) or in the perceiver (Kant's or Burke's), the political economists of art began with the very body of the artist and ended with a theory of creative production.[24] Thomas Hardy's character Jude Fawley in *Jude the Obscure* reads the buildings at Christminster (that is, Oxford) like Ruskin "reads" (his own term) the cathedrals at San Marcos or Amiens:[25] "less as an artist-critic of their forms than as an artizan and comrade of the dead handicraftsmen whose muscles had actually executed those forms."[26] One must not underestimate the extent to which the political economists of art were concerned with ethics and reception ("reading"). Indeed, Ruskin is considered the founder of moral consumption, or the appeal to consumers' social responsibility, and he had affinities with physiological aesthetics in his precise calculations of the impact of art on the body, especially the eye (see the role of seeing throughout his work). Yet despite these concerns and affinities, a theory of creative labor motivated the political economists of art; their object was the relations of production and reproduction and the possibilities for human flourishing within them.

We should pause here, in an age of consumer demand, to remark on how seriously the nineteenth century took the labor theory of value, coming at it from a wide range of perspectives, from that of David Ricardo to those of Marx, Mill, Ruskin, Hardy, Olive Schreiner, and many of the women discussed in this volume. According to this theory, the cost of a commodity was the value of the labor power it took to produce it, plus the value of the laborer's wear and tear in production, plus the value of the laborer's family's subsistence, or, as Marx said, the value of labor power was "the necessaries by means of which the muscles, nerves, bones, and brains of existing labourers are reproduced and new labourers are begotten."[27] Much of the outrage in novels like *Jude the Obscure,* written well after the theory had been discredited as a theory of price, is against a society that literally undervalues its producers. And Hardy's terms are, like "labor," those of political economy: production, reproduction, and the body whose labor was its defining feature. They are also specifically Malthusian. From the beginning Jude is conscious of himself, of his "unnecessary life," as part of Thomas Malthus's "surplus population," and his children die "because we are too menny."[28] Correspondingly, Sue's gendered, reproductive labors are what she seeks, hopelessly, to avoid in pursuit of a (bodiless) aesthetic partnership. And reproductive, like productive, labors are, again, embedded in thick social relations (see, for example, how bodies are typically marked by gender, race, and class).

The impulse to historicize art, to read in art or architecture the history of social relations, of course, goes back to G. W. F. Hegel, a student of political economy. Kant's examples of the sublime and the beautiful in the third *Critique* are drawn from nature, for example, sublime cataracts and mountains or the beautiful song of a bird. Hegel, on the other hand, made representation central, deriving the aesthetic impulse from the fact that it was human nature to, as he said, represent ourselves to ourselves. Thus art and architecture are indexes of their time, their producers, and their conditions of production.[29] At the end of the nineteenth century, in his magisterial *History of Aesthetic* (1892), Bernard Bosanquet saw the culmination of this tradition of philosophical aesthetics in the materialism of Ruskin and Morris. Insofar as the worker was free in his producing activity, so far would he produce the work of creative humanity. In England, Bosanquet concluded, aesthetic insight had had a remarkable influence on economic theory. The dissolution of romantic art into excessive internality and subjectivity predicted by Hegel would presage the birth of Morris's unalienated worker, whose "art [was] the expression of pleasure in labour."[30] Unlike the monumentally abstract eighteenth-century science of aesthetics, for the Victorians aesthetics was the realm of daily life, its "sense data" or sensuous experience, its pains and pleasures. Bosanquet, for example, was particularly interested in Morris's production in the domestic arts of furniture making, tapestries, textiles, and carpets.

For the purposes of this volume one might want to consider how Morris's productivist, or socialist, aesthetic looks when its actual *products* are compared with Mary Eliza Haweis's, mentioned above. Both Haweis and Morris were interested in such diverse crafts as book production, typesetting, fashion, and furniture design; both were deeply influenced by medievalism; and both produced commodities suburbanites could use to beautify their homes. Is it the quality of Morris's work, his status as a socialist, or his gender as a crafts*man* that distinguishes him from Haweis as a home decorator, or does his socialist theory but make his unintentional participation in a high-end niche market all the more ironic?[31] Another way of putting the point is, was the manifestly productivist aesthetic of Ruskin and Morris always implicated in consumer culture, their aestheticism an "elite form of consumerism," as Matthews says, but its commodification displaced onto women? Already, at the height of productivism, Arnold uneasily accepted the fact that his time was an age of criticism, or consumption, rather than creation, or production ("The Function of Criticism at the Present Time"), to be answered by Wilde in "The Critic as Artist" that criticism or consumption was indeed a higher form than creation or production.[32] It is arguable that the commodification so resisted by Morris and Arnold, from their very different but equally elevated platforms (it was "exploitation" in Morris and "machinery" in Arnold), was typically displaced onto the products of women or homosexuals, resulting in the ultimate trivialization of their labor.

The Pleasured Body

In contrast was biological or physiological aesthetics, as in Grant Allen's *Physiological Aesthetics* (1877), which, through its position of authority in the academy, rapidly gained dominance over the applied aesthetics of Ruskin and Morris and in which the cultivation of a distinctive taste in the consumption of art replaced concern for its producers. The roots went back to Hume and Burke, who had analyzed the psychological bases of taste. According to Hume, the structure of the mind made some objects naturally inclined to give pleasure or to inspire fear. In his fin-de-siècle *Philosophy of the Beautiful* (1895) William Knight estimated that Burke's influential essay of 1757 had reduced aesthetics to the lowest empirical level, identifying the beautiful with the source of pleasant sensations.[33] In Burkean sensationism the experience of an elite group of Anglo-Irish takes on the appearance of universalism; the irrational feelings associated with the sublime are given equal place with the sociable feelings associated with the beautiful; and enlightenment or reason is subordinated to mechanism. Burke's very constrained subject — increasingly the subject of political conservatism — is chained to physiology and driven by self-preservation and, to a lesser extent, benevolence. "We submit to what we admire, but we love what submits to us," Burke famously said of our respective reactions to the sublime and the beautiful.[34] We admire the sublime in the form of the vast, the rugged, the jagged, the massive, and the dark. We respond naturally to the beautiful in the form of the small, the smooth, the curvilinear, the delicate, and the bright. Erasmus Darwin perceived the associational basis of the beautiful when he named it a characteristic of beauty to be an object of love. We love the smooth, the soft, and the warm because we were once nourished thence. His grandson Charles later theorized the sense of beauty in relation to sexual selection. Many have remarked on the gender implications of Burke's theory.[35]

After Hume biological aesthetics had included custom with physiology in conditioning our response to the beautiful.[36] In the course of the nineteenth century biological aesthetics merged with established associationist psychology, which gained legitimacy as an academic discipline under Herbert Spencer and Alexander Bain in the second half of the century. As it came to dominate economics, psychology, and sociology, it also came to dominate aesthetics, shifting the study from its German roots in ethics or reason and its Victorian roots in production to a focus on reception, consumption, or individual pleasure. Indeed, for our purposes, the empiricist tradition in the aesthetics of Hume and Burke, which is typically opposed to Kantian reason, is significant for its grounding in sense, in the pleasures of consumption. Bain banished everything but pleasure from aesthetics. Following Bain, in *Physiological Aesthetics* Allen defined the beautiful as that which afforded the maximum of stimulation with the minimum of fatigue or waste in processes not directly connected with life-serving functions.

Allen wrote, "The aesthetic pleasure is the subjective concomitant of the normal amount of activity, not directly connected with life-serving functions, in the peripheral end-organs of the cerebro-spinal nervous system."[37] Although taste had its source in the brain's hardware, whole societies could cultivate it with Lamarckian consequences. Conditions of leisure give rise to two classes of impulse, play and aesthetic pleasure. In play we exercise our limbs and muscles; in aesthetic pleasure we exercise our eyes and ears — the organs of higher sense as opposed to those of the more functional senses of taste and smell. In this aesthetic, whose proponents included Spencer as well as Bain, the highest quality or quantity of human pleasure was to be derived from art.[38]

Contrary to the expressed goals of social justice and egalitarianism among the political economists of art, the experiencers of this pleasure fall into predictable hierarchies, and here is where aesthetics most heavily draws on a lexicon of civilization and barbarism, or stages of development. Elsewhere I have discussed how the late-Victorian "Man of Taste" was distinguished from both savage others, who were perceived as external threats to Britain's dominion, and internal barbarians, or those, like decadent aristocrats, who willfully refused the constraints of taste.[39] With painstaking discussions of the physical origins of aesthetic feelings, Allen ultimately argued that existing likes and dislikes in aesthetic matters were the result of natural selection. From thence it was but a short step to distinguish between stages of aesthetic development, and Aesthetic Man, like Economic Man, was distinguished from others lower in the scale of civilization (whom Allen, following Spencer, Bain, and other associationists, interprets, after Burke, as "children" or "savages"). Barbarians, on the other hand, while capable of making fine distinctions, refused to restrain themselves according to the dictates of taste.[40] Poor taste might be a consequence of a lower stage of development or of an advanced one — degeneration. "Bad taste," wrote Allen, "is the concomitant of a coarse and indiscriminate nervous organization, an untrained attention, a low emotional nature, and an imperfect intelligence; while good taste is the progressive product of progressing fineness and discrimination in the nerves, educated attention, high and noble emotional constitution, and increasing intellectual faculties" (48). "The common mind," as he put it, "translated the outward impression too rapidly into the reality which it symbolized, interpreting the sensations instead of observing them" (51). Rather than immediately translating the impression into its "real" analogue, on the other hand, the aesthetic mind "dwelled rather upon the actual impression received in all the minuteness of its slightest detail" (51). This, of course, meant that persons of taste dwelled on the representation and their subjective response to it rather than on any referent it might have in the external world. (The aesthete Pater, as I have argued elsewhere, emphasized this subjective and formalist response in his aesthetic.)[41] Today, institutionalists like Pierre Bourdieu have shown how the tendencies to "dwell in the referent" or the representation are distinctive marks of social class.[42]

In Allen's influential article "The New Hedonism" (*Fortnightly Review*, March 1894), the author of *Physiological Aesthetics* and by then publicist of the New Woman, specifically contrasted the new hedonism, or the philosophy of pleasure and pain, with the old asceticism, which he associated with the work ethic and self-restraint, specifically targeting the productivist tradition represented by Thomas Carlyle.[43] "Self-development," he proclaimed, "is greater than self-sacrifice" (382). Yet although Allen's interest is in pleasure, feeling, and sensation, these are inextricably linked with sexual reproduction, and the document is specifically an argument in favor of sex: "Now there is one test case which marks the difference between the hedonistic and ascetic conception of life better than any other. I am not going to shirk it. . . . From beginning to end, there is no feeling of our nature against which asceticism has made so dead a set as the sexual instinct" (383–84). In lists comparable to those in *Physiological Aesthetics* Allen argues that, from the beautiful song of the bird to the pleasing physical properties of animals, flowers, and fruits, "every lovely object in organic nature owes its loveliness direct [*sic*] to sexual selection" (385). He goes on to attribute all our "higher emotions" — "our sense of duty, parental responsibility, paternal and maternal love, domestic affections, . . . pathos and fidelity, in one word, the soul itself in embryo" (387) — to "the instinct of sex." Thus the reproductive body returns at the fin de siècle to haunt the consuming or pleasured body, in direct evolutionary descent. Throughout the 1890s Allen's heterosexual aesthetic, with its beautiful body of sexual selection, was in cultural dialectic, both implicit and explicit, with other, perverse aesthetics. In some cases, as I wrote some years ago, art for art's sake was allied with a defense of sex for sex's sake, or nonreproductive sex. In other cases the aesthetic was not beautiful at all, but sublime and terrible, and its body was often abject, repulsive. We have come to call this other body the gothic body.[44]

Physiological aesthetics — aesthetics that calculated immediate pleasure — was pervasive in the fin de siècle not just in Pater's *The Renaissance: Studies in Art and Poetry,* in which he wrote that our object was "to get as many pulsations as possible into the given time," but also in Vernon Lee's "psychological aesthetics."[45] (Physiological and psychological were used interchangeably.) Based on her reading of Allen, Lee experimented on the sensitive body of her lesbian lover, Clementina Anstruther-Thomson; these aesthetic experiments compromised the ethical aesthetics Lee had inherited from Ruskin and the missionary aesthetics the aristocratic Anstruther-Thomson had inherited from a tradition of women's philanthropy (see Diana Maltz's essay). As Hamilton argues in her essay, the biological model seemed particularly attractive to the first generation of New Women, who were striving to distinguish, or dissociate, themselves from their decadent male counterparts (who themselves were more critical of biological or physiological models).

In fiction we could find many examples, but I shall stay with Hardy's *Jude the Obscure,* which seems to me exquisitely divided between two aesthetics, one productivist, deriving from Ruskinian principles of work and creativity, and one physiological, discriminatory, an aesthetics of taste. The example of *Jude the Obscure* takes us full circle, for of course the novel is about desire: the desire to be free of one's class, one's gender, one's marriage and reproductive function. It is about the desire to live aesthetically the life of rich and varied sensations that Jude associates with the mental life and material beauty of Oxford. But unlike Jude the idealist, Hardy is a realist, and his novel is ultimately an anti-aesthetic, showing how social institutions oppose the aesthetic life.

Yet the desire for the good things of the world persists and is exacerbated in our own time. When political theorists say, as they do today, that economic liberalism is the total subordination of the economy and politics to culture, they are defining *culture* for our time as the desires, needs, and tastes of individuals: the end of history in consumer culture. Economists today have a principle that "tastes are exogenous." This means that the construction of taste is external to their models, that they no longer ask why people buy what they buy or do not buy what they do not. The principle is often extended further, to an aesthetic laissez-faire, claiming that it is of no concern what others like, that it is an intrusion on people's liberty to speculate on the rightness — or even the origins — of their tastes. Revealed preference theory ensured that the only preferences revealed were those revealed by consumption patterns, whether or not such preferences were determined by financial constraint or even coercion. Yet as economists have abandoned inquiry into the complexity of choice and preference, cultural critics have become more sophisticated at analyzing precisely this complexity. The leveling of high and low in the broader conception of culture that characterizes most literature and cultural studies departments today has resulted in superb research on why people have the tastes they have. And at no time in history has the construction of taste been more significant.

The sociologist J. Urry describes contemporary global culture as images, language, and information flowing through "scapes" of geographically dispersed agents and technologies.[46] This cultural flow gives rise to a cosmopolitan civil society that "precipitates new modes of personal and collective self-fashioning as individualization and cultural formations are . . . combined and recombined."[47] Urry insists that it is important to see how heavily *culturalized* the flows are, how much global *cultures* have to do with global constructions of preferences of taste: "Increasingly economies are economies of signs. . . . [T]his has implications for the occupations structure and hence for the increasingly culturally constructed preferences of taste."[48] It is precisely this cultural construction of taste that is the province of critics of culture.

But as we study what statistical price lists and microeconomics cannot tell us, that is, as we study the construction of taste, we must remember that people are not only consumers. Although there has been a shift in emphasis from production to consumption, and the dominant tendency today within rich nations is to think more of individuals than social groups and more of desire than scarcity, there is more to be said about the relationship between production and consumption in both economics and aesthetics. An aesthetics and economics of pleasure became salient in ideological terms at the fin de siècle, having competed with ethical, political-economic, and evaluative models. It was doubtless Anglo-American society in the 1980s, with its construction of society as individuals maximizing their self-interest and pursuing happiness, that sensitized us to this development and that led to our emphasis on consumption and excess rather than production or self-regulation. Yet the record of alternative models is worth keeping if we want less reductive accounts of market society. Considering women's complex and often self-conscious roles in the production and consumption of Victorian aestheticism illuminates the history and possible ways forward.

NOTES

Parts of this essay have been previously published in another form in *Victorian Sexual Dissidence,* ed. Richard Dellamora (Chicago: University of Chicago Press, 1999).

1. Ian Small, "The Economies of Taste: Literary Markets and Literary Value in the Late Nineteenth Century," *ELT* 39, no. 1 (1996): 7–18.

2. Regenia Gagnier, *Idylls of the Marketplace: Oscar Wilde and the Victorian Public* (Stanford, Calif.: Stanford University Press, 1986); Andrew H. Miller, *Novels behind Glass: Commodity Culture and Victorian Narrative* (Cambridge, U.K.: Cambridge University Press, 1995); Anne McClintock, *Imperial Leather: Race, Gender, and Sexuality in the Colonial Contest* (New York: Routledge, 1995); Rita Felski, *The Gender of Modernity* (Cambridge, Mass.: Harvard University Press, 1995); Kathy Alexis Psomiades, *Beauty's Body: Femininity and Representation in British Aestheticism* (Stanford, Calif.: Stanford University Press, 1997); Laurel Brake, *Subjugated Knowledges: Journalism, Gender, and Literature in the Nineteenth Century* (London: Macmillan, 1994).

3. Richard Dellamora, "Wildean Economics" (paper presented at the City University of New York Graduate Center, May 1995).

4. Christopher Lane, *The Ruling Passion: British Colonial Allegory and the Paradox of Homosexual Desire* (Durham, N.C.: Duke University Press, 1995).

5. Talia Schaffer, "The Women's World of British Aestheticism" (Ph.D. diss., Cornell University, 1996), especially chap. 2, "The Home Is the Proper Sphere for the Man: Inventing Interior Design, 1870–1910."

6. Versions of this argument are developed in Felski; Carolyn Kay Steedman, *Landscape for a Good Woman* (New Brunswick, N.J.: Rutgers University Press, 1987); and Pamela Fox, *Class Fictions: Shame and Resistance in the British Working-Class Novel, 1890–1945* (Durham, N.C.: Duke University Press, 1994).

7. Lawrence Birken, *Consuming Desires: Sexual Science and the Emergence of a Culture of Abundance, 1871–1914* (Ithaca, N.Y.: Cornell University Press, 1988).

8. Charles Baudelaire, *The Painter of Modern Life and Other Essays,* trans. Jonathan Mayne (London: Phaidon, 1966), 28–29.

9. Charles Baudelaire, *My Heart Laid Bare and Other Prose Writings,* trans. Norman Cameron (London: Soho, 1986), 175–210, 213.

10. J.-K. Huysmans, *Against Nature,* trans. Robert Baldick (Harmondsworth, U.K.: Penguin, 1982), 27.

11. George Moore, *Mike Fletcher* (1889; reprint, New York: Garland, 1977), 261.

12. *The Picture of Dorian Gray,* in *The Portable Oscar Wilde,* ed. Richard Aldington (Middlesex, U.K.: Penguin, 1978), 228.

13. See, for example, Peter J. Taylor, "What's Modern about the Modern World-System? Introducing Ordinary Modernity through World Hegemony," *Review of International Political Economy* 3, no. 2 (1996): 260–86.

14. Probably the best-known recent reification of the Aesthetic is Terry Eagleton's in *The Ideology of the Aesthetic* (Oxford: Blackwell, 1990); for a similar treatment of Value, see Steven Connor, *Theory and Cultural Value* (Oxford: Blackwell, 1992). For an alternative approach, see Martha Woodmansee, *The Author, Art, and the Market* (New York: Columbia University Press, 1994).

15. Immanuel Kant, *Critique of Judgment,* trans. Werner Pluhar (Indianapolis: Hackett, 1987).

16. Immanuel Kant, *Anthropology from a Pragmatic Point of View,* trans. Mary J. Gregor (The Hague: Martinus Nijhoff, 1974), 111–12.

17. See especially Pierre Bourdieu, *Distinction: A Critique of the Judgment of Taste* (Cambridge, Mass.: Harvard University Press, 1988); Stanley Fish, *Doing What Comes Naturally* (Durham, N.C.: Duke University Press, 1989); and Barbara Herrnstein Smith, *Contingencies of Value: Alternative Perspectives for Critical Theory* (Cambridge, Mass.: Harvard University Press, 1988).

18. "What Is Poetry?" and "The Two Kinds of Poetry," in *The Collected Works of John Stuart Mill,* ed. John M. Robson (Toronto: University of Toronto Press, 1963–91), 1:341–53, 354–65.

19. For a detailed analysis of Mill's aesthetic and of its compatibility with his larger views in *On Liberty,* see Kenneth Brewer, "The Absorption of John Stuart Mill," in "Lost in a Book: Aesthetic Absorption, 1820–1880" (Ph.D. diss., Stanford University, 1998), 41–57.

20. "On the Genealogy of Ethics," in *The Foucault Reader,* ed. Paul Rabinow (New York: Pantheon, 1984), 340–73.

21. Tony Bennett, *Outside Literature* (New York: Routledge, 1990), 117–92.

22. Ibid., 181.

23. Ian Hunter, "Cultural Studies and Aesthetics," in *Cultural Studies,* ed. Lawrence Grossberg et al. (New York: Routledge, 1992), 356.

24. See John Ruskin, *The Political Economy of Art,* in *Unto This Last and Other Essays* (London: Dent, 1932), 1–106.

25. See John Ruskin, "The Nature of Gothic," in *Unto This Last and Other Writings,* ed. Clive Wilmer (London: Penguin, 1985), and John Ruskin, *The Bible of Amiens,* in *On Reading Ruskin,* trans. and ed. Jean Autret et al. (New Haven, Conn.: Yale University Press, 1987).

26. Thomas Hardy, *Jude the Obscure* (London: Macmillan, 1984), 103.

27. Karl Marx, *Capital* (New York: International, 1967), 572.

28. Hardy, 36, 356.

29. G. W. F. Hegel, *Hegel's Aesthetics: Lectures on Fine Art,* trans. T. M. Knox (Oxford: Oxford University Press, 1975).

30. Bernard Bosanquet, *History of Aesthetic* (London: Allen and Unwin, 1892), 441–71. The definition of art as "the expression of Man's pleasure in his labour" is Morris's in his preface to John Ruskin, *The Nature of Gothic: A Chapter of* The Stones of Venice (London: George Allen, 1892).

31. See Schaffer, chap. 2.

32. For this concise formulation I am grateful to Gerhard Joseph.

33. William Knight, *Philosophy of the Beautiful* (London: Murray, 1895).

34. Edmund Burke, *A Philosophical Enquiry into the Origin of Our Ideas of the Sublime and Beautiful,* ed. James T. Boulton (Notre Dame, Ind.: University of Notre Dame Press, 1986), 113.

35. See, for example, Peter de Bolla, *The Discourse of the Sublime: Readings in History, Aesthetics, and the Subject* (Oxford: Blackwell, 1989), 56–58; Terry Eagleton, "Aesthetics and Politics in Edmund Burke," in *Irish Literature and Culture,* ed. Michael Kenneally (Gerrards Cross, U.K.: Colin Smythe, 1992), 25–34; Mary Poovey, "Aesthetics and Political Economy in the Eighteenth Century: The Place of Gender in the Social Constitution of Knowledge," in *Aesthetics and Ideology,* ed. George Levine (New Brunswick, N.J.: Rutgers University Press, 1994), 79–105.

36. David Hume, "Of the Standard of Taste," in *Essays Moral, Political, and Literary,* ed. Eugene F. Miller (Indianapolis: Liberty, 1963), 226–52.

37. Grant Allen, *Physiological Aesthetics* (London: King, 1877), 34. All further citations will be noted parenthetically in the text and are taken from this edition.

38. See Herbert Spencer, "Use and Beauty," *Leader,* 3 January 1852; reprinted in *Essays: Scientific, Political, and Speculative* (London: Williams and Norgate, 1883), 1:433–37; and Alexander Bain, *The Emotions and the Will* (New York: Appleton, 1888), especially chap. 14, "The Aesthetic Emotions," 225–63.

39. Regenia Gagnier, "Modernity and Progress in Economics and Aesthetics," in *Rethinking Victorian Culture,* ed. Alice Jenkins and Juliet Johns (London: Macmillan, forthcoming).

40. See ibid.

41. Regenia Gagnier, "On the Insatiability of Human Wants: Economic and Aesthetic Man," *Victorian Studies* (winter 1993): 125–54; and Regenia Gagnier, "Is Market Society the *Fin* of History?" in *Cultural Politics at the Fin de Siècle,* ed.

Sally Ledger and Scott McCracken (Cambridge, U.K.: Cambridge University Press, 1995): 290–310.

42. Bourdieu.

43. Gagnier, *Idylls,* 137–76.

44. See Kelly Hurley, *The Gothic Body: Sexuality, Materialism, and Degeneration at the Fin de Siècle* (Cambridge, U.K.: Cambridge University Press, 1996).

45. Walter Pater, *Selected Writings,* ed. Harold Bloom (New York: Signet, 1974), 17.

46. J. Urry, "Is the Global a New Space of Analysis?" *Environment and Planning A* 28 (1996): 61–66.

47. Ibid., 64.

48. Ibid., 65.

Contributors

ANN ARDIS is associate professor of English at the University of Delaware. She is the author of *New Women, New Novels: Feminism and Early Modernism* as well as numerous articles on late nineteenth- and twentieth-century British literature.

MARGARET DEBELIUS is a doctoral candidate in English literature at Princeton University, where she is writing a dissertation on the figure of the sphinx in fin-de-siècle literature. She has taught at Princeton, Georgetown University, and Smithsonian's Campus on the Mall.

DENNIS DENISOFF is assistant professor of English at the University of Waterloo. He is the author of *Erin Mouré, Her Life and Works,* the editor of *Queeries: An Anthology of Gay Male Prose,* and the coeditor of *Perennial Decay: On the Politics and Aesthetics of Decadence.*

ANNETTE R. FEDERICO is associate professor of English at James Madison University, where she teaches Victorian literature and women's studies. She is the author of *Masculine Identity in Hardy and Gissing* and the forthcoming *Idol of Suburbia: Marie Corelli and Late-Victorian Literary Culture.*

REGENIA GAGNIER is professor of English at the University of Exeter, where she teaches Victorian studies, social theory, feminist theory, and interdisciplinary studies. Her books include *Idylls of the Marketplace, Subjectivities,* and an edited collection, *Critical Essays on Oscar Wilde.* She is currently completing a book on the comparative histories of economics and aesthetics in market society.

BARBARA T. GATES is Alumni Distinguished Professor of English and Women's Studies at the University of Delaware. She is the author of *Kindred Nature: Victorian and Edwardian Women Embrace the Living World, Victorian Suicide: Mad Crimes and Sad Histories,* and numerous essays and reviews. Her edited works include *Critical Essays on Charlotte Brontë, Journal of Emily Shore,* and, with Ann B. Shteir, *Natural Eloquence: Women Reinscribe Science.* She is currently compiling an anthology of nature writing by Victorian and Edwardian women.

LISA K. HAMILTON is a lecturer at Harvard University. In 1999 she was an Ahmanson-Getty Postdoctoral Fellow at the William Andrews Clark Memorial Library at UCLA, participating in its program "Oscar Wilde and the Culture of the Fin de Siècle."

LINDA K. HUGHES is Addie Levy Professor of Literature at Texas Christian University in Fort Worth. She is the author of *The Manyfaced Glass: Tennyson's Dramatic Monologues,* coauthor, with Michael Lund, of *Victorian Publishing and Mrs. Gaskell's Work* and *The Victorian Serial,* and guest editor of the special issue of *Victorian Poetry* on women poets (spring 1995). Her essays in books and journals are devoted to Victorian literature and periodicals and to Arthurian studies. She is at work on a biography of Rosamund Marriott Watson.

DIANA MALTZ is assistant professor of English at Southern Oregon University. In 1999 she was an Ahmanson-Getty Postdoctoral Fellow at UCLA, researching Oscar Wilde and social-reform movements of the 1880s and 1890s. She is working on a book on aestheticism's mission to the working classes.

EDWARD MARX has taught at the University of Minnesota and the City College of New York and has published numerous articles on cross-culturalism in modern poetry. He is currently a lecturer in English in the Department of International Cultural Studies at Kyoto University and is completing a book on Yone Noguchi.

ALISON VICTORIA MATTHEWS is a doctoral candidate in nineteenth-century European art at Stanford University. Her dissertation challenges traditional gender stereotypes by studying the visual culture and clothing of sportswomen and soldiers in late-nineteenth-century Paris.

KATHY ALEXIS PSOMIADES is associate professor of English at the University of Notre Dame. She is the author of *Beauty's Body: Femininity and Representation in British Aestheticism.* She is currently working on a project on the late-Victorian novel and anthropology.

TALIA SCHAFFER is assistant professor of English at Queens College, CUNY. She has published articles on fin-de-siècle writing in the *Henry James Review, Women's Writing, Genders, ELH,* and *Victorian Poetry* and is the author of the forthcoming book *The Forgotten Female Aesthetes: Literary Culture in Late-Victorian England.*

MARGARET D. STETZ is associate professor of English and women's studies at Georgetown University. With Mark Samuels Lasner, she is coauthor of *England in the 1880s: Old Guard and Avant-Garde, England in the 1890s: Literary Publishing at the Bodley Head,* and *The Yellow Book: A Centenary Exhibition.* She has published numerous articles on nineteenth- and twentieth-century literature and culture and is coeditor, with Bonnie Oh, of the forthcoming *Legacies of the Comfort Women of WWII.*

Index